Reeves, ERIC
360 395-8847
vikingReeves@gmail.com

THE HUNTER KILLERS

THE HUNTER KILLERS

THE EXTRAORDINARY STORY
OF THE FIRST WILD WEASELS,
THE BAND OF MAVERICK AVIATORS
WHO FLEW THE MOST DANGEROUS
MISSIONS OF THE VIETNAM WAR

DAN HAMPTON

wm

WILLIAM MORROW
An Imprint of HarperCollins*Publishers*

HarperCollins books may be purchased for educational, business, or sales promotional use. For information please e-mail the Special Markets Department at Spsales@harpercollins.com.

FIRST EDITION

Designed by Jamie Lynn Kerner

Library of Congress Cataloging-in-Publication Data has been applied for.

ISBN 978-0-06-237513-1

15 16 17 18 19 DIX/RRD 10 9 8 7 6 5 4 3 2 1

For those who wore the silver wings and never came back from Southeast Asia—and for all Wild Weasels who have flown into the guns to bring others home alive.

"First In, Last Out . . ."

CONTENTS

AUTHOR'S NOTE

LONG BEFORE THE "Hunter Killer" appellation was borrowed by others, there was an elite group of aviators called the Wild Weasels who truly earned the title. These men weren't watching on a screen thousands of miles from danger. They were right *there,* firing their cannons and dropping bombs; hunting and killing the most lethal anti-aircraft systems created by man. They knew that real combat is not pushing a button from the safety of an air-conditioned bunker or a trailer.

It takes a unique, intelligent, and very dangerous man to duel with missiles and to knife-fight with anti-aircraft guns. With unproven tactics, experimental equipment, and sheer guts these first Hunter Killers never hesitated. They attacked threats hundreds of miles behind enemy lines and too often they never came back. Sometimes they simply disappeared, leaving friends and family waiting for answers that never came.

This story begins in 1965, in the Southeast Asia theater of operations, an area rapidly escalating into war. During the previous decade the Korean War had been largely fought with technology and pilots brought back into service, often reluctantly, from World War II because there was no other choice. Even when new methods and technology became available the tactical mentality hadn't changed much since the Second World War, nor were there many reasons to do so.

But by the early 1960s jet aircraft had proliferated, and so had countertactics against these complex, fast-moving threats. Radar systems had vastly improved from the primitive Freya and Chain Home stations of the 1940s, and they were now being used to precisely aim weapons. As the threat posed by high-altitude, nuclear-armed bombers grew in the minds of world leaders, so did the necessity to bring them down.

Enter the surface-to-air missile.

Through the eyes of those who fought, I present certain seminal events to illustrate the technology, threats, abilities, and challenges of the Hunter Killers. The cockpit viewpoints were written after extensive interviews with the surviving men who flew the missions, and this book was reviewed and rewritten until they approved. In the cases of those missing or killed, narratives were reconstructed utilizing eyewitnesses, squadron mates, government records, and POW network archives.

As in my previous works, real men and actual combat situations are utilized to reveal the historical and political context that put them there. This is done for those of us who came later—those of us who were neither taught the reasons for the conflict nor encouraged to discover them for ourselves.

The war in Southeast Asia was a Gordian knot of issues, and most will never be unraveled or satisfactorily explained. This is not an intentionally political work, yet in one sense it is impossible to accurately describe any post–World War II struggle without accounting for politics. For Americans there hasn't been a black-and-white, unambiguous war since 1945 and Vietnam, in the minds of many, is a perfect train wreck of idealism, shortsighted diplomacy, and failed opportunities. Politics, like geography, history, and technology, are discussed within these pages, as they are the very sinews of any war.

One challenge with this type of approach is to objectively expose error without casting the slightest shadow on those who took the oath and honorably fought for their country. Two words, *fought* and *honorably,* are key. Many protested the war—not the soldiers, but the war—out of genuine conviction, and they had every right to do so. The belief in such liberties was one reason the men in this book were fighting, and our fellow citizens who exercise such hard-won privileges would do well to remember that. Those who physically fought, bravely and honorably, deserve the respect, obligation, and admiration of us all.

Finally, this book is a tribute. To those maintainers, crew chiefs, flight docs, and everyone else who made certain that even if the Weasels went to combat with one hand tied behind their backs, then the hand they had was the best it could be. Most of all this is for the pilots and electronic warfare officers who fought, and often died. It is for those who languished in the hell of captivity, tortured and lonely, and to everyone who found their way home and went on with life.

The men I was fortunate enough to interview and meet became living heroes to me personally, and as I researched those who had died fighting in Southeast Asia they became very real to me, much more than nearly forgotten names on a page. Each had once been a small boy growing up somewhere in America, had gone to school, played sports, graduated from college, and found himself in a Wild Weasel cockpit. They all had a story; they'd all been men with families, hopes, and dreams. Each said goodbye to someone and, with the unique confidence of warriors, each planned someday to return.

As a former Wild Weasel myself, I fervently wish every tale could be told; as an author I know they cannot. But my sincere hope is that wherever warriors spend eternity they will feel that this story is enough of a tribute—for now, anyway. In the end, this is not my story . . . it is theirs.

Dan Hampton

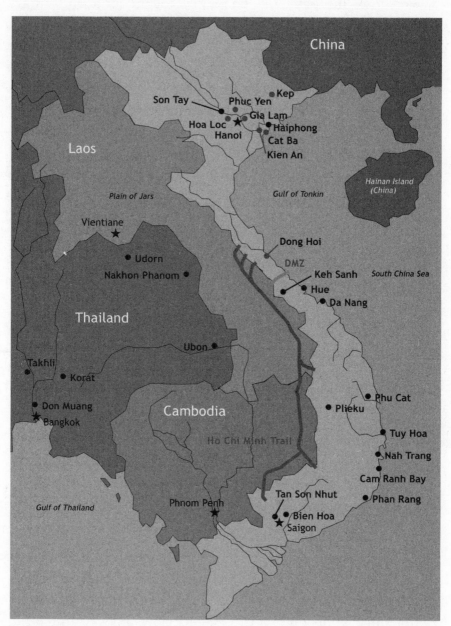

South East Asia Theater of Operations, 1965–1972. (courtesy of Guy Aceto)

Route Pack Structure of North Vietnam. (courtesy of the U.S. Military Academy)

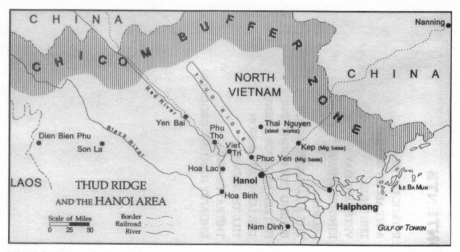

Thud Ridge and the Hanoi Area. (courtesy of Colonel Jack Broughton)

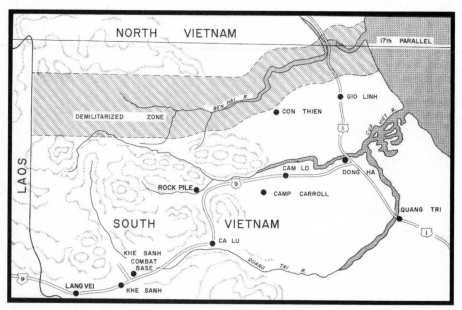

The Demilitarized Zone (DMZ) between North and South Vietnam. (courtesy of Colonel Jack Broughton

THE HUNTER KILLERS

PROLOGUE

A VIOLENT, THUNDERCLAP explosion shattered the quiet, heavy air over the river. Anyone within five miles would have heard it. Those closer would see an intense, forty-foot flame stabbing upward from a rolling brown cloud of dirty smoke. In a second the surface-to-air missile (SAM)* was several hundred feet in the air, glowing bright gold, and streaking up toward the low gray clouds. Moments later the rocket booster burned out and dropped away as the sustainer motor kicked in. Trailing thick white exhaust, the SAM began receiving guidance signals from the ground, and it jerked sideways when its control fins unlocked. Twice the speed of sound now and accelerating, the Fakel 11D missile, called an SA-2 Guideline by NATO, shallowed its trajectory then headed southwest and disappeared into the overcast sky towards its target.

---

*A glossary of potentially unfamiliar terms and acronyms appears on page 357.

EIGHT MINUTES EARLIER several specially trained men crouched in an olive drab trailer, straining to see in the dim light and to hear over the humming equipment. This trailer was mounted on one of two big, six-wheeled Soviet ZIL trucks parked side by side and connected with stout black cables. Other cables ran from the back of each trailer to four generator carts, also green, about thirty feet away. A pair of the generators were running, vibrating, and filling the air with blue-tinted diesel fumes. Atop one of the trucks was a fifty-foot radar antenna array that looked like a huge drying rack. A single pole ran horizontally across the truck top, intersected every eight feet by a vertical post. On both ends of each of the six vertical posts was a four-foot-long horizontal rack called a Yagi directional antenna. Designated the P-12 "Yenisei" surveillance radar by its Soviet creators, it was known to the West as a "Spoon Rest" due to its appearance. All it did was search for aircraft. The Spoon Rest could acquire and track targets out to 100 miles or so, based on their altitude and maneuvering. Not terribly accurate, it worked well enough against targets above 20,000 feet that didn't maneuver much—just like this one.

The radar was Soviet built, as were all the antennas, generators, miles of cables, and, of course, the missiles. Everything mechanical on the site was Russian, as were most of the men seated at the consoles. However, the men standing behind them were not. They were North Vietnamese. Smaller and much thinner, they were dressed in plain, dark green uniforms, and they watched everything.

The actual technicians, all Soviet military personnel, were in the second ZIL. The sides of this trailer were lined with consoles, like big cabinets, about six feet high and two feet wide. At the back near the door one man stood, watching all that took place. Two men closest to him were seated at a large console with a pair of prominent displays. The range height indicator, also called an E-scope or elevation scope, was on the left. It measured altitude and distance to a target, in meters and kilometers, respectively. The larger display on the next console was the planned position indicator (PPI). This displayed range and, by virtue of its circular screen, covered 360 degrees in azimuth. Superimposed over this lay a mustard-colored grid with compass headings marked out in 10-degree increments along its rim. A rotating, amber triangle radiated from the center of the screen to the border. This depicted the actual 30-degree-wide radar beam, and it swept continuously, covering 360 degrees in ten seconds.

A little curved line had appeared near the top of the radar display. The triangle swept through another full rotation and the line appeared again. It was a "hit," a reflection from a target aircraft, and the operator turned a cookie-size black knob protruding beneath the screen. Twisting it brought a single dashed steering line around through the hit, and as the scanning radar beam passed through the contact again it faded significantly. Using his rectangular E-scope the operator manually adjusted the antenna to cover the target's estimated altitude. When the next sweep passed through, the hit was much darker.

Svyazat'sya. Contact.

The Spoon Rest was carefully placed in a revetment, an open-ended horseshoe trench with ten-foot earthen sides that provided just enough shelter to protect the equipment and vehicles. However, the radar rose fifteen feet above the truck, giving it an unrestricted line of sight to any incoming aircraft. In this case, toward the southwest and the U.S. Air Force F-100, F-4, and F-105 fighter jets that flew out of Thailand.*

---

*ProtivoVozdushnaya Oborona Strany: the Soviet Air Defense Force.

Another man, a captain with the PVO Strany and the senior surveillance officer for the missile site, stood behind the operators and watched the displays. The hit had moved closer, but now appeared stuck at the same place on the screen, about fifty kilometers away to the southwest and well beyond the tactical range of the SA-2. Gently, and with surprising finesse, the operator twiddled the steering knob to keep it intersecting the target. Tick marks bisected the white line at ten-kilometer intervals and the hit had moved again, nearly due west of the radar and sixty kilometers away.

Still, this was plainly an enemy aircraft and since it could move closer at any time there was no reason not to transfer the targeting data. The operator kept the steering line centered, and the officer behind him rested a finger against a small, red button near the display. As he pressed and held, the button instantly closed a circuit. This transmitted an electrical signal from beneath the console, which passed through a metal conduit in the floor and into a heavily insulated black cable. The cable ran out of the revetment, across a muddy path and past another, larger revetment. Six of these earthen blisters, heaped with branches and leaves, each about seventy-five feet long, were arranged in a star-shaped pattern around the perimeter of the missile site. Poking up from five of the six revetments was a thirty-five-foot-long, two-ton missile mounted on a splayed, olive drab launcher. Draped with sections of tattered netting, the SA-2's lethal shape was partially obscured by more leafy foliage.

Cables streamed from the rear of each launcher toward another berm, much larger than the others, in the center of the site. There were half a dozen large-field generators here and several thirty-foot-long vans, their immense knobbled wheels resting on matting above the mud. Pairs of men tended the equipment, and several bicycles leaned against a misshapen trailer in the center of the emplacement. This particular structure was twenty feet long by ten feet wide, and here the cable clusters converged, running beneath it and disappearing up through the base. Actually, it wasn't a trailer at all, but a target engagement radar. The Soviet technicians sweating inside called it an Almaz RSN-75, known to Americans as a "Fansong." Where early warning and search radars like the Spoon Rest would find targets at great distances, they could not provide the tracking and guidance for a surface-to-air missile.

The Fansong could.

A heavy metal frame lay atop the van and supported two rectangular antennas, about fifteen feet long. Shaped like a horse trough, one was on its end, pointed up at the sky, and the other lay horizontally across the top of the trailer. Only microseconds after the Spoon Rest transferred the target data, the radar and its trailer swung smoothly around toward the west. A half second later the horizontal antenna moved slightly, then the whole frame twitched when the vertical antenna angled upward. Both troughs were now transmitting powerful, invisible, fan-shaped waves at the American aircraft far out to the west.

Even as the trailer rotated, a target appeared on several consoles fifty feet away inside another green van. This was the command vehicle for the entire site, called a UV cabin. Standing four feet off the ground on eight massive wheels, there were little rectangular windows along its top and bottom, all shut tightly to keep the cool air inside.

Seated at a single console just inside the door, a guidance specialist would physically control the missile once it had been launched. This man, like all the Russians, wore no rank but he also was a senior air defense captain and currently attached to the North Vietnamese 236th Air Defense Regiment. A technical "advisor."

So, too, was the officer standing inside the door. By taking just a few steps he could see any of the consoles along the left bulkhead and, in so doing, decide when to fire site's missiles. Ordinarily the battery fire control officer (FCO) would be running the operation, but this was not a normal day. Major Il'inykh was the commander of the 4th battalion, 1st Surface-to-Air Missile Regiment, yet on this very important of days he was acting as the FCO.

The first console along the row was for tracking the horizontal direction, or azimuth, of the target. The operator was a *praporshchik,* a warrant officer, and had been picked for this assignment due to his long history of operational expertise. Like the guidance officer and the fire control officer, all the Russians had served in Cuba before coming to this miserable place.

The man at the middle console was not a Russian, although the Soviet *praporshchik* was standing directly behind him watching every movement he made. Nguyen Xuan Dai was a Vietnamese officer, one of the most promising from the initial training class. His technical knowledge was very good and he could speak fluent, though heavily accented, Russian.

The target was obviously flying in an orbit, a cap, but for what purpose? Told to assist their communist allies in every way, the major also had been cautioned about giving away too much information. The fear was not the Vietnamese, of course, but that this advanced Soviet technology would fall into Chinese hands.

China was barely 150 kilometers north of this elevated rice paddy on the Red River and their officers had been here the night before, Il'inykh heard, disparaging the Russian system. This was why General-Major Ivanov, the Soviet military attaché in Hanoi, ordered the major to personally take command. The Vietnamese had been reluctant to assume responsibility for this first combat test, obviously believing that if the Soviet missiles couldn't kill a Yankee then Hanoi would turn to the Chinese. They were playing both sides of the game, and it was up to Il'inykh to ensure *something* was shot down today.

The azimuth changed again.

The Yankees had flown a minute outbound. Adding the time to turn, they'd be back in missile range within about three minutes. That was enough time for the missiles to warm up and the system to complete a self-check. Outside, just behind the command van and Fansong radar, were three towed ESP-90 trailers, each with three 220-volt diesel electric generators inside. Normally a battery traveled with only two, but this, as the major was very aware, was not an average battery. It was a demonstration of Soviet military power and an operational testing ground for weapons. Knocking down slow, unwieldy spy planes was one thing; shooting down a fighter, if that's what this was, would be something entirely different.

Forty kilometers.

Each leg of the enemy orbit took about ninety seconds and covered nearly sixteen kilometers. It had to be a fighter, since nothing else flew that fast. Last time the Americans had turned in between forty-five and fifty kilometers, but now . . . if they flew their normal distance then they'd approach to within twenty-five kilometers of his position. A near perfect set-up for the standard Soviet three-shot salvo.

Legkiy udar. Easy shot.

The guidance console was the most complex instrument in the van, but the major had been part of the original missile program and was intimately familiar with its operation. Glancing at the electronics and power panel, he was satisfied everything was functioning. Below this panel were two rectangular scopes that mirrored targeting information from the elevation and azimuth stations. Beneath these were the circular control heads that permitted command signals to be uplinked, which would correct the Fakel, if needed.

Blue ready lights were brightly glowing now, indicating that three missiles were ready to fire. Once one was launched, the system would automatically switch to the next of the six missiles. The major spoke briefly into a field phone, then hung up. The regimental commander, Colonel Lubinitsky, was personally commanding one of the other missile batteries.

Il'inykh would fire the first salvo, then twenty seconds later, the neighboring 64th battery would send up three more. The final trio would then be launched from here. Nine missiles against one target was excessive, but, in truth, no one was certain how this equipment would perform.

The major and the captain watched the twin scopes. Glancing up, Major Il'inykh noted from the range scope that the contact was still moving down the screen. The guidance officer's finger slid to the left of three black buttons near the blue status lights as the major counted down.

"Tri, dva, odin . . . Strelyat!"

Fire!

The Fakel missile was enormous. Gray with a red band near the nose, this one hadn't been in country long enough to be camouflaged. The overcast sky was thick, heavy, and wet, but the missile was indifferent. As the booster motor burned out, a nitric acid oxidizer mixed with the TG-02 liquid propellant and ignited, giving the SA-2 another sixty seconds of burn time.

It wouldn't take that long.

Two command guidance waveforms automatically corrected the missile's flight path, causing it to climb, dive, and turn left or right. Designed to shoot down high-flying U.S. strategic bombers, the Fakel normally used *treokh tochek,* a three-point Soviet adaptation of CLOS, or Command Line of Sight guidance. This kept the missile oriented between the target and launching radar and only worked against non-maneuvering targets. Guidance updates occurred every four seconds, had anyone been looking, the missile would have appeared to be flying a series of short, straight lines, always aiming in front of the target.

THE TARGET WAS a fighter, or rather a flight of four USAF Phantoms from the 45th Tactical Fighter Squadron (TFS) out of Ubon, Thailand. Flying today under the call sign "Leopard," the F-4Cs had deployed to Southeast Asia in April 1965 to protect strikers from enemy fighters, a type of mission called a MiGCAP. One group of F-105s was bombing an ammo dump in the Dien Bien Phu area while another was attacking the Lang Chi munitions factory near Hanoi. Lieutenant Colonel Bill Alden, the 45th TFS commander, was leading the MiGCAP and had put his Phantoms right between the two targets. To remain clear of the Washington-imposed thirty-mile circle around Hanoi, the easternmost point of Alden's orbit was thirty-five miles from the city.

Unknown to him, or any Americans at the tactical level, three batteries of the 236th SAM Regiment of the North Vietnamese Army (NVA) had occupied positions a mere ten miles east of Leopard flight. The four American fighters and their eight men were right in the heart of the engagement envelope, with no knowledge of the threat and no warning systems whatsoever except eyeballs—and given the weather, those wouldn't do much good today.

Alden had requested that the F-105s out west call off target so he could get his flight back to base. Fuel was low and the weather was bad, with clouds below and a seemingly thinner cirrus deck up above. So when the striker lead called, the Leopards immediately turned southwest toward the Laotian border and their tanker track. The Phantoms also began a climb to save fuel and, as they approached the wispy cloud deck, the three wingmen moved into a tighter formation.

In Leopard Two's backseat, Captain Ross Fobair sighed and stifled a yawn. The dark-haired, twenty-nine-year-old captain was quiet and easygoing. His friends and family thought of him as a thinker, though that would have made him chuckle. Losing his father when he was a baby, he and his sister, Betty, had been raised on a homestead in Southern California, near the Rodman Mountains outside Barstow. Loving the outdoors, he hiked and hunted with his dog or explored the desert. It had made him self-sufficient and tough, and given him a taste for adventure.

Ross joined the USAF after college and began his career as an electronic warfare officer, or EWO, flying in RB-47 Stratojets. But he'd wanted to be a pilot and, after a long, hard road, had made it into fighters and he'd been excited about his first combat tour. Two of his squadron mates, Ken Holcombe and Tom Roberts, had downed a pair of MiG-17s just fourteen days ago. Ross had hoped to get one himself, but as Leopard was out of gas and heading back to Ubon he supposed it would have to wait for another trip back to Southeast Asia.

As the big Phantom wobbled through the turn and began sliding toward the leader, Ross put his left hand lightly on the throttles, then carefully rested his right hand on his leg, near the stick between his knees. His fingers were curled and ready, but he didn't actually touch the controls. His job today was to complete the newly arrived front seat pilot's local orientation and, though Richard "Pops" Keirn was a pilot himself, he was an older retread from World War II. Pops had flown bombers and then been shot down on his fourteenth mission, so he'd already been unlucky once.

"Leopard Two . . . close it up," Bill Alden's terse, staccato command echoed through their helmets and Ross winced. He was a perfectionist. Normally an in-flight correction of a basic skill would embarrass him, but at the moment it didn't matter. First, he wasn't flying, and second, he was going home. Today— as soon as they landed. His bags were already packed and to-night he'd be on the Freedom Bird, the air transport, back to Hawaii. From there on to California and his family. His sister, Betty; his young nephew, Bruce; and most of all, Ross's wife, Anne. They'd lost a baby, a little boy they'd named David, just two weeks before Ross deployed, and he was worried about her. It was a bad time, but Anne's father was an Air Force officer so she knew the life. Nevertheless, he needed to get home.

THE U.S. FIGHTERS entered the clouds and closed in together.

Just then, the first Fakel burst from the clouds as the Phan-toms rolled out of their turn. This shifted the missle's guidance to *polavinoye spravleniye,* a half-correction algorithm that updated much faster than its previous setting and would fuse the warhead against the first solid mass encountered. Unfor-tunately, the American flight's southerly heading put Leopard Two on the far edge of the formation closest to the incoming missile. Accelerating to more than a half mile per second, the Guideline traveled fifteen miles in roughly eight seconds.

Even though American tactical military aviation was the best in the world, the threat of surface-to-air missiles was still new, and not well known. There had been no countertactics developed, no training, nor were there detection, warning, or self-protection systems on board U.S. fighters in 1965. The fighter pilots simply had no clue they were targeted. When flying over cloud cover, it was impossible to see the missile's launch, and when flying close together in the clouds, they had no chance of evading anything even if they had seen it. Keirn and Fobair were on Leopard One's left wing so both pilots were looking to the right, at their leader. Neither man saw the missile burst from the clouds a mile beneath the flight. Even if they had, the SA-2 covered the remaining distance in less than two seconds, and it was far too late to do anything.

Too near for any flight corrections, the SAM simply flew straight at the radar return, and the missile's Shmel 5E11 fuse received a command to arm itself. When the telephone-pole-sized missile passed below and slightly behind the nearest Phantom, invisible radar pulses radiating from the missile's nose struck Leopard Two, bounced off the metal fighter, and instantly returned to the fuse. Well within its 213-foot blast fragmentation range, the 440-pound warhead immediately detonated.

Made to destroy much larger bombers, the nine thousand exploding bits of metal were overkill against a fighter. Traveling at 8,200 feet per second, the fan-shaped fragment pattern sliced into the Phantom's belly, tail, and left wing. This punctured the rear cockpit, shredded the jet's hydraulics and left engine, and instantly started a fire in the right engine. Mortally wounded, the fighter flipped over and began spinning out of control. Rocked by the concussion and riddled by fragments from the other SAMs, the three remaining Phantoms headed southwest and managed to limp back across the border.

Burning and trailing black smoke, Leopard Two spun down through the clouds and disappeared. Of the nine attempted SA-2 launches, only seven got off the ground and only the first hit. This didn't stop the Soviets from claiming five kills on American jets that grim afternoon in July 1965. After all, it was good propaganda and validation that their program of surface-to-air missiles was effective against U.S. fighters. The Vietnamese came away convinced that such an air defense system was the only way to operationally protect the few assets they had north of the 17th parallel. Despite Chinese entreaties, Hanoi decided to employ Soviet SAM systems—and they wanted more.

As for Leopard Two, Pops Keirn ejected, was promptly captured, and spent the next seven and a half years as a prisoner of war. Ross Fobair was not so fortunate. He never responded to the front seater's calls and did not eject.*

In addition to Washington's shock and disbelief, the events over the Red River on July 24, 1965, produced two immediate results. Foremost, in long term, the tragedy led to a revolution in combat aviation. Radar-guided missile systems were now a legitimate threat to tactical aviation, the very type of flying needed to fight the rapidly expanding war in Southeast Asia. Something had to be done, and quickly. Soon talk grew of creating a special band of highly trained and specially equipped aviators to fight the missiles—if the Pentagon could find men crazy enough to do it.

The second response to Leopard Two's loss was short term. Very short term, indeed.

Payback.

---

*It was not until his nephew, Bruce Giffin, traveled to Vietnam in 1997 that his uncle's remains were finally identified. In 2001, Lieutenant Colonel Ross Fobair finally made his trip home and was laid to rest in Goleta, California.

PART ONE

The end of the fight is a tombstone white
With the name of the late deceased.
And the epitaph drear, a fool lies here
Who tried to hustle the East.
RUDYARD KIPLING

CHAPTER 1

SPRING HIGH

A LONG WHITE tongue.

That was it. The pilot shoved up the helmet visor, squinted, and shook his head. Well . . . that's what it looked like, he thought, leaning forward to stare over the canopy rail. Sunlight sparkled on the water, edges feathering as it spat from the green cliffs, then tumbled onto rocks a thousand feet below. Amazing. The pilot risked another long look and saw a copper-colored pool wrapped in floating gray mist.

"Isn't that beautiful?"

He flinched, startled. Not the normal type of radio call one heard on a combat mission. Especially this one. Captain Vic Vizcarra, flying as Rambler Two today, watched the magnificent sight disappear as the four F-105 fighters rumbled past, accelerating to 480 knots over northern Laos. Extra chatter on the way into Vietnam was never good, so he merely double-clicked the mike. Vic was certain the flight leader, Major Art Mearns, would have something to say about it later when they landed.

Powerful and big, the F-105 was built to fly fast and dangerously low. Nicknamed the "Thud," it was designed to drop tactical nuclear bombs on the Soviet Union, though by necessity it was now being used in a different war for completely different reasons. Wriggling his shoulders against the seat harness, Vic stared out at the untamed highlands of the border provinces, struck, as always, by their untamed beauty. *Hope I never go down here.* The pilot shook his head.

Weathered gray rock formations poked up like old teeth through the startling green foliage. Far off to the right, layered in shimmering indigo shades, lay the Gulf of Tonkin. Left of the fighters, some sixty miles north between Vietnam and Laos, he could see the peanut-shaped valley of Dien Bien Phu. France's colonial empire had met its fate there, and Vic had very nearly met his own three days ago on another strike mission. *Another place I hope I never see again.* He chuckled humorlessly. Today was different. This was revenge. Forty-eight F-105s out of Thailand were headed into North Vietnam to obliterate the SAM sites that killed Ross Fobair three days earlier.* Rambler was part of six flights from Takhli air base, named for classic automobiles, while Korat's six flights of four Thuds were named for trees.

As the distant valley passed away under his wing, the four fighters headed northeast and began dropping steadily. Vic's eyes continuously measured distances, speeds, and the other jets around him. His left hand subtly slid the throttle forward and back, adding and taking away power while his right hand gently twitched the stick.

Well designed and relatively roomy, the Thud cockpit was set up around a T-shaped center console. Every few seconds Vic glanced inside the cockpit and cross-checked a gauge or switch. He didn't bother with the big attitude indicator or hor-

---

*Forty-six actually got over the target. Two Thuds from Korat aborted.

izontal situation indicator in the middle console just forward of the stick. Neither did the side consoles, by his knees, concern him, as they mostly contained the UHF radio, navigation control panels, lighting, and other miscellaneous systems he'd set up on the ground. The combining glass, a transparent rectangle mounted directly above the glare shield, did get a look and Vic could plainly see its multi-ringed, bright orange circle glowing against the afternoon sun. Normally he would use it for aiming, and it could be set for the airspeed, altitude, and weapons required on an attack. Not that it would matter today, since they would be dropping on their leader's command. *Revenge.* His dark eyes blazed briefly at the thought of Leopard Two.

Passing through 10,000 feet, Vic looked around at Laos. The Plain of Jars was well behind them; just to the right of his nose lay the Barthelemy Pass, a narrow gap through the border mountains. In the steep valley along the foothills he caught the metallic gleam of the Ma River, and he frowned. They'd have to get down quicker since the ingress plan was to cross into North Vietnam at 100 feet and 480 knots. Hidden in rough terrain the Thuds should be invisible to any watching radars, and at that speed they'd cover sixty miles to the next turn point in eight minutes. Too quick, hopefully, for any sort of detection or counterattack from the North Vietnamese Air Force and its MiG fighters.

"Green 'em up."

Major Mearns sounded tense. Passing 5,000 feet, the dive steepened as the mountains loomed ahead, and Vic cracked the throttle back a bit. Eyeballing the armament selector switches at the bottom left of the center console, he knew there'd be no time to check again in a few minutes. The WPN SEL knob was set for CONV BOMBS, meaning no nukes, and the MODE selected was for a manual delivery. It was really the only way to use the four big BLU-27 canisters, two under the wings and two more on a belly-mounted multiple-ejector rack. Glancing left again, he caught Rambler One rocking his wings. Taking another quick glimpse inside, he squinted as he scanned the smaller engine and fuel gauges on the bottom right of the center console.

Tachometer, oil pressure, and all three hydraulic systems were "in the green," reading just what they should.

Nudging the stick left and inching the throttle up, Vic smoothly slid in closer. All four fighters were now within several hundred feet of each other as the earth rose up to meet them. Shallowing the dive at about a thousand feet, Rambler One then carefully dropped lower. Vic swallowed again, flexing his shoulders against the straps. This is what Thuds did—fly low and fast. Its system accuracy, however, was problematic and would be an ongoing issue for the F-105. It began the war with a circular error average in excess of 1,000 feet,* because accuracy wasn't really important for its original mission of delivering a combination of nuclear weapons with a two-megaton yield. They weren't engineered for formation mass attacks against a forewarned, alert enemy—and *this* target had been printed in the *New York Times*!

Up ahead, just left of where the Ma River bent back to the south, a string of valleys wound their way north into Vietnam. Mearns veered off to fly along the western side of the foothills rather than going straight up the valley. Not as much fun, Vic thought, but easier on the wingmen, and they could all remain concealed a bit longer. On the far right side of the formation Vic lagged back, flying more aft of the leader so he could keep the hills in the corner of his eye. For the last eight miles through the

---

*Circular error average, or CEA, is essentially the "miss distance" of a bomb impact from the target.

passes, Vic felt the familiar pure joy of flying. The jet he loved throbbed in his hands, stick and throttle moving in time with his eyes, instantly making countless little adjustments. Terrain blurred past, but his mind took snapshots: a hut perched on a terraced hillside; strange red-brown hills that were bald at the bottom but forested along the top, just the opposite of anywhere else in the world.

Lit up by the sun, the startling, jade-colored valley floor stretched away south and west, but it was gloomier up ahead, where they were going. Maybe it was the mountains or the shadowy ravines, but Vic felt like he was flying from light to darkness. For a minute he was totally occupied with the jet: weaving through the higher terrain, pulling hard when Rambler One angled away, then snapping upright, his eyes catching the bobbing shapes of Rambler Three and Four on the other side of the narrow gorges. Hamlets flashed past, ramshackle wooden shacks clustered in tiny clearings, the thin smoke trails from cooking fires very gray against the green trees.

Suddenly the fighters crested a ridge, and he blinked.

A wide, flat valley stretched out before them, running west to east as far as he could see. Rambler One dropped into the last, funnel-shaped gorge and Vic followed, bumping the stick forward and grunting as cockpit dust floated up in his face. Shoving the throttle forward, he nudged the fighter right and spread out slightly. As the terrain flattened, the Thuds leveled off at 100 feet, so low he could plainly see details on the ground: a wooden sign, a man on a bicycle, farms.

Feeling exposed as the fighter shot into the open, Vic's skin tingled with adrenaline, his chin slippery against the rubber oxygen mask. He held the Thud steady. Letting go of the throttle, he slid the dark helmet visor down just as the other fighters emerged out of the gorge into North Vietnam's sunlit Son La valley. Rain-swollen and churning, the Da River flashed beneath his wings. Up ahead, the emerald and tan valley floor fell away against the mottled dark green mountains jutting up before him. Beneath a brilliant powder blue sky it was a striking picture—then voices crackled loudly in his helmet.

"Stay with it, Two!" The voice crackled through his helmet and Vic flinched.

". . . smo . . . got smoke in . . . the cockpit."

"Stay with it . . . try to get over the next ridge!"

Weaving through the hills, Rambler had been unable to hear what was happening to the front end of the strike package, but now, in the flats, everything suddenly came through. Someone was hit. Vic swallowed. Who was up ahead now? His eyes flickered to the clock. Based on the timing it was most likely one of the Korat flights. Vic swallowed. Or maybe Healy flight, the first fighters over the target from Takhli.

"BEE-EAR BEE-EAR BEE-EAR BEE-EAR."

The chilling wail from an emergency beacon made him wince. Beacons activated automatically when a pilot ejected—somebody was down. With one quick movement Vic flipped up the visor, wiped his forehead, turned the radio volume down a notch, and dropped his hand back onto the throttle.

". . . in the river! Saw a chute . . . over the river."

"Blue Bells are singing." This came from an orbiting RB-66 aircraft and meant that Fansong radars were on air.

"BEE-EAR BEE-EAR BEE-EAR BEE-EAR."

The first twelve Takhli jets were all from the Ace of Spades, the 563rd Tactical Fighter Squadron, and he didn't know any of them well.* Maybe, he thought, maybe it was a Korat guy. *I knew it.* He thumped his knee, anger boiling up from his

---

*The 563rd deployed to Takhli in April 1965, from McConnell Air Force Base, Kansas.

gut. What the hell did Washington know about killing SAMs in Vietnam? Somebody sure thought they did. It was a stupid plan, but there was nothing any of them could do about it.

Takhli was putting twenty-four Thuds against Site 7, supposedly one of the SAMs that shot down Leopard Two, the F-4C from Ubon, three days earlier. Coming in from the north, flying down along the Red River, were Healy, Austin, Hudson, Valiant, Rambler, and Corvette. Each four ship of fighters would plaster the SAM site or support facilities with a mix of cluster bombs and napalm. Korat's flights of Pepper, Willow, Redwood, Cedar, Hickory, and Dogwood would come up from the south to simultaneously hit Site 6.*

"Redwood and Cedars . . . Healy One is west of the river at two K. Capping."

"Roger that . . . two minutes out for Redwood."

"Triple A . . . Yen Bai . . . both sides of the river."

Triple A. Anti-Aircraft Artillery fire and apparently lots of it. Like all fighter pilots Vic was well aware that the rapid firing guns were a deadly threat. He listened and tried to build the picture in his head. Healy One was capping west of the Black River at 2,000 feet. Only reason for that was to look for a wingman. So it had to be Healy Two who'd gone down. This got the leader out of the way of the incoming flights, but in the heart of the envelope for anti-aircraft fire or any waiting SAMs. Nodding slightly, he figured the timing and decided it had to be Hudson calling out anti-aircraft fire over Yen Bai. Two other flights would be over each target right now and behind Hudson came Valiant . . . then Rambler.

Vic stared ahead at the rocky karst terrain and tree-topped, jagged hills. The Thuds were skirting the southern edge of the

---

*Redwood Two was Captain Chuck Horner, who would later command all coalition air forces during the 1991 Gulf War.

Hoang Lien mountain range, which ought to keep them shielded from prying radars. The other jets were gradually moving closer together as the valley narrowed, hills rising steeply up on both sides. *What got Healy Two?* Vic wondered. *Triple A or a SAM?* The "blue bells" call came from an orbiting RB-66 electronic warfare aircraft and meant that enemy radars were operating. But he'd never heard anyone call out SAMs.

"Two went in! Just south of the target!"

Which Number Two?

Vic's mouth dried up. Had to be one of the Korat guys. He took a deep breath. Everyone shot down so far was a Number Two, just like him. Shit. The radios sucked, too; that was the problem with forcing forty-six jets to use the same frequency. Confusion. He sighed and concentrated on flying.

"Blue bells are silent."

"Pickle . . . pickle . . ."

". . . on fire . . . didn't see a chute from Two."

Which Number Two, dammit!

"Valiant Two is now Valiant Five."

Bursting from the dark valley, the four Thuds suddenly shot out into the sunlight and everyone wobbled a bit in the glare. Instinctively, the pilots moved out and Vic's eyes darted back inside the cockpit. Yen Bai, the last turn point before the target, was two minutes ahead. Rambler One was staying a bit north but the terrain was flatter and this would keep the fighters lower for longer. It also kept another line of low, bumpy hills between them and the Red River valley, where all the SAMs were supposed to be.

"BEE-EAR BEE-EAR BEE-EAR BEE-EAR."

Another beacon! Vic shook his head and forced himself to breathe normally. It was 1405 . . . five minutes past 2 P.M., and he tried to remember the target area flow. Healy and Austin should be off the northern target, but he wasn't sure about the Korat guys to the south. Valiant, twenty miles in front of Rambler, should be near the Red River turning south and Hudson would be about over the target.

"Valiant . . . take it down. Triple A . . . over Yen Bai . . ."

"Redwoods, hard left!"

"Triple A . . . ah, over Yen Bai . . ."

"BEE-EAR BEE-EAR BEE-EAR BEE-EAR."

So Valiant was over the river heading south. Vic risked a last look at his weapon switches; three green lights were on, one for the centerline pylon that carried a pair of napalm canisters and a light for each outboard pylon. Everything was getting power and set correctly to release: all he had to do was hit the pickle button. *If I live that long,* he thought grimly. They cleared another smaller ridgeline, and from the corner of his left eye there it was . . . a wide, tan-colored river snaking off to the southeast.

"Pickle!"

"Blue Bells are silent."

"Three is Bingo."

Head swiveling, Vic watched the other three jets and the picture unfolding off to the south. The hills rapidly fell away, spreading the Red River valley out before him, and off at his right at two o'clock there was smoke. Lots of it. Black columns reaching up stark and clear against the blue sky. The target. Hudson was carrying sixteen canisters filled with JP-4, a jelling solution, and a powdered aluminum soap called naphthalene palmitate—napalm. Despite sucking the oxygen from the air, the stuff burned everything. Worse, it stuck to whatever it hit. But it was an area weapon, designed to flatten forests and kill soft things like people. It wasn't great against entrenchments, and the detonations obscured everything for minutes afterward . . . tough on whoever was coming in behind it.

Like Valiant and Rambler.

Nodding again, he glanced at his fuel, the clock, then the map on his left knee. Yep . . . right where the Black and Red rivers joined up about twenty miles to his southeast. It was 1411.

"Hudson Two's hit!"

Vic groaned. No, not again. Then another voice, nearly screaming. "Hudson Two . . . pull up!"

"Kile . . . get out! Eject . . . *eject*!" That sounded like Billy Sparks or Hudson Four, Marty Case.

Rambler One rolled up slightly, cheating off to the left of a small line of hills. As the other three corrected, he rolled the wings level, sunlight flashing from the polished silver skin. *Easy to see . . . too easy.* Vic shook his head and swallowed. None of the jets had been camouflaged and they still wore their peacetime, stateside bright colors over shiny metal. As they'd taken off, he'd seen red and white stripes on the tails and wingtips of the 563rd jets. *Stupid.*

Suddenly a flash overhead caught his eye. Then another.

Lifting his eyes, Vic saw a string of ugly black and gray popcorn balls erupt in the sky over the river. They were maybe three miles off the nose, but he knew what they were. He'd seen them before. Anti-aircraft guns . . . 37 mm junk from Yen Bai.

"Triple A. Eleven o'clock high," someone said, but he couldn't tell who it was.

"Two went in." The voice was angry and shocked.

"Four . . . did you see a chute?" That was Paul Craw, the Hudson flight leader.

"Negative."

Ramping down the last hillside, Vic sat straight up in the seat, the heavy stick solid in his right hand as he jockeyed the throttle. Incredibly, Rambler One was still creeping lower, and at that altitude Vic could do nothing but fly and stare at the other Thud. Barely fifty feet above the trees . . . if he sneezed he'd be splattered all over North Vietnam. Ignoring the chatter, the Triple A, and his own thumping heart, Vic tensed up for what was coming. A curve in the river filled his right eye and buildings from Yen Bai appeared, along with roads and a few boats.

He swallowed. Surely they wouldn't blast over the town at fifty feet.

"C'mon," he muttered. "C'mon!"

"BEE-EAR BEE-EAR BEE-EAR BEE-EAR."

Another one down. Three Thuds lost in less than fifteen minutes . . .

Rambler One suddenly rolled up toward him, and Vic instantly yanked the throttle back, pulling back hard on the stick. The big 105's wings were perpendicular to the ground, vapor streaming from the wingtips as it slid across the horizon toward him. Vic immediately let the nose drop off, flicked his wrist sideways, and pulled away.

"Shit . . . we're lined up with the SAM!"

Vic blinked. That wasn't Art Mearns, but it might be Valiant One, Major Phil Coll. Unlike the first Takhli flights, Valiant, Rambler, and Corvette were all "Headhunters" from the 80th Tactical Fighter Squadron, and he knew their voices.

"Well don't make another pass!"

Despite himself, he smiled at that. It was his buddy J. C. Atkinson, Valiant Two. Overbanking, he cobbed the power back a bit, then snapped the fighter halfway out of the roll, staring off his left wing. Vic saw immediately that he'd done it right and was actually a bit aft of where he should be. Rolling out, he shoved the throttle forward and exhaled loudly. *What a stupid way to fly.* . . . He was more worried about hitting the other Ramblers than he was about the SAMs, Triple A, or the target.

"Blue Bells are singing." The distant voice was disembodied, almost mechanical.

"Redwoods . . . roll out heading two-two-zero . . . climb!"

Rambler One began rocking his wings to bring everyone into close formation. Vic took a deep breath, added more power, and nudged the stick left. Darting a last look at his fuel and the weapons switches one more time, he ran a dry tongue over his dry lips.

Mearns was going lower.

The lead Thud leveled off at 20 feet over the valley and held 500 knots. Vic swallowed, the spit catching in his dry throat. *This is crazy.* As his breathing quickened he closed up to fifteen feet off Rambler One's right wing. Not fingertip formation, but close enough. Too close for combat. Apparently the others felt the same way, and he saw visored faces from Three and Four staring down at Mearns as the fighters bobbled slightly in the hot air. Everyone else was stacked a bit higher than the leader, so Vic could see his whole plane, not just the wingtip. They'd cut across a big bend in the Red River but were now directly over the water, following it into the target.

"Valiant . . . pickle . . . pickle."

It was the dust that caught Vic's eye and his mouth dropped open slightly. Rambler flight was so low over the rice paddies that their exhaust was shooting rooster tails of dirt into the air. Blinking several times, he desperately wanted to sneak a look ahead but didn't dare. Not at 30 feet above Vietnam at 600 knots and eleven miles from the target. But the corner of his right eye picked up the bright orange flash from Valiant's cluster bomb attack.

"Heads up, heads up! Thuds on the nose!"

"Hard left . . . hard left!"

"Valiant, take it *down*!"

Vic didn't have to see it to know what happened. Forty-six fighters simultaneously hitting two targets barely three miles apart from opposite directions. Now, on top of the wrong weapons, Triple A, and every gomer down there with an AK-47, they all had to worry about hitting one another.

Brown against green, the river appeared, disappeared, then reappeared under the wings. Paddies in orderly rectangles zipped past, and thin smoke fingers rose up from cooking fires. *Close,* he thought. *We gotta be close.*

"BEE-EAR BEE-EAR BEE-EAR BEE-EAR."

"Four is Bingo."

". . . left ten o'clock low!"

Wide, flat, and muddy, the Red River was in plain sight beyond Number Four's wing. Green fields stretched out past it to the east, and he could see a long, prominent ridge stretching south, pointing like a finger to the sea—and to Hanoi. He took another deep breath. The North Vietnamese capital was only forty miles away.

Gray paths ran alongside the water and he was surprised to see people on them. Near the banks the soil changed to the deep red color that gave the river its name. Suddenly Rambler One bumped up slightly and the others followed. He didn't go far, though, maybe up to fifty feet, then banked slightly left. Everyone corrected, and as Vic rolled wings level again, Mearns began to count.

"Ramblers . . . five . . . four . . ."

Vic moved his right thumb slightly, hovering over the red button on the top of the stick. Chalky blue water from the Black River suddenly appeared under him, then vanished as they flashed overhead.

"BEE-EAR BEE-EAR BEE-EAR BEE-EAR."

"Triple A! Yen Bai."

"... three ... two ..."

There. Red tin roofs!

"... one ..."

From the corners of his eyes Vic picked up a cluster of white-washed, two-story buildings. Red tin roofs ... the barracks for the SAM support facility that was their target.

... pickle!"

He mashed down quickly and smoothly on the release button, then held it. The four BLU-27s fell away and the jet kicked up slightly as the extra weight came off. In the blink of an eye, he saw twelve canisters peel away from the bellies of the other fighters.

"Vic ..."

Hearing his name, he instantly broke to the right, slammed the throttle forward to the stop, and pulled the stick into his lap.

"You have the lead!"

They had to clear off right immediately to avoid the Korat flights that were attacking from the south. Grunting, he concentrated on a perfectly level turn ... not easy at 30 feet while getting shot at. He tried not to think about going belly-up to the guns and the other Thuds.

"Hickory ... pickle!"

It felt good to look right instead of left, and Vic braced his helmet against the red leather headrest as the 105 muscled its way across the horizon. Normally you'd drop low in a turn but there was no low here ... only dirt and death. For an instant he saw the whole target area, like a snapshot: billowing black smoke, particles hanging in the air, and fire blazing on the ground.

As his nose came through south, he spotted a huge oily cloud hanging above the other SAM site. At that moment Rambler was over a U-shaped flat area between the rivers, maybe two miles wide. Anti-aircraft fire was everywhere. Nasty little yellow or orange explosions that became ugly gray smudges . . . hundreds of them.

Sweat leaked from under his mask and ran down his chin. Another drop trickled into his eye, stinging it. The radio was garbage; everyone still talking so he mentally tuned it down to background noise. As the Black River appeared in the corner of his right eye, Vic snapped the fighter upright, bunted forward on the stick, and leveled off so low that he could see rocks under the shallow water.* Also two other smoke pillars, thinner and darker than anything caused by napalm. He gritted his teeth; Hudson Two and Healy Two . . . had to be.

Roaring down the Black River, Rambler sprinted for the safety of the hills to the southwest. Sunlight flickered on the water, then disappeared as they crossed to the west bank. Vic glanced left and saw the other three Thuds. They'd made it out . . . so far. Dark specks were everywhere along the horizon as the Korat fighters hit their target and then dashed for higher terrain away from the guns.

"Rambler One's got the lead on the left."

The other Thud surged ahead as Mearns lit his afterburner. Vic double-clicked the mike, rotated the throttle outboard and shoved it forward. More flashes overhead . . . and off the left wing.

"C'mon . . ." He was leaning forward, willing the big jet past 600 knots and into the foothills.

"BEE-EAR BEE-EAR BEE-EAR BEE-EAR."

"Hudson Three . . ."

---

* "Bunting" forward puts an aircraft into zero, then negative g's. Temporarily released from positive gravity's pull, the control surfaces are easier to move. This permits rapid maneuvering, though the "light in the seat" feeling is uncomfortable for more than a few seconds.

"Blue . . ."

"Bingo."

". . . are singing."

Then they were there.

Green mountains suddenly stretched from eyeball to eyeball, filling his vision as they made it to the foothills. Falling farther aft, Vic mirrored Rambler One as he wove through the rising hills, putting them between the 105s and the SAMs.

Mearns began a slight climb up to 500 feet and Vic took a deep breath.

"Sonuva . . ." He reached up and unclipped the mask. A wave of cold air immediately hit his sweaty face and it felt marvelous. Four more minutes and they'd be in Laos, then a zoom climb up and straight to the tanker. *Survived again!* His skin prickled and a wave of relief swept through him as he tried to relax his muscles. They were still thirty-five miles inside North Vietnam, but there weren't any known threats between them and the border. None they knew of, anyway, he thought with a grin, pulling the power back to avoid flying ahead of Rambler One.

The thrill faded as he thought of the guys who went down. Dead . . . or worse. Too far into Indian Country to be rescued. Alone. One of the Cedars from Korat had also gone in, and he sighed, dragging a gloved hand across his forehead, up under his helmet.

Was it worth it?

Mearns banked into him and the four Thuds skirted around the western slope of a jagged peak. As they passed by, heading for the basin beyond and the Laotian border, their thundering engines shook trees and vibrated the earth. Hidden from view along the base of that peak, sad metal fragments were strewn about, twisted, charred, and barely recognizable. A wingtip, colored strands of badly melted wire, and attached to a mangled strut was a perfectly intact nose wheel from an American fighter jet.

A large piece of metal, torn at the bottom, lay at the base of a tree. Fin shaped, about six feet tall, it was partially burned, but some markings remained since it hadn't been on the ground long—maybe only three or four days. There was a painted shield, blue on the top and red on the bottom, with a sword on top. A long, yellow lightning bolt ran diagonally through it and disappeared into the burned area. Had there been anyone to see, the numbers on the strut were plain to see: 63-7599.

It was all that remained of an F-4 Phantom called Leopard Two.

CHAPTER 2

HITCHHIKER IN A HAILSTORM

WHY WERE YOUNG American men fighting, and often dying, in a river valley so far from home? The short answer is that they were ordered there, and the military was at the mercy of elected government officials. It was not the Pentagon's decision when, where, and whom to fight, so, having no real choice, they went. Unfortunately, many of them, like Leopard Two's Ross Fobair, never came back. We must turn to Washington for answers: why did the greatest nation on earth find itself embroiled in a small, globally inconsequential region like Southeast Asia?

It is impossible to answer this or understand the Vietnam War, let alone the SAM threat, without understanding something of that country itself, at least in the modern context.* As with most present-day issues, the conflict in Vietnam was partially derived from its tumultuous past. Rice, rubber, and drugs: it is reasonable to say that the last great struggle in Vietnam's history, what they call the War of Independence (1954–75), had its roots here. In 1858, the French Empire, attempting to rival

---

*For additional background on the origins of the Vietnam War, see Appendix C.

British interests in India, landed soldiers, and by the following year they had captured Saigon. After decades of fighting, French colonial hegemony managed to absorb the three Vietnamese regions of Cochinchina, Annam, and the northern province of Tonkin. Cambodia and Laos were eventually added, and the territory collectively known as Indochina became the jewel in France's empire.

While the region was a valuable source of rice, coal, and rubber, it was opium that provided the largest profit margin, one-third of France's total colonial income. Vietnamese land was owned by absentee French landlords and a local aristocracy completely dependent on French patronage for position, titles, and wealth. As so often occurs with such a system, excess privileges and cruelty would fan the grassfire of rebellion. All the scientific and cultural benefits from French cultural influence were negated by mismanagement, avarice, and indifference. To the Vietnamese populace, all the evils besetting Indochina became synonymous with colonialism and, by association, with capitalism. This in turn gave rise to a communist-flavored nationalist resistance movement and fired the imagination of a young man named Nguyen Sinh Cung—later known to the world as Ho Chi Minh.

Much like China's Mao Zedong, the Vietnamese leader was a reluctant communist who used the ideology as a means to an end. Ho Chi Minh wanted sovereignty for Vietnam, nothing else, and would say, "Why drive the tiger [Japan] out the front door while letting the wolf [France] in through the back?" Forming the League of Independence for Vietnam, abbreviated to "Viet Minh," he prepared to fight and expected support from the Allies—namely the Americans.* How, he reasoned, could

---

*Việt Nam Độc Lập Đồng Minh Hội, or League of Independence for Vietnam.

Allied nations combating fascism, militarism, and national so-
cialism then turn around and promote a colonial servitude only
marginally better than the systems they'd vanquished? It was an
understandable but naïve viewpoint.

It was naïve because Indochina was a matter of indifference
to Americans far more concerned with the state of affairs in
Europe. This attitude was encouraged by the French, who desperately needed help reclaiming their prewar possessions and
whatever remained of their national prestige. Paris had also enthusiastically volunteered a reconstituted French Army to help
with an invasion of Japan, assuming, of course, that the Americans would clothe them, give them weapons, and transport the
army to the Far East.

Despite losing to the Axis in 1940 and collaborating with
the Japanese throughout the war, French businessmen felt en-
titled to have their investments returned to them. Vietnamese
nationalist resistance to this notion began to spread and subsequently destabilize the entire area. To achieve this the French
were willing to use deception and diplomatic pressure *and* to
shamelessly risk the lives of their own soldiers, as well as those
of Britain and the United States—two nations that had already
shed much blood for France.* Nevertheless, the British government was in no position to object to French colonial pretensions
since Britain had similar plans for retaining its own empire,
namely in India.

The postwar Potsdam Agreement set the stage for the next
thirty years of military and political troubles by dividing French
Indochina at the 16th parallel. The region north of the line would

---

*According to the British Commonwealth War Graves Commission, there are
473,427 British soldiers buried in France. The American Battlefield Memorial
Commission lists 60,869 U.S. graves in France.

be controlled by the Chinese while the southern areas would be occupied by the British, who, after being handed a complex, unstable, and dangerous situation, pulled out of Cochinchina in October 1945 and left the whole mess to the French—those least likely to solve it.

In a remarkably prophetic assessment, an American OSS officer, Lieutenant Colonel A. Peter Dewey, wrote to his superiors that "Cochinchina is burning, the French and British are finished here, and we ought to clear out of Southeast Asia."*

The Viet Minh reacted predictably against French troops and northern Vietnam began to burn. On November 23, 1946, French warships shelled the port of Haiphong in retaliation for the uprising and the situation rapidly deteriorated.† Viet Minh guerrillas faded into the Tonkinese hills or the Central Highlands, fighting back with a few outdated weapons, and even spears. The conflict that followed became the First Indochina War.

Dien Bien Phu is a forsaken, narrow valley in far northwestern Vietnam. It was here during March 1954 that French Indochina ceased to exist and the window of American involvement was opened. Viet Minh guerrillas had infiltrated the area all winter and, under cover of the spring rains, attacked and laid siege to the French garrison. Aided by the weather, the Vietnamese ambushed aerial resupply attempts and methodi-

---

*A Yale graduate, World War II veteran, and son of a congressman, Colonel Dewey was the first American combat casualty in Vietnam. During an ambush near Hanoi on September 26, 1945, Dewey called out in French and was mistakenly killed.

†Claims that the French cruiser *Suffren* was involved are problematic. The channel into the port is only twenty-five-feet deep, about the same draft as the warship. However, the sloops *Chevreuil* and *Savorgnan de Brazza* were certainly present. Casualty statistics are equally unreliable—but damage was done and lives were lost. Certainly the backlash by the Viet Minh outweighed any military value of the attack.

cally annihilated the defenders. The chairman of the U.S. Joint Chiefs of Staff, Admiral Arthur Radford, and the Air Force chief, General Nathan Twining, responded with Operation Vulture. A far-fetched and dangerous plan, it entailed the use of sixty B-29 bombers, including three with atomic bombs, to hit the perimeter around Dien Bien Phu. Apparently no one gave much thought to the effect this would have on the French defenders, but they did consider the Chinese reaction. General Matthew Ridgway, fresh from Korea, and most of the other chiefs disagreed with the whole scheme. Fortunately sanity prevailed, the plan was scrapped, and no nukes were dropped to save the French.

On the evening of May 7, 1954, the French commander surrendered, shocking the world and bolstering the Viet Minh. The French commanders thought very little of their opposition and tended to ignore intelligence reports contradicting their prejudices. They did not take into account terrain, weather, or indigenous support for the nationalist movement. The collapse at Dien Bien Phu was more than just the shocking defeat of a modern, professional force by poorly trained and equipped peasant militia. It was an unmistakable warning of things to come.

PRESIDENT JOHN F. KENNEDY brought great hope to the United States. The economy was booming; science, technology, and American lifestyles were envied around the world. Five months into his term, in May 1961, Freedom 7 rocketed Alan Shepard into space, captivating the nation with pride and hope. Kennedy was handsome and sophisticated, scion of a wealthy family, with a beautiful wife and young children. He was also a decorated combat veteran who knew the risks of war, and who was well aware that U.S. involvement in Southeast Asia was a potential catastrophe. Yet Kennedy also believed that the Cold War was a real conflict, perhaps not with open battlefields, or proud memories, but a war nonetheless. During his election campaign he had accused his Republican rival, Vice President Richard M. Nixon, of being "soft" on communism and therefore could not afford that perception of his own presidency. So Castro's Cuba seemed an ideal place to send a message to Moscow about the dangers of spreading communism in the Western Hemisphere. The CIA was given permission to activate a plan that would insert 1,400 Cubans onto two beaches in the Bahía de Cochinos, the Bay of Pigs, along the island's southern coast. These men made up Brigade 2506, which would then rouse the countryside in a counterrevolution against Fidel Castro.

That was the assumption, anyway.

Air cover, provided by obsolete, repainted American B-26 bombers flown by Cuban pilots, took off at 0228 on Sunday, April 15, 1961, from Puerto Cabezas, Nicaragua. They subsequently missed most of their targets and left the majority of Castro's Revolutionary Air Force operational.* When the 1,400-man brigade landed on the Blue beach at Playa Girón, and the Red beach at Playa Larga, they were virtually alone. Despite the nearby presence of a U.S. aircraft carrier (the *Essex*) and five destroyers, Washington decided not to intervene, subsequently abandoning the Brigade to its fate. Attacked by 20,000 regular Cuban troops, 114 brigade soldiers were killed and 1,189 were captured.† The operation was a disaster.

---

*Defensa Anti-Aérea y Fuerza Aérea Revolucionaria.
†After nearly two years in prison, the survivors were returned to the United States following a ransom worth $53 million of medical supplies and baby food.

The next year Kennedy lost face again over the same island during the Cuban Missile Crisis. Nikita Khrushchev, the Soviet premier, had come away from a summit meeting with Kennedy believing that the president was a dilettante, unsuited or unwilling to project American power. Moscow was also deeply concerned about U.S. Jupiter missiles based in Turkey, so in response to all this *and* the Bay of Pigs fiasco, Khrushchev increased arms shipments to Havana. These included SS-4 "Sandal" medium-range ballistic missiles (MRBM) that put most of the American eastern seaboard at risk. Further complicating matters was the August 29, 1962, discovery that a pair of SAM sites were operational in Cuba with an additional six in various stages of construction. This type of air defense system, a radar-guided SA-2, was well known to the CIA after the downing of an agency U-2 in May 1960 deep inside the Soviet Union.

On September 8, a U.S. Navy Neptune photoreconnaissance plane caught the Soviet freighter *Omsk* inbound for Havana, her deck covered by missile storage containers. Additional U-2 flights discovered more SS-4 site construction around Cuba and additional sorties were ordered. By mid-September the SAM threat was so great that the military officially took over flight operations from the CIA. Using agency-modified U-2Es with the latest electronic countermeasures (ECM) gear, the USAF began flying from Barksdale, Laughlin, and McCoy air force bases on October 10, 1962. A few days later low-altitude, high-speed reconnaissance from RF-101 Voodoos out of Shaw Air Force Base, South Carolina, revealed probable intercontinental ballistic missile (ICBM) sites.

Negotiations and secret meetings abounded. Many in Washington thought the Soviets were simply bluffing since they'd never bothered to camouflage the Cuban sites. Others believed it was a deliberate provocation and the world was indeed going back to war—this time with nuclear weapons. Strategic Air Command B-52 bombers went on full alert and dispersed for combat operations and on October 22, President Kennedy instituted a naval blockade 500 miles off the Cuban coast. He also sent Task Force 135, formed around the carriers *Enterprise* and *Independence,* with 8,000 Marines to Guantánamo Bay. This was followed by Task Force 136, a 180-ship fleet containing five more aircraft carriers.* Kennedy sent a message to the Soviet premier stating, in part:

> *If certain developments in Cuba took place, the United States would do whatever must be done to protect its own security and that of its allies. . . . I must tell you that the United States is determined that this threat to the security of this hemisphere be removed.*

Khrushchev replied the following day, October 23, by affirming that the weapons sold to Cuba were solely for defensive purposes, and that he hoped the Americans would "display wisdom and renounce the actions pursued by you [Kennedy] which may lead to catastrophic consequences for world peace." Tensions escalated on Friday, October 26, when the Lebanese-flagged *Marucla* was detained and searched by the destroyer *Joseph P. Kennedy, Jr.* (DD-850), named for President Kennedy's older brother, a Navy pilot who had died during World War II.† Secret negotiations, which did not include the Cubans, continued with Soviet ambassador Anatoly Dobrynin.

---

*USS *Shangri-La* (CVS-38), *Wasp* (CVS-18), *Essex* (CVS-9), *Randolph* (CVS-15), and *Lake Champlain* (CVS-39).
†Joe Kennedy Jr. was the older brother of President John F. Kennedy. A naval aviator, he volunteered for a nearly suicidal mission and was killed in 1944.

Castro then sent a message to Moscow urging a Soviet nuclear strike on the United States if Cuba was invaded a second time.

The high point of the crisis arguably occurred the next day when a U-2 out of McCoy Air Force Base, Florida, was hit by an SA-2 above the eastern tip of Cuba. The pilot, Major Rudy Anderson of the 4080th Strategic Reconnaissance Wing, a South Carolina native and Korean War veteran, was likely killed when his pressure suit was punctured by shrapnel. The CIA then confirmed that the Cuban SS-4 sites at Sagua la Grande and San Cristóbal were now operational. Soviet air defenses went on high alert, and their ICBMs prepared to launch on October 28 when a U-2 passed over the Bering Sea into the Russian Far East near Chukotka. The entire world, it seemed, was holding its breath. Waiting.

Then, as it's often said, Khrushchev "blinked."

Moscow would agree to dismantle its missiles in Cuba if Washington promised publicly not to invade the country again. Secretly, the United States would also agree to close down its Jupiter sites in Turkey. Khrushchev announced the end of the crisis over Radio Moscow on Sunday, October 28, 1962. In the end, neither side was willing to go to war. Cuba would never have survived it, and a 6,000-mile Soviet supply line was unsustainable across the American-dominated Atlantic and Caribbean. Only an attack on the U.S. mainland would have changed the outcome and Moscow was unwilling to risk this for Cuba.

So on November 5 and 7, respectively, the freighters *Divinogorsk* and *Metallurg Anosov* left Mariel Bay, west of Havana, with twelve SS-4 missiles aboard.* *Bratsk* put to sea on Novem-

---

*Mariel Hemingway, granddaughter of Ernest Hemingway, was named after the town. Incidentally, her father, Jack Hemingway, was an OSS officer who worked undercover in occupied France during World War II.

ber 9 with six more missiles, and Washington figuratively ex-haled. It was decided by the White House that if decisive action in Cuba had been taken earlier the entire crisis would have been moot. Kennedy was especially sensitive to this viewpoint and resolved never to be bullied again. Right or wrong, this mindset would figure prominently in the events fast unfolding on the other side of the world.

THE RED PRINCE spoke eight languages, including Latin and Greek. Schooled in France as a lawyer, he returned to Laos and at age forty-one was a founding member of the Lao Freedom Front, commonly known as the Pathet Lao. Prince Souphanouvong was a devout nationalist and had organized the Pathet Lao to fight the French. Like their Viet Minh neigh-bors to the east they equated communism with anticolonialism and nationalism. Following Dien Bien Phu and the Geneva Ac-cords of 1954, Laos was declared both independent and neu-tral, yet the Red Prince lost no time in seizing control of the government in Vientiane. This aroused Washington's paranoia and convinced many that the dominoes in Southeast Asia were falling, just as President Dwight Eisenhower had predicted in April 1954.

In 1960, following a series of Laotian coups, the United States began flying reconnaissance sorties in support of the current right-wing government. Operations Pipe Stem and Able Mable deployed RF-101Cs to Tan Son Nhut Air Base, South Vietnam, and Don Muang near Bangkok, Thailand. Laotian communists aside, another major tactical concern was the growing influx of weapons, ammunition, and men from North Vietnam through to their communist brethren in South Vietnam—known as the Viet Cong. This was done through a veritable spiderweb of obscure paths cut through the hills, jungle, and forest that Hanoi designated the Truong Son supply route—known to the Americans as the Ho Chi Minh Trail.

Laos was also important to the Central Intelligence Agency. Per the Geneva Accords, there could be no regular military presence in a neutral country, so American interests were advanced through other means—namely the agency. Highly classified Lima Sites, usually airstrips built to service the agency's private air force, popped up all over the country. (By the end of the war there were more than 200 of these.) When the Pathet Lao infested the Plain of Jars, the United States supported the Royal Lao Army, under Prince Souvanna Phouma, half brother to the Red Prince. As Kennedy surveyed the situation it seemed that Laos, not Vietnam, was the place to make a stand against communism. In fact, as President Dwight Eisenhower left office he'd specifically warned Kennedy that the situation in Laos was the *real* threat in Southeast Asia.

This all changed after the Cuban Missile Crisis. The president couldn't afford another setback, political or personal, with respect to communist containment. He concluded that bolstering the Saigon regime and making a stand in South Vietnam was more practical. After President Ngo Dinh Diem begged for a bilateral defense treaty in late 1961, Kennedy began increasing the American presence in several logical ways. U.S. Special Operations advisors, newly endowed with their famous green berets, had been slowly filtering into country to train the South Vietnamese, interdict along the Ho Chi Minh Trail, and gather intelligence.

Project Farm Gate, composed of Detachment 2A of the 4400th Combat Crew Training Squadron (CCTS), arrived at Bien Hoa Air Base in South Vietnam during November 1961. Flying a mix of rotary and fixed-wing aircraft, including eight

T-28Bs and four B-26s, they were there ostensibly to provide training for the fledgling South Vietnamese Air Force. In reality, they were flying combat close air support missions for the Army of the Republic of Viet Nam (ARVN; the South Vietnamese army) and Green Berets.

All through 1962 the American presence in Southeast Asia slowly but steadily increased. Spurious radar contacts believed to be Soviet Il-28 bombers prompted the deployment of F-102A interceptors in March 1962; the first F-100 fighters arrived in May 1962.* A variety of projects were initiated. Jungle Jim Air Commandos, Mule Train for tactical transport, and Ranch Hand, a highly controversial defoliation operation, were all utilized during this ambiguous and often secretive period. Using Rainbow herbicides, C-123s sprayed huge areas of Vietnam, Laos, and Cambodia with chemicals in an effort to kill trees and food crops.† Like so many initiatives aimed at destroying the enemy through advanced technology, it achieved only marginal results and was a warning, albeit ignored, of things to come. In any event, the president, the White House, and the Pentagon were fully occupied with Cuban issues until the fall.

Yet by early 1963 the Military Assistance Command Vietnam (MACV) had replaced the old Military Assistance Advisory Group (MAAG), and Joint Task Force 116, originally deployed in 1962 to fight the Pathet Lao, was fully reactivated. However, none of this slowed the northern-based National Liberation Front (NLF) or prevented Viet Cong insurgents from occupying the southern half of the Mekong Delta. As the provinces in the region produced most of the rice and food crops for

---

*The 428th TFS out of Cannon AFB, New Mexico.
†Agents Pink, Green, Purple, Blue, White, and Orange.

the Republic of South Vietnam, this was a highly dangerous situation.

The ARVN 7th Division was responsible for the area and, most important to President Diem, for security around Saigon, including the delta. Unfortunately, this division's senior officers were trusted political appointees, not combat field commanders. In point of fact, Diem regarded successful or aggressive ARVN commanders as a threat to his hold on power. Taking casualties was also certain to attract unfavorable attention from Saigon, and ARVN officers at this stage of the war were generally cautious men owing their positions to President Diem, not to competence. This inevitably led to exaggerated claims of success and extremely optimistic, unrealistic reports on the conduct of the war.

The MACV commander, General Paul D. Harkins, did little to alleviate the difficult situation. Aware of American domestic political difficulties, he seemed generally content to "hold the line," as it were, rather than actively fight. A 1929 graduate of West Point who'd served under Patton in France, Harkin has been described as a "black-and-white" style of officer who did not see shades of gray. Nor was he inclined to accept the opinions or reports of his own embedded advisors, most notably Lieutenant Colonel John Paul Vann with the 7th ARVN Division. Vann was a U.S. Army Ranger commander and Korean War veteran who knew the Viet Cong (VC) were not simply the "raggedy-ass little bastards" Harkin believed them to be. Like the French before him, the MACV commander woefully underestimated his opponent and it would cost him dearly.

Early on the morning of January 2, 1963, elements of the 7th Division attacked Ap Bac, a tiny village in the Dinh Tuong province west of the Delta—"Indian Country," as the Americans called it, deep within VC-held territory. Intelligence had discovered Cong units resting in the area and deemed this a perfect opportunity to demonstrate the mobile combined arms warfare concept: air-mobile assault troops acting in conjunction with artillery and close air support. It would also demonstrate to reluctant ARVN commanders the benefits of a strong offensive while revealing NLF weaknesses to the two million peasants in the Mekong Delta.

Unfortunately the assault began to fall apart from the onset; only one of three helicopter waves made it in on time and the other two were held up due to fog. Two battalions of South Vietnamese Civil Guards came in over land and ran straight into carefully placed elements of the enemy's 514th Regional Battalion and 261st Main Force Battalion—twice the number of VC expected. With artillery, air support, and good tactical leadership the situation was salvageable, but the ARVN commanders, fearful of taking casualties and incurring Diem's wrath, refused to advance. Colonel Vann struggled in vain to recover the situation. But the senior Vietnamese commanders led from the rear and were basically out of the fight; without their orders those on the battlefield would not move. General Harkin stopped by 7th Division headquarters at My Tho for a briefing, accepted what he was told, and left without ever visiting the battle. That night, after inflicting some 200 casualties on the ARVN, the Viet Cong slipped away, taking their wounded with them.

The real victory at Ap Bac was far more complex. The National Liberation Front, and specifically the Viet Cong, had demonstrated their ability to stand and fight a modern, mechanized force. Not only that, they could win. This clearly showed Hanoi and the mass of delta peasants that the southern liberation movement was militarily viable. It also graphically illustrated the dysfunctional nature of the ARVN in 1963, not only to the communists but to those fighting for South Vietnam. Ap Bac was the beginning of the end for President Diem and the end of the beginning of American involvement in Southeast Asia.

Washington had at last realized Diem and his sycophants must go if South Vietnam was to stand a chance. This was conveyed through the CIA to several ARVN generals, and on November 1, 1963, General Duong Van Minh led a coup to topple the government.* A hard, ruthless man, he was determined to take power, and the next day units of the 7th Division, under new leadership, captured the Gia Long Palace in Saigon, and Diem surrendered with his younger brother. The South Vietnamese president called the U.S. ambassador to Vietnam, Henry Cabot Lodge Jr., and was promptly put on hold.

Later that evening Minh appeared at the palace for a surrender ceremony only to discover that his prisoners had somehow escaped. After a sweep of the city, the brothers, both Catholics, were discovered in the courtyard of St. Francis Xavier Church in the Cholon district. They were immediately apprehended and put in a military convoy for Tan Son Nhut Air Base. It was reported later that somewhere en route both brothers committed suicide, which was a bit difficult to explain when their bullet-riddled and knife-slashed corpses arrived at South Vietnamese Joint General Staff headquarters. With Diem's demise, the Americans now had a free hand to remake the Republic of South Vietnam. Unfortunately for the millions of Vietnamese and hundreds of thousands of Americans who would be caught up in the Vietnam War, three weeks later on a Friday afternoon in Dallas, Texas, John F. Kennedy was also assassinated.

---

*Minh, a graduate of the French École Militaire, had lost all his front teeth save one to the Japanese.

There is solid evidence that Kennedy intended to extricate the United States from Vietnam *after* the 1964 election, and his correct analysis of the situation in Laos lends credence to this supposition. JFK was also capable of making up his own mind; he was also not overly swayed or dominated by his advisors. Finally, as a combat veteran himself, he would not lightly risk American lives, nor engage in a protracted armed struggle without tangible benefits to the United States. Sadly, whatever plans he had, and whatever hope remained for a realistic resolution in Vietnam, died with him.

America's last step into the Vietnam quagmire came on November 22, 1963, when Lyndon Baines Johnson was sworn in as the thirty-sixth president of the United States. Unlike Kennedy, Johnson was no real veteran. During World War II he used his influence as a congressman to become a naval officer, and, despite an utter lack of military training, he arranged a direct commission as a lieutenant commander. Fully aware that "combat" exposure would make him more electable, the ambitious Johnson managed an appointment to an observation team that was traveling to the Pacific.

Once there, he was able to get a seat on a B-26 combat mission near New Guinea. The bomber had to turn back due to mechanical problems and briefly came under attack from Japanese fighters. The pilot got the damaged plane safely back to its base and Johnson left the very next day. This nonevent, which LBJ had absolutely no active part of, turned into his war story. The engine had been "knocked out" by enemy fighters, not simply a routine malfunction; he, LBJ, had been part of a "suicide mission," not just riding along as baggage. The fabrication grew over time, including, according to LBJ, the nickname of "Raider" Johnson given to him by the awestruck 22nd Bomber Group. The entire incident was aided and abetted by General

Douglas MacArthur, who astutely understood the advantage to having an up-and-coming congressman indebted to him. So much so that he processed a decoration, the Silver Star no less, to recognize Congressman Johnson's "gallantry."*

JOHNSON FACED TWO main problems where Vietnam was concerned. First was the known instability of the Saigon government—there were at least a half dozen coups in 1964 alone. To counter this, the president sanctioned Operations Plan (OPLAN) 34-A, aimed at securing the South Vietnamese border with American forces. He also sent the U.S. Navy and Task Force 77 into the South China Sea. Johnson's critical problem was U.S. domestic support—or lack of it. Weighing heavy on his mind was a May 1964 American Institute of Public Opinion poll that revealed nearly two-thirds of the population had given no thought to Vietnam whatsoever. Only 9 percent of the rest favored any kind of tougher stance regarding Southeast Asia. As he himself said regarding the looming war, "I feel like a hitchhiker caught in a hailstorm. . . . I can't run. I can't hide. And I can't make it stop."

Being the type of president who made most of his decisions according to poll results, LBJ was well aware that something had to change. What he needed was a pivot point, an *incident,* to rally support for action in Vietnam. Something that would portray him as a leader in his own right, the decisive man of action, as he saw himself, not just John Kennedy's unlikely successor. Yet 1964 would be an election year, and LBJ was far too ambitious to merely serve out a few months of his predecessor's

---

* No one else on the crew of the B-26, including the pilot who actually saved the aircraft, received a decoration.

term. He suspected Kennedy had planned to replace him on the ballot and that his own career was finished unless he could win the next election. If any politician needed a cause in the summer of 1964 it was Lyndon Baines Johnson.

On August 2, 1964, a *Sumner*-class American destroyer was lurking off the Vietnamese coast in the Gulf of Tonkin. The USS *Maddox* had been running what was called a "Desoto" patrol, gathering electronic intelligence on North Vietnamese radar installations.* As she approached Hòn Mê Island, three enemy P-4 attack boats from the 135th Torpedo Squadron attacked the warship. Opening fire with her five-inch guns, *Maddox* hit one of the boats while a flight of four F-8 Crusaders from VF-51 (the Screaming Eagles) off the USS *Ticonderoga* strafed the other pair with their 20 mm cannons.† Several days later the *Maddox,* now accompanied by the *C. Turner Joy,* reported another attack by Democratic Republic of Vietnam (DRV, i.e., North Vietnamese) torpedo boats.

Though highly questionable, this second incident, real or not, gave President Johnson exactly the pretext he needed, and on August 7, 1964, Congress passed the Southeast Asia Resolution.‡ Essentially, the resolution gave the president authority to use conventional military force in Southeast Asia *without* a congressional declaration of war. This was vehemently opposed by some, including Democratic senator Ernest Gruening of Alaska, who said the resolution meant "sending our American boys into combat in a war in which we have no business, which is not our war, into which we have been misguidedly drawn, which is steadily being escalated."

---

* *DE Haven Special Operations off TsingtaO.*
† Commander James Stockdale, later the highest-ranking U.S. Navy POW, was leading the flight.
‡ Commonly known as the Gulf of Tonkin Resolution.

The day after the incident, Operation Pierce Arrow, a twenty-aircraft limited retaliation strike, was launched by the U.S. Navy. *Ticonderoga* sent six F-8 Crusaders against the torpedo bases at Ben Thuy and Quang Khe, while twenty-six others were to hit the Vinh oil storage depot. *Constellation*'s F-4 Phantoms, A-1 Skyraiders, and A-4 Skyhawks struck the Hon Gay and Loc Chao naval bases, respectively. It was an aggressive, respectable assault, except that President Johnson made a televised announcement that the missions would occur and, as expected, the North Vietnamese were on full alert. A Skyraider from the *Conny*'s VA-145 was hit by AAA, crashing offshore, and Lieutenant (jg) Richard Christian Sather became the first naval aviator killed in action in this war. Flying an A-4C Skyhawk, Lieutenant (jg) Everett Alvarez of VA-144's "Roadrunners" was also hit by AAA over Hon Gay. Ejecting, he was captured and spent the next eight and a half years in North Vietnamese prisons.*

The USAF, previously operating with the ARVN and covertly in Laos, now began deploying in force. Eighteen F-100s from the 615th TFS and the 405th Fighter Wing deployed to Da Nang and Takhli respectively. Twelve F-102 interceptors left the Philippines and Okinawa for South Vietnam or Thailand. There were also heavy B-52 bombers at Andersen Air Force Base, Guam, B-57B light bombers in South Vietnam, plus essential air tankers and electronic information-gathering aircraft.

By August 9, 1964, eight F-105D Thunderchiefs, nicknamed the "Thud," from the 36th Tactical Fighter Squadron ("Flying

---

*A very brave man, Alvarez was repatriated in 1973. He left the Navy, earned a law degree, and was appointed as deputy director of the Peace Corps followed by the U.S. Veterans Administration. He authored *Chained Eagle* and *Code Of Conduct*, and in March 2014 was appointed to the Vietnam War Commemoration Advisory Council.

Fiends") deployed to the Royal Thai Air Base at Korat.* Five days later, on August 14, Lieutenant David Graben was hit hard by anti-aircraft fire while flying a rescue mission for a downed CIA T-28 in Laos. Zooming his burning jet up to 39,000 feet, he starved the fire of oxygen, then glided down to Korat for a safe landing. The fighter, No. 62-4371, was repaired and sent back into action only to be lost over North Vietnam in September 1966.

Johnson's Republican opponent for the presidency, Senator Barry Goldwater, had accused the president of being soft on communism, so the Gulf of Tonkin incident proved invaluable in disproving this notion. Goldwater doubled down on his rhetoric and proposed to defoliate Vietnam by using tactical nuclear weapons. This didn't appeal to most Americans, nor did his assertion that "extremism in the defense of liberty is no vice!" Johnson's limited escalation suddenly appeared moderate, and, with 61 percent of the vote, the president handily won the November election. Though Johnson had publicly run on a campaign promising peace in Southeast Asia and a "war on poverty" at home, by Christmas eight aircraft carriers were being deployed to the Pacific.

November 1964 through the spring of 1965 was violent and confusing. The VC had attacked Bien Hoa Air Base, then hit the Brinks Hotel in Saigon on Christmas Eve. President Diem was still undependable; Hanoi was intransigent; and American government opinions ranged from ambivalent to belligerent. Despite continued low-level combat and overt armed reconnaissance missions over Laos, there were still opportunities to avoid

---

*The 36th was replaced by the 35th TFS (Black Panthers) in September 1964. They were subsequently relieved by the 80th TFS (Headhunters) in November 1964.

what was coming. Unfortunately Washington was convinced, and would remain so for most of the war, that the North Vietnamese would quickly crumble when faced with overwhelming U.S. airpower.*

In January 1965, the first F-105 was lost in combat when Captain Al Vollmer of the 44th TFS (Vampires) was hit by anti-aircraft fire over Laos.† Then early in February a Viet Cong attack at Pleiku in the Central Highlands left eight Americans dead, and more than one hundred wounded. Operations Flaming Dart I and II, a pair of U.S. air strikes, immediately commenced against targets in the Dong Hai area, resulting in three additional aircraft lost. One F-8 pilot was captured, Lieutenant Commander Robert Shumaker from the "Black Knights" of VF-154, off the USS *Coral Sea*. His back broken, Commander Shumaker was given no medical attention and tortured repeatedly. A member of the "Alcatraz Eleven" due to his years in solitary confinement, it was Shumaker who nicknamed Hoa Loa Prison the "Hanoi Hilton."‡

To Washington's consternation, Hanoi never flinched. This should have been a stark warning to Johnson and Secretary of Defense Robert McNamara, but they failed to see it for what it was. On March 2, 1965, forty-four F-105s, forty F-100s, twenty B-57s, and nineteen VNAF Skyraiders opened Operation Rolling Thunder, the longest sustained air operation in American history, by hitting the Xom Biang ammo depot and Quang Khe naval base in North Vietnam.§ Washington's strategy, if it

---

*This miscalculation would lead to Operation Rolling Thunder.
†F-105 #62-4296. Vollmer was rescued by an Air America (CIA) H-34 helicopter.
‡Commander Shumaker was also repatriated and remained in the Navy, retiring as a rear admiral.
§Combat operations commenced from Royal Thai Air Base Takhli in March with the 36th TFS, redeploying from Yokota Air Base, Japan.

could be called that, was to gradually "roll" attacks north from the demilitarized zone, two missions per week for eight weeks. This would demonstrate U.S. firepower and technology, causing the North to capitulate prior to air strikes against Hanoi and Haiphong. That was the strategy anyway.

It was costly from the beginning.

While suppressing anti-aircraft sites for the main strike package, three Thuds from Korat's 67th TFS were lost, as were two F-100s. Four pilots were recovered, though the fifth, Lieutenant Hayden Lockhart of the 613th TFS, wasn't as fortunate. After his ejection, he evaded the enemy for a week but was finally captured. March also saw the arrival of the first regular American ground units when some 3,000 Marines waded ashore on China Beach. There were already more than 20,000 "military advisors" in country, yet the open commitment of formal combat troops was the final, ominous step toward full-scale war.

North Vietnam did not surrender, nor was it overawed into negotiation. In fact, Rolling Thunder had an opposing effect, as bombing campaigns usually do.* Hanoi was well aware of the danger; they also knew the ninety-four targets drawn up by the Joint U.S. Chiefs, and the rules of engagement (ROE) that Washington forced on American combat aircraft. The DRV, with its potential Soviet and Chinese backers, watched larger regional and global events very closely. National Liberation Front successes in the South against the ARVN, combined with constant political turmoil in Saigon and a vacillating American administration, all indicated a change of situation. If enough support

---

*London in 1917, London in 1940, Germany from 1943 to 45, Yugoslavia in 1997, Iraq from 1991 to 2003. Conventional bombing alone has never won a war and usually psychologically unites those being attacked.

from communist China and the Soviet Union was forthcoming, that is. From Hanoi's point of view, the Gulf of Tonkin incident, Flaming Dart, and now the Rolling Thunder attacks all clearly revealed Washington's intentions, or lack of them, regarding the use of unrestricted airpower.

However, these operations also glaringly illuminated the North's vulnerability, at least in its few industrialized areas, from air attack. Alexei Kosygin, who replaced Khrushchev as premier of the Soviet Union in 1964, traveled to Hanoi in January 1965 with senior air defense experts in preparation for just such an escalation. Two direct results occurred: first, SA-2 missile sites were to be constructed immediately and manned by Soviet advisors until the Vietnamese were trained. Second, shipments of fighter aircraft and training for pilots would be greatly accelerated. The 921st Fighter Regiment of the Vietnamese People's Air Force (VPAF) had been equipped with Soviet-supplied MiG-17s and given advanced training in China. The Tonkin Gulf incident had also provided Hanoi an excuse to bring them home and base them at Phuc Yen in the Red River valley.

On April 3, 1965, a joint Rolling Thunder mission, led by legendary USAF pilot Robbie Risner, attacked a bridge on the north central coast just above Thanh Hoa. This was a major line of communication connecting Hanoi and Haiphong to the southern provinces just north of the DMZ. A bend in the Ma Song River near a line of bulbous low hills gave the appearance from the air of a dragon's head in profile. A small, almond-shaped island provided the eye, and the bridge joining the river with the western hills formed the lower jaw. Inevitably the Ham Rong bridge was nicknamed the "Dragon's Jaw" and the AAA sites surrounding it were attacked by twenty-two Thuds and Huns. One F-100D was lost, killing the pilot, and several F-105s were damaged.

A Navy force off the carriers *Coral Sea* and *Hancock* came next, striking bridges ten miles to the north. Lieutenant Commander Ray Vohden's Skyhawk was hit by ground fire, forcing him to eject.* It was during this strike that the North Vietnamese MiGs made their first combat appearance, damaging an F-8 Crusader. With the bridge still standing, another big mission, composed of forty-eight F-105s with eight F-100s for AAA suppression, launched the next day. The weather was bad and air refueling, always a tedious, risky business, had not gone according to the plan. This forced several flights of Thuds, full of fuel and loaded with bombs, into an orbit south of Thanh Hoa while those ahead made their attacks. One F-105 was lost, and as the radios erupted with shouted warnings, four MiG-17s suddenly dropped through the clouds.

Flying formation in enemy territory, slow and heavy, listening to the emergency beacons and radio traffic, the Thud drivers were unaware of the MiGs. Small and hard to see anyway, the little Soviet-built fighters combined surprise with a close-in, hit-and-run attack. This brought down F-105D (No. 59-1764) of Korat's 354th, TFS, killing Captain James Magnusson. The Thud flight lead, Major Frank Bennett, was also hit by 37 mm cannon fire and immediately headed out to sea. Ejecting from his burning fighter off the coast near Hon Me island, Bennett tragically drowned before he could be rescued. A Skyraider flown by Captain Walter Draeger was on a rescue mission near the bridge and also went down due to ground fire.

Three of the MiGs were also lost, most likely by North Vietnamese anti-aircraft guns. However, Pham Giay, number two in the attacking formation, was shot down by Captain Don

---

*VA-216 ("Black Diamonds"). He was immediately captured and spent more than seven years as a POW. Commander Vohden came home in 1973.

Kilgus with his 20 mm cannons. Four F-100Ds of the 416th TFS (Silver Knights) were capping overhead, waiting to fight the MiGs, and this shootdown was the first American air-to-air kill of the war. Though he was never officially recognized, those who knew Kilgus never doubted him, and Pham Giay's leader did confirm that his wingman was shot down by a U.S. fighter.

In any event, it was an expensive day—and the bridge still stood.

But MiGs could be dealt with now that they were known to be active, and the USAF responded by immediately deploying F-4C Phantoms of the 15th TFW from MacDill Air Force Base, Florida, to Royal Thai Air Base Ubon. American dogfighting skills were well founded and the VPAF knew they'd never prevail in an even air-to-air fight. This was precisely why Hanoi, several months earlier, had insisted upon receiving the latest surface-to-air missile technology from the Soviet Union. On April 5, the day after the Dragon's Jaw mission, reconnaissance photos taken near Hanoi clearly showed several SA-2 sites nearing completion.

Fully realizing the threat, the Joint Chiefs wanted to eliminate them immediately. Secretary of Defense McNamara, continuing his growing legacy of poor choices, steadfastly believed that the Soviets would *never* allow their missiles to actually be used against U.S. aircraft. His assistant John T. McNaughton, an academic with no military qualifications, openly ridiculed the Joint Chiefs, stating, "You don't think the North Vietnamese are going to use them? Putting them in is just a political ploy by the Russians to appease Hanoi."

The 420-pound warhead flying over three times the speed of sound that slammed into Leopard Two on July 24, 1965, was no ploy and no bluff; the missiles of the 63rd and 64th batteries, 236th SAM Regiment, were very real and now fully operational. Three days later, forty-six vengeful F-105s roared out of Korat and Takhli and rendezvoused over the Plain of Jars. They air-refueled, then lifted away from the tankers, joined up in loose formation, and headed northeast toward a miserable little town on the Black River—thirty miles from Hanoi.

CHAPTER 3

WILD WEASEL

"PILOT . . . this is EWO."

What the hell. Allen Lamb shook his head and sighed. He'd never enjoyed flying with anyone else. The questions, the discussion, the whole "crew" concept. The heavy breathing. This was exactly why he'd become a single-seat fighter jock. Now here he was, irritated and sitting in a two-seat F-100F sarcastically called a "family model," on a steamy piece of Florida concrete with a heavy breather five feet behind him. Bad enough to occasionally have to fly with another pilot, but an electronic warfare officer? What the hell was that, anyway? Some kind of bomber thing.

"Pilot, this is EWO. Can you hear me?" Jack Donovan asked again.

"Well, I hope to God that's you back there!" Allen snapped, then busied himself setting up switches, checking onboard systems, the weather, getting his clearance to taxi and depart. Pilot stuff. Maybe the guy in back would get the point.

For his part, Captain Jack Donovan, the EWO, was equally suspicious. It was early October 1965 and he was a long, long way from the belly of a B-52. Exhaling, he looked up from his display at the back of the pilot's head. Donovan understood that these guys weren't complete assholes—they were contending with going off to Southeast Asia, killing surface-to-air missiles, and having someone in the backseat. So far they had Garry Willard, Robert Schwartz, Allen Lamb, John Pitchford, Leslie Lindenmuth, Maury Fricke, and George Kerr—all long-time F-100 pilots with about two thousand hours of flying time each. Donovan and most of the other EWOs, Walt Lifsey, Don McFadden, and Bob Trier, were all volunteers from the Strategic Air Command, while Ed Sandelius had come in from 12th Air Force Headquarters. Volunteers. Only in the military sense, which meant someone higher up had decided that they should volunteer. His orders had read a "temporary duty assignment to the F-100 Command Post."

No one had known what that meant, least of all him. The only good part of it was Florida; he'd imagined white beaches, salt air, and drinks with rum. But even that had been an illusion. He and Walt Lifsey had arrived here in September and immediately been flown to California to meet with the civilian tech reps who were building this thing. Applied Technology Inc. (ATI) was based out of Palo Alto, and they had initially installed Radar Homing And Warning (RHAW) sets into four F-100F fighters on September 12, 1965. Newly mounted antennas on the nose and tail provided 360-degree coverage of incoming radar waves. These were then correlated into either C-, S-, or X-band signals and displayed in the cockpit.

The two EWOs listened to the various proposals, then added suggestions—placement of the displays, adding a knob or switch here or there. On September 16, the first modified Hun lifted off, though with a North American test pilot at the controls. Surprisingly, both the ATI and North American engineers had been enthusiastic and receptive, so everything the EWOs had suggested was done.

Resting his arms on the canopy rail, Jack stared out at the mass of concrete outside, the jets taking off or sliding in to land. Lifting his eyes, he stared up at the powder blue sky. You could see so *much* from the cockpit of a fighter. He suppressed a snort. Plexiglas-topped coffin was more like it. Minutes later the F-100, nicknamed the "Hun," had been cleared for takeoff and Donovan admired the way the younger captain smoothly got the jet airborne and headed out to the test range. No crew effort, no discussion or verbalizing checklists—all the procedures so beloved by SAC. *I might enjoy this after all,* he thought.

Eight minutes later he wasn't so sure. Swallowing hard to keep the bile down, Jack found that if he pointed the air vent directly at his face, used 100 percent oxygen, and didn't look outside much, then he felt less sick. The idea today, and for the remaining sorties to be flown, was to take about six weeks and evaluate the newly installed Vector IV system in both cockpits.

The premise behind the ATI Vector was simple: for a radar-guided SAM to intercept a target, the radar had to stay on long enough to track the target and guide the missile to intercept. If it had to remain "on air" this long, then it could be located by its emissions, and if this was the case, then it should also be possible to locate the radar. The logic then followed that finding it was valuable, but *killing* it was essential. Air Force officers in the Pentagon initially called the new project "Ferret," after the World War II radar-killing program, but this was something new and needed a fresh name. "Mongoose" was chosen, after the ferocious little animal that killed deadly snakes. It seemed appropriate, but had also been previously used by the CIA, so somehow—no one was quite sure why—

it became the "Wild Weasel" program, and that's what stuck. Weasel it was.*

EXHALING LOUDLY, JACK Donovan glanced at the new displays in the backseat while the pilot muttered to himself and talked on the radio. Energy from a SAM or Triple A radar would strike either the forward antennas mounted under the nose, or the rear antenna on the tail. Based on the strength of this signal, a strobe would appear along the direction of arrival, the azimuth, and be shown on a three-inch circular cathode ray tube (CRT) display. Both the SA-2 Fansong radar and the Firecar anti-aircraft radar operated in the S-band portion of the electromagnetic spectrum—2.0 to 4.0 gigahertz (GHz). Signals in this range were shown by a solid line but the Weasel crew's trained ears could easily distinguish the "warble" of a Firecan from the unmistakable "rattlesnake" audio produced by the Fansong. Those for the C-band (4.0–8.0 GHz) were depicted with a dotted line. Airborne intercept (AI) radars in the MiG-17/19 were X-band and displayed a dashed line if detected.

The Vector IV scope was mounted in the center of the rear cockpit console. Like an archery target, the display was divided into three concentric rings that could be used to approximate a distance to the radar based on the length of the strobe. A long strobe meant that the signal was strong and likely very close. A short strobe indicated that the signal was weak, so probably not nearby, though Donovan knew it could also mean that the radar's main beam was simply focused on another target. Azi-

---

*A personal theory is that someone mistook the mongoose for a weasel. They're both quick, have fangs and claws, and are famed for their ferocity. Besides, "Wild Weasel" sounds better than "Wild Mongoose."

muth accuracy was pretty good, but estimating the range was pure guesswork.

One technique was called "station passage": the EWO would give small azimuth corrections to the pilot so he'd fly directly at the signal. Within about a six-mile radius of the SAM there was a "dead" zone, mainly caused by missile launch and guidance limitations, so surviving till this point meant there was a reasonable chance of killing that particular site. When the Weasel got this close, the depicted radar strobe would bend left and right, then curl back to the rear like a waterfall. This was a clear indication that the Weasel was too close for that particular Fansong to engage. However, this gap in coverage was always covered by AAA and, whenever possible, other missile batteries. Yet given the limitations of U.S. weapons, the only way to kill the SAM was to get close—very close. By using this technique, or getting a missile battery to fire at them, the two men would hopefully locate the SAM visually. Once seen, it then could be destroyed with bombs, rockets, or the cannon.

Theoretically.

The other display was rectangular, about eight inches long and five high. Designated an IR-133 panoramic receiver, not only did it detect radars, but he, the EWO, could tune the set to an incoming beam and analyze the signal. All radars were unique, just like aircraft; made with identical components and assembled in the same factory, each nonetheless was slightly different. Given enough time, he could identify, or fingerprint, each SAM radar they found. Upon arriving in theater the first few flights had been made in loose formation with an EB-66 electronic reconnaissance jet. This had been a combination of local area familiarization and the first chance they'd had to evaluate the Vector equipment against real Soviet systems. Jack had realized fairly quickly that analyzing radar signals while bouncing around in the back of a fighter wasn't practical. On hunting missions, maybe, depending on where they were flying, but for killing SAMs it wouldn't work. The scope was too hard to see and meticulously tuning anything on a real tactical mission was out of the question.

But figuring these things out and estimating system accuracy was the point of these sorties. So far they'd learned a few things—starting with the 77-foot accuracy claim following the Eglin tests. Jack snorted. Maybe for big, white buildings and domes that could be seen for miles and never moved, but a real SAM was another matter. It did move. It was also expertly camouflaged, it shot back, and it was protected by dozens of 37 mm or 57 mm guns. Still, they'd done their best.

Eglin Air Force Base, in Florida, had some 135,000 square miles of test ranges, over both water and land. Of primary utility for the Wild Weasel I program, as it was now called, were the Soviet Air Defense Simulator (SADS) systems. These were generally scattered around a long, narrow barrier island south of the base with Santa Rosa Sound on one side and Choctawhatchee Bay on the other. Okaloosa Island was the last bit of land between Florida and the Gulf of Mexico and a good place for the initial aspects of the test. SADS could simulate certain air defense radars by emitting signals in their known frequency ranges and, to a degree, estimate Vector's ability to home in on a site.

There were some problems with this. First, simply emitting a signal in the given frequency range in no way simulates how a real target-engagement radar functions. There was no way to know the pulse repetition interval (PRI) or specific pulse repetition frequencies (PRF) for tracking and guidance. Believing the SADS was a Fansong simply because it could emit in the same frequency range is like believing all cars are the same because they have four wheels. Also, the simulator was easy to see—big, white domes with little buildings attached and surrounded by a fence. They also didn't move, so when the Weasels saw it once, it was nearly impossible not to know where the signal originated from. This skewed the results, like the absurd accuracy claim.

Captain Joe Telford from Eglin's Air Proving Ground Center and Major Jim Odom of the Tactical Air Warfare Center tried to help. They put together a mobile emitter using an S-band radar and mounted it on a blue, USAF flatbed truck. Every other day it would change locations and, being so much smaller, it was hard to see.

Ten sorties would be flown without homing; the EWO would get one cut from the radar, then it would switch off. Five other sorties would be flown with jamming pods to assess the Vector's ability to detect in a "cluttered" environment. Usually four times per mission SADS would come up and stay on air long enough to be detected. Approaching the island from all sides, the Weasel would fly from 100 feet to 10,000 feet. As they flew, the crew would note the different angles of the intercepted signal, called "cuts," and by triangulating they could guess the approximate location. Debriefs made use of the recorders installed in each jet and conversations were analyzed to compare what was seen in flight to what was being presented from the SADS. Accuracy assessments were spotty, to say the least, but it was all they had.

By November 1, 1965, the initial equipment testing was complete and Wild Weasel I moved into a brief tactical phase. No one expected much from this, as information on real SAM sites was very sketchy. Still, they had to try. They also had something new, courtesy of Bill Doyle, director of systems engineering for ATI. One day back in September he'd gotten an idea. Knowing that a SAM used different frequencies for guidance signals after launch, might it not be possible to detect this change? Couldn't a separate antenna be added beneath the jet that would be tuned to that specific signal? If such guidance beams were detected, then this could trigger a light in the cockpit, plus an audible warning so the Weasel would know a missile was in the air.

So a separate test of existing Bendix, Melpar, Loral, and ATI warning receivers was quickly devised to determine their adaptability for this notion. ATI won the contract and the system provided a distinct, shrill tone working in conjunction with a bright red warning light. Though it was technically known as the WR-300, the Weasels called it the "Oh shit!" light.

All the crews talked, formally and informally, about tactics and how to kill a SAM. Allen Lamb and Jack Donovan, now a true team despite their wildly different backgrounds, had learned a great deal. Lamb figured the only way to get rid of the Fansong, blow up the missiles, and kill the technicians was to go right down their throats. In any event, they all knew there was no more time for theory and when the Eglin testing ended on November 18, they were leaving for the program's combat evaluation—125 operational test flights in Southeast Asia. They would have ninety days to discover what really worked, and what did not. What would save American lives and kill the SAMs.

The Weasels were going to war.

"IF THAT SONUVABITCH stays on the air we'll nail his ass to a cross!"

The fighter hit a patch of warm air and bounced hard as Allen Lamb rolled over the ridgeline and pulled. In the rear cockpit Jack Donovan grunted, then blinked, trying to focus on his display. No small feat in a throbbing, gyrating little jet flown through the mountains by a nutty fighter pilot.

"Well . . . that's why we came to the party, right?" Donovan was calm, nearly taciturn, in the backseat, or "pit," as the rear cockpit of the F-100F was called. Allen's eyes flickered to the hillside then back to the round APR-25 display under his glare shield. *Beats the hell outta me how they get guys to fly around back there,* he thought, not for the first time. Using highly trained EWOs had been a necessity for this new program, and it would have gone nowhere without them. But they'd all come from the bomber world, the dignified and rarefied Strategic Air Command—home of the starched flight suit, polished boots, and church every Sunday. He chuckled again. What a shock to get dumped in with the heathens, the killers. The fighter pilots.

"What's funny?"

"Nuthin. Where's the SAM?"

"Ten o'clock . . . no, now eleven o'clock."

Despite being five miles or so from the most dangerous technological threat in existence, Allen Lamb, World's Greatest Fighter Pilot, was enjoying himself. It was a duel, cat and mouse, a game of chicken at nearly 600 miles per hour. The winner gets the kill and the loser . . . well, the loser dies. Jack Donovan, back in the pit, squinted at the screen. It wasn't vibrating, but the damn jet was bouncing and banking so much the screen looked blurry.

"Now," Lamb muttered and reefed back on the stick. The Hun soared up away from the valley floor, but he was already staring to the right as they crested the hill.

"Twelve o'clock!" Donovan called, still head down and panting hard. There were three rings on the scope and the longer a strobe was, the closer it was. This one, directly ahead, was about two rings long. "High PRF!"

Lamb shoved the stick forward again, pushing the fighter back down behind the hills. Leveling off at 300 feet, he glanced left, then right. On either side, about a half mile back, was a pair of F-105s. He held the jet down for a moment, watching the rugged green slope zip past on his left side as he headed north up the valley, and thought about the SAM. The Fansong radar had switched into its high pulse repetition frequency mode—it was ready to shoot. This mode sent a fast, constant stream of nasty little waves out in order to give the radar instant data on a target—in this case Lamb himself, Spruce Five. The trade-off was range. It was only a good mode for short distances.

"Up . . ."

This time Lamb gave his friend a warning, then pulled, angling right a bit. In the pit, Donovan just had time to tense his stomach muscles as the Hun zoomed. *Little bastard loves this,* he thought, still staring at the screen. The strobe was a bundle of solid little lines, like a feather on an arrow, and it had shifted right.

"Two o'clock!"

For a few seconds the pilot could see it all. Directly east of him, off his right wing, were the sluggish dark waters of the Black River. There was a road along the ridge that angled down into the valley before him, a startling white scar against the greens. Above it, all along the horizon beyond the river, nasty little puffy clouds dotted the sky. Charcoal to gray to thinning, widening splotches of white, the anti-aircraft artillery fire was continuous and heavy. The guns were on the other side along the dike and, of course, were off-limits to attack. The White House, imagining reprisals from the Chinese, had severely limited military targets. *What a way to fight a war. They can shoot at us but it wouldn't be fair for us to kill them. Or blow up the fucking dikes.* Lamb shook his head disgustedly.

"And not a damn thing I can do about it . . ." he hissed, then rolled over and pulled again for the ground. As the river vanished beyond the hills he flipped the fighter upright, eye-balled his fuel gauge, and checked the MASTER ARM switch for his weapons. The Hun and four Thuds dropped behind a long north-south hill paralleling the river.

Suddenly the left side of the valley sloped off, opening onto a wide, flat basin with a mountain far up on the north end. Instantly he made up his mind and racked the fighter up in a hard left turn. Tough on the trailing Thuds, but their job right now was to stay with him. He was the Weasel.

Another, bigger mountain loomed ahead so he continued pulling hard left, shoved the throttle into afterburner, and rocketed up into the overcast sky. Twisting in the seat, Lamb strained to see over his left shoulder. Triple A over the river . . . fields and some rice paddies. Where was the fucker? Eyes flickering to the scope, he saw the lines begin to curve, like a water-fall, and he swallowed. That only happened at *very* close range.

"Six o'clock!" Donovan's voice cracked. "Six o'clock!"

Lamb flipped the fighter over again to keep from going too high and pulled back on the stick. Hanging in space, inverted over North Vietnam, he could see the muddy glint of the Red River off to the north. Past the Black River to the east a darker gray smudge hung over the horizon. Hanoi.

The Hun's nose dropped and as he tugged the throttle back Jack yelled again. "To your right . . . your right . . . your right!"

"Left!"

"No—right!"

"We're upside down, dammit. Pull your face outta that scope and look *outside*!"

Straining against the g-forces, Donovan lifted his head and stared to the left . . . nothing there but mountain. *Shit.* He looked right then, realizing they *were* upside down, at less than 2,000 feet above the hills and seventy-five miles inside North

Vietnam. Just then the world swung dizzily, the horizon rotated, and the F-100 popped halfway upright. Eyes watering, Donovan let his chin drop and tried to focus on the scope. They were right on top of the damn thing!

The Hun's left wing was pointed nearly straight down and Allen was belly-up to the river, staring hard in the direction of the strobe. There was a crappy little village . . . some thatched hooches and a few dirt paths but nothing else between it and the river. Lamb had never seen a missile launch, though he had heard plenty about it. Billowing white smoke, a long, orange flame at the end of a flying telephone pole. *Where?*

He bunted over at about a thousand feet, dust particles floating past his face as he flew instinctively, hands and feet moving to keep the fighter in a hard, mostly level turn. Pointed directly at the river now, the pilot knew he had a matter of seconds before the guns corrected or the SAM fired—or both. The strobe was truly curling, which meant they were close, within a few miles, and he followed it again to the village as the five fighters arced eastward. Donovan had stopped panting.

A right angle.

His gaze swiveled back to the village. It shouldn't be there . . . not in a random collection of raggedy huts. There it was again. Eyes narrowing, he leaned against the canopy and . . . there it was. The Fansong. Right in the middle of the fucking village. Once he saw the van the rest of the camouflage melted away. Like knowing a magician's trick, it was obvious once you saw through it. There were the missiles. Three big, white poles under another hut.

"I see the bastard!"

"What?"

Eyes padlocked on the radar so he wouldn't lose sight, Allen keyed the mike. "Center of the village . . . my eleven o'clock."

He didn't bother looking for the Thuds; he simply banked up more and pulled the jet around until the nose was directly on the center of the village, then rolled out. Steep . . . he was too steep! Allen pulled the throttle back more to hold 500 knots and dipped the nose, trying to shallow out the dive. Leaning forward, he squinted through the orange reticle, the gunsight, and fixed it just short of the target.

"Second Fansong!" Jack said over the intercom. "Ah . . . right three o'clock. Must be across the river."

"Guns!" A Thud pilot called. "Guns along the river!"

Flashes . . . up ahead and just across the river. Ignoring the radios, he yanked the throttle back to idle, trying to hold 500 knots, but he was too steep and too fast. Nudging the stick back, he raised the nose and held the glowing gunsight on the van. The ground rushed up; his eyes caught mottled brown and green fields, tree lines, and sunlight glinting off rice paddies. Something was moving along the road by the river and more flashes registered.

Now!

His thumb down on the red pickle button. Hold it . . . hold it . . .

The Hun instantly kicked, yawing the jet back and forth as thirty-eight 2.75-inch rockets snaked out of the tubes. Trailing white smoke, each one was four feet long and weighed nearly twenty pounds. As the earth filled his canopy, Allen pulled the stick into his lap and hit the back of the ejection seat hard as the fighter bottomed out, then began to climb. When the nose came through the horizon, he snapped the Hun sideways, shoving the throttle to the stop. Short . . . he was craning his neck and peering off the left side of the canopy. Rockets hit short. *Sonuva . . .*

The explosion wasn't big, but it was bright. An amazing

flash of yellow that mushroomed out and turned orange on the edges. Must've hit stored fuel, he thought. Maybe the oxidizer tanks.

"I got it . . . I got it!" Allen recognized Spruce One, Captain Don Langwell, the F-105 flight lead.

Well I hope so, he thought, pulling the jet around hard and heading for the safety of the hills. There was a small, peanut-shaped ridge ahead just before the bigger one to the west. Dumping the nose, the Hun leapt forward, passing 500 knots in a few seconds. Zooming over the hill, coming around left to the south, Allen let his eyes jump around the cockpit. Fuel . . . enough for one more pass . . . the red guard over the trigger switch was up.

Smoothly pulling back on the stick, he let the Hun soar up in a climbing left turn. Straining against the straps, his helmet slipped a bit over his wet hair as he twisted around to look at the burning SAM site. One Thud had pulled off target and was following him around, maybe two miles back. As he passed 3,000 feet, Allen saw another 105 directly across from him diving at the target. He'd fired all seventy-six rockets and, trailing black smoke, a massive orange tipped spear reached out and stabbed into the center of the burning huts.

"Two's off . . . One in sight."

"Firecan!" Jack yelled from the pit. "More guns."

Fucking terrific. That was a radar used for guiding Triple A and made the guns much more dangerous. Eyes locked on the flames, Lamb rolled mostly onto his back and sliced back toward the SAM. Hanging upside down, about three miles southwest of the target, he could see everything for a moment. Spruce Two's rockets slammed into the missile site, throwing up dirt, burning thatch, and starting more fires.

Another Thud, it had to be Captain Bob Bush as Spruce

Three, was diving down along the river toward the guns and his wingman was arcing high to the south.* Allen floated the pull a second longer, then snatched the stick back. When the sandbar disappeared and the shoreline filled his canopy, he relaxed the pull and flipped the jet upright.

"Dammit!" Donovan swore from the back as his helmet smacked the canopy again. The pilot never heard it. With the wind from the east, the smoke was blowing toward the hills and though the SAM site was burning he couldn't see it. Rolling out, nose low, he held the Fansong van in the center panel of his canopy just below the mirror. Slapping the throttle back, the stick firm in his right hand, he kept his feet light on the rudder pedals. Any pushing would yaw the jet and likely spoil his aim.

Twenty-five hundred feet and a mile away.

He cracked the throttle back and the jet slowed slightly. *More time to aim* . . . The whole "village," if you could call it that, was a mess. Several distinct columns, white edged with black, rose from the fields. Movement caught the corner of his right eye, and he saw Spruce Three paralleling the riverbank, firing his rockets at the Triple A sites.

Fifteen hundred feet . . . and a half mile.

Swallowing, Allen felt time slowing as the radios seemed to mute themselves, and the gunsight very slowly rose up to the bottom of the weird-looking Fansong radar. Bunting slightly, he then released the pressure, checked the aim, and fired.

"BRRRRUP."

A quick burst . . . maybe thirty rounds of the 20 mm cannon. His eyes flickered inside for a split second. Nine hun-

---

*Bob Bush was shot down by anti-aircraft fire and killed three months later, in March 1966, in the Quang Binh province. He finally came home in December 1988 and was buried at Arlington National Cemetery.

dred feet off the ground and less than a thousand yards from the van. Spurts of mud and dirt shot upward just short of the van. Allen slid the throttle back till it was standing straight up, bunted forward, froze the gunsight on the door of the van, and squeezed the trigger again.

"BRRRUUUPPPPP."

The jet shivered as the cannon emptied. The pilot pulled the nose up slightly and stared out through the canopy. The van rocked sideways, then disappeared in a cloud of dirt and burning metal. Something, probably a generator with fuel in it, burst into flame. Allen brought the stick back to his lap, and as the Hun's nose lifted he rammed the throttle forward.

"Two's Bingo!" That was Van Heywood.

The river, then the mountains on the other side, filled the canopy. Allen grunted, slamming the stick against his left leg and pulling back hard. Left wing down, the F-100 slid sideways, past north and all the way around to the western hills. Snapping upright, he then bunted forward and shoved the throttle in afterburner.

"Four's off . . . good hit! Look at it burn!" Art Brattkus, the last attacking Thud, was excited.

"Spruce One Bingo . . . all Spruces, head two-three-zero. One is visual on Spruce Five."

Allen's head swiveled, unable to find the Thuds. Coasting up slope of the nearest line of hills, he turned around and stared back at the target area. Smoke was rising, thinning as it got higher, and several black popcorn puffs showed up against the lighter horizon. He chuckled.

"We sure made a mess back there."

Donovan was also turned around in the seat, looking at what was left of the SAM. He'd never admit it, but what a ride! As the mountains got bigger and the distance increased away from the deadly valley, he felt an exhilaration run through him that he'd certainly never felt in a B-52. Given enough time, he could identify, or fingerprint, each SAM radar they found. The EWO shook his head at that thought. Well, he could if this flying death trap ever flew straight and level long enough. Glancing up at Lamb's head, he chuckled softly. Not that the paid killer up front would ever fly like that.

And yet that's why they were still alive. Not that an EWO would *ever* admit that to a fighter pilot. Donovan tapped the IR-133 scope with his finger. This would change everything. Today they'd killed a SAM—they'd found it and they'd killed it. Not by accident, but by hunting the fucker down and blowing it to bits.

Sighing, he dropped one corner of his mask and wiped his sweaty face with a glove. He could see the back of Lamb's helmet as he busied himself with fuel, navigation, and flying. Allen was whistling softly, and Donovan caught a glimpse of "World's Greatest Fighter Pilot" on the man's helmet in the rearview mirror.

He grinned. After today . . . he'd go along with that.

ALLEN LAMB SCOWLED at his fuel gauges, doing quick math in his head. It was about fifty miles to the Laotian border, then another 200 miles to the orbiting tanker. He compromised; past the ridgeline they'd climb up to 5,000 feet but slow down to 450 knots once beyond the Son La valley. Smoothly pulling the stick back, he watched the hills fall away. Unclipping the oxygen mask, Allen let it dangle from his left cheek and rubbed his sweaty face with a glove. God, it stunk. Wrinkling his nose, the pilot looked around for his water. Smelled like stale sweat, old Nomex, and jet.

"Fansong's off the air," Jack finally said from the pit. Lamb nodded and took a long pull from the water bottle.

"Damn well hope so . . . I emptied the gun into him."

He was thirsty, so was Donovan, and slurping water sounds filled the intercom. It was a new experience for Lamb, flying with someone. He'd always been a single-seat guy so this crew experience was interesting. Clearing his throat, he stared out over the magnificent valley and thought about that. It had been an interesting month, no doubt about it. *Haven't even been here a month,* he reminded himself.

Major Willard, the Weasel commander, had led the four F-100Fs off the long Eglin runway on the morning of November 21, 1965. The 421st TFS (Fighting Cavaliers), F-105s out of McConnell Air Force Base, Kansas, was deploying to Southeast Asia on the same day. They'd all joined up with tankers over St. Louis and the Weasels tagged along all the way across the Pacific. The Thuds never knew they were there since the F-100s had their own frequency with their own tankers. After Hawaii came Guam, then, on November 24, 1965, the first Weasels arrived at their new home at Korat, in Thailand. And the Thanksgiving Day turkey was gone by the time they'd gotten to the O'Club. That had sucked.

But not nearly as bad as losing a jet and crew two days ago.

"That one's for John and Bob," Donovan suddenly said, as if reading his thoughts.

Maybe, Lamb thought. *Maybe.*

John Pitchford and Bob Trier, flying as Apple 01, had gone down up near Yen Bai two days ago. Losing Americans was never an even trade for a Fansong or the Russian shitheads operating the thing.

"It's not enough," he announced. "I'm gonna get more of the fuckers."

Jack chuckled. He'd been wary of fighter pilots before this
program had kicked off, but he had to admit he thoroughly
enjoyed them now. They had an appalling sense of humor
and acted like twelve-year-olds when they weren't flying. But
they were also utterly contemptuous of danger, bullshit, and
authority—pretty much in equal parts.

Yeah. He liked them.

"*We* are gonna get them. 'We' . . . right?"

"Right."

We. Allen watched the Son La valley pass away off the right
wing, nudged the throttle forward, and lifted the nose. The Hun
began a gradual climb, and he angled a bit right to the southwest and the tanker track in southern Laos. Thinking in terms
of "we" had been a big deal four months ago. Four months . . .
he shook his head. He'd been on the beach in South Carolina.
Colonel Charlie Joseph, an old friend from his time in Japan,
had called him from Tactical Air Command Headquarters at
Langley Air Force Base, in Virginia. Said he was coming down
the next day and wanted to have lunch. Lunch, laughs, and lies
with a buddy—why not?

But it was far from a reunion.

Sitting in the O'Club parking lot, Charlie said that Benny
Putnam, now a major general commanding the Tactical Air
Warfare Center, wanted Allen to volunteer for a special project.
Something so secret that he wouldn't be told what it was until
he volunteered. Saying "special project" to a man like Lamb
was like waving a red flag in front of a bull. Lamb immediately agreed. With that, Charlie pulled a set of orders out of his
pocket and a plane ticket to Fort Walton Beach, Florida.

He peered over the left canopy rail at a rugged, tabletop
plateau. Jutting from the southern end of the valley, it plainly
marked the Laotian–North Vietnamese border. Ahead lay the
Barthelemy Pass, and beyond that the Plain of Jars. Reaching

up, he adjusted the mirror and could see Jack, head down in the back.

"You sick?"

Donovan snorted but didn't look up.

"Well?"

"I'm thinking . . . and trying to write."

Allen chuckled. "Bit early for your memoirs. 'Sides, I did all the work."

That earned him a bleak look and his smile widened. Both men had become good friends and were used to each other by now. Donovan was sketching out the engagement and making notes. The timeline was particularly critical.

"Low-altitude acrobatics . . . that's about it. Any Forward Facing Bird Deflector could do the same. And your singing stinks," he added.*

"Yeah . . . but I *can* sing."

A corner reluctantly turned up on Jack's mouth at that, and he went back to his notes. When did the Fansong pick them up at low altitude and at what range? He frowned. That had been in low PRF, a search mode, at nearly 100 miles. It wasn't supposed to be able to do that. Then the high PRF switch at . . . he glanced at his kneeboard . . . about twenty miles. It was hard to say since the APR-25 didn't give a real range. It just approximated a distance based on signal strength, calculating that a stronger signal meant the radar was close by. Maybe for the Fansong, but Jack had spent years in B-52s and knew radars. At the pace they were developing this probably wouldn't be true much longer.

Allen leveled off at 22,000 feet and pulled the power back

---

* "Forward Facing Bird Deflector," "Nose Gunner," etc., were all relatively friendly rebuttals (in the harsh world of tactical aviation) against the pilots and their references to the "Pitter," "Trained Bear," and other terms of endearment for electronic warfare officers.

to hold 350 knots. Running his eye over the cockpit, he flipped the red trigger guard down, then looked at the column of small gauges on the right of the console. Oil pressure, hydraulics, exhaust temp . . . all in the green. Glancing at his map, he then stared out over the Hun's nose. He could plainly see the immense, tan scar from the Plain of Jars. Beyond that lay the Orange air refueling track with its orbiting KC-135 tankers.

He stretched, yawned, and toggled on the autopilot. Figuring twenty-five minutes to cover the 150 miles to the tanker, he allowed himself to relax a bit and think of what they'd done. Not even a month in Southeast Asia and they'd proven the equipment worked. More important, they'd proven the concept, the idea that SAM radars could be provoked and once operating they could be located, then killed.

Wild Weasel.

He nodded. Had a fierce ring to it that he liked. Like the ferocious little animal it was named for. Of course, the program hadn't always been called that. When he'd landed in Florida, Allen had immediately gone to see Benny Putnam and the project officer, Major Jim Odom. All afternoon he'd sat and listened to the plan for killing SAMs. Spring High, through no fault of the pilots, had been an abortion. It was no secret that the SA-2 was a killer and everyone had their own ideas about dealing with it. What he hadn't known until the briefing was that the Pentagon had been planning a response since the summer of 1964, a year before Leopard Two got whacked.

A California-based company called Applied Technology Inc., ATI for short, had decided to improve the existing APS-54 radar warning receiver mounted in the tail of the B-52 bomber. This had come to the attention of USAF headquarters and they'd sent a young captain named Pierre Levy out to Palo Alto to see what was up. It was a scouting trip, in part to ascertain how far along private industry was in the field of electronic combat. By February 1965, the company allocated a considerable piece of its own budget to develop a replacement for this receiver.

After Spring High, the push was really on, and in hindsight, the Air Force had moved unbelievably fast. On August 3, a mere seven days after the mission and three weeks before Allen Lamb had gotten the invitation to "volunteer," a task force was established to deal with the SAM threat. The USAF Deputy Director for Operational Requirements, Major General K. C. Dempster, invited some two hundred vetted companies to make presentations about their capabilities.

ATI was among them and on August 27, two days after Allen's arrival in Florida, Captain Levy called the company with specific details. The system must have a sensitivity range covering known anti-aircraft radars like the Firecan and Firewheel; it had to detect the Fansong, of course, *and* it had to fit into a fighter. Finally, the first set of two had to be delivered in one month.

Thirty days.

Dr. John Grigsby of ATI immediately assembled his best engineering team to meet the challenge. Tony Taussig, Chuck Wilcox, and Bob Johnson worked through the night, diagramming essential concepts and programming the flow of parts and production. There wasn't time to fabricate components so every piece had to be off the shelf and be made to fit into an existing B-1D size box. This included the CRT displays, filters, and the traveling wave tubes (TWT) that amplified radar signals, permitting the coverage of a wide frequency range.

Lamb glanced at the Vector mounted on the right of his glare shield and remembered the argument over that. Fighter pilots like to turn left, and they'd all wanted it on the left side of the cockpit, something the EWOs just didn't get . . . and he smiled again at that. The first time he'd seen a backseater was there at Eglin in Hanger 68, the same structure used by the Doolittle Raiders twenty-two years earlier. Jack Donovan, Truman Lifsey, Don Madden, Bob Trier, and Bob Schwartz had all come from the B-52. Captain Ed Sandelius had been an RB-66 electronic warfare officer.

Sandelius had come from TAC but the others were SAC toads, definitely used to a different environment and a *very* different type of pilot. Thrown together, it had been left to pilots and EWOs to decide who would fly with whom. At their carefully secured Bachelor Officers' Quarters, they'd gather every night and discuss this new mission. Everyone had their own ideas about it, but Allen had been adamant. The only way to get the bastards was to go straight down their throats and kill them with rockets, bombs, or the gun.

All the EWOs were shocked by this, but it was Jack Donovan who stared at Lamb, appalled, and famously said, "I'm gonna fly with you, and we're gonna shoot a SAM site before it shoots us? You gotta be shittin' me!"*

There was no training program. No classrooms, intelligence briefs, or any of the other things they were all used to in an Air Force program. There just wasn't time. The Pentagon had put all its considerable influence and money into getting them the jets and equipment. The pilots and EWOs were the experts; they were supposed to sort it out somehow.

Just make it work. That's what Benny Putnam had told them. And they had, up to a point. Eglin had a Soviet Air Defense Simulator (SADS) and it at least let them check out their new toys. But, as they'd found out this month, there was a huge

---

*And a tradition was born. Donovan's immortal phrase, "You gotta be shittin' me" was, and still is, used by Weasels when faced with unbelievably dangerous (or unbelievably stupid) situations. Abbreviated as "YGBSM" it is often found on patches.

difference between passive homing runs along a Florida beach and real Weaseling here in Southeast Asia. For one thing, the bad guys didn't cooperate. The missile sites were also extensively camouflaged, and heavily defended by dozens of shitty little 37 mm anti-aircraft guns.

Approximately one hundred sorties had been flown at Eglin against Site A-7 on Okaloosa Island. This was a radar emitter that operated in the same frequency band as the Fansong, but it was obviously not a Soviet-built target tracking radar. Unlike the real sites in Vietnam, this one was stationary and easy to see visually. So it was hard not to cheat by immediately correlating a strobe with the big, white pimple you could see miles away.

But a captain named Joe Telford, assigned to the Air Proving Ground Center, had changed some of that. He had a mobile emitter built that operated in the same frequency band as the SA-2, then had it driven around the Elgin ranges. Using observers on the ground, they were able to report back how close an overflying Weasel came to the actual emitter. This was all fodder for the EWOs and pilots as they tried to work out the best way to go to war with unproven equipment and no counter-tactics against a threat no one had successfully faced.

"Hey . . . will we catch Bob Hope or what?" Jack's voice abruptly came over the intercom.

"Dunno. I'd rather have a drink."

"You got it."

Donovan stared off the left side of the canopy.

A little over a hundred miles to go and they'd be home.

"Twenty more minutes and home sweet home." Allen had finished refueling ten minutes ago, and they'd joined back up with the Thuds. All five were now over Thailand and headed south toward Korat.

"Home?" Jack snorted. "Wooden hooches with planks thrown in the mud for sidewalks?"

The pilot shifted in the front seat and rubbed his eyes. "I bet John Pitchford would trade his left nut for it right about now." Though tired, he was excited and wanted a drink. The rumor was Pitchford had been captured, but Allen wasn't so sure that was better than being dead. Bob Trier, his EWO, had been a USAF competition pistol shooter and had elected to fight it out with the North Vietnamese. He'd lost, apparently.

"I Hope Bob is still around." A chuckle rumbled from the pit. "Get it?"

Lamb glanced back left and right at the trailing F-105s and managed a short laugh. As they'd taxied out for this mission, Bob Hope and his USO touring group were just getting off their transport, and he'd waved to the fighters.

Seventeen minutes later four Thuds, led by the F-100F Wild Weasel, thundered over the show in a tight V formation and the crowd roared. However, the hour-and-a-half-long debrief was all business and not so humorous. Debriefs never are; one lives another day by picking apart every detail, figuring ways to improve what was done correctly, and fixing what was not. In this case, all the Weasels sat in on it, eager to learn how a SAM had finally been killed. There were no cockpit recording devices yet, so Jack's notes were vital.

Now that they knew the radar could be killed, the Weasels debated the best ways to do it. One school of thought was the direct approach, at 5,000 to 8,000 feet. The altitude would keep them out of small arms range, though not Triple A, and right in the heart of the SAM envelope. Not just a single SAM, but any number of them looking in the right direction. Anti-aircraft radars like the Firecan, and the GCI radars used to vector MiGs around, would also see them. But, it was argued, Hanoi knew most of the strike routes for any given mission, courtesy of leaks and spies in Saigon, so why hide? In fact, it was better to be blatant: to stir the pot and shake the tree to see what would fall out.

The other main tactic was to use terrain masking: hiding in the hills or behind mountains and only popping up to get quick "hits" on the SAM, like Lamb and Donovan had done. Lower altitudes would decrease the Fansong's detection capability, so there'd be less clutter and confusion from other radars. This was especially valid while operating anywhere around Hanoi. Low altitude would also keep the MiGs out of their hair, for the most part, but there were always trade-offs. Ingressing that low meant that the pilot's attention would have to be all on flying, and the danger from anti-aircraft fire or small arms was very real.*

In the end, they all agreed to put the matter off until tomorrow. There was, after all, an Officers' Club, cheap libations, and reason enough to celebrate. Once there, Jack Donovan kept pouring martinis down his throat, and eventually decided to see how high the glasses would bounce. To preserve the remaining crystal, Allen borrowed duct tape from the bartender and permanently attached a martini glass to Jack's hand. Sometime during the hilarity a quiet message was dispatched to Washington via Saigon and Honolulu. The dispatch would change lives, forever alter the USAF, and reverberate down to the present day.

It simply read: "Wild Weasel sighted SAM site—Destroyed same!"

---

*By the end of the Vietnam War, 80 percent of all U.S. fixed-wing combat losses were from anti-aircraft guns and small arms fire.

CHAPTER 4

CHARLIE AND SAM

BENEATH A FULL moon on a clear, still night in August 1943, hundreds of British bombers appeared over Usedom in the northern German province of Pomerania. Secluded along the Baltic coast, the island was home to Peenemünde, a secret German research facility and submarine base. The raid was costly: 40 of the 550 bombers never returned and more than 200 RAF aircrew were lost—all for negligible physical damage. However, one general-purpose bomb from an unknown aircraft managed, by luck or by fate, to directly hit a slit trench in a residential area outside Karlshagen. A man, his wife, and two children were killed instantly.

The man was Dr. Walter Thiel, deputy director of the facility. Holding a doctorate in chemistry from Breslau's Polytechnical College, Thiel was a leading expert in rocketry and propulsion and his death caused a significant delay in Hitler's favorite wonder weapon. The Vergeltungswaffe 2 (Vengeance Program), better known as the V-2 rocket, was forty-five feet long and weighed 27,600 pounds, and the liquid-fueled motor propelled it to supersonic speeds. Carrying a 2,000-pound warhead, the missile was also the first man-made object to reach the edge of space.

Its descendants would revolutionize aerial warfare.

German scientists had developed four systems that they hoped would tip the balance of the air war back in their favor. Enzian, Rheintochter, and Schmetterling all were tested and subsequently failed. It wasn't just a matter of building a successful rocket—the Germans were developing a *guided* missile that could hit a specific target. Because the V-2 was employed from extensively surveyed locations, its distance from launch to impact point was precisely known. Guidance, if it could be called that, was simply a trajectory calculation and a motor burnout point that were both set on the ground. This worked fine against stationary, area targets like cities, but an air defense weapon had to track and intercept moving, maneuvering targets.

Wasserfall was their answer.

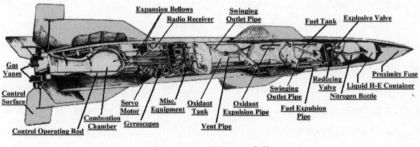

Figure 1. Wasserfall

Based on Thiel's work, the twenty-five-foot-long, nearly 8,000-pound missile was smaller than the V-2 yet retained much of the basic design. One necessary change was the fuel to be used, since Wasserfall, unlike its parent, had to remain in a ready launch status. Alcohol and liquid oxygen wouldn't work, and so a mix of ether with nitric and sulfuric acid was utilized. A hypergolic reaction took place when fuel was forced into a combustion chamber, and ignition automatically occurred.*

However, a responsive guidance system was the real challenge, since without it Wasserfall was just a ballistic missile. One solution was essentially optical: using a joystick, an operator would steer the rocket toward a target all the way to impact. Four graphite rudders protruding into the exhaust were used for early steering commands, then, as the missile accelerated, four additional rudders mounted on the tail took over. Bad weather, supersonic speeds, or low light conditions would render the optics useless, and the Germans realized this was hardly an ideal solution. No, the only practical answer lay with a radar-based control system.

Rheinland was the proposed solution and most of its fundamental principles were later adapted for an entire generation of Soviet and American air defense missile systems. Essentially the radar would track targets and once inside the weapon's launch range—called its "envelope"—the missile would be launched. A signal would be sent from the radar to the missile via a transponder mounted on its tail. This device would recognize the signal and transmit a reply back to the control system. With communication established, the control system would compare the weapon's location to the target and steer it onto the radar beam. Like a moth following a flashlight, the missile could now ride the guidance beam into the target.

There were several limitations with this. First, each radar could only track a single target and had to do so all the way to missile impact or detonation. Also, radar beam widths of

---

*Hypergolic ignitions occur from chemical reactions that begin on contact—no spark is needed.

the time were fairly wide, and a four-inch beam would cover a mile wide area at fifteen miles. Even aimed at a cluster of B-17 bombers, each with a 104-foot wingspan, a direct hit would be sheer luck. Of course, an exploding 674-pound warhead would blow fragments out past a thousand feet in all directions, so damage was quite probable.

This illuminates the last difficulty—fusing. There were several proven, though variously effective, methods of detonating a warhead. Impact or contact fuses of course existed, but these were predicated on directly hitting the target. This was fine for artillery shells since everything that goes up eventually will come down, but it was a less viable method against aircraft as on average 2,500 shells were expended for an aircraft to be destroyed. Timed fuses were most common where the detonator would function after a mechanical delay was exceeded. For anti-aircraft shells this was preset based on the enemy's altitude and became problematic if the guess was incorrect or the target changed altitude. Wasserfall initially had provision for a remote control detonation, but then you still had operator and optics issues. Possible, but again, limited by visibility, time of day, or weather. The only true solution was a proximity fuse.

These had been fielded within the American military since 1943 and were a closely guarded secret. Constructed through the Office of Scientific Research and Development (later the Applied Physics Laboratory), the first proximity fuses were used by the U.S. Navy in the Pacific Theater. Divided between the U.S. carriers *Saratoga* and *Enterprise* along with the cruiser USS *Helena*, the "funny fuse" first saw action on October 1943 off the island of Guadalcanal. It was quickly estimated to be some 300 percent more effective than other fuses and was put into rapid, full-scale production.

The principle was simple enough: a radar transceiver was incorporated into the warhead or artillery shell. When the fuse detected a radio wave that had been reflected from something nearby, usually within seventy feet, it would detonate. Fortunately, perfecting such a fuse and making it tough enough to withstand the shock of firing from a tank, gun, or at the end of a rocket were beyond Germany's capabilities in 1944.

But after the war, it was not beyond the capabilities of the Soviet Union's Nacuhno-issledovaniy (NI-88) scientific research institute. Paranoid about most things, but especially about the United States military, Joseph Stalin demanded a practical defense for Moscow and Leningrad against American B-29 bombers. Using German engineers, techniques, and technology, the Berkut system took up where Wasserfall had left off.* Later changed to Systema 25 (S-25), the missile system was operational in March 1954, becoming known to NATO as the SA-1.

It was unwieldy, of doubtful effectiveness, and expensive. Constructed around Moscow, the two big ring roads built to service the fifty-six SAM regiments had consumed the entire year's production of concrete. Clearly a better and cheaper solution was needed. The Kutepov Beria design bureau, now called Almaz following a political shake-up, had been working on a new system since November 1953. Leaner and more advanced, the S-75 used a two-stage motor to accelerate a Fakel missile to three times the speed of sound. With an approximate tactical engagement range of seventeen miles, the Dvina, as it was known, utilized command guidance from a ground-based RSNA-75 radar.

Command guidance necessitated the radar maintain a track, or "lock," all the way through the missile's time of flight to impact. Unlike later SAMs that would have homing receivers, the SA-2 flew like a puppet on a string. In this case, the strings

---

*Berkut means "golden eagle" and is taken from the first three letters of *Beria* and *Kutepov,* respectively, from the KB-1 design bureau.

were guidance signals (left, right, up, down) that were uplinked to the transponder on the missile's tail. Formal military acceptance occurred on December 11, 1957, and the SA-2, as it was known to NATO, became operational.

An enemy air defense weapon such as this was a game changer to America's Strategic Air Command since both high-altitude reconnaissance aircraft and bombers were threatened by its deployment. Initially the tactical fighters engaged in Southeast Asia countered the SAM threat by attacking at very low altitudes. This was comfortable for USAF pilots; they'd been trained this way to fight the Soviet Union, and the aircraft, especially the F-105, was designed for precisely this mission. Going in low caused problems for the Fansong, though it often guided on low-altitude targets. Low-altitude tactical ingresses also caused problems for the MiGs. Trade-offs were significant; low-altitude flying is physically extremely challenging, often at the cost of navigation, situational awareness, and weapons effectiveness. Then there were the guns. It could be argued that the real lethality of the SAM lay not with the missile itself, but in the *threat* of the missile, which would force fighter-bombers to jettison their bomb loads or drive them down into anti-aircraft artillery range.

Countermeasures were needed.

Electronic warfare wasn't a new field, but it had been a relatively stagnant one for some time. The earliest modern example occurred during the 1904 Sino-Japanese War when Russian radio operators managed to disrupt communications between Japanese battleships. During World War II, noise jamming, which saturates a given frequency range, was used to blind entire sections of German coastal surveillance radars. An aircraft's primary physical countermeasure against radar was chaff, initially sheets of aluminum foil that would reflect radar waves. Joan Curran, a Welsh-born physicist, was the first to cut these sheets into strips, called dipole elements, which measured half of a radar's wavelength.* When RF waves struck chaff, the energy was reradiated and produced an echo, or a false return, that hopefully disguised the original target.

Yet no sooner is a technology or weapon invented than other systems are designed to degrade or destroy it. The Ferret I program began in 1943 by locating Japanese radars on the Aleutian Islands using B-24D bombers and primitive APR-4 receivers. As the program rapidly expanded into Ferret III-IV, the U.S. Army Air Force modified the B-17F to carry a wide range of electronic equipment. They gathered information, collected intelligence, and roughly located German radars all along the Italian and French coasts in preparation for invasion. In the Pacific Theater their counterparts were called Ravens, flying B-24s and B-29s that were equipped for basic spectrum analysis.

Using APA-24 homing receivers during the Korean War, B-26 Hunter aircraft would attempt to ride a detected beam back to its source. When the radar was visually acquired, the accompanying A-26 Killers would strafe the site. By the late 1950s, spot-jamming specific frequencies, deception jamming to generate false targets, and the use of airborne chaff to confuse radar pictures were all in various stages of development or operational use. By this time the original aluminum foil chaff had been replaced by metal-coated glass fiber strips. Developed by Bjorksten Research Laboratories in Wisconsin, the new chaff was stronger and much thinner. This meant that about four times more material could be packed into the same dispenser and, since the glass strips had a rounded cross section, they

*Joan and her husband, Sir Samuel Curran, were member of the Manhattan Project. A brilliant graduate of Cambridge University, she was not awarded her degree in physics until 1935 because she was a woman.

didn't stick together. This permitted better blooming and made the chaff more effective.

None of this saved Captain Ying-Chin Wang of the Republic of China Air Force (Taiwan) from being shot down in an RB-57D Canberra over the Formosa Strait on October 7, 1959, becoming the first confirmed SAM kill in history.* Five weeks later the first *recorded* kill took place inside the Soviet Union when an SA-2 destroyed a U.S. reconnaissance balloon near Stalingrad.† By the time Gary Powers went down over Sary-shagan in 1960 and Major Rudy Anderson was lost during the 1962 Cuban Missile Crisis, the SA-2 was a known, viable threat.

Even so, competing for scarce interwar dollars was ugly; radars and jammers weren't particularly sexy and you couldn't visualize the results the same way you could with shiny jets or impressive new bombs. Besides, in the post–World War II era of atomic weapons, what was the point? Such logic also tried to kill off fighters because they were obviously superfluous in the age of nuclear-armed bombers. The bomber enthusiasts also tried to end funding for aircraft carriers, regarding them as expensive luxuries. Fortunately, saner heads generally prevailed, and though most were convinced that the next war would be nuclear, there were some nagging suspicions that this might not be so.

One positive result from the "bomber mafia," as it was called, retained their interest in electronic countermeasures like jamming. As heavy bombers cannot rely on maneuvering to defeat a threat, the Strategic Air Command had long relied on electronic warfare and countermeasures to increase surviv-

---

*RB-57D No. 5643, on loan to the Republic of China Air Force and part of Diamond Lil—a joint USAF/CIA operation.
†A WS-416L balloon. Stalingrad was renamed Volgograd in 1961.

ability for its planes. They were similarly invested in electronic warfare support measures and the intelligence gathered from signals analysis.

Allen Lamb hadn't been exaggerating when he stated that the USAF mindset regarding SAMs was "just get it done." Yet from the beginning it was realized that the F-100F Wild Weasel was a temporary fix to the problem. A two-seat fighter was needed and they'd been available—but the problem was the jet itself. Designed by North American Aviation, the Hun followed the proud lineage of the P-51 Mustang and F-86 Sabre. Flight testing began in 1953 and the new jet proved to be a handful. The "fly off the drawing board" concept didn't impress legendary test pilots Chuck Yeager or Pete Everest, and the new plane killed George Welch on October 12, 1954.*

Given its performance and the Pentagon's obsession with nuclear war, the redesigned F-100 turned from interceptor to fighter-bomber. Yet for all its problems it had potential. The Hun became the first jet to reach supersonic airspeeds in level flight and had an in-flight air refueling capability.† Possessing six underwing pylons for a variety of weapons with four M-39 20 mm cannons, the F-100 packed a punch. Its relatively small size made it hard to see and the Hun could maneuver well enough to dogfight if needed. Well suited for air-to-air MiGCAPs and close air support, the Hun was initially the workhorse fighter in Southeast Asia.

Alex Kartveli's F-105 was the other choice. Chief designer for Republic, Kartveli also created the P-47 Thunderbolt during

---

* George Welch was one of the two Army Air Corps pilots who got airborne on December 7, 1941, and managed to fight the Japanese over Pearl Harbor.
† Often incorrectly credited as the first U.S. fighter able to air refuel; this honor goes to the F-84, which operationally refueled from the KB-29 during the Korean War.

World War II and the F-84 Thunderjet, which saw widespread service in Korea. In 1927 the Georgian-born Kartveli had immigrated to the United States at the behest of Charles Levine, millionaire entrepreneur and pilot.* It was while working for Levine that the young designer met Alexander de Seversky, another immigrant from Georgia, who formed the Seversky Aircraft Corporation. Following several economic reversals, the little company emerged as Republic Aviation just in time for World War II.

Adept at exceeding military requirements, Kartveli used the success of his P-47 and F-84 programs to submit a proposal for an all-weather, supersonic fighter-bomber. Initially labeled the AP-63-FBX, it featured a fifteen-foot, ten-inch internal bomb bay, an air refueling capability. Powered by the Allison J-71 engine, the jet could reach Mach 1.5 carrying a full load of nuclear weapons. However, eventual redesign made the airframe so large that the original Allison was replaced by the powerful Pratt & Whitney J-75 engine. In any event, the new jet was precisely in line with Pentagon planning for high-speed, low-altitude, nuclear attacks against the Soviet Union, and in September 1952 a contract for 199 aircraft was awarded. The new jet would be called the F-105 Thunderchief, later known as the "Thud," and it would make history.

With the end of the Korean War came Washington's inevitable conclusion that there would be no more wars to fight, therefore scant need of a new fighter-bomber. The initial order of F-105s fell to three. Perhaps anticipating another war, and a nonnuclear one at that, Republic kept the internal cannon and four underwing hard points of the original design. There were

---

*In 1927 Levine had lost the Orteig Prize to Charles Lindbergh, who'd managed to get airborne a few hours earlier.

other innovations, such as forward-swept engine intakes, and the MA-8 fire control system. Like all Kartveli's designs, the pilot was the prime concern, for without the man, the jet was merely 35,600 pounds of useless metal. So the cockpit was comfortable and well laid out, with protective armor, and a near zero-zero ejection seat.*

However, as it became apparent that another war, a conventional war, was ramping up in Southeast Asia, the USAF once again began placing orders.† Following the Spring High disaster, it was obvious the SAMs had to be dealt with if any type of true air campaign was to be successful. Allen Lamb and Wild Weasel I began forming in August, but even with the program taking top priority for testing, personnel, and equipment, there was simply no way to retrofit the first F-100s and get them over to Southeast Asia before November 1965.

So work continued on the Hun at a frenetic pace, despite the limits of small cockpits with little room for the Weasel equipment. Also, the F-100 could air refuel only with a probe-and-drogue system, and though this was commonly used throughout the late 1950s and early 1960s, the Air Force was standardizing boom refueling for fighters. Then there was speed. Even at 860 mph the Hun was hard-pressed to keep up with F-105s during strike missions. Nevertheless, the F-100F was available and the reports of SAMs coming out of Southeast Asia weren't good—something had to be done *now*.

Throughout 1965, Hanoi received three air defense regiments from the USSR along with technical training for an ini-

---

*A safe ejection is possible at zero feet and zero knots of airspeed—sitting on the ground.
†Deliveries were 17 F-105Ds in fiscal year (FY) 1960, 149 in FY 1961, 171 in FY 1962, 198 in FY 1963, and 75 in FY 1964. The production line closed in 1964 after 833 jets were fielded.

tial cadre of North Vietnamese operators.* Organized along Soviet lines, these units were usually based on a three-battery configuration: six SM-63-I launchers with a Fansong radar, a search radar like the Spoon Rest, command vans, generators, and spare missiles. A battery would also have a technical unit to maintain and repair the equipment.

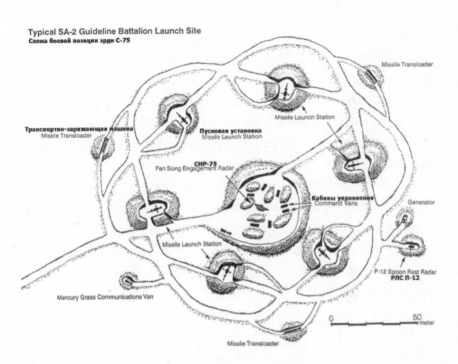

Typical Soviet SA-2 site

Typical Soviet SAM batteries were laid out in a star-shaped pattern of interconnected access paths. Early warning/search radars operated from this outside ring, as did the communications vehicle connecting each battery to its regimental head-

---

*The 236th, 260th, and 274th Air Defense Regiments

quarters. Small outer emplacements held the transporter-loader vehicles and spare missiles, and from this position they could quickly service the missile revetments around the perimeter. The middle of the star contained very substantial earthen berms that protected the Fansong radar and command vans. From here, in theory, each battery commander would receive targeting assignments from headquarters and could operate autonomously if necessitated by combat conditions.

North Vietnamese sites were rarely laid out in the Soviet pattern. The terrain, be it tropical, forested, or a soggy littoral area, wasn't usually conducive to construction. Fixed sites were not important to Hanoi, nor were they preferred. The North Vietnamese were well aware of the American technical prowess and feared concentrated air attacks. Fully expecting the insane constraints against U.S. forces to be lifted, the NVA planned for a relatively mobile air defense system. They knew that if it wasn't able to move and hide, it would be destroyed. So roughly prepared sites were constructed that could be used at will, improved when necessary, then vacated and used again later. Because they moved frequently, and began limiting Firecan and Fansong radar emissions, locating operational SAM sites became highly uncertain.

Using what was available in 1965, the North Vietnamese constructed a rudimentary integrated air defense system. Observers used binoculars, jet noise, and often just plain eyeballs to detect U.S. strike packages. Limited radio eavesdropping on U.S. aircraft transmissions was also attempted, with varying degrees of success. By far the most accurate, effective piece of the air picture was gleaned from a small but steadily improving network of early warning radars. Height finders were large-array radars that provided altitude information; surveillance radars were capable of seeing USAF fighters in their air refueling tracks over Laos and could detect Navy packages in the Gulf of Tonkin.

All of these bits and pieces were then relayed, with varying degree of effectiveness, to the national air defense command center on Hanoi's Bach Mai airfield.* Using landlines, which were secure from U.S. monitoring, and radio communications, which were not, the North Vietnamese attempted to create a composite air battle picture. This was aided by American route and timing predictability, forced on combat commanders from Washington, and by NVA informants within Saigon's military establishment. Because of this, details of nearly every mission were known in Hanoi as soon as Saigon received them. Correlated with all the other information available, a fairly complete air defense picture was available.

North Vietnamese Air Force fighters were equally problematical. There was a mix of MiG-15s left over from the Korean War, along with the newer MiG-17. These had arrived from the Soviet Union with the second group of NVAF pilots and formed the 923rd Fighter Regiment. The initial cadre of MiG-15 pilots had been trained in the USSR at Krasnodar, on the Black Sea, and in China. Heavily dependent on ground-controlled intercept (GCI) procedures, they often lacked the initiative and freedom of their American opponents. On the other hand, they were fighting over their own country, close to base, and weren't burdened by restrictions or bomb loads. The two main MiG bases, Kep and Phuc Yen, were absurdly "off-limits" for attack during much of the conflict. Robert McNamara, the U.S. secre-

---

*Until 1967 this critical piece of air defense infrastructure was also off limits for any U.S. attack due to its proximity to Bach Mai hospital—a facility used to treat North Vietnamese combat casualties. Damaged by bombs in 1972, it was rebuilt by donations from Americans. A special rehab unit was also opened by the Veterans for America.

tary of defense, reasoned that any assault on North Vietnamese air bases *might* provoke a reaction from China.

Until the SAMs arrived in the summer of 1965, anti-aircraft artillery was really the only defense against American air attack. Plentiful and relatively cheap, Triple A has always been the biggest killer of tactical aircraft. In Western Europe during World War II, anti-aircraft fire accounted for approximately 65 percent of the 18,418 aircraft lost, and missions aimed at suppressing the sites were the most dangerous flown. Major General Elwood "Pete" Quesada, commander of the 9th Tactical Air Command, described strafing anti-aircraft positions as being "like a man biting a dog."

Of the 1,230 fixed-wing losses from all services during the Korean War, 88 percent came from the guns.* So with full knowledge of U.S. rules of engagement, their restricted areas, and prohibited targets, Hanoi was able to place their initial 1,200 weapons where they'd do the most damage, and by the end of 1965 the number of anti-aircraft pieces doubled to more than 2,000 guns.†

USAF and Navy tactical aircraft avoided much of the smaller-caliber Triple A and tens of thousands of handheld automatic weapons by simply staying above most of it. In an age before precision-guided weapons, the trade-off here was in bombing accuracy, and this was acceptable until the SA-2 became operational. Now the medium altitudes of 4,000 to 20,000 feet were no longer safe since the SAM could shoot

---

* By the war's end in 1973, NVA anti-aircraft artillery and small arms fire would claim 76 percent of fixed-wing U.S. combat losses.
† The numbers increased, but figures vary according to which source is used. In 1967 the Pentagon estimated there were 4,500 Triple A pieces of all calibers, while the United States' Pacific Air Forces (PACAF) command counted more than 9,000. As always, the truth is likely in between. The number of guns, particularly the 85 mm to 100 mm types, decreased over time.

up past 60,000 feet. Fansongs were not supposed to be able to engage low-level aircraft, below 2,000 feet, so tactical fighters were forced low, thus exposing them to the guns again.*

Spring High had been an unmitigated disaster. Six F-105s had gone down; three highly trained, experienced, and irreplaceable pilots had been killed. Two more would spend more than seven unimaginable, lonely years as prisoners of war.† Today the mission can be viewed as the Vietnam War in microcosm: indecision from policy makers, negligence from planners who should have known better, and amazing courage from those doing their best to fight under such circumstances.

If the Americans had immediately and decisively attacked following Leopard Two's shootdown, or come without warning, the assault might have succeeded despite the silly plan. The 4th SAM battalion commander, Major Il'inykh, had only repositioned his batteries away from the Son Tay region the night before the attack. It was only then that the sham Site 6 and Site 7 were created with cannibalized missile bodies, and sometimes even logs propped up in revetments to resemble operational SAMs. Men stayed behind, appearing busy as they would in a real air defense battery.

But the sites weren't complete fakes. More than one hundred anti-aircraft guns were now carefully emplaced and waiting should the Americans actually attack. No one really thought they would. After all, why would the world's most powerful military come across the globe ready to fight, and then waste their men so senselessly? It would defy logic.

---

*This turned out to be somewhat erroneous. If a Fansong had a clear line of sight and the missile fusing was set to proximity minimums, aircraft at very low altitudes could be engaged—and often were.
†Those responsible, the planners at the Pentagon, PACAF, and 2nd Air Division level, were never held accountable for the debacle.

And still they came.

Yet as bad as it was, Spring High had shown both the Soviets and NVA that the Americans would fight back—hard and viciously. The mission made them blink, figuratively, because for the next two weeks the radars were silent. Perhaps they were assessing the danger or merely working out better tactics for themselves. Perhaps the merciless USAF response made Hanoi realize that their Soviet mentors were incorrect: SAMs in Vietnam could not remain in fixed sites or they'd be eviscerated.

In any event, on August 11, two Navy A-4E pilots near Than Hoa spotted flares glowing through an undercast and circled to investigate. Unfortunately, the hot spots were the sustainer motor exhaust plumes from a pair of SAMs. One Skyhawk was hit and immediately exploded, killing Lieutenant (jg) Donald Brown of VA-23 (the Black Knights). The second A-4, flown by Lieutenant Commander Francis Roberge, was badly damaged but made it back to the USS *Midway*.

Just like the USAF three weeks before, the U.S. Navy wanted revenge. Over the next two days, seventy-six Iron Hand sorties were flown off the USS *Coral Sea* and *Midway* looking for the SAMs that killed Lieutenant Brown. A pair of jets went down to anti-aircraft fire, but it was Friday, August 13, 1965, that became known as "Black Friday."* VA-22 (Fighting Redcocks) lost an A-4C and the *Coral Sea* lost two more, including a Skyhawk flown by Commander Harry Thomas, a Korean War combat veteran and the commanding officer of VA-153 (Blue Tail Flies).†

From August 12 through September 14, 1965, nearly four

---

*September 12 was the same day the initial Vector IV set was delivered for the F-100F.
†Commander Thomas never ejected. His remains were returned to Taft, California, in October 1996.

hundred Iron Hand sorties were flown in a generally futile effort to deal with the missile threat. Little was accomplished, except to categorically prove that World War II and Korean War tactics, even with modern jets and astounding courage, were not the answer for killing SAMs. Low-altitude trolling without specific intelligence and specialized equipment was exceptionally dangerous. In fact, going low with no other purpose but to avoid SAMs caused more fatalities from anti-aircraft guns than the missiles ever did. This was precisely why a group of men were desperately working around the clock on the other side of the world. They were installing antennas, new displays, and rewiring four F-100F Super Sabres that would emerge as the first Wild Weasels.

Clearly something had to be done. It was really no surprise then on October 14, 1965, a mere five days after the F-100F and Wild Weasel I began flight testing, that a USAF colonel named J. T. Johnson got a call from the Pentagon. Before Wild Weasel I even departed for action, he was told to begin Wild Weasel III, with the installation and testing of the ATI equipment on the two-seat F-105F.

He was to do it immediately. They would be needed.

BY EARLY 1966, the war in Southeast Asia had taken on a new character. When Allen Lamb and Jack Donovan killed the first SA-2 near the Black River, two thousand pieces of anti-aircraft artillery were in place in North Vietnam. Some one hundred SAM sites had been constructed or were under construction, and about thirty of these were now occupied.

South of the DMZ, the growing U.S. ground forces fought the Viet Cong, and with no SAMs or large-caliber anti-aircraft fire with which to contend, American close air support ruled the

skies. These air support missions included B-52 *strategic* bombers used against *tactical* targets like bridges, depots, and suspected truck parks.* "Monkey Killers," the B-52 strikes were
called, because each aircraft expended thirty tons of bombs and
often did little but make craters, shred trees, and kill monkeys.
It certainly wasn't the fault of the B-52 units that they were
being used incorrectly, but their employment in an interdiction
role illustrates the dysfunctional use of military power that typ-
ified the conflict.

North of the DMZ was the air war. U.S. Air Force and
Navy strike packages composed of tactical jets faced heavy
Triple A, SAMs, and occasionally MiG fighters to attack strategic targets. As the number of fighters and mission complexity in
the North increased, some method of dividing up the airspace
for coordination was needed. By late December 1965, a joint
Air Force–Navy coordination team cut North Vietnam into six
geographic segments, called "Route Packages," to deconflict
Rolling Thunder missions.

Responsibility for each Route Pack (RP) was divided between the USAF Pacific Air Forces and the Navy's Pacific Fleet,
though in practice fighters went where they had to go, or were
instructed to go. RP One, just north of the demilitarized zone,
was assigned to the Military Assistance Command, Vietnam
(MACV). However, with the exception of VNAF Skyraiders and
shore-based Marine fighters, RP One was primarily worked by
carrier aircraft and USAF fighters based in Thailand. RPs Two,
Three, and Four were coastal zones and well within range of
naval air support. Pack Five stretched from the Red River west
to the Laotian border, then north to China. It was deep inside

---

* "Arc Light" strikes began dumping immense quantities of bombs along the Ho
Chi Minh Trail in December 1965.

the DRV and could realistically only be reached by USAF fighters based in Thailand. All of North Vietnam was dangerous, but no place more so than Pack Six, as it contained Hanoi and Haiphong. Eventually subdivided at the Red River, the eastern portion generally went to carrier air, while Hanoi and the western area remained with the Air Force. Still, jets crossed all the time and the RP system was really only valuable for planning purposes.

Operation Rolling Thunder was barely a year old when Allen Lamb and Frank O'Donnell killed the third SA-2 in March 1966. Conceived the previous year, the operation was intended to attack targets in the South, just above the DMZ, and roll north in a series of graduated assaults. The Pentagon was confident the display of technology and firepower would convince the North Vietnamese leadership that resistance was futile—that they should capitulate, or at least negotiate, before Hanoi and Haiphong became targets. It was an operation that might sound good behind a desk on the Potomac River, but Rolling Thunder reflected Washington's conflictions and indecisiveness about the war.

And yet understanding this operation is central to any discussion of the air war in Southeast Asia from 1965 to 1968. Regarding South Vietnam, National Security Action Memorandum (NSAM) 273 stated that the primary objective of the United States was "to assist the people and government of that country to win their contest against the externally directed and supported communist conspiracy."

This ambiguous language, and that of subsequent White House pronouncements, would unfortunately be used to shape battlefield decisions, which by necessity then dictated tactics. With NSAM 288, McNamara ordered the Joint Chiefs of Staff to develop the idea of graduated, overt pressure, which included, incredibly, a thirty-day notice for scheduled raids and a seventy-two-hour warning to Hanoi for any retaliatory raids. This plainly reveals that the ultimate goal of Rolling Thunder was never military victory achieved through the destruction of the North Vietnamese capacity to fight. Rather, it was to influence the *perception* of certain destruction on Hanoi's part, which would then lead to Washington's desired political outcome of a South Vietnam free from communist influence.

Admiral Harry Felt, commander of the Pacific Fleet, originally articulated the military response with Operations Plan 37-64, and its language clearly illuminates key misunderstandings regarding North Vietnam at the highest levels of the U.S. military. First, it was inconceivable to the leadership in the United States, a modern, industrial society, that Hanoi did not place similar emphasis on power plants, manufacturing facilities, transportation networks, and oil. This led to a predilection, an obsession, really, with any northern target that contained technical value, real or perceived, throughout the war.

The failure in this line of thinking was in ignoring that the North was an agrarian society that could, and did, survive quite well without vehicles, electricity, or factories. The largest DRV power plant had a 32,500-kw generation capacity, which would supply a U.S. city the size of Paducah, Kentucky, or Seguin, Texas.* North Vietnamese still used candles and oil lamps as a primary source of light, and they burned wood for heat. Wood, as well as coal, was used to fuel trains in the North, not oil. Additionally, thousands of portable generators were scattered about the country, so there was no true impact on the population by depriving them of something they didn't rely on anyway.

Factories, the muscle behind superpower economic force,

---

*Cities with a population of about 25,000.

were of negligible strategic value in North Vietnam. Everything required to physically fight the war, such as steel, trucks, weapons, and ammunition, could all be imported from communist allies. These were delivered by sea through the port of Haiphong or overland by rail through China.* Transportation networks were also a natural target choice against an industrial-based enemy but of limited consequence in North Vietnam. Main roads were generally made of clay and were surfaced, if at all, with tar. The vast majority of the network, like the Ho Chi Minh Trail, was simply packed dirt. In any case, Hanoi had an immense pool of at least 500,000 laborers who would quickly repair damage.

Bridges, infrastructure targets beloved by military planners everywhere, were similarly elusive. Most had been built by the French and were of substantial colonial construction. The Paul Doumer (Long Bien) Bridge spanned the Red River and connected Hanoi to the port of Haiphong. Farther south, the Dragon's Jaw (Than Hoa) Bridge across the Song Ma River survived continuous attacks until 1972. Adept at improvisation, the Vietnamese used pontoon bridges, concealed fords, or underwater log crossings that were invisible to air surveillance.

Petroleum, oil, and lubrication (POL) would also become a favored target of Rolling Thunder missions, because, by modern standards, no military could exist without it. By this reasoning, the majority of men and equipment moving along the Ho Chi Minh Trail had to be coming by truck, but in fact they were not. Most of the support for Viet Cong operations in the South came from the South. A mere thirty-four tons per day was all

---

*Narrow-gauge Vietnamese railroad tracks were all replaced to accommodate the standard-gauge arrangement used by the Chinese. Up to 1,000 tons per day were brought by rail into the DRV.

that was required to be brought overland, and most of this arrived via human porter or bicycles. It has been estimated that only 1,600 tons of oil per year were needed to maintain entire vehicular operations along the trail until 1968.

Alarmed by the 170,000 tons of oil imported by Hanoi, National Security Advisor Walt Rostow advocated full-scale strikes against several large storage facilities. Finally approved in late June 1966, Rolling Thunder 51 specifically targeted the POL facilities in Route Pack Six. Within thirty days there was a 50 percent drop in oil reserves, with 80 percent of the holding capacity estimated as destroyed. Significant damage, to be sure, but unfortunately the North Vietnamese economy subsisted on about 32,000 tons of oil per annum, and by late 1966 more than 60,000 tons were dispersed throughout the countryside. Most of this was in smaller holding tanks or fifty-five-gallon drums located alongside dikes or other targets Washington had prohibited U.S. forces from attacking.

Dikes were the true Achilles' hill of the entire North Vietnamese system—the one target that *should* have been targeted. Hanoi actually lay twenty feet below the Red River, and if the dikes had been eliminated then the city would have flooded. Without dikes, the fragile irrigation network of ninety-one locks and dams would also have been overwhelmed, and a significant percentage of the four-million-ton annual rice harvest would have failed.* Starving people don't fight well, nor do they tolerate a government that cannot feed them. Long-range bombing alone, as proven in World War II, has a galvanizing effect on collective morale. Watching your children starve does not.

Surprisingly, military opinion was divided on the matter. The Joint Chiefs never officially pressed for such attacks, and

---

*Only eight waterway targets were officially approved by the Joint Chiefs.

General John P. McConnell, head of the Air Force, considered them of negligible value. Others held the exact opposite view, and not just tactical officers who were being fired upon by the guns emplaced along the dikes. General Earle Wheeler, chairman of the Joint Chiefs, considered that attacks on the waterway system would "exert desirable psychological pressure on both leaders and population." Targeting the food supply would have been a direct attack on the most significant North Vietnamese resource—people.

However, attacking the population, directly or indirectly, ran contrary to the industrial-targeting mindset so engrained within the Pentagon and the White House. The military leadership in particular had committed the cardinal sin of forcing the war to fit their existing doctrines instead of adapting doctrine to fit the existing war. Still, even if there was the strategic will to target dikes and civilian food supply, the decision to do so would have carried appalling human rights consequences. It may have been one thing to target downtown Berlin and Tokyo during World War II, but it would have been quite another to flood villages and starve the countryside of a nation that only the most hardened ideologue could argue posed an existential threat to the United States. Such was the reality of waging a "limited" conflict with a military designed for total war.

Perhaps the most significant strategic error of all was in neither recognizing nor admitting that the conflict in Southeast Asia was a civil war. In Hanoi's view, the fight was always reunification first, and ideology second, if at all. Ho Chi Minh was a communist out of convenience; he was foremost a nationalist, and always had been. Knowing your enemy and his motivation is fundamental to fighting the war you see, and not forcing a war to conform to your own fears regarding global communism or the domino theory. For the NVA, engaged in a nationalist struggle, there would be no sudden bargaining, no paralyzing fear of air strikes, nor a collapse from Hanoi. Likewise, waging a war of attrition was similarly unrealistic against an enemy who did not consider lives lost in combat a high price to pay. In fact, a war of attrition had just the opposite effect. Americans wondered why they were fighting and dying for South Vietnam—the Viet Cong and NVA had no such doubts.

Sensing the White House's tepid commitment, and understanding all the restrictions hampering the U.S. military, Hanoi knew that all it needed was time, with material support from Red China and the Soviet Union. On the other hand, having made the decision to support Saigon, the United States could not walk away without risking a loss of prestige that would have ramifications far beyond Southeast Asia. No one thought America was weak, but then, as now, the perception of indecisiveness, or lack of will, would impact allies and enemies throughout the world.

In later years Lyndon Johnson would reflect:

> *I knew from the start that I was bound to be crucified either way I moved. If I left the woman I really loved—the Great Society—in order to get involved with that bitch of a war on the other side of the world, then I would lose everything at home.*

This was true only if the war was not won.

Johnson's "one foot in, one foot out" approach came to typify Washington's approach to the war. Technology would develop and tactics mature, yet for most of the conflict, Washington was never willing to fight the type of war that had defeated the Axis in 1945. The human cost of waging total war in Vietnam was just too great to ask the American public to condone, and, in truth, the United States was never at war—only the military was, by political will. Further, there were fears that the conflict would escalate into war with the Soviet Union or China, which had tested its first nuclear weapon in 1964. It was known that in 1963 Beijing and Hanoi had signed a mutual defense pact that would activate in the event of U.S. aggression by land, sea, or air. But in the wake of his nation's costly experience against the Americans in Korea, China's Chairman Mao had decided not to fight again. At least not on behalf of another country. As he later remarked, "When we signed the military agreement with Vietnam, our generals were too eager." So by the summer of 1964, Beijing unilaterally abrogated the treaty, and Washington *should* have known this.

DESPITE GRAVE MISGIVINGS, the Pentagon had no choice but obedience to the White House and the Joint Chiefs of Staff drew up a list of ninety-four targets for the initial eight weeks of Rolling Thunder. As with most sensitive information sent to 2nd Air Division Headquarters in Saigon, it was soon known to Hanoi. Naturally enough, the NVA quickly made sanctuaries out of facilities, airfields, and structures (like dikes) that they knew the Americans were prohibited from attacking.

Rolling Thunder was meant to accomplish several objectives. It would, by virtue of its gradual escalation, allay international fears, thus discouraging a military response from China. It was also intended to raise the morale of the South Vietnamese people and firmly establish the Republic of South Vietnam by stopping the Viet Cong's infiltration via the Ho Chi Minh Trail, thus cutting off support from the north. As the eminent aviation historian Walter Boyne stated, "It is worth noting that none of these goals called for the physical destruction of the enemy's capability to wage war."

Nevertheless, interdicting chokepoints along the Ho Chi Minh Trail became a central feature of the air war during the entire conflict. A vital supply line, the "trail" was actually a rough maze of paths through the jungle, not a single, definable line of communication. Created in the late 1950s to support the Viet Cong's insurrection in South Vietnam, Hanoi called it the Troung Son Strategic Supply Route, and it meandered hundreds of miles through Laos and the Central Highlands of Vietnam. By 1965 approximately thirty tons of supplies per day were being moved by thousands of volunteer porters. Trekking southward, they made their way through a series of *binh tram,* or way stations, which eventually contained medical and engineering units, communications, and anti-aircraft detachments.

Now under the control of the NVA 559th Transportation Group, supply hubs, or base camps, directed all troop and material movements south. Located in Laos, Base 604 was the main distribution hub and kept tens of thousands of NVA regulars and Viet Cong guerrillas moving south. Base 611 was located in the Central Highlands, and Base 607 fed directly into South Vietnam through the A Shau Valley. There were those in Washington, and particularly in Saigon, who understood that the war would be won or lost only in South Vietnam. Hanoi certainly knew it, for if the South fell, what did air strikes matter in the north? There were also those who knew that interdicting the Ho Chi Minh Trail was like trying to destroy a jellyfish by attacking the tentacles; they regenerate in a matter of days. The only true way to successfully stop the flow of men and ammunition to the South was by cutting off the sources in the North— namely railroads and Haiphong Harbor.

But this would not happen for another seven years, and in

the meantime American fighting men did the best they could
under Washington's self-imposed political shackles. Laos took
on an even greater importance as the NVA began increasing its
activities along the Laotian portion of the trail, an area theoretically immune to air strikes. Guaranteed neutrality following
the 1954 Geneva Accords, Laos was off-limits to the regular
U.S. military, so nothing that happened there was openly acknowledged.* However, CIA and military special forces operated throughout the country but with no official status should
something go wrong. Added to the diplomatic complexities
were periodic coups, regime changes, and miserable weather;
Laos was just a complicated place to fight. The blurry borders
of Southeast Asia became positively opaque in Laos, which
suited the CIA's counterinsurgency purposes admirably.

However, tacit neutrality could do nothing to prevent American overflight, nor could Laos or Cambodia directly interfere
with U.S. air operations. These rapidly increased from Operation Barrel Roll, along the Bolovens Plateau in Laos, to Operation Steel Tiger, which commenced in April 1965. Both were
flown from bases in Thailand and tried, with variable success,
to interdict the Ho Chi Minh Trail. By December 1965, when
Operation Tiger Hound began, U.S. intelligence sources estimated that at least 4,000 NVA regulars and some 300 tons of
supplies moved through Laos each month.

As America expanded its air operations, the enemy corre-
spondingly beefed up its air defense capabilities. Aircraft continued to be brought down by small arms fire and anti-aircraft
guns that had been moved down from the North. The North
Vietnamese proved to have an inherent genius for logistics, at
least within their own territory. By late 1966, they'd managed

---

*This includes 214 *admitted* American losses.

to move thousands of trucks and artillery pieces, and tons of rice and ammunition. At least seventeen regiments, more than 60,000 fighting men, also made the six-week march. They'd proven over and over again, since Dien Bien Phu in 1954, that anything could be taken apart, packed over hundreds of miles of muddy trails, then reassembled for combat.

Even surface-to-air missiles.

CHAPTER 5

HUNTER KILLERS

"OAK ZERO ONE, Korat Tower . . . winds are zero, six zero at fifteen . . . you are cleared for takeoff."

Major Ed Rock smiled slightly. Winds were right down the runway for a change. As he acknowledged the tower, the pilot smoothly pushed the throttle forward and braced his legs against the rudder pedals. Eyes flickering between the runway centerline stripe and the engine gauges on the bottom right of the instrument panel, he saw everything was in the green. Normal.

"Copy that, Tower. Oak is cleared off."

Releasing the brakes, he slumped back in the seat as the F-105 accelerated. As it lumbered forward, Rock hesitated long enough to check the engine, then shoved the throttle into full afterburner. Nudging the pedals, he kept the jet centered on the runway, let go of the throttle, and flipped the water injection switch by his left knee next to the starter. Water was injected into the big Pratt & Whitney J-75 engine, and as it evaporated the air cooled and became denser. Heavier air made combustion more powerful, causing the turbines to spin more efficiently and generate more thrust.

At 140 knots, Rock flexed his right wrist and held the stick back. The Thunderchief's nose lifted, and the jet paused on two wheels for a moment. Thrust and lift steadily overcame weight and drag, and the jet muscled its way into the air. White hash marks on the runway blurred; as the ground fell away, Rock brought up the landing gear and raised the flaps.

Normally he would be leading a flight of at least four other fighters, keeping an eye on them, listening for problems, and planning ahead. Today was different. On this day they were alone. As Thailand got smaller under the wings, he grinned. It was almost fun. Soon, however, his mind was brought back to the mission. He checked his warning lights and engine gauges and adjusted the seat a bit. Fiddling with the air-conditioning, Rock also squinted at the APR-25 threat warning scope and turned the brightness all the way up. Climbing through 5,000 feet, he began an easy turn toward the northeast and his air refueling (AR) track.

Rock selected Point A on the Doppler navigation system; it was an entry location for the Peach air refueling track over near the Laotian border. Once designated, he'd get a course to the point corrected for winds and a ground speed to fly based on his desired arrival time. All the refueling areas were named for colors: Black, Green, Orange, Red, White, Peach, and so on. Each mission would be scheduled to a certain track within a certain time window. Inside the tracks, KC-135 tankers would be stacked up at different altitudes, holding and waiting to pass fuel to their fighters.

Tankers were absolutely indispensable, as there was no way to make a 1,200-mile round-trip into North Vietnam without refueling. Fighters always did on the way in, and nearly always did on the way out. At least the Thuds had to, given that Korat and Takhli were both 200 miles inside Thailand. Today they'd be sharing the tanker with an EB-66 reconnaissance jet, so Ed Rock would have to use the probe to refuel. About two feet long, the probe would pop up from a panel just forward and left of the cockpit. The other refueling method used a telescoping boom that extended like a big stinger from the back of the tanker.

Air refueling was part science, part Zen. With either system, you first flew the jet to a point, vertically and horizontally, beneath the tanker. The Navy preferred a drogue but most USAF fighter crews liked the boom. With the latter, the pilot would smoothly fly up to a "pre-contact" position where he could see the double row of lights beneath the tanker. The operator, lying flat in a Plexiglas bubble on the KC-135's belly, would use these lights to guide the aircraft into the "contact" position, at which point he'd stick the boom into a receptacle. From there the pilot would correct to keep the boom in the jet. A drogue was worse. The tanker simply streamed the fuel hose out in the wind stream and the fighter pilot flew the drogue into the basket, much like a hummingbird sticking his beak into a flower.

Either way, once connected, the receiving pilot flew in formation, holding the correct horizontal and vertical position, while fuel was passed. It wasn't especially difficult, except at night or in a thunderstorm, but it could be tedious. The F-105 was the only aircraft that could refuel with either the drogue or the boom. Gently banking to line up on the waypoint, Rock leveled off at 15,000 feet, pulling the power back to hold 350 knots. He quickly scanned the engine instruments, checked to see that the centerline fuel tank was feeding, then keyed the mike again.

"Invert, Invert . . . this is Oak Zero One."

"Invert" was the call sign for Detachment 5 of the 621st Tactical Control Squadron, based out of Nakhon Phanom.

Sites like it were responsible for deconfliction between aircraft, tanker rendezvous, and other radar sequencing over Laos, Cambodia, Thailand, and Vietnam.

"Oak Zero One, Invert. Go."

Rock stared out ahead, watching for other fighters. Here in between Takhli, Udorn, Ubon, and Nakhon Phanom they could be anywhere, though this early in the morning, probably not.

"Oak is a single Fox 105, squawking four six zero one . . . inbound for Spirit Zero Two in Peach."

"Copy, Oak. Come right to zero-eight-zero, climb and maintain seventeen thousand."

Rock acknowledged, rolled out on a heading of 080 degrees and added a touch of power for the climb. Leveling off again, he throttled back to hold 420 knots. Korat was in southern Thailand, about seventy-five miles north of the Cambodian border, so they had some distance to go, and he was a few minutes early. He sighed and unhooked the oxygen mask from the right side, letting it dangle against his chin. The tanker was east of him a hundred miles, the Thud was fine, the weather looked decent, and all was right with the world for the moment.

"Oak . . . Spirit Zero Two bears zero-nine-zero for one hundred miles at Base plus five. Maintain present heading."*

"Oak copies all. Wilco."

"Well . . . are we havin' fun yet?" His EWO, Curt Hartzell, finally chimed in from the pit and Rock chuckled. The two men had flown together enough so not much needed to be said. New EWOs, and pilots, too, tended to talk a lot. It was nice flying with the same guys, which they usually tried to do, and the same was true with four ships whenever possible. It was just easier. Everyone knew what was expected, so time wasn't

---

*Base numbers were changed daily. In this case, if the base number was "seven," then the tanker would be at 19,000 feet.

wasted on bullshit and they could concentrate on their mission: killing SAMs.

"Yep. Some fun. How's it all look back there?"

F-105Fs had replaced the F-100 Weasels five months ago, and though the onboard equipment was almost the same as the Hun, there were still issues. Here it was, October 12, 1966, and they still had to rig a sun screen over the APR scope so the EWO could see the damn thing. Still, considering the whole system wasn't even a year old, things weren't too bad.

"Swell," Hartzell griped. "My volume knob is broken, the canopy has a smudge on it, and my ass already hurts."

"So everything's normal." Rock chuckled again and the EWO snorted. The smudge on the right side was from a grease pencil. Some EWOs used it to make sure they didn't confuse right from left in the upside-down, three-dimensional heat of Weasel combat.

Forty-five minutes later the Thud slid slowly back and down away from the tanker. The big gray KC-135 was ponderous, slow moving, and never went into more than 30 degrees of bank as it turned. In fact, it was so slow relative to the fighter that F-105s usually dropped 10 degrees of flaps just to be able to fly with it. But it was beautiful, and Rock was glad to see one every time he flew. Fuel meant time and freedom to maneuver, and that was life around here. The average Thud would take nearly 13,000 pounds of fuel per mission—10,000 going in and another 3,000 coming out. Rock did the math in his head. There were about seven pounds in a gallon, so that was 2,000 gallons per jet per mission. With fighters in theater flying about 5,000 sorties each month, that added up to 10 million gallons every thirty days; 120 *million* gallons per year just on fuel. He whistled softly.

Once he could see the tanker from wingtip to wingtip, Rock added enough power to match the tanker's speed. Switching radio frequencies, he paused a moment, listening so he wouldn't cut anyone off. Everything was quiet, so he cleared his throat and then keyed the mike.

"Cricket . . . Oak Zero One."

"Oak Zero One, this is Cricket." The voice was young and from somewhere in the deep South.

Officially known as an Airborne Command, Control, and Communications platform, Cricket was a specially modified C-130 orbiting somewhere in friendly territory. Flying in relays, they had the unenviable job of staying airborne twenty-four hours per day monitoring all the air missions in theater. Rock keyed the mike.

"Oak is refueling complete . . . as fragged."

This was the short way of saying his mission was proceeding as planned: his type of aircraft, five-digit mission number, air refueling location, and target information.* It saved on radio chatter, assuming the frag was correct, and nothing had changed.

"Cricket copies. When clear of the tanker descend to base plus eight and proceed direct to channel eighty-nine."

Every day was assigned a different "base number," which was used over clear, nonsecure frequencies like this. It could be added or subtracted to altitudes, distances, time, or whatever else was practical. This was done to avoid giving precise information to the North Vietnamese, who listened to everything. Rock glanced at the card on his kneeboard and remembered that today's base number was five, so he was now cleared down to 13,000 feet. There was also a letter and word of the day—today's were Delta and Benji, respectively. He'd also written the three items down in black marker on the back of his left hand so if he had to eject they'd still be around.

---

*This is called a "frag" order because each squadron gets a fragment, or specific section, of the entire tasking.

"Oak copies. Wilco."

He waved goodbye to the boomer and saw a pale flash from the palm of the man's glove. *See you again soon, buddy,* Rock thought, cracking the power back a bit and retracting the flaps. Checking left and right, he dropped the nose, banking away from the tanker, then descended to 13,000 feet.

"Okay . . . so it begins." There was a big sigh from the backseat. "Channel eighty-nine is set."

Rock clicked the knob on his horizontal situation display from NAV, using preset coordinates, to TCN—meaning TACAN. This was a tactical air navigation system tuned to a specific frequency in a specific location. If selected, a channel would provide bearing and range to the station, making it ideal for general navigation and situational awareness. If a pilot dialed up two of them in turn, he could triangulate his position in a matter of seconds, and it could also be used between individual aircraft. In this case Channel 89 was Nakhon Phanom, a U.S. air base near the Mekong River on the Thai–Laotian border. Another one, Channel 85, had been secretly installed on Phou Pha Thi mountain in northern Laos on the Vietnamese border, but they weren't heading that way this morning.

"Got it," Rock answered. "Zero-eight-zero for fifty-six miles. About seven minutes."

"THIS IS A bad idea." Hartzell grunted, apropos of nothing.

Ed Rock was looking over the canopy rail at the hills and trees far below. From two miles up, heading east, it was quite a sight. Thailand's immense plateau stretched out south off the right wing, rising steeply into the dark Laotian hills. Shaped like a boomerang, the mountains along the borders wrapped around the eastern side of the plateau, shielding it from the sea. He'd been a fighter pilot now for thirteen years, having started out with F-86s in Korea. Part of Wild Weasel III, he'd arrived with fifteen other pilots and EWOs in July and ninety days later he was still alive and killing SAMs. As he gazed off the Thud's big nose, the blue haze of the Gulf of Tonkin was plain to see. Between the water and the Laotian highlands lay their destination—the narrow coastal strip of central Vietnam. Glancing north, he saw the fish hook of the Annamite Mountains curve along the Laotian border. Beyond it lay the Route Packs of North Vietnam. Despite many missions up there, and his long experience as a combat pilot, Ed's breathing shallowed a bit at the thought. Guns and missiles and MiGs; and more guns.

But not today.

"A very bad idea." The EWO grumbled again.

"And why's that?" Rock was looking up ahead. Today they were headed for that thin strip of land between the hills and the Gulf of Tonkin. It was still North Vietnam, right above the demilitarized zone. But it was also within gliding distance of the water, or into South Vietnam, both of which were safe locations to ditch. Today they wouldn't be too far into Pack One or Two and nowhere near Hanoi.

"We're here alone, that's why. This is crap. Whoever heard of a single-ship Weasel mission, huh?" Hartzell muttered and began fiddling with his own switches. The APR-25 scope was always tough to see, too small and damn near unreadable when the sun hit it. He sighed. But the little shade they'd rigged helped. He tapped it and leaned forward slightly to see the screen better. As an EWO he thought this was the most important piece of equipment available. The system came from the Huns and Wild Weasel I, but the exterior antennas were better placed on the Thud and the coverage was better.

Rock had the same scope up front, but without the sunshade, so he turned the intensity up all the way. Having just come off the tanker, he checked his fuel tanks, then twisted the little heading indicator a few degrees right. On autopilot, the big F-105F obeyed the command and eased right slightly.

"Two of 'em," the pilot finally replied, shrugging his shoulders under the straps to get a bit more comfortable.

"What?"

"You asked if I ever heard of a single-ship Weasel, and I have. Kennedy and O'Neal were hunting up here yesterday."

Hartzell snorted. "And we're the other one?"

"That's right. There are only five flyable Weasels in the whole damn country right now and they're needed up in Pack Six."

"Sounds like no one at Seventh thinks there's a SAM down here."

Rock watched the rising sun turn the hills from black and gray to dark, mottled greens. That was exactly it. A few months ago the old 2nd Air Division had been replaced by Seventh Air Force, a larger organization to help fight a larger war. Never quite worked out that way. It was just a bigger collection of bullshit, with more paper pushers shoveling it around. This had been a bad summer for the Thuds anyway, with fifty of the big fighters lost since July 1—including five Weasels.

Major Roosevelt Hestle and Captain Charles Morgan, from the 13th TFS (Panthers) 388th Tactical Fighter Wing, Korat, were the first F-105F Weasels down. They'd been hit by anti-aircraft fire near Thai Nguyen, deep in Route Pack Six, on July 6, 1966. Takhli's 355th Tactical Fighter Wing lost their first Weasel on July 23, when Major Gene Pemberton and Major Benjamin Byrd Newsom were likely hit by an SA-2 near Hanoi.

TWO WEEKS AFTER Pemberton and Newsom went down, Ed Larson and Mike Gilroy had been flying as Kingfish One on a strike in Route Pack Six. Air refueling over the water on August 7, they'd crossed the North Vietnamese coast near

Haiphong Harbor, where Gilroy had picked up a Firecan anti-aircraft radar. Towering cumulous clouds were building, covering about half the ground and making visual sightings of missiles or guns very problematic. Yet they followed the signal in, launching a Shrike anti-radiation missile at the Firecan, hoping it would lead them to a SAM site.

And that was exactly what it did.

Larson had seen the first SAM and defeated it with a "last-ditch" maneuver: full afterburner combined with a hard, high-g turn *into* the missile that created too many angles for the SAM to solve. Most of the time it overshot and missed completely, although sometimes the proximity fuse worked well enough to put holes in jets. The downside of the maneuver was that it cost lots of airspeed, so Larson and Gilroy were slow when the second SAM burst from the clouds and exploded under the Weasel team. With smoke filling the cockpit, both men blew the canopies off and Larson nursed the dying fighter out over the Gulf of Tonkin. They managed to eject and were picked up by Grumman Albatross seaplane out of Da Nang.

Altogether, eight aircraft would go down on what became known as "Black Sunday": a Skyraider off the USS *Oriskany*, an A-4 Skyhawk from the *Intrepid,* five Thuds, and one RF-101C out of Tan Son Nhut Air Base.

Bob Sandvick and Tom Pyle weren't so lucky. The pair had been part of another Iron Hand flight about fifty miles farther inland, near Kep, on the same day. On his thirteenth combat mission, Sandvick had been pulling up off target when they'd taken a hit from an 85 mm shell. Turning southeast toward the coast, they'd managed about a dozen miles before ejecting. Word was they'd been captured. Rock hoped so.*

---

*Both men survived and were released on March 4, 1973.

Ten days after Larson and Gilroy's brush with death, the fifth Weasel went down northwest of Hanoi in the Red River valley. Like the others from Takhli, Majors Joe Brand and Don Singer were part of the 354th TFS (Bulldogs) and were leading a Hunter Killer mission. Most likely they'd been hit by anti-aircraft guns guarding the SAM and had little time to do anything but eject. Don Springer's parachute never fully opened, but Brand made it down and contacted the other fighters by radio. That was the last anyone heard of him. Like every member of the tightly knit Wild Weasel community, Rock was anxious to get some word soon.* Hunter Killers were a rare breed and there weren't many of them, so any loss was keenly felt.

A solitary Weasel jet remained at Takhli, but it was hit by Triple A near Hanoi and its pilot, Major Glenn Davis, barely made it into Udorn near the Laotian border. The jet was boxed up and sent to Taiwan for repairs, but Rock doubted it would ever fly again. With guys shot down or hospitalized from wounds, there were only four Weasels left at Takhli. Until more pilots, EWOs, and planes were delivered, SAM killing operations were consolidated with the 13th TFS at Korat's 388th Tactical Fighter Wing.

WITH FIVE OUT of the eleven original F-105F Weasels lost, Ed Rock and Curt Hartzell were forced to go up alone on October 12. Two days earlier, an EB-66 was orbiting near the border and detected Fansong emissions out of Route Pack One. No one had seen a SAM that far south yet, but it was possible.

---

*Project X was instituted to investigate reports of American POWs being held in captivity after the Vietnam War. As of 1976, Major Joe Brand was still listed as missing in action with Project X reference number 0432.

The NVA had shown a disturbing tendency to do the impossible by moving men, supplies, and equipment into places they weren't expected. Putting a SAM that far south would definitely stir things up. It would threaten vulnerable helicopters, slow-moving close air support aircraft, and, above all, the B-52s working against the Ho Chi Minh Trail.

Problem was, no one could find it. Major Jim O'Neal and Captain George Kennedy had gone up yesterday as Cardinal One, and trolled around all the DMZ up to Dong Hoi and found nothing. Maybe the SAM had been testing equipment when the EB-66 caught the trons, or maybe the radar was down for repairs.

"You think there's one out there?" Rock asked the EWO. They were about twenty miles from Nakhon Phanom, better known to Americans as "Naked Fanny," and Rock could see the muddy Mekong River snaking its way along the border. Beyond it lay about seventy-five miles of Laos then Route Pack One and Vietnam. Curt had been thinking about that since last night, when they'd been told of the mission. Like Rock, he thought it very possible the Vietnamese could have moved a radar south, and he also knew the EB-66 EWOs were very good at electronic analysis. They had the luxury of smooth orbits, a jet that didn't gyrate like an epileptic rocket, and sane, predictable pilots. Of course, no one was usually shooting at them, and they were out of range from the SAMs.

"I was thinking it might be the Navy."

Rock nodded, leaned forward, and squinted off the nose. Forward visibility in the F-105 wasn't the greatest, especially now. The canopy was divided into three sections, and the glare shield was cluttered with an APR-25 scope and the combining glass. Still, he could see the fuzzy blue gleam from the Gulf of Tonkin—the Navy's playground.

Closer still was Naked Fanny. The airfield had been built by the Navy Seabees and sat in a bend on the Mekong. The two parallel gray bars of the airfield were surrounded by green plains and even from two miles high Rock could see that the ramp north of the runway was crowded with planes. The 634th Combat Support Wing was there, but there were others, named and unnamed. Rumor had it that in addition to the search-and-rescue (SAR) outfits, there were also air commandos, and the CIA's air force—Air America. It was good to know they were close by. He rolled up on one wing and stared at the base. It was time.

"Cricket, Oak Zero One, channel eighty-nine, as fragged."

The Airborne Battlefield Command and Control Center (ABCCC) aircraft acknowledged his position over Nakhon Phanom, passed the local altimeter setting, and cleared him off to the strike frequency used by all aircraft in Pack One.

"I think you may be right about the Navy." Rock dialed in the altimeter and let his eyes flicker around the cockpit. "Greening it up," he informed Hartzell.

Normally he'd get a bit closer before arming his weapons, but Laos was always tricky and you just never knew. He turned the big wafer knob with his right hand and saw that the centerline fuel tank was dry. The internal tanks were feeding and his engine instruments were all good. Rock glanced up at the glare shield and again twisted the APR-25's brightness knob all the way right. Above his left knee on the central console he checked that the WPN SEL knob was set up for air-to-ground missiles. Below this was a line of four gray switches, like big circuit breakers, for each station that could carry a weapon. By depressing the ones on the end, now his left outboard and right outboard pylons were receiving power and ready to use. Above these and to the left was the red MASTER ARM switch. Rock flipped it up and now his available weapons, two AGM-45 Shrike missiles, were ready to launch.

"Of course I'm right about 'em," Curt went on, still talking about the Navy. "How many ships are there off the coast anyway?"

"Dunno. Coupla dozen at least."

"That's the point. The command and control boats carry Pathfinder radar systems and their guided-missile cruisers use the SPS-39 radar. It has a range of at least a hundred and fifty miles," he added.

"So?"

"Well . . . it operates in the S-band like the Fansong."

"But the EB-66s are crammed fulla guys like you with a lot more equipment. Wouldn't they know it's not a Fansong?"

That, Curt knew, was a very good question. Just because a signal was in the same band didn't mean it was a Fansong. Even dissimilar radars were often parametrically similar, sharing frequencies and other characteristics, such as pulse repetition intervals.

"Maybe. Maybe not. I don't think anyone ever thought of this before."

Crossing the Mekong into Laos, Rock decided to stay up at 13,000 feet, saving fuel and giving them more time in Route Pack One. Also, if there was a SAM out there the Weasel would be easier to see up higher. If the Fansong came on air then Curt would see it sooner and they'd have more time to kill it. Of course, it might not come up at all. It might not be there, or it could be waiting in ambush for something bigger. Like a B-52. The huge bombers had been flying into Laos since 1965 and were exactly what the SA-2 was designed to attack.

Off the nose the Annamite Range stretched away north and Rock could plainly see the mountains lining the entrance of Packs Five and Six. Off to his right they tapered off into the plains down in South Vietnam. Up ahead, another fifty miles or so, the jagged peaks would abruptly drop away at the Gulf of Tonkin coastline—exactly where they were heading.

In the backseat Hartzell pushed his visor up, leaned forward, and frowned at the displays. Near the top of the console were two rows of five little square lights. Theoretically, they'd indicate what type of radar beams were hitting the Weasel: SAM, AAA, or MiGs, all identified by the frequency band. The APR-25, originally the Vector IV, was on the console under them, and directly beneath it was the IR-133. Nothing had appeared on the APR yet, but the 133 showed a strobe. He leaned forward again and squinted. It *was* a signal. Very faint, but there. Alert now, the EWO checked for multiple strobes but saw only one. At this range it had to be an early warning search radar. Still, they were the ones who usually passed information to the SAMs, so it was a good sign.

"Search radar off the nose. Very faint."

"Can you tell what it is?" Rock replied, turning his head slightly and glancing in the mirrors. All he could see was the top of his EWO's helmet.

Adjusting the gain, Hartzell tuned the receiver to the correct band, then watched and listened. Lower frequencies generated longer waves that traveled much farther, so these were ideal for long-range searching. Higher frequencies had a shorter range since the wavelengths were closer together. However, this meant more waves hit a target, bouncing back quickly with better information that was suitable for guiding missiles. Fortunately this wasn't such a signal.

"High twos to low threes," the EWO called out, meaning the frequency range, which was measured in gigahertz. "Barlock . . . maybe a Side Net. Good sign."

"Yep."

Rock ran his seat up a few inches so he was sitting higher.

It helped to see better over the canopy rail at bad things coming up, like gunfire or missiles. He also tugged his lap belt tighter, cinched the oxygen mask a notch closer, and checked that the volumes were up on his radio and APR-25. Up ahead, the Vietnamese border was plain to see along the north-south line of mountains. Valleys appeared like reddish brown scars among the dark green southern ranges. Buried beneath the haze, one of the biggest battles of the war had been fought down there a year ago, in mid-November 1965. Rock stared off the right wing but on this day couldn't see the Drang River valley. It was there that elements of the 1st Cavalry Division famously airlifted into battle against a mixed force of NVA regulars and Viet Cong.* Two hundred thirty-seven Americans didn't make it out and neither did more than one thousand Vietnamese.

There was a much closer, lighter-colored smudge that he could see—the A Shau valley. Six months ago, on March 8, a Special Forces base at the bottom end of the valley was attacked. For two days, seventeen SF troopers with four hundred native strikers held off more than two thousand North Vietnamese regulars. Eight Americans died and all the rest were wounded, but they managed to evacuate the survivors, including a good portion of the Montagnard tribesmen. To the Thud's north the last big cut through the mountain was passing under the left wing. Steep sided and narrow, the Mu Gia Pass pointed straight into Route Pack Two and Rock knew it was time to start down. He pulled the throttle back a crack and nudged the stick forward. There was no hurry since this wasn't going to be a low-level flight, but he wanted to be at 8,000 feet when they popped out near the coast.

Hartzell busied himself tightening straps, shoving papers in

---

*Including the 7th Cavalry of Little Bighorn fame.

his G-suit leg pockets, and taking one last swig of water. Unlike the pilot, he pulled off his gloves and stuck them under his left leg since it was easier to use his system controls without them. Resting one arm along the canopy rail, he looked off the right, craning his neck to see the ground. The terrain got tougher as they crossed the border. A thin river valley suddenly appeared, then disappeared as the Thud zipped past at 500 knots.

"I see ya, Uncle Ho." The EWO flashed a middle finger at the mountains below. This entire area between the Ban Karai and Mu Gia passes was alive with invisible activity. Antlike, thousands of porters marched south along the Ho Chi Minh Trail, covered by the triple canopy forest. The F-105 was right over it, and Hartzell knew there were eyes looking up as the fighter roared overhead.

Rock was sitting up, alert and focused, but he nodded, feeling much the same way. Nothing they'd been allowed to do had interfered much with the trail. A big NVA base camp, BA 611, wasn't too far off to the south. Much closer, though, in the first real valley south of the DMZ, was a Marine combat base named Khe Sanh. "Hey, Rock . . . what's the name of that Jarhead base at two o'clock. Right there where those hills come together?"

"Khe Sanh." The pilot chuckled. His EWO was a mind reader.

"If the gomers ever come south those boys are gonna catch it."

Rock glanced left. It was obvious from here that the base was highly vulnerable. Any invasion from the North wouldn't come along the coast since the Navy would pound them to pieces. It had to come from inland, and since the NVA prepositioned their supplies before an attack, it had to come off the Ho Chi Minh Trail. They also couldn't bypass any American bases that would threaten their rear and Khe Sanh would do exactly that. It was the first big chokepoint south of the DMZ, and if it fell then the entire Quang Tri province would be unhinged. That would give NVA control to the Central Highlands and threaten Da Nang.

"Rock . . . Fansong . . . twelve o'clock. One ring. Weak."

The pilot's eyes swiveled to his APR scope. "Nothing up here."

Dark-shaded mountains suddenly gave way to a narrow belt of coastal flatland. Sage greens and browns abruptly ran into a long, crescent-shaped strip of tan sand stretching from Dong Hoi to the DMZ. Rock banked up slightly to the right and headed for the end of the beach. This would put them right on the 17th parallel at the bottom of Pack One, and it would keep the Fansong, or whatever was out there, off at the eleven o'clock position. If it *was* a real radar, cutting the beams like this would help the EWO nail down an accurate bearing to the site. With the APR-25 any range estimation was pure guess-work, but at least they wouldn't be flying directly at the thing without a better idea of its location.

"What about the Shrike?"

"Nothing."

They were carrying two of the little anti-radiation missiles and Curt Hartzell had already checked them both. If the tiny seeker head in the AGM-45, or Shrike, detected a signal it might give an audio growl. *Might.* The EWO concentrated on his IR-133 set. He didn't place much faith in the missile, but at least he could tune the 133 receiver to threat radar beams if the signal was strong enough.

But it wasn't. The gomers had quickly learned about emissions control, or EMCON, and they rarely stayed on air consistently, or long enough for good location fixes. Due to the

F-100 and F-105 Hunter Killers, the North Vietnamese were now using at least eighteen missiles to kill an aircraft now—twice the number used in 1965. Consequently, the VC air defense commanders had gotten serious about countertactics where Weasels were concerned.* The NVA also used Firecans, or early warning radars, to feed information to the Fansong so it only emitted long enough to shoot and guide the missile.

"Well, if a SAM made it this far south it's got to be banged up a bit." Rock was looking off the wing at the mountains and dark forests. "Trail's gotta be rough on electronics, even without the bomb craters."

"Yeah," Hartzell agreed, sparing a moment to stare outside. "But it is Soviet made. They always overbuild their stuff since the average Russian soldier is dumber than a box of hair."

Chuckling, Rock kept scanning the ground; every thirty seconds or so he'd turn slightly left or right. He did this automatically, a combat habit rather than a conscious thought. Never setting patterns, he also climbed up a few hundred feet, held it for about a minute, then descended. Nothing erratic or violent yet, but flying in straight lines or remaining at constant altitudes was a good way to get shot.

"Let's come north . . . it's got to be up there." Hartzell was still head down in the pit.

"In a minute."

With the rising sun in his face, Rock was looking left up along the beach. Pack One wasn't his favorite place to be but it was safer than the others. If they were hit at this altitude he could probably glide across the DMZ and make it to Khe Sanh

---

*In 1965 there were 109 missiles fired at American fixed-wing aircraft and this resulted in 11–13 losses. By the end of 1966 there would be 649 SAMs fired for 34–35 aircraft losses.

or even Da Nang. The water also meant safety with the Navy right off the coast. So that's what they'd do. Head north up the beach toward Dong Hoi. This would isolate the SAM, if there was one, on the landward side past his left wing. If this signal was some sort of ambiguity with a naval radar then it would show up on his right side. If it wasn't . . . well, that's what they were here for.

"Comin' left," he warned the EWO, then paused and rolled the F-105 up to the north. A few miles off the coast, little Con Co Island disappeared under the wing, but Rock kept his eyes on the plains north of the DMZ and the long ridgeline beyond. *If I were a SAM that's where I'd be,* he thought. Hidden in the foothills with clear line of sight to catch anything coming in off the gulf or over the hills. Camouflaged, ready and waiting.

"Lotsa haze down there," the pilot remarked. The sky was clear and the water was easy to see; bands of blues rippling in the sun lightened farther offshore. But the land was a problem. There were none of the towering clouds that seemed to always build up in the afternoon, but visibility was limited down lower. Like a fuzzy gray carpet, haze hung over the ground from the beach to the foothills, and that would make seeing a missile launch extremely tough.

Hartzell focused on the problem he could control at the moment: detecting radars and figuring out if they were fatal or not. If there was a SAM here it could be getting information from Firecans or any of the early warning radars that had been put up along the coast to see Navy strike packages. A Fansong also took more than a minute to warm up to full power, and though this wasn't significant against unmaneuverable bombers it was a serious deficiency against a fighter. A year ago the SAM operators had left the radar in a standby mode that kept the system on, but not actively emitting. Still, anytime it was on, radar energy "leaked" and could be detected by the Weasel, albeit at a greatly reduced range.

"Left ten o'clock."

Curt looked up. Rock was tapping on the canopy off his left shoulder. "That's where I'd be. See that flat area between the river and the hill? Perfect view up and down the coast . . . and out over the water."

"Makes sense. Only I've got nothing on the scope."

"Doesn't mean he's not there."

Hartzell nodded again and hunched back over the little screens. True enough, especially since the North Vietnamese had also learned about "dummy" loads. Or, more likely, their Soviet buddies told them. A dummy load was a maintenance function used to test a radar's transmitter and electronic circuitry without using the antenna. The system was operating at full power, but not emitting through the antenna, so it couldn't be detected. In this mode, once information was passed from other radars, a Fansong could switch from the dummy to the operating mode, lock on in a few seconds, and shoot.

Rock was enjoying himself, despite the situation. With his right hand wrapped around the stick he could feel the Thud's power. He liked the way the jet responded to the lightest touches on the controls and the way it felt through the rudder pedals to his feet. The cockpit smelled like a fighter—sweat, hot metal, and faint whiffs of mildew. Under a hard blue sky they were here, in Indian Country, doing what they did best. Up ahead the white sand faded into an aquamarine line just off the beach, and for an instant he was reminded of the Florida coast. The most dangerous thing there were the women in the Officers' Club.

Unlike this place. The pewter gray Nhat-Le River ran along the shoreline, actually touching the beach in several spots.

Beyond it the sage green flats stretched west about eight miles, rising suddenly into the mountain range they'd just flown across. It was an ideal place for SAMs, protected by mountains with a clear line of sight over the gulf and south to the DMZ. The whole area could be supplied by the river or National Route 1, which paralleled the coast.

In a visual rectangular pattern Rock methodically scanned the ground, looking for smoke from launches, anti-aircraft flashes, or anything out of the ordinary. Starting just off the nose, he'd work north a few miles, then search the ground west of the river before letting his eyes drift south again. The gomers were too good at camouflage to build Soviet-style, star-shaped emplacements for their SAMs and knew they were much too easy to see. Sometimes you could catch the glint of sun on metal, or find tracks leading off-road to a site. Not today, he sighed. Not yet, anyway. Rock's eyes flickered over the engine gauges, then his fuel. He had more than an hour of on-station time left if he could stay at this altitude.

"Picking up an early warning radar . . . and a Firecan," Curt said from the pit. "Really faint."

"Where?"

The EWO frowned and leaned closer to the scope. He tried to isolate the elevation beam but couldn't. The azimuth was easier, but it was still such a weak signal that he couldn't pinpoint it. "Nine to twelve o'clock."

Rock shook his head. "So pretty much anywhere off the left wing?"

"Yeah." Hartzell knew the pilot was frustrated. Give them something to attack and kill and none of them would hesitate, but vagueness drove them nuts.

"Coming up on Dong Hoi."

The river took a big bend to the west, all the way to the

mountains, then it split. A smaller branch meandered off into Laos, but the bigger one came back around toward the coast and continued north into Dong Hoi.

"Left or right?" Hartzell asked, his eyes on the scope. Left would take them overland and into the heart of Pack One, while a right turn would lead them over the water. Right was much, much safer—but that wasn't why they were here.

The pilot never hesitated, and nudged the stick left. As the Thud rolled up and smoothly turned toward the mountains, Curt chuckled. "That's what I figured."

Rock stared down the left wing at Vietnam. This was a perfect place to get pronged: belly-up in a turn. The river looked sluggish and there was nothing moving on the roads below. Dong Hoi was a decent-size town for Vietnam so there had to be traffic, but they all scuttled for cover when American jets approached. If they hadn't, he would've killed them. Partway through the turn he rolled out and checked the other side for any smoke trails but saw nothing. Pushing the throttle up, he continued left, back toward the DMZ.

"Fansong . . . one to two o'clock," Hartzell called from the pit. "Half a ring."

Reversing the turn, Rock looked down the right wing at the ground between the river and foothills. The circular APR-25 display had four rings that indicated the strength of a received radar beam. A "four ringer" was strong, indicating the site was close. Very close. A "half ringer" was a weak signal that *usually* meant it was far enough away not to worry about. But it could also mean the radar's main lobe, the most powerful beam, was pointed at something else. The APR could detect the lesser beams, called side lobes and back lobes, and these would appear as distant signals when in fact you could be right on top of the site.

"Gone now." Hartzell looked up, craning his neck to see around the Thud's nose. "What's up there, anyway?"

"Nothing to the left but beach. Little villages all over the place on the right side past the river. Farms. Lots of open spaces up to the foothills."

Curt thought about that and squinted at the rising terrain off to the west. "Ho Chi Minh Trail comes out over there, doesn't it?"

"Part of it. See those passes at about two to three o'clock? They all lead to the Trail."

Rock had been angling away from the beach, and they were now smack in the middle of the flatlands. If he was right, and there was a SAM over there, then it would need some bait to bite. *Bait? If the fuckers only knew.* Actually, they probably thought he was a reconnaissance jet since the photo guys were really the only ones who flew around alone in North Vietnam. Whether that would entice the North Vietnamese to shoot was anyone's guess.

Rock nudged the stick left a bit, aiming toward the top of the other big beach down to the south. It roughly marked the DMZ and was about eight miles, or another minute, away. He could see Quang Tri city in South Vietnam, and even from here the valley with Khe Sanh's combat base was plainly visible. *What a shithole.* He'd think of those guys there next time Korat or Takhli seemed bad.

Suddenly a low rattle filled his helmet, like an angry rattlesnake. Rock instantly tensed, shoved the throttle outboard to the MIL power stop, just short of afterburner, and rolled the jet up on its right wing just as Hartzell called out, "Fansong . . . six o'clock. Two and a half rings."

Dropping the nose, he yanked the Thud around in a hard right turn and stared outside, looking for smoke trails. Rock heard the EWO grunt against the g-forces and croak, "Five . . . no, four o'clock!"

West of the river, near the foothills. *Right where I thought.* Overbanking and pulling harder, Rock came around heading north, then snapped upright. This way he could see the whole area without the jet's nose in the way. Then, as quickly as it started, the rattlesnake sound stopped. Glancing at his APR-25, Rock saw it was blank.

"You still got it?"

"No. Got a Barlock, though. North."

The sun was high enough on his right side to begin baking the cockpit. Shoving the visor up, Rock wiped his forehead, ignoring the faintly sweet smell of his Nomex gloves. *There.* He stared hard at a flat, open spot at the base of the mountains. A reservoir glinted in the sunlight and there were several low hills scattered about. Had to be somewhere around there.

"We'll turn sooner this time. I see a few places this bastard might be."

Hartzell grunted and squinted at his IR-133. If he could find a Firecan anti-aircraft radar along the same azimuth he'd feel better, but everything was suddenly quiet again. He felt the jet begin to move, and he clenched his stomach muscles. Rock turned right again, almost a slice back, to get the nose around as fast as possible.

"Nice shot of our butt you're givin' him," the EWO muttered.

"Your butt, not mine. You're closer."

Hartzell chuckled in spite of himself. *Fighter pilots.*

"This way we've got a bit more distance and"—he popped the jet upright—"the sun's behind us."

"Hadn't thought of that."

Rock tapped on the right side of the canopy. "I'm thinking

he's up here . . . two o'clock. We'll get closer . . . try to piss him off or maybe get the guns to shoot."

He left the throttle up and lowered the nose. If they'd been "painted," or detected, by a Barlock, or height finder, then they'd know his altitude. Time to change it. At 540 knots, Rock pulled the power back. If there was a SAM up there, it might think this was an attack and shoot, too.

But it didn't.

Not wanting to get too close to the hills, he cranked the fighter hard to the left until they were pointed south at the beach, then rolled back right and pulled back on the stick. As the F-105 surged upward, Rock squinted off the wing and watched. Still nothing. Glancing in, he saw 9,000 feet on the altimeter and bumped the stick forward, hearing the EWO swear as he floated off the seat. The river flashed under the nose and he leveled off, pushed the throttle back up a bit, and checked his gas. They were about ten miles north of the DMZ heading south when the radar came up again.

"Five o'clock . . . Fansong. Three rings!"

Instantly rolling right, Rock snapped the Weasel around, dropping the nose as he did so. The rattlesnake came on again, and a strobe appeared in his display. Eyes flickering inside, he confirmed that the MASTER ARM switch was up, went to afterburner, and pulled the nose toward the sky.

"Three-zero-zero, Rock," Hartzell called out as the Thud came through the horizon.

"Got it." Using stick and rudder, he nudged and pushed the fighter over to line up on the heading.

Shooting a Shrike was always an educated guess. No one was really sure how well the damn things worked, but it was all they had today—except for the cannon. Holding the wings parallel to the horizon, he kept the nose tracking upward. Ten degrees . . . twenty . . . he bunted forward slightly, hesitated a half second, then jabbed down hard on the red pickle button when the nose hit 30 degrees up.

"Shrike's away!"

It was such a small missile there was barely a kick, but the smoke was hard to miss. Rolling inverted, Rock clenched his stomach muscles and sliced back down toward the beach.

"Still on air," Curt gasped as he rattled around in the pit.

The pilot brought the throttle out of burner, snapped the wings level, then cranked back to the left. They were now paralleling the Shrike's flight path and were between the SAM site and the beach, heading north. Rock squinted against the bright blue sky and flew by peripheral vision so he could watch the Shrike. The Thud felt fast, and he cracked the throttle back another inch or so. Just then the thick white smoke quit as the motor burned out, and the little AGM-45 all but vanished.

"Is it still on air?" he asked, not daring to look away.

"Still up. Bearing two-eight-zero from us."

Rock pictured it in his head and figured that was about right. He'd fired heading northwest, came off right, then back to the left, so the site ought to be at his left ten o'clock or so. The Shrike's gray trail had thinned out, then completely vanished, and it was no good trying to watch the little missile. A few months back, the Weasels had mentioned that difficulty to General William "Spike" Momyer, the Seventh Air Force commander. They'd suggested a flare be attached to the rear, as it was with the Bullpup air-to-ground missile, helping to keep sight. That hadn't worked with the Shrike, but a special charge was added to the warhead so the detonation would be easier to see. White phosphorus, called "Willy Pete," was used by forward air controllers to mark targets.

"How long?" Rock asked, leveling off, setting 540 knots,

and glancing at his fuel. "I figured it was about six miles away when I pickled."

Curt did the math in his head. The AGM-45A-2 they carried used an Aerojet motor that covered six miles in about a minute. The rocket motor burned out ten seconds after launch, and Rock hadn't been supersonic or very high, so both factors would slow the missile down. It had to be lofted so that as it reached its apex and nosed over, or "tripped," the seeker head could see the enemy radar. If they shot along the correct azimuth and if the range was close, and if the Fansong was still operating, and if the seeker head in the Shrike could pick all that up in its tiny field of view . . .

Lots of "ifs."

"About thirty more seconds." Hartzell felt the F-105 rack up to the left as Rock turned in toward the hills. The AGM-45 had started life back in 1958 at the China Lake Naval Weapons Center, in Southern California. In the interest of expediency, Texas Instruments and Sperry Rand built the ASM-N-10, as they called it, from the AIM-7 Sparrow air-to-air missile. This meant the small 149-pound warhead was designed to bring down an aircraft, not destroy ground targets. It was also tuned to cover a specific threat frequency range, in this case the S-band containing the Firecan and Fansong, among others. It came from the factory that way and couldn't be changed in the field, much less in flight.

At the moment, this wasn't a huge limitation, since there were only a few types of radars worth shooting, but Curt could see a time not too far ahead when there'd be many more. Another significant limitation of the Shrike was that it had no memory; if the threat radar shut down, the missile had nothing to guide on and went stupid, or ballistic. Tactically there was still some merit to forcing a radar off the air, but like most Weasels, Curt believed killing the radar was a better answer. In any event, depending on a weapon that assumed enemy cooperation was a flawed way to fight.

"Can you still see the Shrike?"

"Nope. But I know where it was going, and how far it can go. We're gonna arc around to the northeast and try to see where it hits."

"Looks kinda hazy."

Rock nodded, visually padlocked on the little hills about two miles off the nose and hoping the new phosphorus spotting charge would make a difference. He was still flying peripherally, 8,000 feet up, heading north between the river and National Route 1. If it was an SA-2, and *if* it was actually there, then he and Curt were too close for it to shoot at them. It took about four seconds for the missile to physically launch and begin to receive guidance. While it did that, the SA-2 was ballistic, so there was a minimum range of about three to four miles around a site. Of course, there could always be another battery nearby that was also tracking the Weasel. And there were always guns.

"Still on," Hartzell repeated. "Three-ringer bearing two-eight-zero."

Something suddenly caught the corner of his eye, like a camera flash instantly followed by a bright white puff of smoke. There it was!

"We're close," Curt was saying. "I—"

"Shit! Got it."

Rock slammed the throttle back to MIL, and smoothly pulled back on the stick, beginning a climbing left turn. "Left ten o'clock . . . about two miles."

The Willy Pete was brighter than the haze and hung directly over the impact point. Zooming up to keep the area in sight, Rock suddenly saw it all clearly. The gomers had carved an area out of the trees at the base of a hill. The illusion was perfect, and unless you were looking right at it, you'd never realize the thing was there. Squinting, he now saw that some of the trees on the front side were leaning sideways more than they should. He shook his head. The Vietnamese had stuck cut trees and bushes in the ground to cover their tracks in from the road.

"Fansong's off the air."

"Anything else? Firecan maybe?"

"Nothing."

Rock leveled off at 10,000 feet, stood the throttle up, and slowed the fighter to about 450 knots. Shooting a glance at the fuel gauge, he figured they could stay overhead for another forty minutes or so.

"I don't see it," the EWO replied.

"See the hill off the left wing? Look at the base on the east side in the middle . . . you can see the smoke."

"Got it." Hartzell squinted and saw one . . . no, two launchers. Several trucks and command vans . . . the whole thing.

"How'd we miss that?"

"We didn't."

Fair enough. Curt whistled softly. "Bastards really know how to hide things. Means there's probably another one."

That was an excellent thought, Rock knew. It was easy to get fixated on what you could see and forget that there was always more. The one you never see is the one that gets you. That tactical lesson hadn't changed since 1915.

"Well, I got this one; you look north and south for about a mile in each direction and try to find any others. Guns, too," he added. Passing a mile east of the site he saw where the AGM-45 had struck.

"Looks like today we had the one Shrike that actually worked." He rolled up on one wing and tapped the canopy.

"See . . . left of the smoke, that lighter spot? The Fansong's right in the middle." Even from this altitude he could see that the big trailer wasn't sitting upright, but was cocked off sideways like it had been punched. Rock shook his head. The little warhead must have hit the antenna directly.

As they flew around the back side of the site most of it was hidden by the hill. As he looked east now, the sun hit him full in the face, so Rock dropped his visor and looked at the fuel again.

"So what's the plan?"

"You look and listen for anything else . . . I know they're down there. Probably waiting to see what else is gonna show up."

"Then what?"

Coming around south of the hill, Rock glanced at the outboard weapon station under his left wing. Rumor was, the USAF was running out of general-purpose bombs and, more critically, cluster bombs. This was why they'd come out today with only two teeny Shrikes—that and a full load in the 20 mm cannon. Still, it wasn't enough, and he turned his radio volume back up a bit, then keyed the mike. They'd need some help, and if any other fighters were available they could be diverted to attack the SAM.

"Cricket . . . Oak Zero One."

Twenty minutes later he wasn't so sure. With a hundred Navy and Air Force aircraft airborne, Cricket finally managed to divert a flight into Route Pack One. Rock was astounded: it was a pair of F-104 Starfighters. He'd flown them himself in California years before and knew it was a superb high-altitude interceptor. It was also the only fighter in Southeast Asia that could keep up with a Thud, but as a ground attack jet it was very nearly useless. Hell, when he'd flown it, the 104 didn't even have a bomb sight. He sighed and clipped the oxygen mask back over his face. The Starfighters had found the hill, but trying to give them a "talk on" to the target was pointless. Besides, Rock was running out of gas.

"Mallard One . . . Oak is in from the east . . . watch for my hits."

"Ah, copy that Oak. Gotcha in sight. No joy on the target."

Well, you will in a minute.

From long habit Rock scanned the cockpit, then put his left thumb and forefinger on the WPN SEL wafer knob directly above the MASTER ARM switch. He clicked it three notches to the right to AIR TO GROUND GUNS. He'd decided on a high-angle strafe (HAS) attack instead of coming in low since there was just no way of knowing what else was down there. High-angle strafing wasn't very accurate against small targets, or things that moved, but against a SAM site it would work. At least well enough to mark the target for the Starfighters. The biggest virtue of HAS was that it kept you above 4,500 feet—the range for automatic weapons and small arms fire. Taking a deep breath, he raised the visor, paused, then snapped the Weasel to the left. It wouldn't keep you safe from anything else, though. Especially from a SAM.

Vietnam spun beneath him as Rock rolled the Thud nearly inverted. A patchwork of red, dark brown, and orange fields filled his windscreen. Tan roads cut through irregular clumps of trees and little jade green pools of water were everywhere. Popping the fighter upright, he pulled the throttle back to midrange and leaned forward. Staring through the combining glass, Rock held the big orange reticle short of the target and opened the speed brakes.

Eight thousand feet and 40 degrees nose low. *Close enough.*

Tapping the rudder pedals, the pilot kept the nose pointed at the same place on the ground in front of the target. His eyes jumped back and forth between the reticle and the altimeter. Back and forth . . . aimpoint and altitude.

Seven thousand feet. He slid the throttle all the way back to idle and fanned the speed brakes to hold 500 knots.

Rock could see the darker Fansong van very plainly against the mold-colored ground. Little dark spots were moving everywhere and he realized they were men. Suddenly, flashes lit up on both sides of the SAM site, seemingly right out of the earth, but he never flinched.

"Firecan." Curt sounded a bit tense again. "Close!"

Almost . . . almost . . . His right index finger was curled around the trigger, lightly touching it. A bead of sweat ran out from under the helmet and down his cheek but he ignored everything except the reticle and the target. *Aimpoint and altitude.*

Then the ground really lit up. Rippling flashes came from along the road, the base of the hill, and all around the site. Glowing red and orange blobs lifted off the ground, curving lazily toward the Weasel, but Rock held the reticle steady.

"Sheeit." Curt sounded remarkably calm.

Six thousand feet . . . and the center dot touched the base of the Fansong van.

Now!

"BURRRRRPPP." The Gatling cannon spat out a few hundred rounds of 20 mm shells.

He let go, bunted forward, and fired again.

"BURRRRRPPPPPPPPPPPP."

Rock let go of the trigger immediately and reefed back hard on the stick as flaming scraps of metal drifted past the cockpit. When the nose made it through the horizon he slammed the throttle forward and yanked the Thud around hard to the right. Bunting savagely, the pilot rolled back left and kicked the left rudder, sliding the jet sideways.

It probably saved them.

Twisting in the seat, both men looked back and saw the sky light up with explosions. Angry black puffs, orange in the middle, and a dangerous cluster of smaller, white warts exactly where they'd just been. Rock flicked his wrist right and pulled back. The Weasel bounced upward and changed direction in a second. He then nosed over, hesitated, and pulled back up diagonally to the left, jinking erratically to spoil the gunner's aim.

"Look at that!"

Rock continued the turn and stared back in time to see a huge explosion followed instantly by an ugly black and red mushrooming cloud that covered the SAM site. Little yellow-tipped fragments shot out in all directions and dust rolled back against the hillside. He must have hit one of the missiles.

"You got 'em, Rock!" The EWO was exuberant.

"I missed."

Hartzell stared up at the back of Rock's helmet. "You *what*?"

Leveling off at 10,000 feet, Rock squinted at the fuel gauge and knew it was time to go. The SAM site was a mess, though. Fire, death, and destruction. Served the little pricks right.

"You nailed the bastard." The EWO excitedly thumped the canopy rail. "Even that 104 driver can't hardly miss that."

"Nope. I missed."

"You gotta be shittin' me."

"I was aiming at the Fansong."

Curt Hartzell's mouth dropped open, then he heard Rock chuckle. Dropping the corner of his sweaty oxygen mask, he wiped his face and grinned. Taking a deep breath he realized, not for the first time, that fighter pilots were crazy. Then he reminded himself that he and Rock had just found a hidden SAM and blown it apart. So if fighter guys were nuts, then Wild Weasels were downright insane.

CHAPTER 6

MAKE MUD, NOT WAR

ON A TUESDAY morning in November 1965, a thirty-one-year-old man, a college graduate and father of three, poured gasoline over his head and set himself on fire forty feet from Robert McNamara's Pentagon office. Born in Pennsylvania, Norman Morrison had become a Quaker and lived in nearby Baltimore. His self-immolation, and that of Roger LaPorte one week later, were part of the rising antiwar movement in America.* McNamara, as opaque as ever, would later say of Morrison, "How much evil must we do in order to do good? We have certain ideals, certain responsibilities. Recognize that at times you will have to engage in evil, but minimize it."

However one interprets that statement, at the very least that mentality represented a serious disconnect in 1965 between Washington and everyone else. For those fighting the war such ambiguity certainly didn't bode well, and as 1965 ended there were serious doubts, from civilians and military professionals

---

*LaPorte burned to death in New York City, in front of the United Nations headquarters.

alike, about Vietnam. The War Protester's League, the Committee for Non-Violent Action, and scores of other groups were popping up all over the country. Protesters conducted their infamous "Vietnam Day" at the University of California, Berkeley while the Watts District of Los Angeles erupted in riots.

Lyndon Johnson initially held to his Great Society domestic programs, failing to realize that they could never succeed while in competition with a conflict in Southeast Asia.* His wartime budget and supplemental requests ran into the tens of billions of dollars, and he tried tacking on a 10 percent surcharge to federal income taxes to meet the bill. This wasn't only the cost of fuel, machines, food, ammunition. Or the 385,000 men brought over by the end of 1966, and the more than one million tons of supplies per month needed to sustain them.† The tremendous cost also included building an infrastructure to receive the goods, distribute them, and move troops. Vietnam had no real road system, and what did exist was French made. Airfields, bridges, warehouses, and, most critically, deepwater ports all had to be built to meet the vast logistical needs of the conflict. Six deep-draft harbors were constructed from scratch. Most impressive was the massive complex at Camranh Bay, which was put together with prefabricated piers floated across the Pacific. A submarine cable was also laid along the ocean floor, connecting Washington, D.C., to Saigon by telephone, so communication could take place in a matter of seconds.

But manpower remained the central issue, especially to MACV's commander.

---

*A series of programs LBJ wished as his legacy, improving education and medical care and ending poverty.
†Nineteen sixty-four troop levels had increased to 17,280 and by Christmas 1965, they had climbed to 129,611. The Post Exchange in Saigon was about the same size as the Bloomingdale's department store in New York.

William Childs Westmoreland was a 1936 graduate of West Point and had taken over from General Paul Harkins in 1964. A World War II and Korean War veteran, "Westy," as he was known, was an artillery officer by training. He believed that destroying the enemy's will to fight through a war of attrition would bring about Hanoi's capitulation. To this end he perpetuated a "seek and destroy" strategy, based on the central tenet of killing large numbers of NVA or Viet Cong soldiers. This had the advantage of being offensively minded, and permitting the United States and ARVN to choose the battlefield—in most cases. On the other hand, the entire country was a battleground for the Vietnamese, and Westmoreland never understood that Hanoi did not care about losses. To the Viet Cong and NVA this was a war of independence, so no price was too high to pay. Westmoreland's strategy of attrition needed big units, and this meant a drastic increase in American military deployments.

To the Pentagon this meant full mobilization of the National Guard and Reserves, but Johnson demurred for several reasons. The president's legal footing for going to war was never very sound, yet he felt it could be justified to Congress and the American people as long as the fight remained limited in scope. Full mobilization of the National Guard and Reserves would obviate that. Mobilization meant a declared, full-scale war with all the budgetary entanglements, public relations headaches, and diplomatic issues accompanying it. The conflict in Southeast Asia *was* a war, and had been since 1965, in every respect except Washington's official recognition of the situation. To avoid mobilizing and keep up the charade that this was just a temporary action, Johnson had no choice but to increase the draft.

The majority of those deployed to Vietnam belonged to the Army, yet regardless of the branch of service, Westmoreland's plan required tremendous amounts of manpower. All males ages eighteen to twenty-six were required to register in compliance with the Selective Service Act, and under Program 2 the 1966 call-ups increased from 10,000 to 30,000 per month.*

Most of those drafted were good soldiers and did their duty. Colonel David Hackworth, a legendary combat officer, described it like this: "They were all good men, but none in their heart of hearts wanted to be there."† Still, drug use skyrocketed and applications for conscientious objector status climbed some 40 percent in 1966, and continued rising throughout the war. By 1966 the overall absent without leave (AWOL) figure for military personnel was 57 per 1,000 troops.‡ For the U.S. Army alone this would increase to 78 per 1,000 soldiers the following year.

These conditions were exacerbated by Robert McNamara's disastrous Project 100,000. This was a political fix intended to simultaneously solve several problems: first, the military's need for manpower to fight the war in Southeast Asia, and second, Johnson's need for political capital for the War on Poverty. What better way, McNamara reasoned, than to give hundreds of thousands of uneducated, low-income, underperforming kids a chance than by employing them in a military desperate for men?

Men were needed, true, but the correct sort of men. Aptitude measurements had been used for the U.S. military since the

---

*This was renamed the Military Selective Service Act of 1967 and again to Selective Service Amendment Act of 1969 before once again becoming the Military Selective Service Act in 1971.

†Among other decorations, Hackworth earned two Distinguished Service Crosses, ten Silver Stars, and eight Purple Hearts.

‡AWOL status acknowledges the soldier's whereabouts are unknown, and his absence may or may not be justified (usually not). It is one step away from desertion, which is the willful abandonment of a duty or post without the intention to return.

Alpha tests were initiated during World War I. This was adapted to the Army General Classification Tests (or equivalent per service) for World War II, and eventually became the Vietnam-era Armed Forces Qualifications Test (AFQT). By law, no one with an intelligence quotient (IQ) below 80 could be put in uniform and this was expanded to include those who scored lower than Category III on the AFQT. Ratings were percentile based, so those in Category IV scored only better than 10–30 percent of their fellow recruits. Recruits could also be put into lower categories, or exempted outright, for being overweight, illiterate, lacking English language skills, and other similar disqualifiers.

Project 100,000 lowered the entry standards to the point of putting all sorts of individuals in military service who had no business in uniform or carrying a weapon.* They were called the "Moron Corps" by other service members and became one of the larger problems facing the military. According to a 1989 report published by the Office of the Secretary of Defense, being drafted into the military had little quantifiable effect on their later lives, as hoped. It concluded that Project 100,000 military service for low-aptitude veterans

> *did not show veterans to have an advantage. In fact, in terms of unemployment status, educational achievement, and income those who never served appeared better off than those who had been in the military. Veterans were found to be more likely to be unemployed, and to have an average level of ed-*

---

*Cassius Clay, better known as Muhammad Ali, couldn't pass the initial AFQT screening but was retested during Project 100,000 and accepted due to the lower standards. He then applied for conscientious objector (CO) status as a Muslim cleric. Ali stated, "[M]y enemy is the white people, not the Viet Cong." His request was denied by the military.

ucation significantly lower than the nonveterans. Income differences between the two groups ranged from $5,000 to $7,000, depending on the sources included, in favor of the nonveterans. Finally, veterans were less likely than nonveterans to be married, and more likely to have been divorced.

Like most of McNamara's policies, plans, and programs this was an abject failure. However, revisionist criticisms of the project and incorrect statements seeking to reinforce Vietnam service myths are equally dangerous. In fact, 88 percent of those serving in country were Caucasian (which includes Hispanics), 11 percent were black, and 1 percent were classified as "other." Of the 58,128 dead, 87 percent were Caucasian, 12.5 percent were black, and 1.2 percent were "other." There was no magic number, no one group singled out as "cannon fodder" or a specific class of victims. What did exist was a very American military mix of professionals, volunteers, and draftees, engaged in a tremendously ambiguous conflict.* Hanoi suffered no such confusion. In 1965 the People's Army numbered about 195,000 but by the end of 1966 this more than doubled to 400,000 men and women. Three additional fighter regiments had been added to the Vietnamese People's Air Force, and anti-aircraft battalions had increased from fourteen to *forty.*

Most conflicts become more defined over time but as the year wore on there was no indication that this was happening in Southeast Asia. Rolling Thunder rolled on. In 1966 alone, more than 79,000 missions were flown and 136,000 tons of bombs were dropped. At this stage, only Hanoi and Haiphong were off-limits, in addition to a ten-mile prohibited zone along the

---

*More than 60 percent of those who served in World War II were drafted.

Chinese border. On the Ho Chi Minh Trail thousands of trees became toothpicks under Arc Light strikes, but craters were filled in and those streaming into South Vietnam continued their march.* Impressive American science began appearing in the form of electronic sensors designed to hear, and even smell, those on the Trail. Another idea was to seed the clouds over Southeast Asia, forcing additional torrential rain that would make the pathways impassable. It was also hoped that the extra rain might overcome the North Vietnamese dikes and wash out the rice crops. This, it seems, was more humane than simply *bombing* the dikes.

Yet even if all restrictions had been lifted, Rolling Thunder would have very likely still failed. Not only was there a dearth of viable targets, but the military was running short of bombs. Many were leftovers from Korea, and pilots were sometimes sent into combat with partial weapons loads.† Limits were imposed to stretch out the remaining ordnance, and the Pentagon purchased surplus U.S.-made, 500-pound bombs from West Germany.

It should have been obvious by New Year's 1967 that there would be no meaningful negotiations with Hanoi under the current conditions. The Ho Chi Minh Trail was undiminished and actually expanding in capacity. Rolling Thunder and the other air operations, unless their restrictions were lifted and adequate munitions found, would continue to fall short tactically and fail strategically. It should also have been apparent to Washington that the Soviet Union and China would not intervene. Overes-

---

*Arc Light strikes were massive raids by B-52 heavy bombers.
†This is not an isolated occurrence. The author dropped bombs during the 1991 Gulf War that were left over from Vietnam.

timating their potential involvement was therefore limiting U.S. tactical options. American strategy would have to change.

Early in 1967, President Johnson appears to have decided to win the war militarily since none of his diplomatic efforts had succeeded. "Mayflower" had been an abortive attempt to negotiate with the DRV in the spring of 1965 before real escalation commenced. While Blair Seaborn, a Canadian diplomat, acted as an emissary, Johnson halted Rolling Thunder in May as a show of good faith. Hanoi agreed to talk, paid lip service to the process, and used the bombing pause to finish building up its air defenses, including the SAM site that killed Leopard Two in July.

In December 1966, Italian and Polish diplomats began the secret "Marigold" initiative in Warsaw to discuss peace proposals as Hanoi finally realized the Americans weren't just going to give up and leave. To this end, Nguyen Dinh Phuong arrived in Poland with the authority to open negotiations and perhaps end the war. Unfortunately, on the eve of the talks, Hanoi was bombed. A Rolling Thunder mission that had been postponed due to bad weather hit the city and, convinced that Washington was being duplicitous, the North Vietnamese called off the meeting.

Hanoi had always publicly stated it had four demands as preconditions to any peace discussions: 1) a U.S. withdrawal from Indochina; 2) the freedom of South Vietnam to manage its own affairs; 3) the guarantee that South Vietnam would remain neutral and peaceful; and 4) that Vietnam would be reunified. Harrison Salisbury, an assistant editor from the *New York Times,* had spent some weeks in Vietnam in 1966 to observe the bombing. During his stay the Vietnamese communicated to him that the four points were no longer inviolable obstacles and Salisbury subsequently reported this to Washington, as Hanoi hoped he would. "Sunflower" was then initiated through U.S. and DRV diplomats in Moscow, but it failed as well.

Lyndon Johnson then complicated the issue by sending a personal letter to Ho Chi Minh that intimated a bombing halt in return for providing evidence that the DRV had ceased infiltration operations into South Vietnam. The letter and the overture were rejected by Hanoi, who felt that Washington really had no firm bargaining position. This was true, as long as total war and tactical nuclear weapons were off the table. So with the continued failure of diplomacy, Johnson approved several big ground operations that he hoped would break the stalemate.

Twelve miles north of the South Vietnamese capital two rivers run together forming the apex of a triangle—the Saigon River to the west and the Thi Tinh River to the east. The base of the triangle is formed by the Than Dien forest a few miles to the north. Long a stronghold for the National Liberation Front and Viet Cong, this "Iron Triangle" was the perfect target for a major ground operation. Operation Cedar Falls was designed to sweep the enemy out of the area to where they could be cut apart by American airpower. Devastating the NLF military capability would signal to Hanoi that the insurgency had failed, and would likewise demonstrate to South Vietnamese civilians that joining the VC was pointless.

In what would be the largest ground operation of the war, 16,000 American soldiers and 14,000 ARVN troops would execute a hammer-and-anvil attack. Elements of the 25th Infantry Division (Tropic Lightning) and 1st Infantry Division (Big Red One) would be the anvil, taking positions east and southwest of the rivers. Saturation bombing from B-52s began on January 4, 1967, and the next day the 173rd Airborne Brigade with the 11th Armored Cavalry began their hammer sweep into the Iron Triangle.

Air assaulting by helicopter into the village of Ben Suc, headquarters of the NLF Military Region IV, the Americans quickly captured the town. ARVN units then moved in to interrogate the villagers and relocate them; Ben Suc was then leveled. Unfortunately, the NVA 272nd Regiment, local militias, and the 165th Viet Cong Regiment simply melted away into the forests and hills. Most went into Cambodia or Laos, though others were discovered in a truly impressive network of tunnels stretching fifteen miles southwest to Cu Chi. Altogether some 1,500 NVA and VC fighters were killed, wounded, or surrendered. On the American side, 72 men died and 337 were wounded; the ARVN lost 11 killed with 8 wounded.

The operation was officially terminated on January 26, and General Westmoreland promptly declared a victory, impressed by the results. Lieutenant General Jonathan Seaman, a career artillery officer like Westy, commanded the II Field Force and was convinced that the NLF would have to "re-evaluate the relative capabilities of their forces as opposed to ours." However, as with most issues in Vietnam, the reality was somewhat more complicated. True, enemy operations were disrupted; more than one hundred bunkers were destroyed, as were twenty-five major tunnels. Enough rice was captured to feed an enemy division for a year, along with sixty thousand rounds of ammunition and six hundred weapons. VC and NVA regulars were scattered and the Iron Triangle was declared clear.

But two days after the U.S. forces pulled out, the Viet Cong came back and reoccupied the Triangle. So in the short term, Cedar Falls was a tactical success and Hanoi had definitely received a message—but *what* message, exactly? As with so many American ground operations designed for fast, decisive victory, this one lacked staying power, and that fact was certainly noted in the North. The long-term results were more difficult to quantify, though Hanoi was again reminded of the awesome capabilities of the American military. No doubt this had a major effect on Hanoi's strategic planning and would manifest itself early the following year.

It was also apparent that the NLF was not yet strong enough to achieve a military triumph and that the South would not fall through Viet Cong operations alone. This drove home the point that victory, which for the North meant reunification, would only be achieved through a major invasion south of the DMZ. Cedar Falls and other similar operations unintentionally laid the groundwork for this through the forced relocation of hundreds of thousands of South Vietnamese. As Saigon and MACV uprooted peasants and redistributed them around the Mekong Delta, many who had remained detached, or neutral, were now thoroughly angry, destitute, and more than ready to believe what the NLF and Viet Cong were telling them. This would remain true throughout large-scale U.S. occupation of the South. As one American advisor succinctly phrased it, "We lose more through the death of one innocent civilian than through . . . dead VC."

No matter how it is debated, Cedar Falls did not ultimately achieve its objectives, nor did President Johnson get the military knockout punch he'd so desired. This led to a much more ambitious operation to clear the entire region north of Saigon all the way to the Cambodian border. Operation Junction City commenced on February 22, 1967, with the largest U.S. airborne drop since World War II.* Two U.S. infantry divisions were positioned in the northern Tay Ninh province along the Cambodian border to prevent the escape of the 9th Viet Cong Regiment. A sweep was then accomplished, just as in Cedar Falls, driving the hammer onto the anvil.

Likely tipped off by a highly placed North Vietnamese agent

---

*Operation Market Garden in 1944.

in Saigon, most of the enemy had already escaped into Cambodia. As before, U.S. forces captured significant amounts of food and ammunition and more than a half million documents. Nearly 3,000 VC casualties were claimed against 282 Americans killed and some 1,100 wounded. More than 3,200 tons of bombs were dropped with 366,000 artillery rounds expended. Yet, as in the Iron Triangle, when the Americans moved on, the Viet Cong came back.

A plethora of causes, politics, egos, and errors brought the war to 1967, but Johnson and McNamara unequivocally bear the blame for its continuance past this point. Every year of the war contained a turning point, and each new year held opportunities to win or lose, both diplomatically and militarily. Given the American political system and civilian control of the Pentagon, the U.S. military could not fight the war as it would have wished—for better or worse. Had the Joint Chiefs been permitted, or been more forceful, they might have waged a ruthless, unrestricted conflict that would have produced much different tactical results. This could not have happened because the American system, thankfully, doesn't function in that manner. Civilian control is a cornerstone of our existence as a nation and implies a trust unseen in much of the world. The military agrees to forgo its inherent violent strength to do as it pleases and permits governance by elected officials. In return, those elected agree to do so with wisdom, intelligence, and daily recognition of the awesome responsibility to the lives of fighting men whom they hold in their hands.

Yet it is simplistic to blame civilian amateurism alone, since professional military officers generally expect this from any political administration. However, those in uniform who fail others in uniform are more culpable. If General Westmoreland, as the MACV commander, didn't know how to better conduct the war, then he *should* have known. Others did. During a Saigon cocktail party, Major General Frederick Weyand, commander of III Corps, whispered to CBS News correspondent Murray Fromson, "Westy just doesn't get it. The war is unwinnable. We've reached a stalemate, and we should find a dignified way out." As a former intelligence officer, Weyand did not view the war in Southeast Asia in conventional terms, and he was among the many officers who knew it could not be won by fighting that way. Weyand later agreed, on condition of anonymity, to be interviewed by CBS:

> "*I've destroyed a single division three times,*" *a senior American general* [Weyand] *said the other day.* "*I've chased main-force units all over the country and the impact was zilch. It meant nothing to the people. Unless a more positive and more stirring theme than simple anti-communism can be found, the war appears likely to go on until someone gets tired and quits, which could take generations.*"

Westmoreland would tell the president, at McNamara's request, that the conflict would take another two to five years, depending on troop levels. This was at odds with the optimistic picture the general continuously painted publicly, so why would the war take so long to win? Johnson was facing an election year in 1968, and if he was to survive politically, he desperately needed a way out of Vietnam without appearing weak. There were three main options available, and the first was to do nothing, accept the status quo, and wait. With waning congressional support and growing domestic unrest, this was not a realistic political option in 1967.

A second choice was invasion.

If Washington's true objective remained a stable South Vietnam, then eliminating DRV support for the National Liberation Front was essential. There were two ways to do this: cut the supply at the head, in North Vietnam, or block the Ho Chi Minh Trail at the DMZ and in Laos. Both were given serious thought, and a plan called York was detailed that would clear the area between Pleiku and Khe Sanh, then west to the Laotian border. Operation El Paso would be the actual advance into Laos to Tchepone, with at least three divisions. The biggest challenges to a thrust into the interior were weather and supply. At least 2,300 tons of supplies per day would be required, and this was simply beyond the logistical capacity of the few airfields nearby. By virtue of its small size and single runway Khe Sanh, for instance, could only sustain about 300 tons per day. The only road in, Route 9, was truly "Indian Country" and was patently unsafe.

Walt Rostow, the White House national security advisor, advocated an invasion of North Vietnam itself. If a force was landed near Vinh, above the DMZ, and another moved up from the south, then the VPA would be caught in a nutcracker. Rostow proposed an amphibious end-around, just as Doug MacArthur had done at Inchon in 1950; this would bypass the North Vietnamese and land in their rear. Invasion was an ambitious idea but entailed formidable difficulties. It would need to be a joint operation with the ARVN, which meant surprise was likely out of the question, given that Hanoi always seemed aware of Saigon's plans. With or without the ARVN, the U.S. military would still be responsible for the heavy lifting, and for a seaborne attack this meant landing craft.

With the usual shortsightedness following a war, hundreds of landing ships and thousands of Higgins boats were scrapped, sunk, used as targets, or converted to various civilian uses after World War II. By 1967 most of what remained was already being used in Southeast Asia, and the U.S. Navy estimated that only two infantry or Marine divisions could be transported at any given time. One partial solution to this would be to bring the troops in, fully prepared to fight, on their conventional naval transports. But disembarking this way meant deep-draft harbors and there were none close to the DMZ.

Johnson, McNamara, and Secretary of State Dean Rusk were among those who feared that any invasion of the North would trigger Chinese intervention. Walt Rostow did not believe it, probably correctly as it turns out; he calculated that Beijing would not risk another costly conflict with the United States unless absolutely necessary. Invasion would also necessitate increased troop levels, and this could really only be done by mobilizing U.S. reserve forces. However, mobilization would exceed the authority granted the president in the Gulf of Tonkin Resolution to conduct a limited war, and Johnson was fully aware that no expansion of his powers would be granted by Congress. In any event, it was a risk that LBJ would not assume while still contemplating another election run in 1968.

So Robert McNamara's third option—containment through technology—seemed to offer the president an acceptable alternative: a way to appear proactive, with minimal risk that would buy some time. Private sectors and government scientists nicknamed "the Wizards" created an array of programs offering astonishingly diverse solutions. One of the sillier projects was a cloud seeding effort, called Popeye, that would make rain to flood the rice fields and Ho Chi Minh Trail. There was, somewhat hypocritically, opposition on humanitarian grounds from several leading academics to rainmaking.* Concentrated largely between the Mu Gia and Ban Karai passes, the attempt

---

*Donald Hornig, the presidential science advisor, told Johnson that such flooding would cause a food shortage and pose health risks due to poor sanitation.

to induce rain was made, though if the enemy along the Trail noticed, it wasn't obvious. They simply did what they'd always done and found other paths, or laid bamboo matting and logs over the mud. They went on.

The Wizards also concluded that mud was an excellent by-product of rain. If mud was a sticky mess then surely there was a way to make mud even muddier. The Dow Chemical Company modified a popular detergent called Calgon to increase the saturation point of the iron-rich soil in the Annamite mountain range. Somewhat implausibly named "Commando Lava," the top-secret mud-making project used C-130s to drop huge bags of the compound all over Laos. John Prados relates a story in *The Blood Road* about an American helicopter pilot who was warned not to call in air strikes on friendly elephants in Laos. No doubt blinking a few times in disbelief, the man understandably asked how he would know a friendly pachyderm from one with hostile intentions. He was told that "enemy elephants would have their bellies tinged with red from the clay mud of The Trail." And so it was. The detergent caused a chemical reaction that not only thickened the mud, but brightened its iron red color to the point where it was visible on elephant bellies.

But McNamara's real emphasis was a barrier—a fortified line by which infiltration could be stopped and the North contained. Called "an iron-curtain counter-infiltration system," it would stretch from the South China Sea across the DMZ and Laos into Thailand. If interdiction could not be halted by bombing, then the Viet Cong could be strangled when the Ho Chi Minh Trail was permanently cut. Again, this illustrates a fundamental miscalculation regarding the trail's logistical importance, since most support for the VC was indigenous, and the few tons of required supplies leaked through to South Vietnam despite American efforts. The barrier would also contain the People's Army, or so McNamara believed. In fact, discussions about such a plan went back as far as 1965, but ultimately it was quite correctly regarded by the military as totally impractical.

All through the summer of 1966 various studies had been commissioned, including those by the Institute for Defense Analysis and the JASON group.* By that September, disregarding all practical opposition, cost, and wasted manpower, the secretary of defense ordered the barrier implemented in one year. Phase One would run from the coastal area near Gio Linh, just below the DMZ, west to Con Thien. Phase Two would extend farther west into Laos and would be constructed at a later date. More than 50,000 miles of barbed wire, five million fence posts, and 200,000 tons of other materials were needed. The initial cost hovered around $1.6 billion, which included $600 million for a command center at Nakhon Phanom in Thailand. Phase One fell entirely within the 3rd Marine Division's area of operations and General Lewis Walt, the Marine commander, was not at all happy about it.

McNamara brushed off Walt's very real operational concerns, just as he had ignored the Joint Chiefs; construction commenced. Under the title Joint Task Force 738, also called "Practice Nine," the bulldozers, Rome plows, and engineers began clearing terrain. The main concept was an overlapping system of physical obstacles and sensors tied into a centralized, computerized command center. Seismic and sonic sensors would detect movement and sound, respectively. Electrochem-

---

*JASON was created to use a younger generation of scientists with no ties to older Los Alamos, Manhattan Project, or Massachusetts Institute of Technology cadres. It is run through the MITRE Corporation and takes its name from Greek myth, not from "Junior Achiever, Somewhat Older Now."

ical sniffers like the XM-2 personnel detector were supposed to detect urine on the premise that where there was urine there were people. Others were employed that would find the enemy by smell, though no one seemed quite sure of body odor differences among Vietnamese, or even Americans who'd been living off native food.

However it was to happen, when the infiltrators were detected, cluster bombs, mines, and barbed wire would discourage them, or at least give a warning to close air support aircraft or ground teams, who would then respond. To the surprise of no one, except perhaps the secretary of defense, the barrier didn't work. As axiomatic as it sounds, the greatest vulnerability to high technology often seems to be low-technology solutions. The North Vietnamese promptly blew up the initial fourteen guard towers along the cleared trace then moved the acoustic sensors far off the Trail. They also draped urine bags near the chemical sniffers and herded domestic animals in all directions to mislead the seismic sensors.

Practice Nine was headed by Lieutenant General Alfred Starbird, a 1933 graduate of West Point who competed as a pentathlete in the 1936 Olympics, then earned a master's in engineering from Princeton in 1937. A Wizard by training, Starbird was also a combat engineer who'd been in the first unit to cross the Rhine River during World War II. Following the mediocre results of Cedar Falls and Junction City in early 1967, the pressure was on to make the barrier—the McNamara Line, as it came to be known—a success. So despite the failure of fixed fortifications in history from Hadrian's Wall to the Maginot Line, Starbird persisted. By early September 1967, McNamara overlooked test results and complaints by those in the field and declared the system operational.

Some of these projects were interesting, some marginally

effective, and some, as shown, were outright wastes of time. As such, these projects illustrated the fact that winning the war was no longer Washington's priority, if it ever had been. What is certain is that vast amounts of men, materials, and money were diverted from real fighting, where a difference could have been made if Washington had decided upon a military solution.

IN THE MEANTIME, Americans were still fighting and dying in Southeast Asia. The White House might not have known whom to fight or how to do it, but the Weasels suffered no such dilemma. Missions like Major Ed Rock's fight on October 12 continued to demonstrate how surface-to-air missile sites could be provoked, then precisely located and killed. This Hunter Killer tactic was increasingly valid in a theater where a creative enemy made the most of what he had—mobility and camouflage—and minimized his vulnerabilities.

The Weasels did the same.

Ed Rock had found the SA-2 but lacked the mix of weapons to kill it. He was forced to rely on F-104s that were not expecting to attack a missile site, had limited experience in dropping bombs, and subsequently missed the SAM. In the end, he had to use his own 20 mm cannon, which, though extremely reliable and lethal under the correct circumstances, would be no one's first choice for attacking heavily defended ground targets. Through Cricket, the orbiting ABCCC, Ed passed the location of the SA-2. A photorecon flight was immediately sent north into the target area, and it discovered two additional SAM sites nearby. Back at Korat a flight of four F-105Ds, each armed with six 750-pound bombs, were readied for a strike. As soon as he landed, Ed ran over to the waiting flight lead on Thud Row and passed him coordinates for the missile site. The 105s immediately launched, but by the time they air refueled and made it over to Route Pack One the SAMs were gone, having been dispersed and relocated.

But the mission did illustrate what could be done with proper weapons, flexibility, and accurate intelligence. These hard lessons, and dozens more gleaned from both initial Wild Weasel programs, were used to create the Wild Weasel College at Nellis Air Force Base. Since 1929, on 11,000 acres north of Las Vegas, Nevada had been home to a unique airfield operating under various names. Western Air Express, a contract air-mail carrier, used the field until the Army acquired it in 1941.* It was redesignated Nellis Air Force Base in 1948 in tribute to William Harrell Nellis, a Las Vegas native and P-47 pilot killed during the Battle of the Bulge in 1944.

By early 1954, realizing that air combat was not passé, and dogfighting skills were still vital, the Air Force established the Fighter Weapons School. It became the clearinghouse for honing combat tactics, sharing lessons learned, and operational testing. Immense bombing ranges, electronic warfare complexes, and top-secret evaluations of new equipment, weapons, and aircraft would be conducted here—and still are.† It was the perfect place for the surviving Hunter Killers to establish the 4537th Wild Weasel Electronic Warfare Squadron, better known as the Wild Weasel College—and pass on what they'd learned to those heading to Southeast Asia to fight the SAMs.

But improvements emerged from other sources as well. One of the most significant innovations, and one that would have long-term implications for all U.S. combat aircraft, came from

---

*The "WA" tail flash is still used today on Nellis-based aircraft.
†Nellis is still the "Home of the Fighter Pilot"; the base also hosts Red Flag, the Aggressors, and the 422nd Test and Evaluation Squadron, among others.

a young airman based at Takhli. California native Weldon Bauman enlisted in the Air Force and was trained as an electronic warfare repair technician. Arriving in Thailand in October 1966, Bauman had been in the Air Force for two years and was barely twenty-three years old. Assigned to the Vector shop maintaining APR-25/26 sets for the Weasels, he listened for months as pilots and EWOs discussed missions. He watched them roar off the runway heading north, and waited for many to return who never did.

At that time the F-105F had a Stancil-Hoffman tape deck that recorded all radio calls, cockpit conversions, and audio signals from threat radars. Bauman listened to this data as well. The biggest complaint coming from combat crews was the sheer density of the received signals. Barlocks, Firecans, Fansongs, and all the early warning or GCI radars were saturating the threat display unit (TDU). Although enemy radars were displayed, it was impossible to tell *which* Fansong was shooting because so many signals appeared. "When I heard the tapes, I knew I had to help," Weldon related. "I figured if I could hear the audio then there had to be a way to see the signal."

One day in March, acting on his own, Weldon hooked a mission tape up to an oscilloscope, which would display the recorded audio as an electrical signal. This data could then be measured over time, and graphed into a waveform to measure pulse repetition interval, frequency, amplitude, and other characteristics. He discovered that the radar pulse densities in the S frequency band, where the Fansong resided, were so dense that the PRI filters were saturated and ineffective. But Weldon also thought he'd found a pattern that he hadn't known existed. When a Fansong was engaging a Weasel, there appeared to be a measurable interval between a tracking beam and the transponder beacon guiding the missile. It was tiny, less than four microseconds, but if he could prove this, it should be possible to identify which Fansongs were shooting and which were not. If signals were farther apart than four microseconds then the beams were not synchronized and were *not* coming from the same radar. It would, he reasoned, be fairly simple to vary the threat displays seen in cockpits based on this correlation. This would instantly tell the Weasels which SAM had fired and where it was.

Bauman was excited. He knew the 41st Tactical Electronic Warfare Squadron flew EB-66 Destroyers out of Takhli, and in addition to warning of Fansong activity, they also gathered signals for analysis. If he could talk to them and confirm his theory, then he could work out the engineering aspects himself. Weldon explained his idea to Captain Paul Chesley, a Weasel EWO, who got Bauman into the Skywarrior's top-secret compound. Bauman asked a technician about the interval, and the man agreed that he'd never seen more than a four-microsecond spread between correlated signals. The EB-66 EWOs had known it all along but had not understood its significance.

Weldon Bauman did.

Any type of wiring modification or changes to hardware would enter the Byzantine world of Air Force acquisitions and procurement. If it did work, the 355th TFW commander could approve the modification's use for his aircraft without going through outside channels. This was the fastest, most direct method, so Weldon started by dissecting the APR-25. Basically the old three-inch Vector scope in both cockpits, it was composed of the TDU and the analyzer box that processed signals. "I fed several mission recordings of raw SAM and AAA audio pulses directly into the APR-25 processor to determine where the processing choke point was," he recalled.

He changed a switch function on one of the circuit cards

so that the four-microsecond signals could be isolated from the cluttered, dense, and barely usable display.* But pilots and EWO like choices, so this had to be something they could select, only when needed. Also, Weldon wasn't 100 percent certain it would really work, and he was painfully aware of the difference between a bench test in a hangar and real SAMs outside Hanoi. His stomach knotted at the thought that his tinkering might cost a jet—and two lives.

However, Captain Chesley, known as "Cool Bear," was convinced and obtained permission to have his jet modified.† Bauman took the unused C-band test button on the APR-25 and wired it such that when depressed, the system would only display the SAM radar actually firing a missile. It worked so well that within months every Thud at Takhli was modified, and similarly bypassing the convoluted Air Force bureaucracy, the Korat Weasels were also retrofitted later that fall.

By the time Weldon Bauman left Thailand in the fall of 1967, Rolling Thunder was at its height and the North Vietnamese were fighting back ferociously. MiGs claimed 27 aircraft, and anti-aircraft fire caused at least 89 percent of the remaining 566 fixed-wing losses for the year. Five hundred and eighty-four men lost their lives and another 163 were captured. From a single SA-2 battalion in 1965, there were now at least thirty. Firings had risen from about 30 per month to over 600 by the fall of 1967. During that year approximately 1,950 missiles would be launched during 1,104 engagements, and this caused 62 U.S. fixed-wing combat losses from SAMs. Still, it was taking more than three times the number of missiles to shoot down an aircraft than it had just two years earlier. Hunter

---

*The Gate Logic card.
†F-105F No. 63-8349.

Killer tactics were much better, and the Bauman modification, RHAW equipment, and advanced predeployment training at Nellis all increased the odds.

Another game changer had been the belated introduction of QRC-160 jamming pods onto fighter aircraft. Developed by General Electric, this detachable, underwing pod was 7.5 feet long and weighed 200 pounds. Powered by a ram air turbine, four 75-watt magnetron transmitters generated noise jamming against the Fansong and Firecan radars. The programs were selected based on the mission threats and manually set on the ground to the desired bandwidth and frequency—all the pilot had to do was switch it on or off.

One hundred fifty of these Quick Reaction Capability (QRC) pods were built, painted, numbered, and promptly put into storage in 1963. Tactical Air Command, in general, and fighter pilots in particular, saw them as unnecessary. And why wouldn't they? The SAM threat wasn't well understood, and anything under the wing of a fighter should either carry fuel or be dropped on an enemy's head. Jamming was something done by heavy bombers because they couldn't crank and bank like fighters. However, due to increasing combat losses in Southeast Asia, the pods' usefulness had been evaluated in 1965 using RF-101 Voodoo reconnaissance jets. From its onset the test was a cock-up; the pods weren't mounted correctly, interfaces weren't checked, nor had the units been properly stored or tuned. Not surprisingly, the results were horrible and the PACAF commander had them removed from Southeast Asia.

This was certainly not new technology, since the Navy had been using ALQ-51 deception jammers on their A-6 and A-4 strike aircraft for years.* The USAF had initially passed on the

---

*Unlike the USAF, the Navy also used airborne chaff.

idea, since the presence of false targets seemed to result in heavy barrage fire from the enemy. Further ahead in their thinking, naval air built the jammer into each aircraft instead of using pods. This aided maintenance, made ECM an integral part of aviation rather than an afterthought, and did not occupy a weapons station. As early as 1965, each carrier had a dedicated electronic warfare detachment, usually four aircraft, on board. Fleet air primarily utilized the EA-3B Skywarrior or the EA-1B, while shore-based Navy and Marine pilots flew the EF-10B Skyknight out of Da Nang.

Determined to catch up, the USAF began testing an improved version of its pod at the Air Proving Ground Center in Florida early in 1966. Designated QRC-160A-1, by the fall it was ready for field evaluation and, with fixed-wing combat aircraft losses mounting, twenty-five pods were shipped to the 355th TFW at Takhli for testing.

The results of the program, called "Vampyrus," were startling. Earlier that year, seventy-two F-105s had been lost all over North Vietnam, with fifty-two Air Force planes going down in Route Pack Six alone.* This equated to a loss rate of 28.3 aircraft per 1,000 sorties. In September, following the pod employment, the rate fell to 16.4 per 1,000 sorties. Of course, the monsoon season had arrived so there were fewer missions, but clearly pods helped. As Colonel William Chairsell of the 388th Tactical Fighter Wing stated to Seventh Air Force Director of Operations:

> *The introduction of the QRC 160A-1 pod to the F-105 weapons system represents one of the most effective operational innovations I have ever encountered.*

---

* Forty-five of these were F-105s.

Seldom has a technological advance of this nature so degraded an enemy's defensive posture. It has literally transformed the hostile air defense environment we once faced, to one in which we can operate with a latitude of permissibility.

This was fortunate, since the year had been as lethal as it had been confusing and would get worse. Just as the U.S. military was studying SAMs, exploiting their weaknesses, and developing new technology, the enemy was also striving to stay ahead of emerging American systems. With every countertactic comes a counter-countertactic, and SAMs were no exception. The coming year, 1967, would be the bloodiest yet: the Wild Weasels would need every edge they could get to keep killing the missiles and guns.

PART TWO

The thundering line of battle stands,
And in the air death moans and sings;
But Day shall clasp him with strong hands,
And Night shall fold him in soft wings.
JULIAN GRENFELL ("INTO BATTLE")

CHAPTER 7

A FULL DAY'S WORK

"THERE . . . there he goes!"

"Yep."

Captains Jerry Hoblit and Tom Wilson watched the lead F-105's wings rock so hard they could see into the cockpit. Hoblit shoved the throttle forward, glanced left to check that his own wingman was out of the way, then slammed the stick left. Rolling heavily to the north, the pilot dropped the nose to keep the airspeed up. It was too soon to use afterburner, and besides, they'd likely need all that fuel a little farther north. The open funnel-shaped end of the Son La valley disappeared as he snapped upright, heading north, heart pumping, along the Black River. Kingfish flight, four F-105Fs, was about five minutes ahead of sixteen D-model Thuds loaded up to kill to-day's target—the North Vietnamese Army barracks at Xuan Mai. Barely twenty miles southwest of Hanoi, the whole area was ringed with anti-aircraft guns and there were at least five known SAM sites within range.

"Guns. Got Firecans and Barlocks all over the place," Tom Wilson remarked calmly, considering the situation.

"Fansongs?"

"At least four. Bearing northeast . . . weak . . . one to two rings."

Jerry nodded and tightened his mask. Two rings was real enough, but not too close. The little bastards were up and ready to play. Soon. Having four Weasels today permitted Kingfish to try a new tactic. Major Leo Thorsness, the flight lead, with Harry Johnson in his pit, was splitting them up into two pairs; Hoblit and Bear were Kingfish Three, so he and Number Four were arcing to the north around Hanoi while Kingfish One and Two stayed south. The idea was to troll for SAMs and give the enemy radars more than one big target to watch. Hopefully, faced with a multidirectional threat, the Fansongs would all have to come up, then stay up. Then the four Weasels could find them and kill them.

Hopefully.

In the back cockpit, Tom Wilson hunched forward and squinted at the APR-25 threat display. Grunting, he straightened and pulled the circular hood off the console. The sun wasn't too bad this afternoon, and he hated flying bent over. It hurt when Jerry pulled g's. Glancing off the left wing at the Black River, he then looked to the right at the big peaks. They were still more than thirty miles from Hanoi, and even if there was a nearer SAM, it would still be too far away to engage. "Bear," as he was known, chuckled at that thought. Actually you never really knew *where* they were, which was precisely the point of having Weasels.

"Harpoon Zero One . . . Fansongs active."

Both men flinched at the loud voice in their helmets. Harpoon 01 was an EB-66 orbiting somewhere over Laos watching all electronic emissions in North Vietnam. If early warning radars were up, he might be skeptical, but SAM, GCI, and airborne intercept (AI) radars always necessitated a warning on the GUARD frequency. This permitted a simultaneous broadcast over all frequencies and was intended only for emergencies. It was annoying, and pilots could disable the function, but they rarely did. Wilson remembered hearing that the first F-4 shootdown happened because the pilot had turned off GUARD and so got no warning about the SAMs. With only a single radio, sometimes GUARD was the only way to get critical information across to fifty jets over North Vietnam.

"Hey, Jerry."

"Whaddya want, Tom." It was a standing joke. Tom and Jerry. Like the cartoon cat and mouse.

"That F-4 that got whacked in '65 by the SAM . . . the first one. Remember his call sign?"

Indeed he did. Up front, Hoblit looked off the Thud's nose at left ten o'clock. Poor son of a bitch went down about twenty miles from here, just beyond that ridgeline.

"Leopard." He rolled up on one wing and looked down at the narrow river valley. "I think he was Number Two."

The pilot eased back to wings level and dropped the nose a few degrees. Holding 540 knots, the Thud felt heavy, solid, and fast. He craned his neck to look down again.

"Spring High . . . that was the mission. The Korat guys flew in directly below us when they went in to take out the SAM that got the Phantom."

Bear grunted again. He wasn't much interested in whatever happened two years ago—not when there were SAMs nearby right now. Still, he stole a quick glance at the gray-blue water two miles below; it was because of those Thuds and Spring High that four Weasels were here now hunting and killing missiles.

But back to business. Below the threat display was the larger ER-142 panoramic receiver, which let him pick apart radar signals. Fortunately it was angled up so he didn't have to crouch to see it, which wouldn't work anyway with Jerry's cranking and banking. Checking to make sure the three-position toggle switch was in the center S-band position, he tuned in azimuth first and isolated a two-ringer signal directly east of them.

"Kingfish, Kingfish . . . Harpoon Zero One. AI radars."

They heard Leo acknowledge and Jerry did the same. Airborne intercept radars meant MiGs and Tom glanced at the APR-25. It was cluttered with everything now: early warning radars, GCI stuff for the MiGs, guns . . .

"Looks to be quite a party," Jerry said with a chuckle.

"Gotta Fansong bearing zero-eight-zero." Bear twiddled the elevation knob with his right thumb and forefinger while watching the FREQ and PRF windows mounted to the left of the ER-142. Had to be it . . . The 2.175 gigahertz and the pulse repetition matched a Fansong.

"Range guesstimate?"

The EWO frowned, squinting at the scope. The signal faded at a 5-degree down angle but flickered back to life anytime he went more than 12 degrees in elevation. Visualizing the triangle in his head, Bear replied, "Ten to twenty miles."

Jerry stared off the right wing, glanced at his map, then looked off to the east again at the striker's target. Bearing to the SAM cut right through the target about twelve miles away, and he could see it. Well, the target area anyway. A chalky road snaked its way past the mountains and where it emerged, just past the foothills, was the army barracks. Past that, he could see when he lifted his head slightly, was Hanoi. The low-lying mist having burned away, the visibility was good enough to see the city's gray smudge on the banks of the Red River.

"That's the SAM that Leo and Harry are after. Look outside."

Bear opened up the search again, then looked up. "Good look at the river today."

"Yep. Dunno why they call it the Red River, though. Always looks muddy and brown."

"One guess why that is."

Jerry chuckled again, letting his eyes roam over the cockpit. "World's biggest crapper?"

"You got it. Two Fansongs . . . bearing zero-six-zero . . . ah, no range yet."

Gas, engine, and switches. The pilot had already "greened it up," and his pylon lights were on. He had two Shrike anti-radiation missiles on the outboard stations and CBU-24 cluster bombs inboard. And the cannon, of course.

"Guns," Tom called again from the backseat. "Lots of guns. All north and northeast."

Jerry nodded to himself and pushed forward on the stick. Time to go down; the gomers had taken the bait. Eyeballing the airspeed indicator, he kept it right around 550 knots, pulling the throttle back a bit in the descent. The river blurred by; beneath the Thud now was the SAM site that Lamb and Donovan killed eighteen months ago. But Jerry was watching the mountain peak east of the river—Tan Vien, according to his map.

As it zipped under his wing, he leveled off at 4,000 feet, pushed the throttle back up, and cranked the fighter hard over to the right. Three minutes and thirty miles had passed since they'd split from Kingfish One. The plan was for Kingfish Three to stay north of the peak and work along Route 87, paralleling the Red River, from Son Tay to Hanoi. Right now they were only five miles south of the junction between the Black and Red rivers, and the Spring High target area was still visible if he cared to look. But he was scanning the ground for Triple A flashes, and smoke from SAM launches.

And he was watching Hanoi.

THIRTY ONE MILES to the southeast, just past the mountain range, Kingfish One was also watching the city. The whole area west of the North Vietnamese capital was a nest of SAMs and anti-aircraft guns. After splitting up, Leo Thorsness had angled his pair of fighters away from the target area and skirted over the high terrain to the south. This would hopefully force the radars to come up and track him, as well as Kingfish Three, since they were so far apart. He also didn't want to fly straight to Xuan Mai and warn the Vietnamese of what was coming. This way, Harry could work the signals, and they'd pop out over the flats heading north just about when Kingfish Three was turning east toward Hanoi.

It actually worked out that way.

The rough terrain dropped away behind him, and Leo stared over the Thud's nose at the plains. There were two long, prominent hills a few miles in front of him, like whales swimming side by side. Beyond that there was nothing but farmland and Hanoi. It was much easier to see the ground out here but he felt naked and very exposed. Shoving the throttle up to hold 500 knots, the pilot rolled left and headed north, feeling his heart slowly thump against his chest.

Well, that's the way it was supposed to be. First in, last out.

"Kingfish . . . Harpoon Zero One. Fansong's active."

"Guns, too, Leo . . . all over the place. Like a damn pinball machine. Fansongs . . . one to three o'clock."

The pilot nudged the Thud left, closer to the hills. It was safer over there. No SAMs and a place to hide if they needed it. "Who's closest? Gotta be the one by the strike target."

"Dunno . . . too many signals. Scope's trashed."

Thorsness bunted a bit lower, holding the big fighter steady at 6,000 feet. He was still above the range of all the gomers with "AyKays"—AK-47s—but close enough to the ground to get lower, fast, if he needed to.* They were also high enough to be seen by any Fansong within thirty miles.

---

*AK-47 assault rifles were preferred by the NVA and Viet Cong, though they would use anything that would shoot. Categorized as "small arms," they had an effective vertical range of about 4,000 feet.

"Try Bauman's switch. We're a minute out."

The Thud was nine miles south of the target, streaking north with the ridgeline off the left wing and Hanoi off the right. Leo held the stick lightly but firmly in his right hand, turning sideways to look back over his left shoulder at his wingman. Kingfish Two, Major Tom Madison and Major Tom Sterling, was right where it was supposed to be. About a half mile back and stacked a bit high so he was looking *through* his flight lead at the ground: a good position to see Triple A or SAMs, and made it easy for Leo to find him.

"Got it!" Harry sounded surprised. "Fansong, two o'clock . . . three-ringer." Both men looked toward Hanoi and picked up two smoke trails lifting away from the ground. Bauman's modification obviously worked. But the SAMs he could see visually were not from the same Fansong that Bear found. These were too far away and shooting at someone else.

Gas, engine, and switches—his eyes flickered around the cockpit, then stared ahead. The afternoon sun was off his left shoulder and shadows filled the little valleys zipping past. Shoving up his visor, Leo rechecked the manual reticle setting he'd use for the bombs and glanced again at the pylon buttons. All four were lit: two Shrikes and four CBUs were ready.

"Fansong . . . three-five-zero. Two rings!"

Just saw us, he thought, nodding. Maybe the radar operator had been looking at Jerry or munching rice, but Leo's pair of Weasels just slipped in the back door. Flicking his wrist, the pilot centered the steering to 350 degrees, shoved the throttle forward, and smoothly pulled the stick back. The nose instantly rose and the F-105 shot upward, blue sky filling the corners of his eyes as the jet rocketed up from the foothills.

"Kingfish, Harpoon . . . Fansong active."

No shit.

Leo ignored the call and focused on the angle, his right

thumb poised over the pickle button as he bunted forward to freeze the climb at 35 degrees. His eyes darted around the cockpit . . . 5.6 miles from the target at 490 knots.

Now. He stabbed with his thumb and held the button down. From the corner of his left eye he caught the flash, then a trail of white smoke when the AGM-45 snaked away. As the Thud passed 9,000 feet, sound exploded everywhere; audio warnings for the threat scope and radio calls filled his helmet.

"BEEP BEEP BEEP BEEP!"

"Harpoon Zero One . . . GCI active."

Leo rolled off left toward the mountains as the earth spun around beneath him and he got a face full of Vietnam. The earth spread out before him, huge green peaks flanked by smaller hills, woven together with lighter green valleys and a spiderweb of chalky roads.

"Fansong, Leo." Harry's voice was gravelly, almost like he had his mask down. "Ah . . . north . . . to the north."

Leo slammed the stick against his right knee, dumped the nose even farther, and headed nearly straight down toward a line of low, knobby hills. Stark against the lighter ground, gray karst jutted from the dark green ridge like a moss-covered skeleton. When it filled the windscreen, Leo slid the throttle back and pulled.

"Guns . . . guns north."

Eyes swiveling to the threat display, he saw the curving dashed lines and kept pulling. "Got 'em."

When the nose came through the horizon, Leo shoved the throttle forward to the stop and snapped level. A wide, flat valley opened up in front of them, and he stared to the right. Remembering the targeting pictures from the briefing, he picked up an east–west running road—National Route 6—with two prominent hills on either side.

"Triple A . . . one o'clock."

Over the road and between the hills. Leo saw the ugly little gray clusters against blue sky and looked at the ground below them. Anti-aircraft guns were there for a reason: to protect something. The pilot's eyes swept through the cockpit. He was at 8,200 feet and 550 knots with Xuan Mai about two miles off the nose to the right.

He saw the missile launch just as Harry called, "Fansong . . . one o'clock . . . three rings."

"Packard's three minutes out."

Packard was the leader of Thud strikers about to plaster the barracks. Four flights of four F-105Ds from Takhli, and they were less than twenty-five miles away. He had to do this *now*. The spreading cloud of dirty smoke rolled away, but Leo kept his eyes padlocked on the site. It was plain to see now—they always were after they fired. It was just south of the road near rows of narrow buildings that could only be army barracks.

The picture was as good as it was going to get, and they were on a near-perfect 20-degree wire for a dive-bomb attack. Keying the mike in the bank, he broke in over the radio chatter with "Missile off the ground . . . Xuan Mai . . . northbound."

"Hope it's not after Jerry."

BEAR WILSON WAS appalled.

His ER-142 was nearly useless—there was so much shit out there ahead of them. Every Barlock, Spoon Rest, Firecan, and Fansong in North Vietnam seemed to be burning holes in his Thud. And why not? They were twenty miles west of Hanoi and any gomer with a gun was going to shoot. Rattlesnake audio filled both helmets and the bright red launch warning lights suddenly lit up.

"SAM in the air," Jerry called, quite calmly. "Two of 'em . . . twelve o'clock."

Bear looked up and saw the telltale gray smoke trails arcing upward, stretching like obscenely long fingers. This close to the ground the Fansong wasn't supposed to be able to track and guide missiles, but sometimes that wasn't true. Reaching up, he jabbed the C-band test button on the APR-35 and held it down. The system cycled and the scope cleared except for a single Fansong. Eleven o'clock and three rings. *Sonuvabitch.* The kid's modification worked.

The Thud was *fast:* 600 knots and bouncing in the heated air close to the ground. Bear tried to keep his fingers steady, attempting to synchronize the 142 receiver along the Fansong's azimuth beam.

"Third missile up," Jerry added. "All heading southwest."

Bear nodded. "Valid. They're tracking us."

The Weasel nosed over as Jerry took it down lower. The rice paddies off the left wing were a blur, along with the brown stain of the Red River just beyond. Behind him the comforting shield of mountains dropped away, leaving them horribly exposed in the open. His right wingtip was practically on Route 87, which was empty of any vehicles as it led straight east into Hanoi.

"How far to the city?" Bear asked, without looking up.

Jerry's eyes were glued to the first two SAMs. They always shot three. Shoot, shoot, look, and shoot again; one bit of Soviet doctrine the gomers used. "About twelve miles. First two SAMs passing off south and high."

"Roger that . . . zero-two-zero for the Fansong . . . pull at ten miles."

But the third one seemed like it had corrected. The smoke trail had a big bend in it and looked shorter—this was bad since the missile was now headed in their direction. Before the SAM's motor burned out and he lost the trail, Jerry darted a quick glance around cockpit. Engine, temperature, and oil were good. Fuel . . . well, they were always low. Both outboard pylon buttons were green and ready. As he started up at the incoming missile it seemed to be drifting aft, more toward the mountains than at him. *We'll see.*

"Ten miles . . . up we go!"

With his left hand Jerry shoved the throttle into burner and pulled with his right into a steady, 4-g climb. With Vietnam falling away under the wings, he bunted forward and held the nose at 35 degrees nose high.

Eight miles. His thumb rested lightly on the pickle button, eyes flickering to his wingman, the airspeed, nose-high attitude, then back outside to the SAM. The missile tried to correct, but the Weasel's explosive transition from low altitude into a climb seemed to have thrown the guidance off. The SAM had flattened out, then streaked past a half mile overhead, heading west.

"SAM's ballistic." Harry thumped on the canopy. "Guns," he craned forward, trying to see past the 105's enormous snout. Jerry nudged the left rudder pedal with his boot, lining up perfectly on 020 degrees, then mashed down with his right thumb.

"Shrike's away!"

The 600-knot loft from seven miles away would get the little missile to Hanoi and there wasn't anything else to do for it—except stay alive to finish the job. Rolling left, Jerry let the fighter's heavy nose fall through the horizon and brought the throttle back to MIL power. They'd bug out west, then come back for—

"Holy shit!"

No backseater likes to hear that from the front and Tom Wilson was certainly no exception. "What?"

Even as he asked, Bear felt the burner kick in again and Jerry's hard pull on the stick.

Dishing out of the dive, the Thud began muscling its way into a climbing, left turn right at the g limit.

"MiGs . . . four of 'em," the pilot grunted. "Two by two at left nine o'clock!"

Jerry was straining against the g's, head sideways, staring up and left, so Bear did the same. And there they were, bright and shiny, sunlight glinting from their wings as they swarmed down on the Thud.

"MiGs," Kingfish Four yelled, then, "my burner won't light!" *Sonuvabitch!*

"You see Number Four?" Jerry asked, reaching for the GUN switch without looking away from the enemy fighters.

"I see MiGs!"

Swept wings and a snub nose. MiG-17s or 19s . . . he couldn't tell. Not that it mattered. Going up, even in burner, the heavier F-105 was slowing, and with less airspeed his own turn circle was getting bigger. The MiGs were cutting down across the horizon, moving incredibly fast, and turning well inside his own circle.

"I got 'em," Jerry replied calmly, in spite of having his guts in his throat. Both men were breathing heavily. "See if you can spot Four."

Nearly rolling the Thud onto its back, the pilot yanked the throttle back to MIL and sliced back toward the southwest, watching the MiG's noses. If any of them got a bead on him then he'd have to jink to spoil the gunshots.

"Overshot! The lead MiG overshot." Bear sounded like he was being strangled. Glancing in the mirrors, Jerry saw his EWO turned all the way around in the seat, arms braced against the canopy rail and head back, staring over the tail.

"Now I gotta chase him down to kill him." Jerry snapped the jet upright, lit the burner, and shoved the nose forward, silently laughing at his own joke. He caught a glimpse of another MiG, probably the leader's wingman, zip past a thousand feet above, up on one wing, looking down at the Thud. Dust floated from the negative g's, and as the powerful 105 surged forward, Jerry lifted his left hand and shot the MiG the finger. In the back, Bear's head hit the canopy, but his swearing turned to chuckling when he saw his pilot flip the bird. Jerry heard it and, amid the strangeness understood only by those who've seen combat, laughed too.

Quilted green fields splattered with brown patches filled the windscreen as the F-105 dropped earthward. Swollen and sluggish, the Red River snaked off under the right wing as Jerry headed for the biggest hill on the north end of the mountain range. Fifteen miles, then safety; nothing could catch a Thud in full afterburner.

"Any sign of Four?" Bear Wilson asked, sneaking a peek at his APR-25. Why bother? It looked like a plate of spaghetti.

"You watch the MiGs . . . I'll find that guy." Jerry keyed the mike. "Kingfish Four . . . position?" Jerry made the call on the strike frequency. "Kingfish Four, say position."

Bear twisted around again, looking east toward Hanoi. He hadn't seen any more SAMs, but that was because the MiGs had shown up. There had been some smoke rising to the southwest, though this had to be the 105s hitting Xuan Mai.

"We're not leavin,' are we?"

Jerry pulled out of the dive a few thousand feet above the paddies, leveled off, and at 700 knots pulled the throttle back to MIL. The foothills were near . . . maybe ten miles now. Beyond that there were no SAMs and MiGs, only safety, the tanker, and then home. Behind them were the guns and SAMs.

And the MiGs.

He didn't even hesitate.

"Hell no." The pilot began a relatively easy climbing turn to the right, not watching the river or Thud Ridge off to the north, but searching for MiGs.* "With three or four gomers waiting to become stars on our jet? You gotta be shittin' me."

LEO THORSNESS GRUNTED, increased the bank, and sliced back toward the thinning smoke. Suddenly a call came through that shattered all the mental radio filters that fighter pilots have in combat.

"MiGs," blurted Kingfish Four, "my burner won't light!"

At this distance there was nothing Thorsness and Johnson could do for Jerry Hoblit and Bear Wilson. Leo slapped his knee and kept his eyes on the target. This was one reason why four ships didn't split up . . . more eyeballs to see MiGs and SAMs. It had been a calculated risk, and he prayed Jerry and Bear didn't get bagged.

Flying by feel and peripheral vision, Leo played the stick and throttle for the target roll-in. Finally aware of the real danger, the NVA anti-aircraft gunners opened up with a vengeance. Ignoring the airbursts and constant radio calls, Leo froze the reticle on a 20-degree line just below the target, then rolled the big fighter upright. Dozens of blue-gray ponds were scattered about, and he noticed a canal just south of the SAM site. Cracking the throttle back an inch, he tried to stay at 550 knots as the altimeter spun down.

Sixty-five hundred feet . . . almost . . . he focused on some

---

*Thud Ridge was the American nickname for the Tam Dao mountains; a forty mile ridgeline northwest of Hanoi used by U.S. fighters to mask low altitude ingress routes in Route Pack Six.

vans at the edge of the smoke and didn't think about the yellow flashes suddenly rippling around the whole area.

At 5,500 feet the orange pipper touched a van and Leo pickled. Unlike launching a Shrike, he felt the 3,600-pound loss from four CBU-24s falling off the right inboard station. Silently dropping away, they would open like clamshells, scattering 2,600 tennis-ball-size bomblets all over the doomed SA-2 site.

"Kingfish Four, say position." That was Jerry Hoblit, separated from his wingman somehow. Jamming the throttle forward, Leo pulled up, then rolled hard to the right along the horizon. There was only one way to go—southeast. If he went in any other direction he'd either hit a wall of Triple A or get a face full of inbound Thuds. Heart pounding, he planned to extend a bit to the south, then hook left over the plains to head north and help Kingfish Three. Maybe he could stop it from getting any worse.

SEVENTEEN MILES NORTHEAST, Jerry Hoblit would have been okay with that. He and Bear Wilson had pitched back toward Hanoi and, between the building cumulus clouds, discovered a solitary MiG cavorting in the sun.

"Right one o'clock . . . low. See? Right over that light green patch between the clouds."

Bear saw him. Almost like the silly son of a bitch was doing acrobatics on a training mission. He said as much to the pilot.

Jerry chuckled. "Well then, this'll be a lesson he remembers till he dies . . . in about one minute." Sliding the throttle forward, he held the Thud in a slight right bank. A bit closer, then—

"MiG!" Tom yelled. Jerry jumped, snapping his head around. All he saw was the intake of a MiG.

We're dead . . .

Even as the thought flashed through his shocked brain, the pilot's hands and feet were moving. Yanking the stick back into his lap, he kicked the right rudder hard and the Thud corkscrewed wildly as the nose lifted. Eyes graying from the sudden g's, Jerry shoved the stick forward, forcing the nose over, and tensed, waiting for cannon shells to rip through the jet . . . and him.

"He missed!" Bear shouted. "Overshooting . . . low . . . right."

Jerry swallowed and rolled back right. *There!* Silver, shiny wings and the orange glow of an afterburner. His eyes narrowed, and he stared harder. Two orange spots . . . then the MiGs were gone, disappearing into the clouds.

Enough. Outnumbered four to one, ten miles from Hanoi and out of gas, they weren't going to win anything here today. Except maybe a chance to fight again. Continuing the roll, Jerry snapped the Thud inverted and went to afterburner.

"Good idea," Bear chimed in as Vietnam rushed up again for the second time in four minutes. "Let's let the bastard live another day."

Jerry headed for the hills, leveling off at 100 feet and 650 knots. Glancing at the APR-25, he saw nothing but Fansongs, and since MiGs couldn't find their own asses without GCI he thought maybe they'd gotten away. Jerry took a deep breath and peered out at the mountains, then eyeballed the fuel gauge and thought about the orange spots. *Two* burner cans . . . and MiG-17s only had a single engine.

What the hell had that been?

"KINGFISH LEAD . . . Kingfish Two is hit!"

Pulling off the southern target, Leo Thorsness in Kingfish One yanked the Thud around to the right, overbanking so he could see past the tail. Snapping his head around, he gazed back at Xuan Mai, looking for his wingman.

"Ya see him?"

"No." Harry was straining against the g's, twisted almost backward in the seat, looking toward the target. Both men caught the thousands of sparkling flashes from the cluster bombs, though, like a shotgun blast right through the middle of the SAM site. The pilot continued to turn and keyed the mike.

"Kingfish Two . . . head southeast toward the hills, plug in burner, keep transmitting, and I'll home in on you."

"Roger that . . . west of the target, ah . . . six miles."

Madison must have turned immediately if he was already west of Xuan Mai. Made sense. Shortest direction out of North Vietnam. Leo dropped his hand off the throttle to the radio control panel on the left console. Glancing down, he found the big gray switch, twisted it to the ADF position on the far right, and held it. The white arrowhead in the big HSI indicator on the center console jumped to the left as the ARC-70 radio homed in on Tom Madison's transmissions.

". . . got more warning cockpit lights," he was saying, the strain obvious in his voice. Leo followed the arrow's direction with his eyes. Left eleven o'clock, and Tom had said he was about six miles from the target.

C'mon . . . he tried to will the other fighter to stay in the air. Just a few more miles. If they could limp across the Mai Chau valley then their odds increased dramatically.

"It's getting worse." Tom Madison's voice sounded hollow.

Straining to catch sight of the F-105, he caught a glimpse of the river valley. Past that it was only fifty miles to the Laotian border, barely six minutes of flying time under normal conditions. Every yard they made south and west meant a better chance of getting picked up. *C'mon* . . .

"BEE EAR BEE EAR BEE EAR."

Oh shit.

An emergency beacon had activated from someone's parachute. Leo swallowed hard, mouth dry and his stomach tight; Kingfish Two, Major Tom Madison and Major Tom Sterling, had ejected. Pulling the nose up, he angled off a little left of where he'd been pointing. Until he could see the chutes he didn't want to blast overhead.

"BEE EAR BEE EAR BEE EAR."

A second beacon . . . they were both out.

"Fuck it." Harry Johnson began to swear softly, earnestly, and with total fluency.

As his eyes swept over the impossibly thick green trees below, Leo's mind registered that something was not quite right. There! He focused and saw it again: bright, unnatural white against green. Parachutes.

"Got 'em, Harry. Left eleven, low . . . about two miles."

"Right. I got the co-ords . . . about twenty fifty-two north, and one-oh-five twenty-four east."

Leo nodded and was about to key the mike when in the corner of his left eye he saw something move. Glancing away from the drifting chutes, he looked southwest. For a long half second his brain was shocked; then he knew what he was seeing.

A MiG.

"MiG! Ten o'clock high."

Unmistakable.

Swept wings, blunt nose, a shark fin for a tail, and it was bright silver in the afternoon sunlight. *Where in the hell had it come from?* His eyes widened as he realized it was dropping like a vulture and pointed straight at the drifting parachutes. Instantly shoving the throttle forward, Leo Thorsness slapped the stick against his left knee and pulled.

"Harry . . . keep your eyes peeled, I'm setting up the MiG!"

He'd intended to just barrel roll into position behind it, but the ugly little fighter had lost altitude and angled into him—which solved most of the geometrical problems. Leo reversed, snapped back to the right, plugged in the burner, and followed the Soviet-built MiG down. It was less than a mile away, but he had to get the thing before it strafed Madison and Sterling. *Little bastard* . . . Hot anger lanced through him. Killing a man in a fair fight was one thing, but this was sheer cowardice.

Without taking his eyes off the other fighter, he reached up to the WPN SEL knob and clicked it twice to the right, selecting air-to-air GUNS. The gray jet banked up slightly to the right, lining up on the lower parachute, and Leo saw rounded wingtips with a high tail—a MiG-17. It carried a 37 mm and two 23 mm cannons in the nose; maybe Atoll heat-seeking missiles, too.* NATO called it a Fresco and the jet could outclimb and out-turn the Thud if it got the chance.

A faint smile ghosted across Leo's face—this one had no chance at all.

Fast. *Too fast!* At 2,000 feet the pilot yanked the throttle back, pulled the orange gun reticle above the MiG's canopy, and opened fire at 1,500 feet.

"BRRRRPPP."

One thousand feet and still closing!

Leo released the trigger, tugged the throttle to idle, and watched the line of 20 mm shells pass above the enemy fighter. Instantly fanning the speed brakes, he twitched the stick sideways, sliding below the MiG and to its left. Intent on killing helpless Americans, the North Vietnamese pilot never saw the tracers.

As Leo bumped the Thud's nose up slightly, everything

---

*This particular MiG-17F came from the 921st Fighter Regiment's "Red Star" squadron, based at Noi Bai, northwest of Hanoi and only twenty-five miles away from Kingfish.

seemingly froze for a microsecond; white parachutes spotting the mottled green background, the silver fighter against the blue sky with the orange reticle balanced on its wing. As the orange "death dot" led the cigar shaped fuselage, Leo fired again.

"BRRRRRRRPPPPPPPP."

The longer burst at 700 feet did it and shredded the MiG's wing. Shoving the throttle forward as he retracted the speed brakes, Leo pulled up and away from the spinning debris. *A kill!* Exhilaration shot through him as the enemy jet spun toward the trees, just like a bird with a broken wing.

He was starting to grin when Harry shouted, "Leo, we got MiGs on our ass!"

His elation vanished. Twisting frantically in the seat, Leo stared to the left and a MiG's belly less than a thousand feet back.

We're dead meat.

Instinct took over and the pilot flipped the Thud right, slammed the stick forward, and shoved the throttle into burner. The MiG fired, but Leo's reaction saved them and the shells passed high to the left. Green trees filled his windscreen, and he pulled up.

"Can't see him anymore!" Harry managed to gasp out against the g-forces and wild flips.

Deep inside North Vietnam, skimming the trees at 800 mph, the pilot's heart pounded. Streaking out of the foothills, the Weasels flashed across the Black River and headed for the high terrain to the southwest. Leo risked a few left and right banks to clear his six o'clock, but neither he nor Harry could see any MiGs.

"Fuel."

Leo nodded; he'd seen the lights. "I know . . . coming left, hang on."

Banking up to the southwest, he pulled back gently on the stick and the Thud rocketed upward away from the hills. The deep cut of a river valley suddenly appeared off the left wing, stretching north behind his tail. To the right lay the wide, flat trench of the Son La valley and up ahead, Laos. Passing 10,000 feet, he shallowed the climb to hold 450 knots, then leveled off seconds later at 15,000 feet. Pulling the power back to save fuel, Leo turned the IFF back on and keyed the mike.

"Brigham Control, this is Kingfish Lead."

Like Invert in the south, Brigham was an airborne command-and-control aircraft orbiting over Laos. It kept track of all flights into the northern Route Packs, passed weather or intel updates, and monitored the flow of jets into the tanker tracks.

"Kingfish this is Brigham. Go ahead."

"Brigham . . . Kingfish is a single Weasel, squawking four two six seven . . . flash."

Leo depressed the tiny IDENT button that transmitted his identification code—his "squawk." He also flipped the red cover down over the MASTER ARM switch, checked his gas, engine gauges, and dialed up the TACAN in northern Laos. His bearing pointer immediately swung to the left about 10 degrees and the little DME window read 91 miles to Channel 85.* Leo nudged the fighter more to the southwest, and far to the south the C-130 picked up a sudden bright blip with a 4267 code next to it.

"Kingfish . . . Brigham is contact. Come left heading two four five direct Lima Sierra Eight Five, climb and maintain flight level one-eight-zero. Say intentions?"

---

*DME—distance measuring equipment. A TACAN provides both bearing *to* the selected station and distance *from* it.

"Brigham . . . stand by to copy." Leo paused, slowly adding power and beginning a gentle climb, one eye on his dwindling fuel. "Kingfish Two, an F-105F with two crew is down at twenty fifty-two north latitude and one-oh-five twenty-four east longitude."

"Roger that Kingfish lead, copy; Kingfish Two is down. Did you see parachutes?"

He leveled off again at 18,000 feet, set the altimeter, and pulled the power back to hold 350 knots.

"Affirmative, and two good beepers." He swallowed and stared off the left wing back at North Vietnam. "Advise any rescue aircraft there are a bunch of MiGs around, and the location is in SAM range."

"Brigham copies all. Say intentions?"

Leo had been thinking about that. The sixteen Thuds attacking Xuan Mai had come and gone. So had Kingfish Three and his malfunctioning wingman, meaning he and Harry were alone with only a few seconds worth of 20 mm shells, no bombs, and no Shrike. But he was a fighter pilot; he was supposed to wade in and kill things. Besides, those were his buddies down there.

Someday it might be me.

"Brigham . . . Kingfish lead requests a snap to the closest tanker and a clear boom. We'll refuel and head back in to cover the rescue."

There was a long pause, and he was about to repeat it when a new voice came over the air. "Brigham copies all. Red Anchor bears two-zero-zero degrees for eighty-one miles. Come up air-to-air Nineteen Yankee."

Leo brought the Thud around heading 200 degrees and switched to 19Y on the TACAN, which could also be used between aircraft. A red flag appeared and the bearing pointer lazily began spinning around the dial. Too far away, but with a tanker willing to take him they could go much, much faster. He pushed the throttle up and the powerful 105 surged ahead. At 480 knots, he'd get to the tanker in about ten minutes with enough gas to refuel. Another ten minutes to refuel, then about twenty minutes back to the Black River. Add five minutes for slop and he'd be back over the two Toms in forty-five minutes.

Hang on, guys.

"Brigham, Kingfish lead . . . keep working on anyone you can divert to the area. I'll be off the tanker in"—he glanced at his watch—" 'bout twenty minutes. Have the tanker come to the north end of the track."

"Brigham copies. Sandy Four One is inbound with Jolly Green Six Nine. Both are up this freq."

Outstanding, Leo thought, and glanced at his map. *This might work.*

The Sandys were A-1E Skyraiders, and, like the Jollys, they had detachments scattered all over Southeast Asia. He'd heard a squadron had just moved to Udorn a few weeks ago, part of the 56th Air Commando Wing, and he hoped the helo was at Nakhon Phanom or else it would be dark by the time it got so far north. "Shit hot." Harry thumped the canopy. "We gotta little help anyway."

Maybe. A Skyraider, also called a Spad, was a piston-engined retread that had served the Navy and Marines extremely well during the Korean War. Made by Douglas, they were heavy, tough, well armed, and slow. Excellent for close air support or combat rescue down south, they stood almost no chance against MiGs or SAMs in the North.

"How fast is a Spad?"

"Oh, about two fifty, I think. Maybe three hundred knots on a good day," Harry replied.

Leo glanced at the map again. Udorn to Kingfish Two's position was about 350 miles, though from Naked Fanny it was shorter, maybe 275 miles. Either way it would still take a Jolly HH-3 nearly two hours to get up near the Black River. His eyes flickered around the cockpit again. Everything was good, except for the fuel, and they were about halfway to the tanker track.

"Brigham . . . Kingfish lead . . . have the tanker hold at the north end of the track. We're five out."

"Brigham copies all."

Leo continued. "Sandy Four One . . . Kingfish lead."

"Go ahead." The voice was calm and deep.

"Sandy . . . be on your toes as you near the bailout area . . . there are MiGs in the area, and it's in SAM range."

"Kingfish . . . we copy that. Beeper plots to north twenty forty-one, east one-oh-five thirty-two. Bit farther north than we've ever gone."

Leo could see the tanker now. Beautiful, big silver wings just above the horizon in a wide left turn. The air-to-air TACAN read twenty-seven miles, and he stayed pointed at the north end, knowing the KC-135 would just make a big circle.

"Roger that." He had to help this guy. "SAM radars aren't much good against low, slow targets, so if you see a smoke trail, put it off one wing and take yourself down to the treetops. If you're looking at one when the smoke goes away, count to four, then pull hard toward the last place you saw it."

"Sandy copies. So I'm a Weasel now?"

Despite the situation, Leo laughed. The Sandy driver had big enough balls to go into North Vietnam and make jokes. But the threat was no laughing matter, as he and Harry knew well. The Spad driver knew it also. Opening the Thud's air refueling door to depressurize his tanks, he switched on his white anti-collision beacon so the tanker could see him.

"You bet. Heads-up for MiGs. I got one but there're probably at least three left. Maybe waiting for SAR."

The radio clicked.

"Stay low," Leo went on. "Heat from the trees and the ground will spoil their missile shots. If one gets behind you for a gunshot, pull the power and break hard into him. They go too fast to turn with you."

The radio clicked again.

"Sandy . . . Kingfish will refuel and should be back overhead in thirty minutes."

"Sandy Four One copies all. We'll be feet dry in five mikes . . . overhead the bailout area in twenty."

Leo Thorsness nodded, admiring the other pilot's matter-of-fact attitude, and clicked the mike. That would put the two Skyraiders over hostile territory alone and without protection for about ten minutes.

"Those guys are hangin' it out, aren't they?"

"Yep." He played the stick and throttle, sweeping in on the tanker from the northeast as it turned. Switching to the air refueling frequency, Leo asked the 135 pilot to stay as far north as possible, and the man cheerfully acknowledged. He'd been listening to the whole discussion and knew what was at stake.

Thirteen minutes later Leo disconnected from the boom with a puff of vaporized residual fuel. Cracking the throttle back, he slid aft and down, changing radio freqs on the way. The pilot held the Thud motionless in space, staring up at the tanker's shiny belly.

"Harry . . . if we go back we go it alone."

"Yeah. But you heard Brigham . . . Packard and the other strikers already RTB'd. Looks like we're it."

"Bad odds."

"Worse for the Toms."

Leo Thorsness took a last look at the big tanker as it began a turn to the safety of the south, and without another word he banked up hard, passed under the KC-135, and headed north, back toward Route Pack Six. Mountains rippled away in all directions, their western slopes splattered with shades of light green in the afternoon sun. The eastern slopes, and all the valleys, were already darkening. A childhood memory stirred, something about not fearing the Valley of the Shadow of Death, and Leo felt a knot tighten in his stomach.

"I've got the last known location . . . bearing zero-two-five for a hundred thirty-five miles." Both men had written the coordinates down and Harry had punched them into the computer while they'd refueled.

"Same. Looks like some thin clouds up near the border. Let's stay above it and see what we can see." He added power and eased the Thud into a climb.

"You mean, be bait."

That was exactly what he had in mind. "Right. If we can attract the attention of whatever is still up there, maybe they'll leave the Sandys alone and the chopper can get in."

"Makes sense to me." Harry sounded utterly unperturbed, like they were dropping bombs on a practice mission at Nellis. Whether the EWO really felt that way or not, Leo appreciated the man's calm courage.

Leveling at 20,000 feet, he set the throttle to hold 540 knots and centered the bearing pointer on 025 degrees. At this speed they'd be overhead the Toms in fifteen minutes, about the same time as the Spads. He hoped so, for their sake. One combat loss today was more than enough. *How,* he asked himself again, *had it happened?* Should they have stayed in the covering hills longer or come in from a different heading after firing the Shrike? Had the smoke from that thing given them away? Leo sighed heavily and tried not to think of it—there'd be time enough for that back at Takhli. The thing now was to get the Toms back. But what if they couldn't? What if they were already captured . . . or worse. And what would he write to their wives?

Eight minutes later they crossed the Laotian border into North Vietnam. His hands moved around the cockpit, flipping up the red guard and arming his gun. Checking that his exterior lights were all off, Leo turned up the volume on the APR-25, then adjusted the orange reticle intensity. With the Barthelemy Pass off the left wing, he caught the blue sheen from the Gulf of Tonkin off to his right. Jagged, dark green peaks loomed ahead, and just beyond lay the Mai Chau valley with Kingfish Two. Hopefully.

Switching to GUARD, he took a deep breath. "Kingfish Two . . . Lead here. Do you read?"

Nothing. He swallowed and tried again.

"SAM acquisition radar has us, Leo," Harry said quietly. "Still at a safe range."

"Roger that."

The EB-66 suddenly broke in over GUARD with "Harpoon has MiGs active . . . SAMs active."

Nothing unexpected there. "Hopin' they'd be gone by now," the EWO muttered, and the pilot shook his head. "Only if our luck changed."

Crossing the Mai Chau valley, Leo raised his dark visor and stared down through the thin gray cloud. The wider, northern end opened up to relatively flat farmland that bordered the Black River. Unfortunately, there was a good-size town about twelve miles away with decent roads leading southeast down the smaller valley where Kingfish Two had gone down. He squinted, picturing the parachutes and MiGs; he'd been coming from the opposite direction but recognized several of the peaks. Right there . . . he could see where the crash site had to be on the western slope.

"Kingfish Two, this is lead . . . please come up."

Static, like grease frying, suddenly filled his headset and Leo blinked. *A voice!* A very faint voice. Could they still be alive and free?

"Hear that?"

"Yeah," Harry answered. "Whaddya think?"

A good question. He hoped it was one of the Toms, but the gomers had long ago figured out how to use captured radios. They liked to slowly close in on downed fliers, then let them roam around free and act as live bait. Once the rescue aircraft arrived overhead, the North Vietnamese would spring the trap and bag as many as they could.

"Dunno . . . I—" Suddenly he saw movement.

Aircraft. His first thought was that the Spads had beaten them to the site. Too fast, he immediately realized. This thing was too high and too . . . shiny.

"MiGs!" Harry shouted at the same time the pilot was opening his mouth. "Leo, MiG . . . eight o'clock!"

"Another at eleven low."

Then he saw the others. Four silvery MiG-17s orbiting over the valley in a big circle that fighter pilots called a wagon wheel.

"The Spads'll never get in with those pricks around."

"Well, let's bag 'em!" Harry was twisting back and forth, looking over both sides of the canopy. Leo simply rolled right into a sliceback, padlocking on the enemy fighter off his right wing. For a moment it was perfect; the late afternoon sunlight struck his shoulders, glinting off the glass gauges, and making the mirrors sparkle. Dust floated up from the floor, and the heat amplified the cockpit smells of hot nylon, jet fuel, sweat, and the faint odor of urine.

But now it was the People's Air Force's turn to be surprised. Looking for rescue aircraft far below, the enemy pilots never saw the vengeful Weasel dropping down through the wispy veil. Pulling the power back to midrange, Leo overbanked and pulled his nose around onto the MiG.

"Ughhhh," Harry grunted. "MiG at five o'clock!"

"And another at two o'clock." The snub-nosed fighters were all turning clockwise along the horizon.

This one dies.

For the second time that day, Thorsness pulled the double orange circles over the jet in front of him, paused, and as the reticle settled between the MiG's T-shaped tail and its nose, he squeezed the trigger.

"BRRRRPPPPPPPPP."

The Thud shuddered as the cannon spat out the last few hundred cannon shells, then abruptly stopped. A blinding flash of yellow exploded beneath the MiG, then pieces of metal flew up and off. As the enemy jet corkscrewed right and down, Leo snapped inverted, shoved the throttle forward, and pulled.

"Ya got 'em! You nailed the bastard!" Harry shouted over the intercom.

The heavy 105 fell like a stone, straight down at the mountains. With wind ripping over the canopy and the sun filling his left eye, Leo felt the controls stiffen with speed and shot a glance at the airspeed indicator. Fast enough. Playing the pullout, he leveled off just above the hilltops, screaming north at 700 knots. Tugging the throttle back, he keyed the mike.

"Sandy, Kingfish Lead."

"Go." The Spad's big radial engine was rumbling in the background.

"Kingfish picked up a garbled transmission in the area . . . might be one of the crew."

"Copy that . . . Sandy's overhead now."

"Heads-up for MiGs. We got one but there's at least three left."

Leo shot a quick look at his engine gauges and fuel, then tipped up on his left wing, so low that individual trees stood out. Going back into burner, he pulled toward the west, aiming at the jagged spine of the hills bordering the valley.

"Kingfish Two . . . this is lead. Come up."

Another voice immediately broke in, high pitched and desperate. "Sandy One is going in!" That had to be the number-two Spad watching his leader go down.

Leo swore and bumped the Weasel up so he could see over the hills.

"Sandy One is going in! MiGs got 'em."

Keying the mike, Leo called, "Sandy Two get on the treetops! Get as low, slow as you can." The Thud crested the hills and the valley yawned open. "Turn as hard as you can and the MiGs can't get you."

"Copy . . . I'll try."

The Spad flew at 300 knots . . . maybe 350, and had little chance in a dogfight, but if he and Harry could distract the MiGs then the rescue plane might get away. Cranking up again on his left wing, Kingfish One popped over the slopes and roared into the little valley like an avenging angel.

"MiG . . . one o'clock."

"Another one at nine o'clock," Harry added. "We're empty, ya know."

Leo went back to burner and pulled hard right, watching the swept-wing fighter turn against the mountains. "He doesn't know that."

Good point. Johnson strained hard to keep the other one in sight. But there had to be more of them . . . *where?*

The MiGs had seen them. The closest one racked up in a hard turn, vapor streaming from its wingtips, to meet the insane American who was attacking them alone. As the snub nose came around in his direction, Leo bunted forward, then rolled up hard to the left toward the other MiG.

"Third one . . . uhhh . . . seven o'clock . . . comin' around!"

The fighter to the left of the nose suddenly overbanked and pulled hard into the Thud. The one on the other side was just off the right wing, trying to bring his nose to bear. All of the MiGs seemed to have forgotten the Spad and were trying to kill the Weasel.

His fuel lights were flashing and both men were breathing heavily. *Good enough.* Reefing back on the stick, Leo got enough altitude to make the MiGs flinch, then rolled inverted. As he pulled through, a solitary black pillar of smoke off in the trees caught his eye. *Sandy One.* He'd think about that brave man later.*

A narrow pass on the west side of the valley filled the windscreen, and he dropped down, heading for it at 600 knots. "Watch 'em, Harry!"

"They're turning . . . ah, but not at us. They're all . . . ah . . . all back up over the hills to the east."

Leo took the Thud up the pass, aiming just above the hard green ridgeline at the darkening sky beyond. Thundering over the rocky humps with the Mai Chau valley spread out before them, Leo yanked the throttle out of burner and turned southeast.

"Switching to the tanker freq . . . keep checkin' six."

Fuel was critical now; both men tried not to look at the gauge and ignored the glowing warning light.

---

*Major John S. Hamilton flying A1-E No. 52-133905; from the 602nd Air Commando Squadron out of Udorn. He was declared MIA until March 1979; his remains were returned to Fort Bayard, New Mexico, in October 1997.

Leo made one more call on GUARD, hoping against all hope. "Kingfish Two . . . this is lead. Come up."

Silence.

He took a deep breath, licked his dry lips, and called Brigham.

"Ask the tanker to come north," he repeated. "We're emergency fuel right now."

Zooming past 15,000 feet, he called up the nav point for the tanker track and gently banked up to the southwest. One hundred thirty-three miles to the Red air refueling track and twenty-eight miles to the Laotian border. Leo bunted over to catch 20,000 feet, then pulled the power back to hold 375 knots. Staring out ahead, he saw the sun had been swallowed by a wall of black clouds. Sudden orange flashes lit up the sky far off to the south, and he shook his head.

Thunderstorms. *Perfect.*

Unclipping his sweaty mask, the pilot heard Brigham talking with Sandy Two and was grateful, at least, that he'd gotten away. But the chopper had been turned around and the rescue canceled. The Toms were screwed, and a bitter lump settled in his gut. He pulled a plastic canteen from his g-suit ankle pocket and took a long swig of the warm water.

"We gonna make it?" Harry finally asked, rather subdued. Both men felt the guilt settle over them, like a wet, heavy blanket. It was the risk of combat; everyone who did this knew that. There was nothing that could have been done differently, but the responsibility was still his. Crushing. Permanent.

"We'll make it." It would be tight, but they could fill up with fuel and then deal with the thunderstorms. Seemed a minor problem after everything else that had happened today. He switched to the tanker freq and squeezed his tired eyes shut for a moment. Keying the mike, he called, "Red Anchor, Red Anchor . . . Kingfish One."

"Go ahead, Kingfish . . . happy to hear from you again."

Me, too, Leo thought. "Kingfish is single ship, one hundred fifteen miles northeast of Red, inbound."

"Copy, King—"

Another voice suddenly came over, quiet but very, very tense. "Leo . . . Panda Four here."

Leo? Thorsness was shocked. No one *ever* used real names in the clear over the radio. ". . . got six hundred pounds, am lost . . . can you help?"

Panda was a Takhli call sign, and this guy clearly knew him. What in the hell was he doing up here? Six hundred pounds? That was fumes. That was actually the fumes of fumes. Whoever it was had less than ten minutes of flying time before he flamed out.

"Panda Four . . . count."

Leo moved the radio switch to ADF as the other pilot counted down from five, then back up. The bearing pointer swung around to the east northeast, behind him, and the distance read forty-seven miles. Too far apart to rejoin, and the other Thud was in enemy territory. The tanker could get to one or the other but not both. Panda Four was a young wingman, lost and alone over North Vietnam and running out of fuel.

Easy choice.

"Red Anchor One . . . you have about six minutes to rendezvous with Panda Four, or he ejects. You gotta come farther north."

Some of the tanker guys were Strategic Air Command pricks who would never deviate from their assigned mission. Others were not. He hoped they'd gotten the right sort tonight.

"Ah, roger that, Kingfish . . . we'll do our best." Leo managed a sigh. *God love the guy.* ". . . and Panda Four, we are transmitting . . . home in on us."

"He's all yours, Panda . . . adios. Thanks Red."

"Put in the coordinates for Udorn," he told Harry. "We'll point that way and at least try to get across the Mekong."

If they could do that, if they could at least get into Thailand, then they'd be safe enough. Ejecting over Laos was better than North Vietnam because it was closer for rescue aircraft, but just as dangerous with the Pathet Lao running around. In any event, no one would come get them at night in either place. Not waiting for a reply, Leo switched back to Brigham, dumped the nose, and went to full MIL power.

"Udorn bears two-zero-zero for three hundred miles," Harry said, and Leo corrected the heading.

"Terrific." Leo blinked to clear his eyes. Shrugging off the physical, emotional, and miserable mental weariness, he forced himself to concentrate. *Thailand,* he told himself. *We've gotta get to Thailand.*

". . . and now for the last act."

"Let's hope not," Harry replied drily. Let's hope *not.*

FEW THINGS OUTSIDE of combat are as disconcerting as being in a fighter jet, at night, with horrible weather, while running out of fuel. Leo Thorsness zoomed the F-105 up to 35,000 feet heading southwest into the lightning and thunder. Just past the Plain of Jars in Laos, he pulled the throttle back to idle and dropped the nose to hold 270 knots—the Thud's best glide speed. It was seventy miles to the Thai border, and if they could glide that far they'd make the Mekong, even with a pitiful few hundred pounds of fuel showing on the gauge.

But for the first time during this seemingly endless day, fate cracked a smile. Leo and Harry made the river, crossed the border, and had nothing to lose by trying to glide the rest of the way into Udorn. Everyone on the air base knew the situation; those who could stood outside watching the dark sky to the north. When the battle-scarred F-105F loomed out of the blackness, with lightning flashing all around, cheers floated up along the flight line.*

Coasting in for a long approach on Udorn's runway 12, Kingfish One finally crossed the threshold, and that beautiful 10,000-foot strip rose up to meet them. Rolling out and slowing, lights flashing by on either side, the big Pratt & Whitney J-75 engine flamed out at last, utterly starved of fuel. Lurching to a stop, the two men sat and watched as the emergency response trucks and their flashing lights careened toward them. Despite the dead engine, the pilot moved the throttle to OFF out of habit; he turned the generator and inverter off, then raised the canopy. Leo unclipped his mask; as it dangled against his chin and the wet, heavy air brushed his face, he leaned back and closed his eyes.

"Well," Harry Johnson managed to say. "That was a full day's work."

Indeed it was.

Leo Thorsness and Harry Johnson were numb in every sense of the word. They had no idea that Brigham finally diverted Panda flight into the Mai Chau valley, and that the last three MiGs had been shot down.† Nor did Jerry Hoblit and Bear Wilson, Kingfish Three, know what had happened to Kingfish One and Two until they were back on the ground at Takhli. In addition to everything else, one SA-2 site had been destroyed by cluster bombs, and no strikers were lost during the Xuan Mai

---

*F-105F No. 63-8301.
†Jack Hunt, Fred Tolman, and William Eskew of the 354th TFS (Fighting Bulldogs) were each credited with a MiG. Leo Thorsness and Harry Johnson were officially credited with one MiG-17 destroyed and one probable because Leo's KA-71 gun camera ran out of film. It was certainly another kill.

attack. A deputy political commissar for North Vietnam's Air Defense Command wrote in his memoirs:

> *The battle becomes more savage day by day and the enemy has begun to attack our missile positions on a regular basis. As soon as we fire a missile, enemy aircraft swarm in and destroy our firing positions. Could it be that our people are afraid to fight?*

Maybe.

But afraid to fight or not, the North Vietnamese definitely knew the Weasels and feared them. They knew that if they turned on their Fansong or Firecan radars, the Weasels would hunt them down and kill them. It was also obvious that in the spring of 1967, Hanoi did not rule the sky over their own country—the Americans did, and would continue to do so despite the MiGs and SAMs.

CHAPTER 8

YEAR OF THE MONKEY

CHRISTMAS 1967 WAS a grim one for the Weasels in Southeast Asia. Eleven F-105Fs had gone down in action—more than *50 percent* of the available jets—and sixteen priceless men were killed or captured. Only six of the twenty-two lost fliers were recovered. Major Larry Biediger and First Lieutenant Claude Silva had been killed over Thud Ridge northwest of Hanoi, and Major John Dudash died when his Thud, No. 63-8277, exploded after a direct hit from an SA-2. He'd evaded the first two missiles fired, but the last one got the Weasel. In November 1967, Captain Earl Cobeil ejected from F-105F 62-4430 over the Red River after being hit by multiple 57 mm shells. He was captured, tortured, and beaten so badly by Cuban and Vietnamese guards that he died in captivity three years later. A week before Thanksgiving, Major Oscar Dardeau and Captain Edward Lehnhoff Jr. were clearing SAMs for a strike on Phuc Yen Air Base in Route Pack Six. Their Thud, *Mugley Other,* was hit by an Atoll air-to-air missile fired from a MiG-21 and disintegrated in flight.

Ten other Weasels were captured and would spend the next

six years as prisoners of war. Captains David Duart and Jay Jensen went down in February 1967, over Route Pack Three near Vinh. Vietnam's first steel mill was located on the Cau River near Thai Nguyen and, as it was vital to Hanoi's fragile economy, the factory was heavily protected.* The first U.S. strike against the mill was sent in on March 10, with Majors David Everson and Captain Jose Luna leading the Weasels. Hit by 85 mm anti-aircraft fire, they ejected, and both men survived a long captivity to return home in 1973.†

April 1967 was a deadly month for the Weasels, beginning with Majors Tom Madison and Tom Sterling, who went down near the Black River on April 19.‡ Captain Alton Meyer, ejecting on April 26 with Major John Dudash, was captured and imprisoned. On the last day of the month, a stray MiG claimed F-105F No. 62-4447 and Leo Thorsness and Harry Johnson ran out of luck. The day had started well enough; 0430 wake-up with a morning mission protecting a strike package in North Vietnam. All twenty-four jets arrived back safely and the two Weasels crossed off their ninety-first mission—only eight more to go and they'd be headed home.

Missions into the North normally took about four hours; that didn't include briefing, debriefing, ground operations, and all the other details of a combat sortie. Because of this, and the time needed to plan the next day's package, crews flying out of Thailand rarely, if ever, flew more than one mission per day. Unfortunately, on April 30, 1967, one of the Weasel crews on

---

*The first Medal of Honor for a Wild Weasel was awarded to Captain Merlyn Hans Dethlefsen for his role in this flight. His EWO, Captain Mike Gilroy, was awarded the Air Force Cross.

†March 10 was also the day President Johnson publicly admitted to basing U.S. aircraft in Thailand—three years after the fact.

‡Madison's flight lead was Major Leo Thorsness, who would become the second, and last, Wild Weasel to date to earn the Medal of Honor. See page 178.

the afternoon sortie aborted for a maintenance issue. Leo and Harry were the only crew available so they launched as "Carbine Three" and headed back into North Vietnam.

On the surface it didn't appear too bad; the target area was about fifty miles west of Hanoi and away from most of the SAMs and guns—but not the MiGs. A pair of MiG-17s were hiding in the valley just east of Muong Do peak, waiting for the Americans. When Carbine Three roared overhead at 600 knots, the North Vietnamese pilots, cued by their GCI controllers, simply pulled their noses up and fired. The clear sky was an ideal background for the AA-2 Atoll infrared missiles and the big, all-metal F-105s offered a perfect hot target. Leo Thorsness would later write: "[I]t felt like we'd been smacked by a massive sledgehammer. The stick and rudder pedals immediately went limp; the cockpit filled with heavy black smoke."

Damaged Thuds had a nasty habit of exploding and others had died trying to slow down enough for a safe ejection. Harry Johnson knew that if the pilot bailed out first, the blast from his seat would likely fry the EWO. Even though the maximum speed for ejection was 525 knots and they were well over 600 knots when the missile hit, Harry pulled the handle and Leo went a split second later. Floating down into the Yen Bai province as the North Vietnamese shot at him, Leo could only think of his wife, Gaylee, and daughter, Dawn. With two destroyed knees he was unable to evade and was captured quickly. Harry Johnson had also been captured. Both men would suffer though nearly six years of the Hanoi Hilton before returning to the United States in 1973.

On May 15, Takhli's run of bad luck temporarily transferred to Korat's 388 TFW with the loss of Captain Donald Lester Heiliger and Major Ben Pollard over Kep. Four months later, also over Kep, Captains Joe Howard and George Shamblee were hit by an Atoll air-to-air missile. Howard managed to nurse the damaged Weasel out over the Gulf of Tonkin north of Da Nang, where he and his Bear ejected. Both men were picked up by rescue helicopters. Early the next month, on November 5, Major Dick Dutton bailed out with Captain Earl Cobeil.

Two weeks later, on November 19, Major Gerald Gustafson and Captain Russell Brownlee were hit by a SAM over Hanoi. Luckily, they cleared the target and limped back across the border into Laos. Though wounded, Major Bruce Stocks flew cover until the two were picked up by an Air America helicopter.* Others who were lucky enough to be recovered were Major Mike Muscat and Captain Kyle Stouder from the Korat's 44th Tactical Fighter Squadron (Vampires).

AS CHRISTMAS APPROACHED there were other causes for concern—seventy thousand of them. All through the fall of 1967 into early 1968, the People's Army and Viet Cong had massed along the DMZ and infiltrated into South Vietnam. Following the American offenses in early 1967, Hanoi decided that the war had stagnated for too long and it was time for a major assault of their own. Both China and the Soviet Union were losing enthusiasm for the fight; without their continued support, there could be no fight. Relations between Moscow and Beijing, always tense, were becoming worse. Eventually Hanoi would have to choose a side.

More ominous for the NVA, relations between Washington and both communist powers were thawing. The Soviet Union desperately required American grain, and Red China needed an economic injection brought about through trade and international acceptance. Both Moscow and Beijing now needed the

---

*CIA operating out of Laos.

United States more than they did the Democratic Republic of Vietnam. Hanoi knew this, so a victory in the field was critical. It would either cause the Americans a military and political defeat, or give Hanoi a strong negotiating position. Or both.

There were also factions within the Lao Dong, the Vietnamese Worker's Party. Military officers and party officials were typically aligned with the pro-Soviet bloc; they favored big-unit, conventional warfare. General Van Tien Dung, the People's Army chief of staff, supported this strategy as it enhanced his power. Opposing him was Vo Nguyen Giap, the defense minister and senior field commander. Cognizant of American military might, Giap believed a protracted guerrilla war with Chinese support was the best path to victory. Ho Chi Minh was seventy-eight years old and ailing, so the problem of succession added to the overall friction. His prime minister and most likely successor, Pham Van Dong, was even advocating negotiations with the Americans.

If Washington had turned the military loose in 1967 with clear-cut goals and limited restrictions, it is very possible the war would have ended. But that never happened, and 1967 became the conflict's bloodiest year, with more than 650 combat aircraft lost and 19 percent of the war's casualties sustained. Keenly aware of the domestic turmoil in the United States, and the upcoming 1968 presidential electi   Hanoi's leaders felt the situation could swing either way. If Lyndon Johnson won reelection and the war continued, then antiwar pressure would mount, eventually forcing a withdrawal of U.S. forces. On the other hand, if a new administration won the election then the full weight of American military power might be unleashed to end the war. If that occurred, and China or Soviet intervention did not occur, then the DRV would lose the war. Hanoi reasoned that a stunning victory in early 1968 might win the war outright, or at least force the current administration to negotiate.

Either way, it was time to act.

In the aftermath of Operations Cedar Rapids and Junction City, Hanoi had begun planning in earnest. By midsummer of 1967 the details had been worked out and movement to the forward areas initiated. Signs of the People's Army intentions were not lost on those Americans closest to the action. From October 1967 through January 1968, more than 20,000 soldiers were estimated to have moved south down the Ho Chi Minh Trail. Base camps were stockpiled with ammunition, weapons, and medicine of all types. This by itself was enough to make the Special Forces and Marine patrols around the DMZ wary. Aware of its own logistical shortcomings, NVA and NLF forces prepositioned supplies in advance of an attack, rather than using the American method of continuous resupply.

Though the summer had been relatively quiet as the People's Army moved south, there were ongoing probing attacks against U.S. outposts near the DMZ—shortly to be given the grim nickname "Dead Marine Zone." Four bases in particular—Gio Linh, Dong Ha, Cam Lo, and Con Thien—bore the brunt of NVA assaults. Called "Leatherneck Square," these were key concentrations of American combat troops standing in the way of any real enemy thrust into the south. Nevertheless, NVA units, including the 324B Division, had been digging in between the Marines and the DMZ for more than a year.*

At the northwest tip of the square, barely two miles from the DMZ, the Marine firebase at Nui Con Thien was hard hit beginning in May 1967.† At 0400 on the morning of May 8, two battalions of the 812th Regiment from the 324B Division

---

*The "B" suffix denotes a North Vietnamese unit. *Bac*—from the North.
†Con Thien roughly translates as the "place of angels."

attacked. Ferociously defended by the 1st Battalion/4th Marines, the "Hill of Angels" held at the cost of 44 dead and 110 wounded. Two months later Operation Buffalo was launched to clear the enemy from the immediate area north of Leatherneck Square. Eventually elements of four Marine battalions, a recon detachment, and two artillery companies engaged the 90th Regiment of the 324B Division. By the time fighting ended on July 14, 1967, at least 1,300 North Vietnamese were dead and several hundred wounded. Marine casualties stood at 159 dead and 345 wounded, including several platoon leaders and a company commander.*

But now it was the North Vietnamese Army's turn to miscalculate. There was often a perception among NVA and NLF soldiers that Americans were pampered, spoiled, and overly dependent upon technology. The hill battles with their associated operations should have been a red flag to Hanoi—a stark warning that although electronic sensors, gunships, close air support, and artillery were tremendous advantages, the Americans didn't necessarily need them to win. U.S. fighting men were perfectly capable of close-in, hand-to-hand combat and proved it many times over.

Con Thien was again attacked in force in September, with much the same result. More than three thousand rounds of 82–122 mm mortars, Katyusha rockets, and heavy artillery turned the miserable little hill into a bloody mud pile, and still the Marines refused to budge. Farther south, in the Central Highlands, Loc Ninh was hit on October 27 by the 273rd NLF Regiment. Near an active rubber plantation, it was home to an ARVN regional headquarters and, unfortunately for the attack-

---

*Captain Sterling K. Coates, commanding officer, B Company, 1st Battalion, 9th Marines.

ers, a Special Forces A-Team.* Unable to overrun the Americans, two days later the NLF 272nd Regiment was thrown into the grinder and cut to pieces. By November 2, the North Vietnamese entered the fray with the 141st and 165th Regiments. The Americans countered by unleashing a four-thousand-round artillery barrage and eight B-52 Arc Light strikes that vaporized most of the attackers.

Dak To, also in the Highlands, was assaulted during the same time and a running series of bloody battles was fought among the hills in the area. Failing to defeat the U.S. 173rd Airborne Brigade and elements of the 4th Infantry Division, NVA and Cong units melted back into the Cambodian and Laotian hills. But the cost was high; the 173rd Airborne suffered nearly 30 percent casualties and 376 Americans from all units were killed in action; 150,000 artillery shells had been expended in conjunction with 2,096 tactical close air support missions, and an additional 2,000 Army helicopter sorties. Nearly 1,500 enemy casualties were claimed, but the actual number was likely smaller as only 94 crew served weapons, and fewer than 300 individual weapons were recovered. In any event, the Americans held. From the safety of the National Press Club in Washington, General Westmoreland declared, "I think it's the beginning of a great defeat for the enemy."

If so, it certainly wasn't apparent to Hanoi or U.S. troops on the ground. Far off to the northwest the Marine combat base at Khe Sanh formed the left anchor point of the McNamara Line. Just below the DMZ it was the jumping-off point for Long-Range Patrols deep inside Indian Country. Unlike their French predecessors, the Marine officers knew the terrain and knew their enemy. Colonel David Lownds, commander of the 26th

---

*A-331 of the 5th Special Forces Group.

Marines, had first seen combat as a young platoon leader in the Pacific during World War II. Fighting on Kwajalein, Saipan, and Iwo Jima, he'd been wounded twice. Recalled to fight in Korea, Colonel Lownds had stayed in the military and had assumed command at Khe Sanh in August 1967. Tough, realistic, and a skilled combat leader, he had no intention of letting his base become an American Dien Bien Phu.

True, they were both in low places surrounded by hills but at Khe Sanh the Marines controlled the hills. This meant the base was a bit safer from bombardment, and that enemy anti-aircraft guns could not control the airstrip. Both garrisons were defended by relatively small numbers of men and were solely dependent upon airlifts for survival. Both were also strategically important: Dien Bien Phu had threatened the opium route into Laos while Khe Sanh, barely twenty-three miles from Tchepone, directly threatened the Ho Chi Minh Trail. But while Dien Bien Phu had been 150 miles from Hanoi and difficult to resupply, Khe Sanh was only twenty-five miles from its support base near Quang Tri city.

Also, though Colonel Lownds only had about 6,700 men, half the French force, he was defending an area nearly one-seventh the size. Airlift, absolutely essential to both, was equally imbalanced. The French garrison had required nearly 150 tons per day and, at best, averaged 100 tons with barely a three-day supply of ammunition. The Marines needed 65–150 tons per day, depending on their varying numbers and ongoing reinforcement. USAF transports and Marine helicopters together would manage 260 tons per day during the seventy-seven-day siege of Khe Sanh, and the base maintained a thirty-day supply of ammunition. But the biggest difference was the men themselves. Though individual French soldiers, especially the paratroopers and Legionnaires, fought bravely, they were not U.S. Marines or Special Forces. Their senior leadership was arrogant, made foolish tactical choices, and failed their men.*

Colonel Lownds, on the other hand, disliked static, defensive warfare and preferred to attack the enemy whenever possible. Lownds also correctly sited his artillery and had the inestimable advantage of effective tactical air support. In the end, it was a mismatched situation; the NVA units were somewhat under strength, and not experienced or equipped for protracted siege warfare, while the Americans were grossly outnumbered, but heavily armed and extremely aggressive fighters.

So on January 2, 1968, when pale wet faces appeared across the wire along Khe Sanh's perimeter, the Marines immediately opened fire and killed the intruders. It was discovered the following morning that the enemy scouts were all wearing American battle dress. Other signs appeared that could not be ignored. Captain Robert Simmons, a young intelligence officer with Major General Frederick Weyand's II Field Force, noticed that the known NLF post office boxes for the Saigon region had been changed.† Drawn out on a map, it was plain to see that the command areas had been reorganized and were centered on the South Vietnamese capital. Funerals in the city also increased, though it wasn't discovered till later that the coffins had been used to smuggle in weapons. Weyand used the recent events to add twenty-seven U.S. battalions to those already in the Saigon area and added another battalion to Khe Sanh's defenses. Westmoreland had always believed the attack would be directed at the Marine base and was only too happy to send reinforcements north.

---

*Consider French colonel Charles Piroth, who committed suicide rather than stand by his soldiers. See Appendix C.
†Rob Simmons later went on to the CIA as an operations officer, then became a Connecticut state representative in 1990. Elected to the U.S. House of Representatives, he served from 2001 to 2007.

Knowing Washington would avoid a repeat of the French disaster at Dien Bien Phu, Giap calculated that Khe Sanh would make an ideal red herring, a distraction from the real assault during the Tet Offensive. That attacks against the combat base began here ten days prior to the main holiday offensive bears this out. Hanoi hoped the Americans viewed Khe Sanh as the offensive's primary objective. If Washington was committed to avoiding a repeat of the French disaster, then the battle would hopefully draw in U.S. and ARVN forces from the entire area. This would weaken defenses elsewhere so when the Tet assault actually occurred there would be fewer American forces available to deal with it.

This was the gamble and the key to Hanoi's audacious plan. The main goal of the offensive was to spark a country-wide, full-scale rebellion against Saigon. If this occurred then the Americans, who could not be defeated militarily, would lose by default. Washington's entire pretext for overt action in Southeast Asia was to secure a free and independent Republic of South Vietnam, so if the South didn't want the Yankees, as a revolt would prove, then U.S. forces would have to pull out. In any event, a successful uprising would make the southern military situation untenable.

Though not totally in favor of the offensive, Giap was given his orders and made the best of it. He knew Westmoreland was fixated on the border area and wished to invade Laos. He also knew of CIA operations along the roads, and had witnessed the folly of the McNamara Line. So if the Americans valued the area so much, this could be used against them to draw attention away from the real objective: the rest of South Vietnam. An assault on Khe Sanh would also hopefully require large numbers of U.S. and ARVN reinforcements, concentrating them in a single area while the NVA and Viet Cong struck elsewhere.

Giap had been in command during Dien Bien Phu and knew it was certainly possible to take the firebase. Also, as a political prisoner in 1930, he'd been incarcerated at Lao Bao, less than fifteen miles from Khe Sanh, so he knew the terrain intimately.

If a major victory *was* achieved it would clear his left flank. The fall of Khe Sanh could also lead to control of the entire Quang Tri province and threaten the huge U.S. base at Da Nang. If not, at the very least it would divert attention, cause confusion, and kill many South Vietnamese or American soldiers. It was obvious that the Americans were planning for, and even desiring, a large, set-piece battle along the DMZ, so what better way to deceive them than to give them what they expected?

To support the Khe Sanh garrison, Operation Niagara I had commenced early in January 1968, verifying the NVA buildup in northwestern South Vietnam and Laos. Composed of aerial surveillance, Special Operations Group (SOG) and CIA road watch teams uncovered the 304th, 325C, and 320th divisions, totaling 24,600 men, moving into place. A fourth division, 324B with 9,500 men, would be kept in reserve. The prescient Colonel Lownds stated on January 10 that he expected an attack on Khe Sanh within ten days, and that was precisely what occurred.

Giap's Tet Offensive actually began during the evening of January 20 when NVA artillery trapped a Marine patrol on Hill 869, just southwest of the base. This was followed right after midnight by 300 NVA soldiers of the 4th Battalion, 95th Regiment assaulting on Hill 861 near the airstrip. Ferociously defended by K Company, 3rd Battalion of the 26th Marines, the fighting was close in and often hand-to-hand. The company commander, Captain Norman Jasper, was wounded three times. The executive officer, Lieutenant Jerry Saulsbury, hadn't made it as an aviator, but was a natural combat leader and took over. At the end of the day forty-seven NVA bodies were counted and Hill 861 held, at the cost of four Marines dead and eleven wounded.

As the shaken North Vietnamese withdrew down the hill, the east end of the combat base erupted in a tremendous, ear-splitting explosion. A chance artillery round hit Ammunition Supply Point 1 and more than one thousand tons of shells blew up. Worse, tear gas canisters exploded and the wind blew the noxious cloud down over the base. Despite it all, the perimeter held, though Khe Sanh village fell the next day to the NVA 102nd Regiment. A few days later, as General Westmoreland was announcing a thirty-six-hour cease-fire for the Tet holiday, the 37th ARVN Ranger Battalion arrived and took up positions on the eastern perimeter. The Marines continued to clear away rubble, dig in, and improve their positions as best they could.

Lyndon Johnson, viewing the battle with his own political interests in mind, told the chairman of the Joint Chiefs, General Earle Wheeler, that "I don't want any damn Dinbinphoo." In a sentiment ominously paralleling the French fourteen years before, U.S. military leaders proclaimed that Khe Sanh would not fall, because "it afforded an opportunity to draw large enemy forces to battle, then destroy them with a combination of superior firepower and a counterthrust into Laos."

Air support and tenacity had always been the keys to holding Khe Sanh, so while the Marines, Army Special Forces, and South Vietnamese Rangers provided the latter, Niagara II accomplished the former. A transport fleet of C-123, C-7, Marine KC-130F, and C-130 fixed-wing aircraft began twenty-four hour operations, weather dependent, to keep the combat base supplied. The hill outposts were best serviced directly by helicopter; these included Hueys and the UH-34D Sea Horse for utility operations, Sea Stallions (CH-53A), and Sea Knight

(CH-46A) for heavy cargo. Marine Aircraft Group (MAG) 16 and 36 provided most of the rotary-wing support sorties flown into Khe Sanh. The 1st Marine Air Wing (MAW) averaged approximately 7,000 helicopter sorties per month and 17,900 countrywide during the siege. Of these, 9,109 went into the battlefield to deliver 4,661 tons of cargo.

Fixed wing transport operations brought in most of the bulk supplies, ammunition, and heavy weapons. USAF C-130s premiered a new tactical delivery system during fifty-two of these missions. Called LAPES (Low-Altitude Parachute Extraction System), it worked like this: Nine high-speed pallets, each weighing a ton, were loaded on roller racks across the cargo bay. The 130 would make its approach, flying down the runway barely five feet above the ground. With the cargo door open, a drogue parachute was deployed that yanked the pallet out the back of the aircraft. A braking parachute was automatically released that delivered the pallet to the earth, runway, or landing zone. Precision airdrops were used more frequently and as cargo was released at 400–500 feet, most of it landed within 150 yards of the target. All told, USAF transports accounted for 12,430 tons while Marine KC-130Fs brought in 2,000 more tons.

Even though the hills around Khe Sanh were never captured by the North Vietnamese, the base would have been overwhelmed by sheer numbers without tactical air support. Personnel from the 1st MAW arrived at the base on January 21 to set up a Direct Air Support Coordination (DASC) center for fighter control. Marine A-4 Skyhawks, F-8E Crusaders, and F-4B Phantoms flew 7,078 sorties and delivered 17,015 tons of ordnance. The Navy provided its own Skyhawks, Crusaders, Phantoms, A-6 Intruders, and the indomitable A-1 Skyraider for 5,337 combat missions over Khe Sanh. USAF F-100s, Phantoms, and T-28 Nomads sent 9,681 sorties into the battle for a total of 14,223 tons of ordnance on NVA and Cong positions. Perhaps the biggest surprise for the North Vietnamese were the 2,602 B-52 missions and 75,631 tons of bombs dropped on their heads from 35,000 feet.

Throughout the siege some four hundred aircraft per day circled overhead watching and waiting for their clearance to drop. Weather, everyone's enemy to some degree, was a perennial problem. Dry wind from China passed over the South China Sea, picking up moisture that became rain over the Vietnamese highlands. Drizzle was frequent and lowered visibility accordingly. Dusk to dawn brought fog and low clouds, and early morning visibilities were typically less than a half mile. Late mornings to afternoon brought clearing, but the NVA used the weather to shield movement, reposition, and attack.

However, the enemy wasn't completely concealed, as Navy and Marine A-6A Intruders had the only true onboard, all-weather attack capability in theater. Called DIANE (Digital Integrated Attack and Navigation Equipment), it provided steering cues to the pilot through the inertial navigation system, terrain-following radar, radar altimeter, and ASQ-61 ballistic computer. Other Navy or Marine attack jets were able to bomb through the weather by using controllers and a TPQ-10 radar, but were far less accurate. This was basic ground-directed bombing where the radar locked the aircraft, and a controller guided the pilot to a release point based on the target location, wind, restrictions, and weapon's ballistics.

The USAF used the MSQ-77 "Skyspot" system, which continuously computed predicted bomb impact points based upon the aircraft's current parameters. A B-52 would arrive at the designated initial point (IP) for his bomb run and the computer would correct for winds, ballistics, and plot the attack heading to a release point. To designate areas for saturation bombing the "Bugle Note" system was used; this divided the area into 1x2-kilometer grids, which were then specifically assigned to incoming flights. A single B-52 could carry *twenty-seven tons* of bombs; either 108 500-pounders or a mix of 500- and 750-pound bombs. Known as BUFFs, the huge bombers usually arrived in cells of three jets every ninety minutes around the clock.*

Official estimates put enemy losses between 9,000 to 13,000 dead and wounded, nearly two divisions, or 50 percent of the attacking force. One NVA prisoner stated that 75 percent of his regiment was destroyed by a single Arc Light strike. The MACV commander would later report to Admiral U. S. Grant Sharp Jr., CINCPAC, that use of the B-52s to drop within 1,000 yards of the Marine perimeter "was quite possibly the deciding factor at Khe Sanh."

Courage and aggressiveness on the ground combined with heavy bombing, sustainable airlift, and flexible tactical air support were impossible to defeat. Safe at high altitude, the bombers were spared the dangers below but all aircraft performing close air support or cargo drops were vulnerable to anti-aircraft fire. The Marines lost two A-4Es from VMA-311 ("Tomcats") in the first few days of the siege, including the commanding officer of VMFA 323 ("Death Rattlers"), who went down in a Phantom near the base; fortunately the aviators were all rescued by the mud Marines.

Though numerous, enemy guns were almost exclusively the lighter 37 mm variety, as nothing heavier had been brought down the Trail, and there were thankfully no SAMs. This lends further credence to the theory that the NVA never intended to conquer the base. If the opportunity presented itself, fine, but

---

*BUFF; Big Ugly Fat Fucker.

the idea was to wait for the general uprising, and once that happened the Americans would be isolated and much easier to defeat. The NVA divisions on the plateau then attacked where they could, held where they couldn't, and waited for the beginning of the coming offensive that would win the battle for them. Time, they knew, was on their side.

But it wasn't.

Though Vietnam had officially adopted the western Gregorian calendar in 1954 for governmental and administrative purposes, the civilian population still used the traditional, lunisolar calendar. This measured annual solar time, and also used lunar phases to account for seasons. Like the Chinese calendar it was animistic, and this new year would be, appropriately enough, the Year of the Monkey.

Traditionally a time to return to family, venerate one's ancestors, and forget the past year's troubles, in the early days of the war Tet usually occasioned a semimutual cease-fire. To some degree, hostilities slacked off as Vietnamese on both sides tried to observe the holiday. In 1968, Tet Nguyen Dan, the "Feast of the First Morning of the First Day," would fall on January 30. In an effort to accommodate its own soldiers, Hanoi adjusted the calendar so Tet would formally begin on January 31, not the night before. So now hundreds of thousands of fighters were spread all over Vietnam, using relatively primitive communications, and not utilizing the same calendar.*

Inexperience with complex, large force deployments was another disastrous factor for the North Vietnamese Army. Ill-equipped to resolve the coordination nightmares associated with moving large numbers of combatants, Hanoi exacerbated

---

*This timing error was confirmed thirty years after the fact by Vietnamese historian Ngo Vinh Long.

this by failing to designate a single command point of contact, an on-scene commander. Small commando outfits had been briefed in advance and moved accordingly, but this was not the case with larger units. In the name of secrecy, the majority weren't informed of their orders until twenty-four hours prior to the assault. Because they were traveling fast and hard at the last moment, their heavy weapons were generally left behind, and this would quickly become a decisive factor in the coming battle.

Finally, the whole offensive hinged upon instigating a rebellion throughout South Vietnam; the people were to rise up, turning against both the Saigon government and the Americans. Southerners would then provide intelligence, logistical support, and reinforcements, for without local support, NVA and Cong units would be grossly overextended, cut off from resupply and too far from home to fight. The uprising was supposed to be facilitated by a major attack on Saigon itself, for if ARVN headquarters, the U.S. embassy, Independence Palace, and the National Radio Station were all captured this would, Hanoi assumed, spark the revolt. The calendar issue probably saved Saigon. Units assigned to attack the northernmost targets, especially the area around Da Nang, began their attack on January 30, a day earlier than expected.

Called Military District 5 by Hanoi, and Military Region 4 by the United States and ARVN, it was a crucial zone that contained the old Vietnamese imperial capital at Hue, Khe Sanh, Da Nang, Nha Trang, and Cam Ranh Bay. Da Nang was among the first areas attacked near midnight on January 30. Home to the port of Da Nang and China Beach, the 2,300-plus acre facility also had a fine air base with several tactical wings, helicopters, gunships, and transport aircraft. The ARVN I Corps was headquartered nearby, as was the Vietnamese Navy's I Coastal

Zone Command. Unfortunately, the 5th Marines had departed a few weeks earlier, and the remaining defenders were spread thin.

Less than 100 miles below the DMZ, Da Nang was especially vulnerable in the event of a large-scale ground attack and the 1st Marine Division commander, Major General Donn Robertson, knew it well. Despite General Westmoreland's announcement of a Tet cease-fire, commencing on January 27, the marines around Da Nang were on edge. Reliable locals had informed the defenders that by 0130 hours on January 20 there would be a major enemy attack in the region. Large hostile concentrations, including the 2nd NVA Division, were discovered near Go Noi, south of the base. Informants also warned of a pending attack against the main U.S. transmitter site on Marble Mountain, barely six miles from Da Nang. Recon patrols from the 7th Marines found more enemy troops just west of their position in the hills near Hieu Duc. This was enough for General Robertson, so the 1st Marines went on 100 percent alert.

When the first barrages of rockets and mortars began falling shortly after midnight, no one in Da Nang was really surprised. Despite instant and heavy fighting, by 0230 the outer perimeter was breached by elements of the 402nd NVA Sapper Battalion, and enemy soldiers advanced to within one hundred yards of the main division command post. The VC 25th Battalion made it across the Cau Do River an hour later, reaching the ARVN I Corps headquarters compound. But the failure to take the defenders by surprise, combined with the tenacity of the Marines and South Vietnamese, lost the initiative for the attackers.

But sunrise brought the attack jets and helicopters. Rockets firing, bombs exploding, and guns strafing, the resulting close air support broke the assault. The enemy tried to get away, and some did, yet others had no choice but to turn and fight. The

VC 20th Regiment got caught west of the Cam La bridge, and the pursuers swarmed in. Marine F-4Bs dropped napalm and high explosives and strafed till their cannons were empty; C-130 gunships wheeled overhead and shredded anything that moved. By January 31, the VC tried to run again, with a few making it to the hills, but more than 190 dead and wounded did not. Qui Nhon, Nha Trang, Ban Me, and Pleiku were also assaulted with no permanent results. When the rest of the offensive began early in the morning of January 31, attacks occurred in 39 of 44 provincial capitals and more than 100 cities, villages, and towns, along with dozens of American bases.

But the main target was always Saigon.

Westmoreland would say in a 1998 interview, "I knew the attack was coming, but I did not want to let the enemy know I knew."

If the general was truly aware that thirty-five enemy battalions were descending on the city, then why was he at home on Tran Huy Cap Street, and not at MACV headquarters, or in the U.S. embassy? Both his chief of staff, General Walter Kerwin, and the SOG chief, Colonel John Singlaub, were in their quarters, as was General Phillip Davidson, chief of combined intelligence. If, as Westmoreland claimed, he knew all about the attack, then so would these other officers. If they all were expecting an offensive then they certainly would *not* be at home in their underwear, especially given the siege at Khe Sanh and the scope of premature assaults the previous evening.

After midnight on January 31, several vehicles pulled up to the Nguyen Du Street gate of Independence Palace, home of South Vietnam's President Thieu.* The fourteen men and one woman of the 3rd Commando Team tried to storm the gates

---

* It was attacked in 1962 by two rogue South Vietnamese pilots flying U.S. A-1D Skyraiders. Rebuilt on a grand scale, it was funded with American tax dollars.

but didn't make it in. They'd expected a huge, carefully planned student rally at the nearby Tan Dao gardens and once the gates were attacked by the commandos, then thousands of youths would pour into the palace. This would overwhelm the defenders and provide top-quality film footage to be shown later. However, due to the sporadic attacks on January 30 a curfew had been imposed in Saigon, so the rally never occurred. Third Commando retreated across the street to fight it out, and by early morning all were dead except two who were captured.

The woman got away.

At 0245, disguised as ARVN soldiers, seventeen men of the 11th Commando Team pulled up to the U.S. embassy on Thon Nhat Boulevard. They destroyed the gate and charged the embassy itself, which the Marine guards just managed to close up. Fighting till daybreak, the beleaguered Americans held out until a quick reaction team of 101st Airborne paratroopers arrived by helicopter, and elements of the 716th Military Police Battalion attacked from the street.

The entire commando team was killed.

Fourth Commando Team, wearing National Police uniforms, attacked and captured the National Radio Station. This was key to the plan since Hanoi assumed that broadcasts of the U.S. embassy takeover and images of thousands of Vietnamese storming Independence Palace would set the South afire. South Vietnamese would then throw off the puppet Saigon regime, the Americans would have to pull out, and the Tet Offensive would be a success. Of course, neither the palace nor the embassy was taken, and even if they had the 4th Commandos only captured the studios. The audio feed was controlled from a downtown location and was cut off at the source. By early morning the South Vietnamese military had killed the commandos and regained complete control of the complex.

Northeast of Saigon, Bien Hoa Air Base, home of the 3rd

Tactical Fighter Wing, and Long Binh Naval Headquarters, home of General Weyand's II Field Force, were also under attack. Unlike Westmoreland, General Weyand *had* truly anticipated the attack and brought several units back from the field to protect the base. The VC 274th and 275th regiments found themselves up against frontline U.S. troops and were no match for the 199th Infantry Brigade, the "Redcatchers," and the "Screaming Eagles" of the 101st Airborne. In the village of Ho Noi, near the air base, two platoons of the 2nd Battalion, 47th Infantry ran across two jeeploads of National Police accompanied by an American military police colonel and, quite bizarrely, a Los Angeles sheriff's deputy—in full uniform. The MP officer told Army Lieutenant John E. Gross that infantrymen didn't know how to search a house, so they would show him how it was done. The lieutenant sarcastically replied that they weren't in a police station, but in combat. Nevertheless, the colonel and deputy sheriff kicked open the door, got a face full of VC machine gun fire, and ran for their jeep.

Bien Hoa and Long Binh held.

Another primary objective of the Tet attacks was Tan Son Nhut Air Base, located in the heart of Saigon. Containing MACV headquarters, also known as "Pentagon East," the headquarters of both the USAF in Vietnam (Seventh Air Force) and the South Vietnamese Air Force, the air base was a prize. Destroying it or even gaining temporary access to the trove of documents, studies, and war plans would be an intelligence windfall. The capture of the defense attaché and Air America compounds would be a disaster for U.S. operations in Southeast Asia. Tan Son Nhut was also home to the South Vietnamese Joint General Staff, so the capture or killing of the dozen generals living there would be a coup indeed.

The assault was three pronged. To the northeast the VC

268th Regiment would make a diversionary attack, focusing the defenders in that direction and away from the southwest perimeter. The 6th and 9th commando teams were then to take control of Gate Four, giving access to MACV headquarters on the south side, and Gate Five, which would open up the flight line. Once it was breached, a combined VC task force of about 1,200 men under Colonel Nguyen Van Ho would pour into the base to deal with individual targets.

However, as with the rest of the offensive, nothing worked out according to plan. The 268th VC regiment got lost on its way into Saigon, so the diversion never happened. This allowed the 377th Security Police Squadron, elements of the ARVN 8th Airborne, two battalions of South Vietnamese Marines, and armored cavalry units from the 25th Division (Tropic Lightning) to concentrate on the attackers. In the end, the base was secured by noon the next day. More than a dozen planes were damaged or destroyed; the Americans lost 23 killed and 86 wounded, while the South Vietnamese lost 32 dead and 89 wounded. NVA and VC figures vary, as always, but 600–1,000 enemy dead is an accurate range.

Hue, the old Vietnamese imperial capital, was especially hard hit. Located north of Da Nang, the city lay on the banks of the Perfume River about fifty miles south of the demilitarized zone. At 0233 on January 31 a flare lit up the sky and ten enemy battalions began their assault. Primary targets were MACV headquarters on the south side of the Perfume River, the ARVN 1st Division Headquarters in the citadel, and Tay Loc airfield in the old city.

The 6th NVA regiment stormed the western gate of the citadel while the 4th Regiment attacked the MACV compound on the southern bank. With the perimeter breached, two NVA battalions entered the city and by 0800 a communist flag was flying from the citadel. For nearly a month fighting raged, house to house and hand to hand, while U.S. Marines, the ARVN "Black Panthers," and elements of the 1st Cavalry Division counterattacked to reclaim the city. On February 28, having isolated or killed the last enemy soldiers defending the citadel, Marines and the Black Panthers cut down the NVA battle flag.

U.S. and ARVN forces lost 688 killed with 3,707 wounded. As always, enemy figures were understated by Hanoi and usually overestimated by American sources, but the best approximation puts communist losses at about 8,000 killed. From Hue itself nearly 3,500 citizens were abducted; they were never seen again, though a mass grave containing 3,000 bodies was later discovered.

Elsewhere, the offensive began playing itself out. Shocked by the lack of success, Hanoi simply didn't know how to react initially. In some places, like Hue, fighting continued unabated, while farther south the attackers vanished into the countryside. Khe Sanh, due to its proximity to the trail, was easier to reinforce and resupply, so a fifth NVA division was committed. On April 1, 1968, the Americans began Operation Pegasus to break the siege by airlifting three battalions of the 1st Cavalry Division into positions around the base. The combination of the angry, aggressive Marines attacking from within and the Cav's "Sky Soldiers" dropping in from above was enough. By that time, stragglers coming back up the trail had passed the news of the failed Tet Offensive so the NVA broke contact and faded back into the Laotian hills.

Assessing the aftermath of Tet is complex and controversial and, even after nearly five decades, is by no means conclusive. From a strictly military standpoint the offensive was a resounding North Vietnamese defeat. Excepting Hue, none of the primary or secondary objectives was achieved. Figures vary widely, but according to the Department of Defense, communist casualties range between 67,000 and 84,000 killed, with an unknown number of wounded. Many of the wounded never survived to fight again. The Americans lost 3,326 killed in action with 16,947 wounded, while ARVN and Free World Forces* suffered 8,188 casualties.

Much has been made of the fact that the Viet Cong, as a fighting force, was essentially destroyed. Yet if Hanoi expected eventual victory, which it did, then would not a powerful National Liberation Front in the South be almost as big a threat as the combined ARVN and U.S. forces? If so, what better way to weaken them, or eliminate them outright as a fighting force, than by bleeding the NLF through the Tet Offensive? Victorious or not, southern communists in the Viet Cong would bear the brunt of the casualties. Either way, in victory or defeat, the NLF would be easier to eventually deal with.

Psychologically and politically, Hanoi broke even with Tet. True, American domestic opinion was severely impacted after the offensive, with the antiwar movement, including Vietnam Veterans Against the War, expanding dramatically. Facing re-election, Lyndon Johnson was typically indecisive. Public approval had plummeted with Westmoreland, his top general in Vietnam, emerging from Tet with egg on his face and blood on his hands. The president had fired Robert Strange McNamara, who subsequently departed on February 29 to head the World Bank. Now Johnson was being seriously challenged, not only by the Republicans and Richard Nixon, but by his own party.

Incumbent presidents nearly always secure their own party's

---

*These were military forces of South Korea, Philippines, Thailand, Australia, New Zealand, and Spain that augmented the U.S. military presence in Southeast Asia.

nomination, but that was far from certain in 1968. Minnesota Democrat Eugene McCarthy made a bid for the ticket stating, "[W]ith the evident intention to intensify the war in Vietnam and, on the other hand, the absence of any positive indications or suggestions for a compromise or for a negotiated settlement, I am concerned that the administration seems to have set no limits to the price that it is willing to pay for a military victory."

On March 16, after watching McCarthy win 42 percent of the New Hampshire primary, Senator Robert Kennedy announced his own intentions by declaring, "I do not run for the presidency merely to oppose any man, but to propose new policies. I run because I am convinced that this country is on a perilous course and because I have such strong feelings about what must be done, and I feel that I'm obliged to do all I can."

Johnson, confused and disheartened by the Vietnam War, called a meeting of his top advisors during the final week of March. While the Marines at Khe Sanh fought for their lives, the president was sorting out damage control. It was obvious that Westmoreland had either fabricated the "light at the end of the tunnel" viewpoint regarding Hanoi's ability to wage war, or he simply didn't know the truth. Either way there was no political cover left for a man who'd called Tet a "great victory" and in doing so permanently undermined Johnson's fragile credibility. The president's advisors, who had supported the various operations, buildups, and escalations of the war, now told LBJ that he needed to disengage from Vietnam. Realizing he was a liability and would very likely become his party's scapegoat, Johnson decided not to risk losing the Democratic nomination. On March 31, 1968, he abruptly announced, "I shall not seek, and will not accept, the nomination of my party for another term as your president."

This gave hope to a nation disillusioned by Johnson's failures, yet once again fate took a hand. After handily winning the California primary early in June 1968, Bobby Kennedy left the congratulatory reception and took a shortcut through the kitchen of the Ambassador Hotel in Los Angeles. Gunned down by Sirhan Sirhan, a Palestinian-born Christian who worked as a stable boy, the presidential hopeful died the following morning. Four days later, on June 10, hope glimmered again as General Creighton Abrams took over MACV from William Childs Westmoreland. Abrams, a far better commander and much better soldier than his predecessor, had very different ideas about the war in Southeast Asia.

Though Tet was a defeat in many ways, the much-trumpeted political success of the campaign was a double-edged sword. Hanoi might have won the South sooner, with less blood spilled, if Johnson, McNamara, Westmoreland, and the rest of that ilk had remained in charge. In any event, it was done. Regardless of politics, military successes, or defeats and body counts, no one doubted that in 1968 a corner had indeed been turned.

CHAPTER 9

WARTS ON A FROG

LIKE MANY AMERICAN boys who'd grown up during World War II, Stan Goldstein was fascinated with aviation. He began flying at age twelve, then entered Air Force ROTC at New York University while earning an engineering degree. After graduating in 1956 he wanted to serve his country and fly, but he was hampered by 20-50 eyesight.* So Stan chose navigator training and went off to Texas, which in and of itself was quite a shock for a guy from the Bronx. Lackland Air Force Base, Texas, was the first stop for preflight, then he was sent farther south to Harlingen for nav school, joining class 57-18C.

In a world before Inertial Navigation Systems (not to mention the satellite-based Global Positioning System), a navigator could make or break a mission. Flying around Texas in a T-29C, Stan learned to use basic grid references and LORAN and became adept at celestial navigation. Still, he was dreading the prospects. Most navigators were sent off to feed the Stra-

---

*One of the inviolate rules then, and now, is that candidates for flight school have at least 20-20 vision.

North Vietnamese air defense personnel. Note the early unpainted SA-2 missile, and the cut foliage used for camouflage.

SA-2 hit on a Phantom. Captains Ed Atterberry and Tom Parrott ejected and were captured. Captain Atterberry was killed in captivity. (USAF)

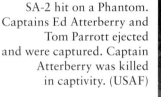

(Left) Ross Fobair and Ed Sihler at Ubon. Flying as Leopard Two, Fobair was the first fighter pilot to fall prey to a surface-to-air missile on July 24, 1965, just west of the Red River in Vietnam.

Captain Vic Vizcarra in 1965. Vic would fly as Rambler Two on the ill-fated Spring High Raid to avenge Ross Fobair. Vic survived the war and his two sons became Navy flyers. (Colonel Vic Vizcarra)

Group photo of Wild Weasel I, 6234th Tactical Fighter Wing, Korat, Thailand. (USAF)

Wild Weasel III-2, 1966: After 45 days, only four of the fifteen pictured here remained to be transferred to Korat. Standing, left to right: Tom Pyle (POW), Bob Marts (medical), Norb Maier (shot down; recovered 11/72), Mike Gilroy (shot down; recovered 7/66), Bobby Martin, Ed Larson (shot down; recovered 7/66), Gene Pemberton (KIA), Buddy Reinbold (WIA). Kneeling, left to right: Bob Sandvick (POW), Curt Hartzell, Ed Rock, Joe Brand (KIA), Ben Newsom (KIA), Glen Davis, George Metcalf (MIA), Don Singer (KIA). (Courtesy of Colonel Ed Rock)

Wild Weasel I patch.

Major Garry Willard, first Weasel commander, Korat, 1965. He would survive the war and retire as a brigadier general. (Allen Lamb)

F-100F. (USAF)

Captains Lamb and Donovan after their SAM kill on December 22, 1965. (Allen Lamb)

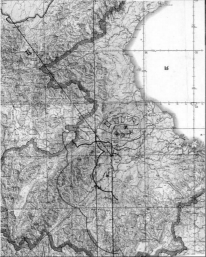

Captain Allen Lamb's flight map used for the SAM attack, showing lethal ranges for the missile. (Allen Lamb)

YGBSM! ("You Gotta Be Shittin' Me!"—Jack Donovan) patch. Still proudly worn by Weasels today.

"F-100F used by Lamb and Donovan on the first kill." (USAF; caption courtesy of National Museum of the US Air Force)

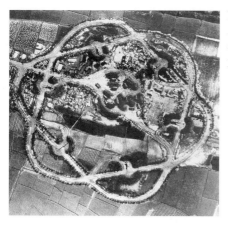

North Vietnamese SA-2 site. The Fansong radar and command vehicles are on the center berm, and individual launchers can be seen in the six points of the star around the perimeter.

Later-model SA-2 Fansong radar with the "birdcage" on top used for optical target acquisition. The circular antenna is used for guidance uplinks to the missile.

Spoon Rest Surveillance radar. (Hungarian Ministry of Defense)

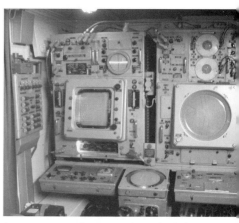

Spoon Rest radar consoles. The left display is the range height indicator (RHI), while the circular scope on the right is the planned position indicator (PPI).

North Vietnamese SA-2 missile (known as a "Fakel" or "Guideline") atop its SM-90 launcher. (httppeters-ada.de)

MiG-17 shot down by an F-105D. Thuds accounted for 30 of the approximately 210 North Vietnamese fighter losses.

North Vietnamese MiG-17 pilots.

"North Vietnamese soldier preparing to fire an SA-7 surface-to-air missile." (USAF; caption courtesy of NMUSAF)

Tough Thud! Major Bill McClelland, 80th TFS, stands in the hole made by an 85mm shell.

Ed Rock, then a captain, in 1963. Ed began his fighter career flying F-86s in Korea. (Colonel Ed Rock)

Major Leo Thorsness (left) and Captain Harry Johnson, Takhli, 1967.

John Revak and Stan Goldstein (left).

Major Leo Thorsness. Awarded the Medal of Honor, two Silver Stars, six Distinguished Flying Crosses and two Purple Hearts, he would survive captivity and the war, becoming an inspiration to all future Wild Weasels. (Colonel Leo Thorsness)

Captains Jerry Hoblit and Tom Wilson, 1967. (Jerry Hoblit and Maxine Macaffrey)

Major John Hamilton, 602nd Air Commando Squadron. He died trying to rescue Majors Mark Madison and Tom Sterling, a Weasel crew downed on April 19, 1967.

100 missions complete! Flyers were always greeted with champagne and beer if they survived one hundred missions over North Vietnam.

In addition to booze, crews completing one hundred missions over North Vietnam were always met with a fire hose.

F-105G.

"F-105 attempting to dodge an SA-2 over North Vietnam." (USAF; caption courtesy of NMUSAF)

F-105 damaged by a near miss from a SAM. (USAF)

Two-seat F-105F Weasel with a single seat F-105D operating as a Hunter Killer pair. Summer 1966.

"SAM Slayer" patch for a confirmed surface-to-air missile kill.

"SAM site being destroyed. After initial attack by a Wild Weasel, it was struck with bombs that set off secondary explosions." (USAF; caption courtesy of NMUSAF)

SA-2 site being annihilated by cluster bombs. (USAF)

Wild Weasel operations for the
13th Tactical Fighter Squadron
(Panthers). Korat, 1966.
(Colonel Ed Rock)

Standing, Left to Right: Rick Westcott (WW Pilot), Don Quigley, Walt Williams, Ted Ballard, Jim O'Neil (WW Pilot), Clyde Hayman (WW EWO), Jimmy Goode, John Buick (WW EWO), George Williams, Ken Ryckman (WW Pilot), Jim McKee, Roger Hegstrom, Mack Angel (WW Pilot), George Kennedy (WW EWO), Gordy McLeod, Tom Lockhart, Ed McCabe, Roger Counts, John Hill (WW Pilot), Dick Fleitz.

Kneeling, Left to Right: Bill Cargal, Max Hatcher, Ed Stanford, Wally Frazier, Jim Flood, Ed McGauley, Mike Lanning, Bob Tondreau (WW EWO), Bob Brinckman (WW Pilot and "Head Weasel"), Herb Friesen (WW EWO), Col. Dick Baughn (Squadron Commander), Don Hidge, Turk Turley, Ed Rock, Vince Scungio (WW EWO), Mike Thomas, Joe Trickey, Chuck Haberstich, Bill Coleman, Sgt. ???

13th TFS Wild Weasels. Korat, 1966. (Colonel Ed Rock)

Mass briefing before a
mission, Korat.

388 Tactical Fighter Wing headquarters, Korat. It was named after the beleaguered US fort in the 1948 film. (Colonel Ed Rock)

Following a flight line and base parade, one-hundred-mission crews ended up in the pool before the celebratory Officer's Club bash.

Work hard, play hard! The KABOOM was the Korat Air Base Officer's Club and had the longest bar (85 feet) in Southeast Asia.

Comic relief!

Nose art from the days when fighting spirit and a sense of humor were virtues. "Pussy Galore II," F-105 # 62-4364 was hand painted by Captain Vic Vizcarra in October, 1966. (Colonel Vic Vizcarra)

Korat RTAB—probably late 1966.

Korat F-105 ramp.

Scenes from Korat—ground support
personnel were vital. They worked
long, hard hours in bad conditions to
keep the Weasels in the fight.

Ken Williams and
Guillermo Valdez
working on a
Thud, Korat.

Loading an AGM-78
STARM missile. The
USAF alone consumed
more than six million
tons of ammunition in
Vietnam, more than
WWII and the Korean
War combined.

AGM-45 SHRIKE missile.

Korat, maintenance personnel installing
fuel tanks, August 1973. Over eight
billion pounds of fuel was offloaded
during the Vietnam War.

In clear weather, returning fighters joined-up in close formation to "pitch-out" over the base. If the mission had been a success, this was usually preceded by a "V" for victory pass over the field.

Lieutenant Colonel Ed Rock, 17th Wild Weasel squadron commander, 1972. Note the "100 Mission" patch and extra ammunition stitched onto his harness. Colonel Rock flew of total of 183 combat missions, 164 into North Vietnam as a Wild Weasel.

F-105F front cockpit. Note the threat warning display mounted on the upper right of the glare shield.

F-105G rear cockpit. Note the more extensive threat warning equipment and the spectrum analysis set in the center.

Captain Mike Bosiljevac at Korat, Royal Thai AFB, 1972. Mike went missing in action on September 29, 1972. (Colonel Ed Rock)

Wild Weasel IV patch.

F-4 Phantom Wild Weasels Captains Bob Tidwell and Denny Haney. Linebacker II, 1972. (Denny Haney)

Captains Mike Herndon and Phil Steeves, 17th Wild Weasel Squadron. Korat, November 1972. (Dr. Phil Steeves)

"Dec. 29, 1972, the end of an era—Capts. Jim Boyd and Kim Pepperell landing after one of the last Wild Weasel missions of the Southeast Asia war during Operation Linebacker." (USAF; caption courtesy of NMUSAF)

Declassified intelligence reports on downed Weasels Clifford Fieszel and Howard Smith.

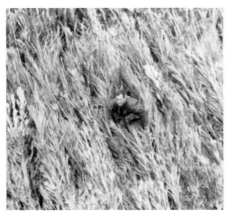

"Downed F-105 pilot being rescued in 1972." (USAF; caption courtesy of NMUSAF)

American POWs on their way to freedom! 1973.

Wild Weasel Memorial Bench at the National Museum of the US Air Force in Dayton, Ohio.

Today's Wild Weasel patch—the legend lives on.

tegic Air Command's insatiable appetite for fresh meat. As he put it, "I thought SAC stood for Simulate, Authenticate, and Cheat." Endless evaluations, exercises, and mind-numbing nuclear readiness alert cycles was not what he wanted, so Stan volunteered to become an electronic warfare officer—an EWO. At that time, EWOs were still a comparative oddity and their mission largely misunderstood, if at all. Assigned to fly aircraft crammed with temperamental, rudimentary equipment, an EWO was a long, long way from the sexy aviator image; Stan likened tactical electronic warfare to being "a wart on a frog."

But as radar-guided threats such as SAMs proliferated, this perception rapidly changed and electronic combat was suddenly a high priority. Becoming an EWO meant starting off in Biloxi, Mississippi, learning to operate the AN/APR-9 radar and ALT-6/8 jamming equipment.* Stan was fortunate to have a fellow classmate like Major Kermit T. Beahan who'd learned his trade the hard way during World War II and Korea. Beahan had been the bombardier aboard *Bockscar* and dropped the second atomic bomb ("Fat Man") over Nagasaki on August 9, 1945. He also taught the younger officers the finer points of chilling gin and making a first-class martini.

Twenty-two months after entering the Air Force, Lieutenant Stan Goldstein arrived in West Germany to fly RB-66s with the 42nd Tactical Reconnaissance Squadron at Spangdahlem Air Base. The RB-66C was the electronic surveillance variant of the versatile B-66 Destroyer light bomber. It was new and interesting, yet spending a few hundred hours sitting in a downward-firing ejection seat, *in the bomb bay,* confirmed

---

* "AN" for Army/Navy. The "AP" designation is a military notation for "airborne radar equipment" and "APR" denotes an "airborne radar receiver." Likewise, "AL" means "airborne countermeasure equipment," with "ALT" designating an "airborne countermeasure transmitter."

Stan's fears that he was way down on the pecking order. Offered a chance to fly up front as a navigator, with a real ejection
seat, he grabbed it. This meant flying in all the jets, not just the
electronic reconnaissance types, while seeing Europe and the
Middle East through a window. Operation Golf Ball was going
on at the time, which meant frequent trips to Wheelus Air Base
in Libya.*

Summertime in 1960 saw Stan and the 42nd TRS relocate to
RAF Chelveston, seventy miles north of London. This was nec-
essary because despite 9,387 Americans buried in Normandy,
French president Charles de Gaulle ordered all nuclear-capable
American fighters out of Libya. The 49th Tactical Fighter Wing
was then moved from Étain-Rouvres Air Base in France to
Spangdahlem Air Base, Germany. Being a footloose bachelor,
Stan rolled with it and was quite happy in a medieval manor
house complete with a maid, stables, and squash courts.

Coming up on a permanent change of station assignment
in 1961, he was sent back to the States to Hill Air Force Base,
Utah, as part of the 4677th Defense Systems Evaluation Squadron. The RB-57E Canberra carried an electronic countermeasures suite and was used to evaluate the U.S. Air Defense
Command's ability to intercept bombers capable of jamming.
Not great work, but Stan got to fly all over the country and ski
when he was at home. He also applied for, and was accepted to,
the Air Force Institute of Technology. Sent to the University of
Missouri, he earned a master's degree in industrial engineering
in 1964 and also a private pilot's license.

If not actually invented by the Pentagon, the concept of payback was certainly perfected by the military. All officers get
sent off for career "broadening" assignments, usually just as

---

*A truly dangerous time—Frenchmen in Algeria were preparing to detonate a
nuclear bomb over the Sahara Desert.

they become very, very good at what they've been trained to do. It's an annoying, usually worthless fact of military life. Now a major, Stan went to Air Training Command Headquarters at Randolph Air Force Base, Texas, to the whimsically named Management Engineering Division. Being trapped in a staff job—a predicament nearly all true aviators despise—was not a happy way to begin 1965, but then he heard about the F-4 shootdown in July and the Spring High mission to avenge it. It was very clear, even in San Antonio, Texas, that the situation in Southeast Asia had become a war.

His problem was how to get into it.

OTHERS ALREADY WERE.

On January 5, 1968, *Miss Molly,* F-105F No. 63-8356, thundered off the runway at Takhli. As it angled off to the northeast, three other Thuds from the 355th Tactical Fighter Squadron joined up and climbed toward the air refueling track. Major Jim Hartney, a long way from his home beaches of Florida, led the four fighters up to the tanker, then into North Vietnam and Route Pack Six.

Strikers were hitting a railroad bridge in the Bac Giang province, northeast of Hanoi. Paralleling National Route 1, the railway continued over the bridge into the Lang Son province all the way to the Chinese Communist (Chicom) border.* Here the narrow-gauge tracks in northeast Vietnam had been modified to fit standard gauge Chinese railcars for the trip south. On any given day, more than a thousand tons of material passed into the DRV in this manner, so destroying the bridge would have a real impact farther south.

Like everyone else, Hartney had heard the rumors about

---

* "Chinese communist" was frequently shortened to "Chicom."

lots of enemy movement down the Ho Chi Minh Trail. He and his EWO, South Dakota native Captain Sam Fantle, had discussed it and were briefed daily by the squadron intelligence officer. Everything pointed to something big happening their way soon. But that was the war in the South: a ground war, a grunt's war. Rolling Thunder was still an active operation, so he and the other Wild Weasels had to keep flying north into the SAMs to protect strike packages.

Missions such as this were truly in the belly of the beast. The target today was on the northeast side of Hanoi, between the heavily defended capital and the Chicom border. There was Triple A everywhere and, of course, SAMs on both sides of the city, which was precisely why the Weasels were there. The bridge was also within ten miles of the MiG-17 base at Kep.

From 1966 to 1967, the VPAF had shot down nineteen U.S. aircraft, which prompted legendary fighter pilot Colonel Robin Olds, a double ace in World War II, to conceive Operation Bolo. On January 2, 1967, as commander of the Wolfpack, Olds led the 8th TFW F-4 Phantoms down Thud Ridge toward the MiG base at Phuc Yen. Using F-105 call signs, routes, and jamming pods the idea was to impersonate a strike package, sucker the MiGs into a dogfight, and kill them all. No combat plan goes off without a hitch, and Bolo was no exception. Yet the Wolfpack still shot down seven MiGs without a loss and forced the VPAF 921st Regiment to stand down. It hadn't stopped the MiGs permanently, though, and twenty-seven American aircraft were lost in air-to-air combat during 1967. However, U.S. fighter jets shot down seventy-nine confirmed MiGs and put the VPAF on the defensive.

But not today.

Concentrating on attacking an SA-2, Jim Hartney and Sam Fantle never saw the MiG-17F at their six o'clock. Small and crudely constructed, the Soviet-made fighter was nevertheless extremely maneuverable and difficult to see. Twin NR 23mm cannons shredded the Americans' left wing, putting the Weasel out of control and forcing both men to eject. Two good parachutes were observed, and a pair of beeper signals were heard in a little basin where the Bac Giang, Thai Nguyen, and Lang Son provinces meet. No voice communications were ever received, and no rescue attempt could be attempted so deep inside North Vietnam. Neither man was seen again.

By Americans, that is.

NEVADA IN THE wintertime can be a bleak place. Like the surface of the moon, but with wind. Cold air sweeps in from the north, accelerates through the Pahranagat Valley, and spits out over Las Vegas. Between the foothills and the city lies Nellis Air Force Base, where in January 1968, Stan Goldstein and John Revak were stationed. Arriving as part of Wild Weasel III-17 (68-EW), their group of eight pilots and eight EWOs had started class on Halloween. Stan breezed through the main gate in his 1963 Pontiac Catalina convertible, and spent the normal first few days checking in. Paperwork, official records dropped off, and a local medical clearance to fly. The EWOs had never been in a fighter before, meaning they all needed to be fitted up with g-suits, which fighter guys called "speed jeans."

The front-seaters were all high-time, experienced pilots—most from the F-105, but a few had come from F-4 Phantoms.* The backseaters were, according to Stan, a "different and mixed kettle of fish." A few were electronic warfare instructors; others

---

*John Doyle, Gobel James, Vern Harris, Bill Finn, Charley Hart, Tom Murch, Harry Matthews, and John Revak.

were electronic intelligence (ELINT) specialists, or staff officers with varying degrees of experience.* They would all have
to learn about the threat systems they'd face, tactics, countertactics, and the specialized equipment on the F-105F Weasel.
They'd also have to learn about each other.

It was much more than simply scheduling a crew in the same
jet. It was putting two strangers together who would have to live
with each other, fly with each other, and fight as a pair. There
was a very good chance they would also die together: casualty
rates were still north of 50 percent. The Weasels called it the
"mating dance," and it hadn't changed since Allen Lamb and
Jack Donovan's day. You had single-seat fighter pilots who'd
never flown as a crew, and you had EWOs who'd never done
anything else. During the initial week, the men generally sorted
each other out, usually in class and at the O'Club bar. According to Stan, they made their own arrangements by background,
personality, lifestyles, and "viewpoints on life, wine, women,
and song."

Whatever method they chose, it worked. In describing their
choices, Stan recalls, "John Revak and I were a natural fit in
that we were both bachelors, and had grown up in New York
City. He was calm and somewhat more reserved, which balanced my more boisterous approach to life. This was the start
of a team and friendship that lasts to this day." [†] The class cele-
brated their "marriages" by attending the Johnny Carson show
at the Sahara on the Vegas Strip that night. Carson was in on it
himself, arranging VIP seating and announcing the new Wild
Weasels to his cheering audience.

---

* Jerry Knotts, Dan Handley, Kemper Gleason, Larry Martin, Dave Brog, Don
Lavigne, Kim Pepperell, and Stan Goldstein.
† Forty-seven years as of 2015.

But none of them ever forgot why they were there. They knew that more than 2,500 surface-to-air missiles had been fired at their fellow Americans since 1965, and that at least 105 aircraft had been lost to the SA-2. They also knew that since the Weasels had been flying, it was taking more and more SAMs to bring down U.S. combat aircraft—17 per jet in 1966 and up to 32 per jet in 1967. Stan and the others paid close attention to their instructors in the 4535th Fighter Weapons Squadron: their lives depended on what they learned. All of the instructors, pilots as well as backseaters, were combat veterans, and all the EWOs had been Weasels, not SAC switch operators. Some, like Jack Donovan and Rick Morgan, were legends from the F-100F Wild Weasel I program.

EWO students began flying in the T-39F Sabreliner for familiarization with the APR-25/26 and ER-142 panoramic receiver. The copilot's console had also been removed and the F-105 R-14 radar installed in its place. All told, the students would fly four or five T-39 flights, and about twenty-two sorties in the F-105F. The full Wild Weasel course normally took ninety days, so for Class WWIII-17 this meant a graduation date of February 5, 1968.

But that changed.

On January 21, the same day Khe Sanh was attacked, thirty-one North Korean infiltrators got to within a half mile of the Blue House; the office of the president of South Korea. Nineteen divisions of the South Korean First Army went to full combat alert status as clashes erupted up and down the demilitarized zone. The USS *Pueblo,* a former cargo ship converted to gather electronic intelligence, was approached and harassed by a North Korean sub chaser. Part of Operation Clickbeetle, the ship was primarily engaged in locating inland radars and intercepting Soviet–North Korean communications but did so offshore in international waters. Forty-eight hours later four communist torpedo boats, two sub chasers, and a pair of MiGs attacked and captured the *Pueblo*.

Three days after this, on the morning of January 26, Stan Goldstein was sitting in class learning the finer points of cluster bombs and their fuses. The squadron operations officer appeared through the doorway waving a sheaf of papers and interrupting the lecture. Reading off sixteen names, including Goldstein and Revak, he informed them that in response to the *Pueblo* crisis, they are being sent to Korea in preparation for a second Korean War. Clear out and begin packing, the officer said, because you leave tomorrow.

Class was over.

ONE OF THE great strengths of the U.S. military is its collective ability, when desired, to dedicate a tremendous amount of talent, funding, and creativity to a given problem. Despite initial neglect of the field of electronic warfare, significant advances had been made by 1968. This was partially accomplished in response to combat losses incurred by the proliferation of radar threats like the Fansong and Firecan. But there were those who also realized that with enough effort American technical prowess could create a capability gap that our enemies could not match. Such an area of exclusion in electronic countermeasures would permit future wars to be fought exclusively on our terms, or very nearly so.

In addition to electronic countermeasures, antiradiation missile technology was also continuously evolving as a more active response to the radar threat. First fired by the USAF on April 18, 1966, near Dong Hoi, the AGM-45 Shrike had proven less than optimal. For the next three months, 107 of the missiles were lobbed at enemy emitters, resulting in many puzzled farmers and a single confirmed radar hit. With 116 aircraft losses to the SA-2 between July 1965 and February 1968, clearly the Shrike wasn't the answer. It was, according to the legendary Jack Donovan, "like fighting a long sword with a pen knife." Development continued on the AGM-78 Standard Anti-Radiation Missile, or STARM.

Like the Shrike, STARM was initially a Navy project that mandated off-the-shelf technology, in this case the RIM-66A/B surface-to-surface missile. Designed to target ships, it was big, at 1,400 pounds and fifteen feet long. Over 210 pounds of this was a blast fragmentation warhead, a vast improvement from the minuscule 149-pounder in the Shrike. Due to the larger rocket motor and better seeker head, the STARM could potentially be employed fifty miles from the target, though this assumed near-perfect target cooperation. In any event, the AGM-78 had a longer range than the SA-2, thus for the first time American fighters had a standoff capability and could attack without venturing into anti-aircraft gun range.

But antiradiation missiles only truly functioned if the enemy radar cooperated by continuing to transmit. If a Fansong or Firecan blinked off temporarily, or shut down altogether, a Shrike simply went stupid and stuck itself in the earth somewhere. Later-model STARMs made some provision for this by incorporating a memory circuit, and if the radar signal vanished the missile would guide itself to the approximate last known location and detonate. This was certainly better than nothing, but the drift error of circa-1968 inertial navigation technology was slightly over 50 feet per minute. So even for a twenty-mile shot the AGM-78 could impact well over 100 feet away if it was forced to rely on INS memory rather than homing.

North Vietnamese countertactics had also improved significantly, and emissions control, or limiting radar transmission times, was consistently practiced. With very short on-air times, a SAM radar would emit long enough to launch a missile, guide it to intercept, then shut down. Such a tactic usually prevented a Fansong from being located, and even if it was, there would rarely be enough time to hand this off to a STARM and have it guide to impact. Cooperative feed tactics were also used where Firecans and early warning radars provided rough target information to the Fansong. The target-tracking radar would stand by in a dummy-load configuration and then come on-air just long enough to acquire the target and guide the missile. Spare antennas were on-site whenever possible and kept ready to replace any that were damaged or destroyed.

Assessing the damage or destruction of a radar was uncertain at best. Effectiveness of conventional weapons like bombs, guided rockets, kinetic missiles, etc. was (and is) measured according to a "probability of kill" (Pk). Also referred to as a K-kill, this is a measurement of how many weapons of any given type it will take to irreparably damage a target. The value obviously changes based on the weapon employed and the type of target. Antiradiation missiles (ARMs) were never designed to truly kill radars, but rather to damage them, thus a probability of hit (sometimes referred to as probability of success) was used. This takes into account the complex acquisition and launch sequence, ARM guidance to the target, and a successful detonation, which renders the target radar inoperable for at least three hours.

None of this is to say that antiradiation missiles were wholly ineffective, since they were not. In fact, the *threat* of Shrikes and STARMs actually counted for more than the missiles themselves. If the North Vietnamese could be forced into degraded modes of operations, or forced to shut down with missiles in flight, then ARMs were partially successful—much like MiGs were considered successful if they could force American fighters to jettison their bomb loads prior to attacking. But in neither case was it a permanent solution. In the case of the SAMs, *any* left alive and operating meant there still were systems that could shoot down and kill Americans the next day. Therefore the most effective use of ARM technology enabled fighters to get close enough to kill the radar sites with bombs.

North Vietnamese air defense regiments scrambled to meet the adaptive U.S. threat, and did so with several variously effective methods. "Birdhouses," little metal boxes with four viewing hatches, began appearing atop the Fansong F (RSN-75V2) horizontal antenna array. There was room inside for a pair of observers who could optically track and guide the missile if needed. Using this method, a SAM was fired blind and flew a ballistic flight path during the initial four seconds of the launch. With high-powered scopes, the men in the birdhouse would then use only two signals: guidance, which most fighter RHAWs were very late in detecting, and the "down link," which indicated an accurate trajectory. Besides being impervious to jamming and nearly impossible to detect, optical guidance permitted missile launches against aircraft flying below the Fansong's capability. It was a very dangerous tactic, and fortunately it was extremely difficult to execute under normal conditions. Optical guidance could be defeated by defensive maneuvering, terrain masking, night operations, and bad weather.

In the late fall of 1967, the 236th Missile Regiment also modified the Fansong engagement sequence by switching to "three-point" guidance. This technique used the normal automatic mode to launch the radar, then the operator would switch to manual control once the missile was safely airborne and tracking its target. With a few seconds remaining to interception, the operator would switch back again to auto mode. This abrupt change in guidance signals permitted combat under heavy U.S. jamming and potentially neutralized the EB-66s and APR-25/ER-142 receivers in the Wild Weasels.

Yet interfering with Fansong or Firecan radars was only part of the solution to the SAM problem. From the beginning of the war, both the military and the CIA had made numerous attempts to intercept the SA-2 uplink signal. These guidance commands were transmitted to a beacon transponder located on the rear of the missile, which would then reply and establish two-way communication. If that coded reply could be acquired and dissected, then a jamming program could be created to jam it. The biggest problem was that the uplink-downlink sequence only occurred when a missile had been fired and was guiding to impact. A way had to be found to provoke the Fansong under relatively controlled circumstances when snooping EW aircraft could capture the signal.

Operation United Effort was a CIA initiative to do just that, and for more than a year Firebee drones were used in conjunction with RB-47H ELINT gatherers to acquire the vital data. During mid-February 1966, a drone finally antagonized a Fansong near Thanh Hoa into firing. The Firebee retransmitted not only the guidance and downlink signals before it was destroyed, but also the proximity fuse detonation command signal.* Analysts discovered that the missile's beacon receiver had a narrow bandwidth just 20 MHz wide, and operated in a single frequency. Now it was entirely possible to jam a Fansong's radar guidance signals using the power available from

---

*Initially called the Q-2, the drone was made by Ryan. Twelve feet long and weighing 2,062 pounds, it had a range of about 200 miles with a maximum speed that exceeded 500 mph.

onboard pods. Colonel Marty Selmanovitz, the assistant to the commander for electronic warfare at Seventh Air Force headquarters, would state:

> *Power density was the problem. All the beacons operated in the same 20 MHz wide band, so we could narrow the jamming to that particular band of frequencies. So we set one pod on each plane to the beacon frequency, with all four [magnetrons] running on the same center frequency. The other jamming pod we left tuned to the Fansong and Firecan radars. . . .*

This information, combined with all the data compiled to date about North Vietnamese threats, was included in countermeasure research on how to beat the radars. As mentioned earlier, the QRC-160A-1 pod was at the center of this effort, yet despite self-protection jamming, the SAMs shot down eight jets in five days following the Vampyrus test. The results indicated that specialized pod formations, optimized for electronic coverage, would be most effective against radars. Both the 388th Fighter Wing at Korat and Takhli's 355th Fighter Wing experimented and came up with similar solutions. Takhli flew in four ships spaced about 1,000 feet apart, with an altitude stack of 750 feet from top to bottom. Korat flew a bit wider, with 1,500 feet between jets, and a deeper top-to-bottom stack of nearly 2,000 feet. This initially played havoc with the SAMs, causing 66 percent of all the missiles fired in that period to lose control and crash. During several weeks of air battles over Hanoi, 18 of 37 missiles lost guidance, and crashed. The SAM kill rate against U.S. aircraft utilizing pods fell from 50 percent in 1966 to 16 percent in 1967.

Yet this had consequences for the Americans as well. Hiding behind an electronic cloak is fine for nonmaneuvering bombers, and even air-to-air jets while they cap and wait to engage. But past a certain point in their missions, this usually wasn't feasible for tactical strike fighters, nor for Weasels trolling for MiGs. Flying straight and level was an excellent way to become a guest in the Hanoi Hilton, or worse. Also, when their radar screens became cluttered and unusable, the North Vietnamese began tracking the jamming source itself. Those nice, tight pod formations created a fairly defined noise strobe, so an accurate azimuth to the jammer source was easy to see. Establishing range was trickier, but by using geographically separated Fansongs, Firecans, and other radars, the triangulation calculation could be made and then passed by landline to the launching SAM battery.

During a three-day period at the end of November 1967, eight USAF jets were lost to the SAMs: one F-105F, two RF-4Cs, and five F-105Ds. Neither the Weasel nor the reconnaissance jets used pods because jamming interfered with their own onboard equipment. However, the striker Thuds were all flying tight, nonmaneuvering pod formations to maximize jamming effectiveness. Employing a track-on-jam profile against these fighters, the SAMs cost the lives of four pilots, including Colonel Edward Burke Burdett who died in captivity, the 388 TFW's commander.*

The bitter trade-off for the Americans was decreased situational awareness, and miserable weapons accuracy if they remained in pod-friendly formations. Wingmen concentrating on maintaining a set, rigid position are doing little else other than flying; they aren't searching for targets, and certainly not

---

*The fifth Thud pilot was captured: Major Ray Vissotzky, 34th TFS, 388 TFW.

watching for MiGs or SAMs. As for weapons, according to a 1968 report conducted by the Seventh Air Force director of tactical analysis, "the pod formation, while optimizing electronic countermeasures, complicates the bombing delivery problem."

Sometimes this was as drastic as a 15-degree variation in dive angles, which can cause all sorts of problems. Shallowing a dive angle can mean more time pointed at the target, making an attacker predictable and vulnerable to enemy fire. It can also mean a lower release altitude and may prevent the bomb from fusing correctly. Steeper dive angles can cause less time to aim, which might mean a miss. Being steep also usually means a bomb release below the minimum altitude required for a fuse to function, and if the weapon doesn't arm, or is degraded, then what's the point of the mission? The whole sortie becomes a risky wasted exercise, and some other flight will have to try again another day. Fortunately, following an investigation into the fiasco, close formations over enemy territory were discarded.

Another consequence of the effective U.S. response against SAMs and radar-guided anti-aircraft fire was a marked increase in MiG activity. Though long recognizing the necessity of fighters, Hanoi had primarily relied upon missiles and anti-aircraft guns for defense. This was partly based on cost; SAMs were relatively inexpensive, and guns were downright cheap. Fighter pilots were highly specialized, well educated (for North Vietnamese), and required a great deal of effort to train and maintain. Replacements were needed often, especially during the early days of the war when faced with American combat veterans of World War II and Korea.

The average NVAF pilot was in his early twenties and had been selected after secondary school through Soviet-style qualification tests. If picked, the young man could plan on spending several years away from home learning Russian, basic aerodynamics, and aircraft systems. Flying L-29 trainers and later the MiG-21U, about 10 percent of a given group of students would progress to fighters. From a fighter class of seventeen to twenty candidates, maybe seven or eight would become full-fledged pilots and be sent back to North Vietnam to fly MiG-17s or MiG-21s.

Heavily dependent upon ground-controlled intercepts, a NVAF fighter pilot was essentially just a shooter. The GCI controller managed the geometry and led the flight into a firing position behind the attacking Americans. After shooting, the MiG pilot would invariably dive away and run, so very few turning engagements—true World War II or Korean-style dogfights—occurred. And it worked. If an enemy could be taken by surprise then the likelihood of killing him, or at least shooting him down, was fairly good. The North Vietnamese seemed very aware that they were no match for their U.S. adversaries on anything like even terms. The 1973 USAF "Red Baron" report published by the Fighter Weapons Center found only one instance of an American fighter being outmaneuvered and shot down in a turning fight. On equal terms, called a neutral engagement, U.S. fighters scored 28 kills, and when reacting defensively, the American jets frequently reversed the situation and shot down 18 NVAF fighters. Of 131 North Vietnamese losses, 63 were MiG-17s, 60 were MiG-21s, and the remaining 8 were MiG-19s.

Losses were bad and sometimes an entire NVAF squadron would be lost within a week or so. However, one tremendous advantage of combat over friendly territory was that pilots who survived ejection could be rescued and quickly returned to combat. Pilots could expect to fight for the duration of the war as long as he was physically able to do so. There are no reliable figures regarding North Vietnamese pilots who were shot down and returned to duty, but total fixed-wing combat losses for just the USAF numbered 1,627 aircraft. American combat search and rescue (SAR) was extremely daring and very effective, yet some men were lost too far into Vietnam or too close to population centers to be rescued. The U.S. Department of Defense confirms 766 known POWs, and 591 were returned with Operation Homecoming in 1973. Of these, 325 were USAF fliers.

BY 1968, THE demands of war had changed American military aviation. This was especially true for the USAF, as some two hundred pilots were entering fighter Replacement Training Units each month to meet escalating needs. This requirement was driven primarily by the policy of rotating fliers in and out of combat squadrons rather than rotating the squadrons themselves. This had been done at the beginning of the war so units that had trained together, and knew each other well, then fought together. It was a sound method and made perfect sense in fighting squadrons. Any combat veteran will admit that it's the replacements, the unknown "new guys," who bear watching the closest. But in a ludicrous decision to "spread the wealth" of combat experience, the individual rotation system was put into place. This was exacerbated by USAF policy that a man's tour ended after one year in country, or 100 combat missions over North Vietnam. After all, it wouldn't be fair otherwise. This went deep into the USAF leadership's problem of viewing war in a rather detached, abstract sense—rather than committing to achieving victory, Air Force command approached combat as a box to be checked in one's career.

At any given time a fighter squadron in Southeast Asia would have a wide mix of experience: some who were closing in on the 100-mission mark and others who only had two or three. The new policy required more fighter pilots than even the USAF could produce, so rather than sensibly changing course, the USAF compounded the problem: it lowered the standards. Also, in a head-scratching policy shift, qualified bomber, transport, and tanker pilots were allowed to convert to fighters. A pilot was a pilot, wasn't he?

Actually, no. Not at all.

Make no mistake, the USAF could not survive then, or now, without all the fine fliers and support personnel who are not fighter pilots. Khe Sanh graphically illustrated the absolute necessity of logistics, and any fighter pilot worth his wings will openly acknowledge his debt to tanker crews. But piloting a fighter is a different type of flying, unlike any other in the world. Just because a man can fly a jet, it does not mean he can fly a fighter jet. Split-second decisions, aggressiveness, dogfighting, and a predisposition to controlled violence are just a few traits that separate a fighter pilot from other types of fliers.

Air Force technocrats—undisputedly very, very good at what they do—have always been at odds with those who actually do the fighting. This created a culture that attempted to balance combat realities with the peacetime system of promotions, decorations, and career progression. For instance, fighter Replacement Training Unit commanders were evaluated and promoted based on meeting their allocated class schedules, not on the combat readiness of the pilots they trained. High-value, perishable skills such as surface attack and particularly air-to-air training were subordinated to meeting graduation dates and training quotas.

In the end, a fighter aircraft is a complex weapon delivery system, and without the correct type of pilot who has undergone rigorous specialized training, it is ineffective or fails outright. From 1965 to mid-1967, when 77 percent of the Tactical Air

Command was composed of fighter-qualified pilots, the USAF MiG kill ratio was 3:1. By late 1968 onward, nearly *50 percent* of TAC pilots came from bombers or transports, and the kill ratio dropped to 0.85:1.

Fortunately, John Revak was not one of these pilots. By the time he and Stan Goldstein met at Nellis in October 1967, John had been a fighter pilot for seven years. He'd decided to beat the draft back in 1951 by enlisting in the Air Force, and entered the Aviation Cadet Program four years later. Initially trained as a navigator, John graduated with Class 54-13C from Harlingen and became a flight engineer on B-36 bombers out of Carswell Air Force Base, Texas. Selected for flight school, Captain Revak went through Undergraduate Pilot Training Class 59-C at Bartow Air Force Base, Florida. Then, as now, pilots were chosen for fighters by class ranking; John was selected to fly F-100 Super Sabres. Following tours at Luke, Nellis, and Kadena's 67th TFS, he converted to F-105s and ended up in 1964 as a "Fighting Hawk" with the 23rd TFS, Bitburg Air Base, Germany.* Two years later the squadron converted to the F-4D and so did John. By 1967, eager to get to Southeast Asia, he volunteered to transition back to the Thud. With orders to Nellis in the fall of 1967, John became part of Wild Weasel Class 68 and was on his way to Southeast Asia.

After the *Pueblo* Crisis concluded, John Revak and Stan Goldstein left Korea for Tachikawa, Japan, on March 11, 1968. From there they flew on to Clark Air Base in the Philippines to attend Jungle Survival School, a mandatory course for anyone flying combat in Southeast Asia. As the pair arrived in Korat on March 25, President Johnson had met with his advisors and received the full brief on the Tet Offensive results. While the

---

*The author was proud to serve in the same squadron, though a bit later.

president mulled over his options for the future of Vietnam, Stan and John went through the normal in-briefings, records reviews, intelligence updates, and local orientation flights prior to flying their first combat mission.

Unfortunately this fell on April 1, 1968.

The previous evening, faced with myriad political, personal, and international difficulties, Johnson announced that he would not seek reelection. Desperately trying to salvage a favorable legacy, the president publicly acknowledged that he would seek a negotiated peace with Hanoi. As a show of good faith he curtailed offensive bombing north of the 19th parallel and effectively placed North Vietnam off-limits. This restricted strike and Weasel missions to the southern wedge of North Vietnam between the DMZ and Vinh: roughly Route Packs One and Two.

Launching at 0720, the pair flew with the 44th TFS (Vampires) into Pack One supporting an Arc Light strike against the Mu Gia Pass. If the passes into Laos and South Vietnam could be closed down, the White House reasoned, then the war in the South could be throttled. It didn't work out like that, but to Revak and Goldstein it didn't matter much. Their clock had officially started; ninety-nine missions to go.

AT 0100 ON the morning of March 10, eight Wild Weasels pulled on their flight suits, tied their boots, and, wary of stray cobras, trudged off to the Takhli Officers' Club for breakfast. Cigarettes followed the fish, rice, and coffee as they made their way into the ops building. Weather, NOTAMs, and personal flight gear were all checked out, and at the ops desk they gave a cursory glance to the Flight Crew Information File. Each man also signed out next to his name, noting the tail number of the Thud he'd be flying that morning.

The flight briefing started exactly at 0200.

Two hours and twenty minutes later, gleaming wet in the rain, the lead Weasel released his brakes. Three other bright orange afterburner plumes sliced through the rainy dawn at Takhli and followed him up. Barracuda flight—four F-105s from the 357th TFS (Lickin' Dragons)—roared off the runway and vanished into the heavy, lead-colored clouds.* Each one carried a single QRC-160-1-8 improved ECM pod on the left outboard wing station, a 650-gallon fuel tank on the centerline, and two AGM-78A STARM missiles on both inboard stations. These were Mod O missiles, not production versions, and carried the same T1 seeker head found in the Shrike. This mission, covering sixteen F-4D strikers hitting a target near Hanoi, would be the first USAF operational use of the new antiradiation missile.†

Crossing the Mekong at 0515, the four Weasels had air refueled and armed up and now headed northeast into Vietnam toward Hanoi. They'd picked up Barlock early warning radar emissions 100 miles from the target; missiles and guns were certain to be waiting. As the first golden shafts of sunlight lightened the clouds, all four flights of strikers checked in. Waco, Cheetah, Falcon, and Cactus were on time, loaded to kill and headed for an NVA barracks complex at Ha Dong, about five miles southwest of Hanoi along National Route 6. Unfortunately, broken cloud decks extending up to 12,000 feet and mechanical issues forced half the strikers to turn back, but eight Phantoms still pressed on into the Hanoi suburbs.

Shortly before the 0600 time over target, Barracuda went into a racetrack cap, an elongated orbit, twenty miles from the

---

*Major Harlan Wyman and Captain Ron Davenport; Captain George Acree and Captain Frank O'Donnell; Major Gene Goodwin and Captain Roger Elmer; Captain Warren Kerzon and Captain Scott McIntire.
†On March 6, 1968, four A-6Bs from VA-75 (Sunday Punchers) off the USS *Kitty Hawk* operationally employed the first STARM missiles near Haiphong.

closest Fansong, right at the fringe of its engagement envelope. Six SA-2s launched, its nasty rattlesnake audio filling the Weasel's cockpits. The anti-aircraft radars were up as well and the big stuff—85–100 mm guns—opened up. Orange and red explosions made brief, bright splashes against the darker clouds and the sky lit up with gunfire. Over the next few minutes the four Weasels fired all eight STARMs at valid Fansong radar signals. Two AGM-78s exploded a few miles after launch, and it was later determined that the rocket motors had been damaged in transit. When the STARM made its 5-g pitch up, the cracked motor casing came apart and the propellant exploded. Another one didn't function because the arming lanyard had been inadvertently left off by the ground crew.

Five remaining missiles functioned as they should and disappeared through the clouds toward the radars. Two had no measurable effect, either on signals from the ground or missiles in flight. Three did. Several SA-2s went ballistic very soon after the STARM time of impact, meaning the AGM-78 had either hit the radar, impacted close enough to damage it, or caused the Fansong to shut down simply as a result of its being launched. Whatever the explanation, none of the SAMs found a mark, no Thuds or Phantoms were lost, and the target was successfully destroyed.

The 37 percent success rate for the first combat STARM employment decreased and held around the 20 percent range for subsequent missions, but it was certainly better than the Shrike.* Yet the rapid development of weapons and systems to fight the SAMS would slow considerably following the April 1, 1968, bombing pause above the 19th parallel. Just as operations

---

*Thirteen STARMs were tested at White Sands Missile Range by the USAF Missile Development Center project team and yielded a 28 percent success rate.

and tactics had been modified for Rolling Thunder missions, they would now be adapted for combat in the southernmost Route Packs and along the Ho Chi Minh Trail. Those fighting the war hoped either the newest round of peace talks would succeed, or, if not, that the bombing pause would be lifted soon and they could get back to hunting and killing SAMs.

Unfortunately, neither eventuality occurred.

What did happen was that Hanoi used the new bombing restrictions to immediately begin widespread repairs and reconstruction. Bridges, roads, depots, and railways were put back into commission. Without fear of American air attacks, the NVA could now move as far south as Than Hoa by rail. Arms, ammunition, and supplies of all types were stockpiled in depots as close as Bat Lake, a mere twenty miles north of the DMZ. In Route Pack Two, the air base at Vinh was repaired and put back in service while another was built far to the south near Dong Hoi.

Fully exploiting their new freedom, SAMs moved south as well, and by late spring there were four units below the 19th parallel. One site near Bai Due had a clear line of sight down the Gianh River valley to cover both the Mu Gia and Ban Karai passes. Two more batteries around Vinh now threatened anything flying east of the Truong Song mountain range along the coast. The last unit was very mobile, deploying just north of the DMZ, and from there it could reach into South Vietnam's Quang Tri province. After all, if the Americans were going to impose such a restriction on themselves, that was their business.

Hanoi suffered from no such delusions.

Through the spring and summer of 1968, missions continued into North Vietnam above the 19th parallel. Whether armed reconnaissance flights or B-52 strikes, both required protection from the SAMs and MiGs. With the changing face of the air war, the Weasels also had to adapt. Prior to the bombing pause, Rolling Thunder missions were composed of relatively small groups of strikers operating within a large area. Hanoi, Haiphong, and other comparatively industrialized targets were protected by a gauntlet of point defenses. MiGs would attack incoming U.S. strike packages, hoping to throw off their timing, cause them to jettison their bombs, or occasionally would shoot an American down. Closer to the cities, the SAMs would engage and very often the fighter bombers had to jettison their ordnance to survive. When this occurred, those bombs did not hit a primary target. Finally, if the jet made it all the way in to an attack, then any one of the hundreds of anti-aircraft guns might get lucky.

If a combatant has only a limited number of targets worth protecting, all his defenses can be concentrated around these, but after April 1 this changed. Now everything between the 19th parallel and the DMZ was a target so the NVA had to cover a geographic area, rather than a few specific assets. With the exception of Vinh, nothing in Route Pack One or Two lent itself to point defense, and the terrain was much rougher than the northern flatlands around Hanoi. Consequently, there was less Triple A; what was fired was generally of a lighter caliber. Spare parts and extra missiles now had to travel some 250 miles farther south; as a result, SAMs only fired when they had a high-value, high probability of success target—or if they were deliberately provoked, hunted, and attacked.

So that's what the Weasels did.

With a mobile, well-camouflaged enemy operating in broken terrain this was no easy problem to solve, yet during the month of May alone the F-105Fs made 26 attacks. This increased to 38 in June, and there were 82 Weasel assaults on SAMs south of the 19th parallel in August. Some of these Hunter Killer missions were planned in conjunction with other missions, but often, after a primary target was hit, the Weasels would go trolling for SAMs. This was usually done up in the "shoot me" altitude blocks above 6,000 feet. Purposely easy to see on radar, the F-105s would zoom back and forth close to suspected SA-2 sites, to see if they could provoke a Fansong or Firecan radar long enough to locate it and attack. Sometimes it worked and sometimes not.

One of the days it backfired was July 15, 1968, when the 44th TFS lost its first Weasel since February. They'd been told that a SAM had moved into one of the many prepared locations scattered around Packs One and Two. This site was situated about eight miles northwest of Dong Hoi, between the mountains and National Route 1. On his thirty-eighth mission, Major Gobel James rolled in on the site, pulled the power back slightly, and concentrated on his aim. As they pulled off target the Thud was hit by 37 mm anti-aircraft fire; he and Captain Larry Martin immediately turned southeast toward the coast. On fire and trailing smoke, James's F-105 limped along as far as the beach, but when the hydraulic lines burned through, the jet became uncontrollable. Ejecting safely, Major James came down on the beach in the Dong Hoi suburbs and was captured immediately. He hadn't seen Captain Martin bail out, nor did James hear any word of his EWO's fate once imprisoned.*

Nearly two months later the 333 TFS from Takhli lost a Weasel over the same SAM site. "Root Pack Rat"—F-105F No. 63-8317—was also hit by 37 mm gunfire over its target. Another Weasel flight in the area had heard, "going to egress by Quang Khe and head south," and then there was nothing. Beeper activity was detected near Butterfly Lake, just west of Dong Hoi, and it continued for twenty-four hours. But Captain

---

*Major James was released in March 1973 and Captain Martin's remains were repatriated on November 8, 1989.

Cliff Fieszel and Major Howard Smith, flying as Bison 01 that day, were never seen again.*

Fieszel and Smith were the last of five F-105F Weasel crews lost in action in 1968. Always tragic, this was even more poignant given President Lyndon Johnson's October 31 announcement:

> *We have been engaged in discussions with the North Vietnamese in Paris since last May. The discussions began after I announced on the evening of March 31st in a television speech to the Nation that the United States—in an effort to get talks started on a settlement of the Vietnam war—had stopped the bombing of North Vietnam in the area where 90 percent of the people live.*
>
> *Now, as a result of all of these developments, I have now ordered that all air, naval, and artillery bombardment of North Vietnam cease as of 8 a.m., Washington time, Friday morning. I have reached this decision on the basis of the developments in the Paris talks.*
>
> *And I have reached it in the belief that this action can lead to progress toward a peaceful settlement of the Vietnamese war.*

"YOU GOTTA BE shittin' me."

Stan Goldstein dropped his fork in his fish and rice and leaned back in the chair, openmouthed and astonished.

---

* No remains were ever turned over to U.S. authorities, and as of today their fate is still unknown.

"Nope. Says so right here." John Revak waved the *Bangkok Post* at his friend, who was calmer but no less astonished. The October 31, 1968, front-page article confidently predicted Lyndon Johnson was going to call a halt on Operation Rolling Thunder sometime that night. In September the president had stated there would be no bombing halt until he was certain it would not lead to American deaths. John and Stan had taken that as a good sign, since they'd been closing in on their coveted hundredth mission over North Vietnam. For he and John this was the difference of going home in a few weeks or waiting until March 1969. That very morning, when John pulled the throttle to cutoff and shut down the engine, he, Stan, and their Thud, *Crown Seven,* had finished their ninety-ninth mission.*

They'd taken off at 0520 that morning as Locust 01, leading a two-ship Iron Hand mission against the SAMs in Route Pack One. After air refueling they'd arrived on station over North Vietnam at 0630, waiting for Pistol—the F-105 strikers—to appear. One of the SAM sites was farther north, near the Gianh River, and supposedly it was covering the Mu Gia Pass. Three others were reported to be down south, only a few miles north of the DMZ. The strikers hit the targets and everyone funneled out of Pack One while John and Stan refueled again and landed back at Korat around 0800.

"Ninety-nine missions!" Stan shook his head, exhaled loudly, and thumped the table. They were in the "KABOOM," the Korat Air Base Officer's Open Mess, sitting at the 44 TFS squadron table. Their very cute Thai waitress had walked them through the "No-hab" part of the day's menu, so the pair

---

*F-105F No. 62-4424 would be converted to a G-model Weasel in December 1969. It would go down with Majors Bill Talley and Jim Padgett on May 11, 1972.

had settled on fried fish, with sticky white rice. "It just can't happen."

Revak took a long drink of warm iced tea, hating the clammy feel of his sweaty flight suit under the air-conditioning. Frankly he'd suspected something like this was coming, but, like a lot of guys, he thought it would be closer to Christmas. Politicians and generals always tried to do goofy stuff around the holidays, thinking it would improve morale. *Being allowed to really fight, win quick, and go home . . . that would improve my morale,* Revak thought. Glancing at Stan's grim face, he pushed his chair back and stood. "Let's go see Jack."

Lieutenant Colonel Guy Sherrill, known as "Jack" behind his back or "sir" to his face, had been the Vampire squadron commander since May. Lean, with close-cropped gray hair, he always seemed to have a cigar dangling from his fingers. As the designated spare for Stan and John's mission, Sherrill had also been up since the wee hours today. The cigar wasn't helping much, the coffee was bad, and now this. He listened to the pleading as commanders usually do, even though his mind was already made up. Sherrill sympathized—up to a point.

"Well, sir . . . can we do it?"

The three men were standing in a small office behind the ops desk. Sherrill was propped nonchalantly against a gray metal cabinet and staring with mild disgust at his coffee cup. To be one mission short was agonizing. Still, there was a limit to what the commander could do, or would do. The two officers asked to pull a "double turn"—to fly an afternoon mission. This just wasn't done except in an emergency and was almost always considered a bad idea. Guys were tired, and tired men sometimes make mistakes. Pilots are also superstitious and equated flying up north twice in one day with giving Fate the bird.

"Whattaya worried about anyway?" Sherrill cleared his

scratchy throat and took a cautious sip of coffee. "Might not happen," he said of the recent news. "We all know the rumor mill is usually fulla shit."

The two Weasels didn't believe that any more than he did. John Revak replied softly, "Not this time, sir."

Sherrill sighed and stared at the whiteboards lining the wall—this was the scheduling shop, the pulse of a wartime squadron. It was here men were matched with jets and missions according to the frag order. The time over the target was the hard number. Air refueling tracks and times were backed up from this time, as were takeoffs, taxi, step, and briefing times. He *could* switch the two into a later mission; they'd flown early enough to help plan and brief it. However, if he let it happen once, then everyone would want exceptions made. Blowing noxious smoke sideways out of his mouth, Colonel Sherrill stared at both men and managed a regretful smile. He knew how they felt, but it would set a bad precedent.

"I do not schedule based upon the front page of the *Bangkok Post*." And that was that. Until November 25, 1968.

"THIS SUCKS." MAJOR Stan Goldstein shoved the helmet visor up and stared off the right wingtip at North Vietnam. They were so close. He could see the damn place.

Major John Revak nodded but said nothing. He was flying a loose, half-mile-wide formation off the other F-105G, and watching the cloud deck 10,000 feet below. The Wild Weasel pair was patrolling on the Laotian side of the border covering the passes through the Annam highlands. Starting at the DMZ, they'd flown north past the Ban Karai Pass, then Mu Gia, and were now headed up toward the Nape Pass. They were directly over the heart of the Ho Chi Minh Trail, and both men were casually alert. SAMs weren't supposed to be down this far, but you never knew.

You just never knew.

"One mission . . . one more shitty mission." Stan groused and the pilot grinned under his oxygen mask. His EWO had been fired up for three weeks now, but who could blame him? The pair had flown once since the end of Rolling Thunder, and it had been a noncounter—they hadn't made it into North Vietnam. That had been on November 5, covering a B-52 Arc Light strike against the Ho Chi Minh Trail. He shot a glance to his left at the relatively flat terrain south of the pass. Right there, where the Trail spilled out onto the Xiangkhoang Plateau, it split apart into hundreds of paths and continued toward South Vietnam. If only they could get cleared to cross the border, they'd have their hundredth combat mission.

"Didya hear about the Recce Rhino?"*

"Yeah." Revak shifted back to the flight lead. Ozark One, Major Floyd Dadisman Jr., was about a mile away at his two o'clock position and a little low. "From the Fourteenth Reconnaissance. Squadron at Udorn. That makes what, two this month?"

"Yep. So that's at least a dozen photo birds down since April."

"Tough business."

Stan nodded. "Must really stink to not be able to shoot back."

The frustrated pilot gazed across the cloud-draped peaks. *Can't shoot back.* It didn't make sense to come all the way over here and take the same risks just to get photos of trees, truck parks, and mostly empty SAM sites. "Navy lost a Vigilante this morning up in Pack Four."

---

* "Rhino" and "Double Ugly" were slang terms for the F-4 Phantom.

"Yeah. Now there's a smart idea. Take the biggest jet you've got and send it out to take pictures of things that can kill you."

Revak winced at the dark humor, but Stan had a point. The RA-5 was even bigger than the F-105. Something like eighty feet long compared to sixty-four feet for the Thud. He sighed and wriggled in the seat, flexing his aching shoulders. The pilot reached down into his g-suit right ankle pocket and pulled out a candy bar. It was 1235 and time for his mid-mission treat. Tugging his gloves off one at a time, John squeezed his knees together to hold the stick steady, then carefully unwrapped the bar.

"Couple of weak Firecans . . . right three to four o'clock." The EWO sounded bored.

"How weak?" He glanced in the mirror and saw Stan twisted around in the seat, leaning against the canopy and gazing out toward the coast.

"Thirty miles or so. Maybe in the river valley or around Ban Karai."

The clouds broke up past the mountains and both men could see the blue gleam of the Gulf of Tonkin out beyond the Vietnamese coast. Stan thought about his friends who'd went down and gone missing over there four months ago. Larry Martin and Gobel James had been in the same Wild Weasel class at Nellis, and both being engineers, Stan and James had some interesting discussions.

"BEE EAR, BEE EAR, BEE EAR."

Both helmeted heads snapped up, staring off toward North Vietnam. Emergency beacon signals were blaring—always bad news.

"Ahh . . . shit." John Revak automatically glanced down and checked his fuel. That sound always made his heart quicken; it meant an American was down in enemy territory. A guy like himself, someone with a home and a family, a dog and a car. He sat up straighter and peered at his scopes. *It could be me.*

The radios went berserk.

"Crown Six, Crown Six . . . this is Grommet One!"

"Go for Crown Six."

"BEE EAR, BEE EAR, BEE EAR."

". . . for sixty-one. Repeat, Grommet Two is down at three-zero-zero degrees for sixty-one . . . Channel 109."

From the corner of his eye, John Revak saw Ozark One bank up and begin to turn to the southeast. When the lead Thud crossed the nose, he bunted the stick forward, added power, and stayed a bit high as they turned to follow. Stan pulled out his map and spread it across his lap. He found Dong Ha, which was where the Channel 109 was located. Using his fingers to measure off sixty miles, he placed them along a northwest heading off the TACAN. Marking the spot with his pencil, he looked up and out. Most of the plateau was covered by low clouds, but through a few holes he could see the gray, scabby ground.

"You know where we are?"

The pilot snorted with mock disgust, switching off GUARD so the emergency beacon wouldn't block out other radio transmissions. Rolling out toward the southeast, John floated to the outside of the turn such that he was looking through the other Weasel toward the border. "Laos, right?" He answered sarcastically.

"Okay, okay . . . sorry."

"Right over Mu Gia . . . look left."

Stan did, and through the low-lying weather he saw the distinctive dish-shaped pass through the mountains. Farther east and south the cloud cover filled in solid, blocking his view.

"Did ya plot it out?" Revak asked, glancing at his fuel again, then back at the flight lead.

"Yep." Squinting at the map again, Stan eyeballed the position. "Off the nose for thirty-five miles . . . They're a coupla miles north of the border . . . just east of the pass."

New voices had joined in by now as the search and rescue (SAR) network went into action. Skyraiders sitting alert at Nakhon Phanom had gotten airborne immediately, and the Jolly Green rescue helicopter was just lifting off to follow. It turned out that Grommet Two was the F-4D escort for the RF-4C photoreconnaissance jet, and he'd apparently gotten hit by Triple A near the pass.* Having SAR assets so close was one clear advantage to operating this far south. "Naked Fanny," as the base on the Mekong was known, sat less than 100 miles away, meaning the Spads could be overhead in fifteen or twenty minutes. The RF-4 pilot who'd been leading the recce flight was doing a good job talking, passing information, and getting all the wheels rolling. Fortunately one of the nearby F-100 flights was a Misty FAC, a forward air controller qualified fighter pilot who was used to reading maps, directing fire support, and finding things on the ground.

Stan and John listened as Misty 41 located the wreckage, got the downed pilot on the radio, and then found him visually. As the on-scene commander, the FAC started with a roll call of all the available aircraft, which Stan then jotted down. There was Grommet One, the RF-4, then Nail, an O-2 that was spotting for movers along the trail. A flight of B-52s somewhere high overhead also offered to help.

"All they need now are Weasels," John remarked, hoping they could get in and help.

"Misty 41 . . . Misty 41 . . . this is Ozark One."

---

*Grommet 01 was photographing Route 137, the primary road running from the port of Dong Hoi through the Ban Karai Pass into the North Vietnamese–Laotian border region.

Both listened as their flight lead, Major Floyd Dadisman, called in with their type of aircraft, ordnance, and time available in minutes. "He's a mind reader," Stan remarked, but he was pleased nonetheless. All airborne missions stopped when someone went down, and nothing had a higher priority than recovering brothers who were down in enemy territory. Ozark was cleared into the working area and the two Weasels trolled for threats. Searching electronically for radars and SAMs, they strained their eyes watching for airbursts or missile trails while the rescue unfolded. Major Joe Morrison, the pilot of Grommet Two, and First Lieutenant San Dewayne Francisco, another pilot flying as a weapon systems officer, or WSO, had ejected safely, made it down fairly close together, and were talking to the Skyraiders. The helicopter arrived and visually sighted one of the parachutes tangled in a tree; everything looked good.

Until the extraction was attempted.

Unfortunately the two Americans on the ground had ejected directly over a major artery along the Ho Chi Minh Trail, barely forty-five miles from the Laotian town of Tchepone. Thousands of NVA soldiers and Viet Cong irregulars came through the passes on their way to South Vietnam. Flowing into Laos, the paths and trails converged on Tchepone, the hub of the whole network, before continuing south. Base Area 604 surrounded the town, and farther north, near Grommet Two's crash site, was the Ban Trim Base Area and the 1st VPA Division. Both men had come down within a half mile of a North Vietnamese encampment and had no chance of remaining undetected.

Despite the Skyraiders circling overhead, as the Jolly Green made its approach to pick up the fliers, the surrounding hillsides erupted with small arms fire. Using downed aircrew as bait was an old NVA trick, and it almost worked again. However, the Skyraiders roared in and shredded the hillside, allowing the helicopter to limp away to safety. Then that heavy, helpless feeling settled in among every man listening. It was a mix of guilty relief that someone else was down there in the gathering dark, surrounded by enemies—and the horrible knowledge that you couldn't do a thing about it. The SAR pilots promised to return the next day, and flight by flight everyone wheeled off to the southwest. *Hang tough, guys. Keep the faith . . . we will come back.*

And they did.

The Spads arrived with the rising sun, but they heard nothing from Lieutenant Francisco: sometime during that dark, cold night his enemies had caught up with him. However, Joe Morrison was still very much alive and free. His location was confirmed, so he waited, staring up through the gray mist, desperately straining to hear the beating sound of rotor blades. This time it was the fog that was the problem, and once again the chopper couldn't land. The rescue was postponed a few hours. When the sun finally burned away the mist and the SAR force returned there was nothing: no voice contact, no signal, and no sign of the two Americans.

Later that day, November 26, 1968, the *People's Army* newspaper ran a story congratulating the residents of Quang Binh for shooting down an F-4 fighter: it asserted the pilots were captured alive. Maybe, but neither man made it to a POW camp or was ever seen again by any American. Their maps, dog tags, a driver's license, and other personal effects did turn up in the 280th Air Defense Regiment's museum. Also displayed was a grainy black-and-white photograph showing the dead body of Major Joseph Castleton Morrison.

CAUGHT UP IN the rescue attempt, John and Stan did what they could to help save Grommet Two. It wasn't until they'd cleared the area and headed toward the tanker that both men realized they'd been back across the North Vietnamese border for the one hundredth time. They were done, so with a full load of fuel, the two Weasels put Channel 125 on the nose and rocketed back to Korat in record time. Major Dadisman radioed the 388th Fighter Wing Command Post, aka Fort Apache, and told them they had a hundred-mission flight inbound. Stan flew the high-speed pass and the 105 came scorching down the runway, afterburner lit, and ground shaking. Pulling up in a tight, closed pattern, Revak brought the Thud around, landed, and taxied to park. Everyone in the 44th Fighter Squadron was there, plus the maintainers, support folks, and a few pilots from the newly arrived 469th TFS (Fighting Bulls).*

As the engine wound down, Stan and John clambered off the ladder and were immediately surrounded and hosed down with high-pressure water from a waiting fire truck. The drenching, slippery wrestling match and champagne toasts were all traditional accolades for surviving warriors. This was also the first such mission since early November, and everyone enjoyed it. A slow-moving parade through the base came next, and the line of vehicles threaded its way past the flight line, back shops, and hangars. Puffing cigars and waving, the two Weasels emerged from the smoke and rolled up to the KABOOM for the *real* party.

Mobbed and dragged from the jeep, John and Stan were bodily launched into the Officers' Club pool, then carried inside. At eighty-four feet long, the bar was the longest in Southeast Asia, and by tradition if the bell over the bar was rung then everyone got a free round of drinks.

---

*F-105F No. 63-8306 would be converted to a G model on December 18, 1969. It would fly during the Son Tay raid on November 20, 1970, surviving the war and returning to the United States.

Bedraggled, soggy, and happy, both men jumped up and promptly rang the bell. Eventually every bottle of cognac in the club was dumped into a soup tureen then mixed with champagne—a concoction called a French 75. Everyone drank, sang, and slapped backs until the booze was gone. Stan and John closed out the night by somehow making it to the NCO club, where they bought rounds for all the enlisted guys who serviced and armed the jets.

After they had recovered painfully from the diamond-splinter hangovers, there would be a week of out-processing, packing up, and a private Vampire going-away party—but it was over. On December 4, 1968, Major Stan Goldstein left Korat for the last time and headed to Bangkok. American officers in transit stayed at the Chao Phya Hotel, next to the Siam InterContinental, which accommodated commercial airline stewardesses on their layovers. Stan passed on that opportunity, and also on the "hotsie bath" he was offered when passing a beauty parlor. Relaxing for the first time in a year, he bought jewelry and presents for his family, then three days later lifted off on a military charter bound for California.*

Operation Rolling Thunder was over. During the forty-four months between March 1965 and November 1968, some 864,000 tons of bombs were dropped on the North, more tonnage than was employed in the entire Korean War.† A total of 306,183 combat sorties were flown by U.S. aircraft, of which 153,784 belonged to the USAF alone. It did not force Hanoi to negotiate, nor did it destroy the Ho Chi Minh Trail, though it

---

*Stan actually tried to come home via boat, thinking it might be fun. He was told that returning from Southeast Asia by ship was reserved for those afraid of flying and that plainly didn't apply to someone who'd just completed one hundred missions over North Vietnam.
†There were 653,000 tons dropped during the Korean War.

did severely curtail operations. Supplies and men still moved south, morale was undiminished, and there was little permanent effect on the North's rural, agrarian life. More than half the bridges in North Vietnam were destroyed, as were 9,821 vehicles, 1,966 railcars, and nearly 60 percent of the power generation capacity, yet, as Tet proved, the North Vietnamese were in no way defeated.

But the cost for America was terrible: CIA analysis put the financial cost at $6.60 spent for each dollar's worth of damage to North Vietnam. Operational and combat aircraft losses totaled 506 from the USAF and an additional 416 lost from the Navy and Marines. Heinous as those figures are, they pale next to the cost in lives. More than 450 naval aviators were killed, wounded, or captured. The Air Force lost 255 killed; 222 captured, of whom 23 died in captivity; and 123 missing in action. In the end the political restrictions, diplomatic compromises, and divided U.S. command structure marginalized the success of Rolling Thunder. Those culpable, both in and out of uniform, put true victory out of the hands of those who fought so skillfully and sacrificed so much.

MAJOR JOHN REVAK stopped over at Takhli for several days to attend a tactics conference, passing on some of what he knew to those who would remain behind. On December 15, as his commercial flight left Yakota Air Base, Japan, the pilot leaned back in his seat and let it all sink in. Happy, incredulous, and proud, he'd made it. Relieved to have survived, he, like Stan, was grateful to be spared the quick death of combat or the hell of captivity. Time would not dim the memory of their coveted one hundred Wild Weasel missions nor would they forget the men who never came home.

CHAPTER 10

WINDS OF CHANGE

WINDING THROUGH THE mountains, the pewter-colored Gianh River made a sharp bend to the east, then continued twisting south toward the Mu Gia Pass and the Laotian border. Just west of the bend was a line of hills, higher than the others, stretching about four miles from tip to tail. Between this rugged, arrow-shaped ridge and the river was a narrow, passable area, and here lay the Ho Chi Minh Trail. Using Soviet-supplied four-inch pipe, the North Vietnamese had constructed several pipelines connecting Vinh to the Mu Gia Pass. This section of the Trail contained several such lifelines running through the valley roughly parallel to the path. Next to it, oriented south to protect both trail and pipeline, was a SAM site.

As the two American fighters thundered up the valley, the Fansong target tracking radar found them and went from its dummy load to full power in a matter of seconds. Seabird One was an RF-4C Phantom on a reconnaissance mission and never saw the radar or the guns. Smoking through the hills at 540 knots, it pressed north and continued snapping pictures. The escort, Seabird Two, was an F-105G Wild Weasel—and it did notice the SAM.

The G-model F-105 was one of 64 F-105Fs modified with the latest radar hunting and killing equipment.

Bob Panek Sr., a thirty-year-old captain from Chicago, was the EWO in the back of Seabird Two on that late January day in 1972. The radar picked up a Fansong close off the nose, and he reacted immediately, calling the threat out to the pilot. A long, long way from Portland, Oregon, Captain Richard Mallon had seen muzzle flashes near the river and instantly jinked. Pulling straight back with his right hand, he went into afterburner with his left. As the Thud soared skyward, the pilot shoved the stick forward, forcing their butts off the seat as the nose came down. Tracers from AK-47s shot up past the fighter and Mallon pulled savagely sideways, spoiling the gunner's aim. Dirty white puffs from 37 mm guns spotted against the dark hills, and suddenly both jets were over the hills to the north and safe.

While the RF-4 climbed up out of harm's way, the Weasel spun around to attack. Under the current, inane rules of engagement a fighter could only shoot if first fired upon—assuming he survived, of course. Wild Weasels hadn't carried bombs since 1968, but they always had their 20 mm cannon. Dropping down from the hills, his orange gunsight glowing against the green background, Mallon stared at the flat area nestled against the trees and opened fire. Cannon shells chewed up the earth and the Fansong van disappeared under a cloud of debris. Not sure if he hit it, the pilot muscled the Thud around and attacked again. Emptying the cannon into the clearing, he pulled up and was looking back when sudden, violent blows kicked the fighter sideways. The red fire light glowed as hydraulic pressure dropped. Both men knew the F-105 was finished.

Fear gripped his heart, but the pilot's feet and hands reacted from long training. Nursing the battered Weasel up away from the valley, Seabird Two called to the RF-4 and headed south-west over the hills toward Laos. The coast was closer, only half the distance, but Mallon knew the SAR forces were just eighty miles away, at Nakhon Phanom. The Skyraiders and Jolly Greens would be airborne within minutes and every mile closer increased their chances of rescue. Mouth dry, he was under no illusions about ejecting over the Ho Chi Minh Trail. If they could even make it a dozen miles past the valley then he and Bob Panek would have a chance.

They didn't even get five miles.

Designed as a low-altitude nuclear bomber with no thought given to the threat of anti-aircraft fire, the F-105 had hydraulic lines that all ran along the belly—truly the big jet's Achilles' heel. Once the hydraulics were damaged it was only a matter of time until control was lost. As the controls stiffened and the Thud began an uncommanded roll, the Weasels ejected. Two parachutes were seen; Richard Mallon landed on the trail itself and was captured immediately. Bob Panek came down in the trees; he was surrounded and also taken captive. A pair of A-1s arrived shortly and began circling overhead, waiting for the helicopter. Unfortunately the SA-2 had been lying in wait and opened fire, scattering the Skyraiders. Fortunately the missile couldn't guide against the low, slow aircraft, and it missed. Twenty miles northwest, two HH-53s from the 40th ARRS weren't so lucky. A flight of MiG-21s had appeared from the northeast and attacked the choppers. Jolly Green 71 was hit by an Atoll infrared missile and went down immediately, killing all six crew members.* The SAR attempt fell apart and the remaining aircraft were forced to return to base, though

---

*Major Holly Gene Bell, Captain Leonard Leeser, Senior Master Sergeant William Pruett, Technical Sergeant William Sutton, Sergeant William Shinn, and Sergeant Greg Anderson.

one of the Skyraider pilots reported seeing both Americans in a clearing with their hands up and surrounded by NVA troops. Stripped to their underwear, the Weasels had plainly survived to be taken prisoner.

Neither man was ever seen alive again.*

"I WILL NOT be the first president of the United States to lose a war."

So stated Richard Milhous Nixon on January 20, 1969, after being sworn in as the thirty-seventh American president. Nixon was elected largely because he pledged to end the Vietnam War, and his quandary was how to do this without forsaking the South Vietnamese or losing prestige and honor. Following their military losses during Tet, the Viet Cong effectively ceased to exist, and when Nixon took office there were no real communist zones remaining in the South. Most big NVA units had withdrawn north across the borders to reinforce, replenish, and reconstitute. Some came back up the Ho Chi Minh Trail while others retreated to sanctuaries in Cambodia or Laos.

It was here then that the new fight was to be made. If the previously untargeted strongholds in Laos and Cambodia could be eliminated, and the Ho Chi Minh Trail finally severed, then the Vietnamization of the South would succeed. This control and defense of a stable South Vietnam by its own inhabitants had always been the primary public goal of U.S. involvement in the war. Johnson's administration had believed the way to ensure this was by using American military power to force a policy change in Hanoi—but clearly this hadn't worked. LBJ,

---

*Captain Richard Joseph Mallon and Captain Bob Panek Sr.'s remains were returned in December 1988.

McNamara, and Westmoreland had no realistic understanding about the use of such force in a Southeast Asian scenario, so the war had dragged on.

Nixon had no such qualms about using force.

Also swept aside with the winds of change, General Westmoreland had been promoted, or replaced, depending on one's viewpoint, following Tet. His successor, a West Point classmate and his former deputy commander, immediately put MACV on a different heading. General Creighton Abrams had made his reputation as an aggressive, innovative tank commander during World War II. Abrams had started the war as a captain, and his ability to think obliquely and meet objectives no matter what so impressed George Patton that by April 1945 he was a colonel. This unconventional attitude toward combat was exactly what MACV required and, unlike his predecessor, Abrams understood that the conflict in Southeast Asia was a civil war. It would be won or lost in the countryside of South Vietnam, not in the North.

His strategy was one of "Vietnamization," that is, of returning South Vietnam to its own people. America would eventually have to pull out of Southeast Asia, and if Saigon was no more than a puppet regime then it would collapse in short order. To this end, his approach was to strengthen the ARVN and transform it into a credible, reliable fighting force. Under the cover of U.S. airpower, and with sophisticated logistical support, he felt that the South Vietnamese could make South Vietnam safe. The present lack of security was the crack in the wall that Hanoi was exploiting and that Abrams proposed to fill. His war would be one of winning hearts and minds, not the war of search and destroy.

"I know the fighting is important," Abrams stated to his commanders. "[B]uilding the village and the hamlet, and really building a base there and so on. I really think that, of all the things, that's the most important. That's where the battle ultimately is won."

In this Abrams was aided by the new commander in chief and by outside events. Though outwardly united, the communist bloc of the Soviet Union and People's Republic of China had begun fracturing badly. On March 2, 1969, less than forty-five days into Nixon's term, military units from Red China's People's Liberation Army (PLA) ambushed and killed fifty-nine Soviet border guards on Zhenbao Island in the Ussuri River. Counterattacks and incidents followed all through the summer, and by August Chinese troops attacked Tielieketi, in Soviet Kazakhstan, and were repulsed. Both nations had nuclear weapons, and it was now Moscow and Beijing that were worried about U.S. reaction to a war. As Washington had done over Vietnam, the two communist powers began second-guessing the possible consequences.

Moscow dreaded Chinese hegemony over the Asian Pacific rim, while Beijing, always paranoid about its belligerent neighbor, feared Soviet expansion. This seemed especially apropos given the August 1968 Soviet invasion of Czechoslovakia and the Arab-Israeli conflict. China badly needed U.S. trade, and Beijing had interpreted the halt of Rolling Thunder as a clear sign that the United States had no territorial ambitions in Asia. This, combined with their worsening relations with Moscow, led the Chinese to seek a rapprochement with Washington, sending shock waves rippling through North Vietnam, Laos, and Cambodia.

NORODOM SIHANOUK HAD become the king of Cambodia at the age of nineteen. Educated in Saigon, and later at the École de Cavalerie in western France, the young man was crowned in May 1941. Adroitly sitting on the fence during the Japanese occupation of Indochina, Sihanouk kept Cambodia within the postwar French Union. Though appointed as prime minister by Paris, he was increasingly nationalistic, joining Laos and the Democratic Republic of Vietnam by splintering Indochina into separate nations. Following the French collapse, Sihanouk abdicated in favor of his father and remained prime minister until 1960. After the old king's death, Sihanouk was elected the head of state as a prince of Cambodia, rather than a king.

As the war in Vietnam escalated, he again displayed a talent for survival and remained neutral—at least officially. The prince knew that the United States would not remain in Southeast Asia indefinitely, and without its military might the Republic of South Vietnam was doomed. Sharing Hanoi's nationalistic views and not wishing an open conflict with his neighbors, Sihanouk allied himself with Hanoi. His position was precarious, however, sandwiched between a U.S.-controlled Republic of South Vietnam and Cambodia's age-old enemy, Thailand. Adept politician that he was, Sihanouk reasoned that an alliance with the People's Republic of China was the only sure bet for his nation's safety.

These alliances created key diplomatic, logistical, and strategic difficulties for both Saigon and Washington. No Cambodian airspace privileges were granted, not that Phnom Penh could do anything to stop U.S. aircraft; and, more significant, the port of Kompong Som, better known as Sihanoukville, on the Gulf of Siam, was now open to Chinese vessels. There, neutrally flagged Chinese ships made port with an average of 200 tons of supplies per day that were destined for the Viet Cong. These were brought overland up from the gulf, along what became known as the Sihanouk Trail, to base camps near the Vietnamese border.

But by late 1968 the frigid relations between Washington
and Beijing were already thawing. As they'd done regarding
Hanoi, the pragmatic Chinese reasoned that American trade
and international recognition were more valuable than anything Cambodia could offer. As a result, overt aid declined, and
faced with a loss of Chinese support Sihanouk renewed negotiations with Washington. This was undoubtedly prompted by the
spread of the indigenous Khmer Rouge within his borders, and
the very real fear that large numbers of Vietnamese communists
could eventually overthrow his reign.*

For the newly inaugurated President Nixon this provided an
excellent opportunity to kill off several birds with a big stone.
Free from worry over Chinese intervention, he could now move
against NLF and NVA sanctuaries in Cambodia. This would
very likely cripple logistical support for the Viet Cong, allowing
Vietnamization to really take hold, and thus permit a wide-
scale American withdrawal from Southeast Asia. By wiping out
the communists in Cambodia he could also be potentially re-
cruiting another regional ally in the form of a grateful Prince
Sihanouk. All that was needed was a pretext, an excuse, which
the NLF provided in late February 1969. Nixon maintained that
the latest attacks on Saigon violated the de facto "truce" created
by the halt of Rolling Thunder. So after church in Washington
on Sunday, March 17, he commenced Operation Menu.

Sensitive to his own domestic peace movement issues,
Nixon had the first phase of the operation, called Breakfast,
served in secrecy. Forty-eight of sixty B-52s on an Arc Light
strike veered off at a preplanned point and headed farther west
into Cambodia. A few minutes later Base Area 353, just inside
the border, was suddenly vaporized by 2,400 tons of bombs.

---

*The Khmer Rouge were the predominant Cambodian communists.

Over the next fourteen months other gastronomic strikes would follow: Lunch (Base Area 609), Snack (Base Area 351), Dinner (Base Area 352), Supper (Base Area 740), and Dessert (Base Area 350). All told, 108,823 tons of bombs were dropped from more than 3,600 sorties during the secret bombing of Cambodia.

As for the situation between the Soviet Union and Red China, they wanted to fight over their disputed border but were not prepared for the consequences. In September, Soviet ambassador Aleksei Kosygin and Chinese diplomat Zhou Enlai met at the Beijing airport to begin negotiations. Kosygin was on his way back to Moscow from a state funeral—in North Vietnam. Ho Chi Minh's death had been announced on September 2, 1969, and his burial took place a week later in Hanoi. Many in the West had been hoping that his death would mean a quicker end to the war, but, though still the spiritual leader of Vietnam, he had long since passed operational control to others due to his failing health. Ho was succeeded by a triumvirate of the defense minister, General Vo Nguyen Giap; Le Duan, the Communist Party's first secretary; and Truong Chin, chairman of the National Assembly. Each had his own ideas about the war and leadership by committee is difficult even under the best of circumstances. Clearly these were not the best of times for Hanoi, since a quite different American president now occupied the White House and there had been a material loss of support from its communist allies.

Regarding the war, Nixon had stated back in 1964 that "all that is needed, in short, is the will to win and the courage to use our power—now." If war had been inevitable in 1964, which it was not, then it certainly *could* have been won if conducted clearly, violently, and ruthlessly. Far better to fight viciously, overwhelmingly, and decisively for a short amount of time than

to slug away halfheartedly for years, expending blood and trea-
sure to no avail.

But this was 1969, not 1964, and the situation had changed
both for better and for worse. By April, American combat casualties had exceeded those suffered during the Korean War and
the peace movement was now a serious force with which to contend. Wanting an opinion beyond the State Department, CIA,
and the Pentagon, the new administration had commissioned
the RAND Corporation to explore possible options regarding Vietnam. Among other things, the study concluded that
the DRV expected the United States to withdraw in the face of
mounting domestic opposition. It also discussed the *threat* of
escalation on the DRV, and its willingness to make concessions.
The Madman Theory, as Nixon called it, was one result of this
and in July he let the rumor reach Hanoi that he was considering atomic weapons. By August he said to H. R. Haldeman,
his White House chief of staff, "I want the North Vietnamese
to believe I've reached the point where I might do anything to
stop the war."

Giving strength to the rumors and illustrating his lack of
patience, Nixon dispatched a personal, secret communiqué to
Ho Chi Minh in August. It was a warning that if the Paris
Peace Talks were simply a ruse to gain time, then the United
States would react accordingly. It was hoped that the shadow of
nuclear weapons, bombing, and the threat of resumed bombing
would have an effect on Hanoi. Unfortunately the North Vietnamese called his bluff and refused any concessions. Two weeks
later, on September 3, 1969, Ho Chi Minh was dead.

Nixon decided that November 1, 1969, would be the drop-
dead date for his ultimatum. If negotiations were not produc-
tive then the one-year anniversary of the Rolling Thunder halt
would open a new and final chapter of the war. The planning

phase of this proposed offensive was called Pruning Knife, and responsibility for its success was entrusted to a fighting man, not a staff officer or political advisor. Rear Admiral Fred Bardshar had shot down eight Japanese aircraft as a Hellcat fighter pilot with VF-27 during World War II and had commanded the USS *Constellation* during the Gulf of Tonkin incident. With a Silver Star, three Distinguished Flying Crosses, and a variety of combat commands, he was the man for the job.

Called Duck Hook, the actual operation would accomplish everything that should have been done in 1965. Haiphong was to be mined and the rest of North Vietnam's ports would be blockaded. Massive, carefully timed air strikes would wipe out airfields and air defenses and destroy the North Vietnamese Air Force. Railways and major roads would be cut, bridges destroyed, and vital irrigation dikes obliterated. Interestingly, the subject of invasion also reappeared. If the area around the DMZ was occupied by U.S. and ARVN troops it would send an unmistakable signal to Hanoi, and could provide for a permanent border between the Vietnams.

All of this only confirmed to Nixon what he already knew: military victory was the only way to have leverage and end the war. Still frustrated by missing combat in the Pacific during World War II, the president likely saw this not only as a way to end the conflict in Southeast Asia, but also as a personal vindication. In any event, the sudden, massive blow of Duck Hook would cripple the NVA, send Hanoi reeling, and force peace negotiations on Washington's terms.

However, fate stepped in again under the antiwar banner as cities all over the United States erupted in protest. October 1969 saw the "Days of Rage" in Chicago, courtesy of Students for a Democratic Society (SDS). A national moratorium was organized for October 15 with thousands of American businesses shutting down for the day. A month later 600,000 protestors marched on Washington, D.C., catching Nixon and National Security Advisor Henry Kissinger by surprise with the scope of the demonstrations. In the end, fear of domestic ramifications shelved Duck Hook. Just as Johnson had wasted American lives to placate an unsubstantiated Chinese threat, so Nixon lost his best chance to end the war early by placating the peace movement. Some of these groups were dedicated and well-meaning, while others, like the Black Panthers or the Weathermen, were rabble. Either way, it is ironic and sad that their actions actually prolonged the very war they publicly sought to end.

DESPITE DEMONSTRATIONS OF American resolve, both Prince Sihanouk and the Chinese were playing both sides of the fence, and Nixon knew it. So in March 1970, when the prince was in France for medical treatment, Washington did nothing to stop the coup that deposed the Cambodian ruler. Fronted by Prime Minister Lon Nol, the new government ordered all NLF and NVA forces out of the country within seventy-two hours and another golden pretext fell into Nixon's lap. He immediately ordered the finishing touches on a plan to invade Cambodia that would continue to demonstrate that he was not Lyndon Johnson. This would also show that America's resolve was in no way diminished, and that the ARVN was capable of large-scale, offensive operations. On April 30, 1970, the president went on national television and announced, "It is not our power but our will and character that is being tested tonight. The time has come for action."

At the same time, twelve ARVN battalions crossed the border into Cambodia, followed the next day by 10,000 Americans and 5,000 South Vietnamese soldiers. Striking directly

into the Kampong Cham province, long a Viet Cong stronghold, they hoped to destroy the entire southern communist
organization. True to form, the NVA and Viet Cong stuck to
their tactic of falling back in the face of superior, fixed battles
with the Americans—especially when the latter were backed
by overwhelming airpower. Forewarned, many NVA units had
already left the border and were two days north when the fight
began.

However, the enemy could not take their supplies with them
and the loss of more than 20,000 weapons, 2,000 tons of ammunition, 55 tons of medical equipment, and 8,000 tons of rice
was devastating. U.S. figures put NVA and VC casualties at approximately 10,000, though this is difficult to verify.* Much
was publicized in Saigon and Washington about the ARVN
success, with President Nixon calling it the "most successful
military operation of the entire war." The military was more
circumspect, and the Pentagon realized that at best the NVA
had been disrupted rather than destroyed. Far from ARVN
being a self-sufficient, stand-alone force as portrayed, its victory
was only possible due to the spearhead of U.S. ground forces,
intensive, efficient logistical support, and an umbrella of 6,665
American tactical air sorties.

Reaction to the invasion in the United States was predictable. Antiwar demonstrations, some exceeding 100,000
people, erupted in large cities. ROTC buildings on college
campuses were attacked and at least thirty were burned. On
May 4, Ohio National Guardsmen opened fire on a group of
enraged, rock-throwing protestors at the Kent State University
campus, killing four students. Yet several weeks later 100,000

---

*American losses were 338 killed in action with 1,525 wounded. ARVN losses
were 809 killed and 3,486 wounded.

pro-administration marchers walked through New York City to show support for Nixon's efforts to end the war.

Congress was not so supportive. Many believed Nixon had exceeded the limited authority granted the presidency in the 1964 Southeast Asia Resolution. It was admitted that a president's ability to wage war, without congressional approval, was one reason this war was still being fought. LBJ had gotten away with it, but Republican senator John Cooper of Kentucky and Democratic senator Frank Church of Idaho, both World War II veterans, were determined to ensure Richard Nixon would not. The pair passed an amendment to the Foreign Military Sales Act that would cut off U.S. support for ARVN operations beyond South Vietnamese territorial borders. It would also eliminate funding for American ground operations in Laos and Cambodia after June 30, 1970, and would prohibit air support of Cambodian operations without congressional approval. It was a measure of national discontent with the conduct of the war that the amendment passed by a vote of 58 to 37 in the Senate. Failing in the House of Representatives by a sizable margin, the amendment would nevertheless reappear later in the year.

The invasion and Vietnamese threat were also used by the new government in Phnom Penh to clean house, as it were. The oppressive, genocidal actions that followed certainly alienated the populace and in the long run lost Cambodia to Pol Pot and his Khmer Rouge. The White House additionally claimed victory on the grounds that Cambodia was now denied to the enemy as a base for the future. This is also subjective, however, as the Viet Cong and NVA simply fell back into the hills, gathered their forces in Laos, and waited.

RICHARD NIXON HAD always known that the window of opportunity to effect a "peace with honor," a satisfactory American withdrawal, was limited. This was glaringly apparent in the wake of the fall 1970 Cambodian invasion, and time was running out. Facing reelection in 1972, he had to end the war, and this could only happen with an independent South Vietnam free from Hanoi's threat. The twin pillars of this scenario were built on Vietnamization, and the destruction of the Ho Chi Minh Trail through aerial interdiction. To many, the American incursion into Cambodia had shown what was possible, while to others the situations were totally different.

Interdiction by American aircraft cost the DRV roughly three tons of material for every one ton it managed to get to the bottom of the trail. Yet for an army living off the land and only requiring some 6,000 tons per annum, these were acceptable losses. Also, despite the tremendous expense of the old McNamara Line (which had been abandoned), tens of thousands of sorties, and tons of bombs delivered, the trail still functioned quite well. The NVA 559th Transportation Group had perfected logistical operations by essentially turning the entire network into an interactive human computer. Each section had its own manager, who could route or reroute convoys, determine priorities, and provide air defense.

This also represented a change. In the early days, those on the ground had fought U.S. aircraft using AK-47s and other small arms. With a tactical effective range of 4,000 feet, these were easily defeated by simply flying higher. As they'd done against the French at Dien Bien Phu, the Vietnamese then managed to bring lighter-caliber 37 mm anti-aircraft guns overland to key points. By 1970, courtesy of the Rolling Thunder bombing halt, greater numbers of heavier weapons could now be brought farther down the trail. More than 800 guns of all calibers were now deployed around the Nape, Mu Gia, and Ban Karai passes. Tchepone, the trail's main hub in Laos, was the only area with access to the sea through the North Vietnamese port of Vinh. Vital and heavily defended by guns, Firecan radars, and a few SA-2 batteries, if South Vietnam was to be secure then Tchepone would have to be destroyed.

Washington's answer was Operation Lam Son 719—a limited invasion along the Sepon River in eastern Laos.* There were issues with this, however, and though the Cambodian incursion had been marginally successful, Laos was very different. To begin with, the area was about 400 miles closer to North Vietnam's supply lines and home to several large base areas. These were heavily defended, reasonably well fortified, and would be tenaciously contested. The notion that the ARVN was in any way capable of sustaining an invasion, with untried troops, against NVA regulars on their own ground was deeply flawed.

American support and firepower were deciding factors in the Cambodian invasion but there would be none of that in Laos. Senators Cooper and Church had passed a revised version of their amendment in late December 1970, and though many of the restrictions on airpower were relaxed, there would be no commitment of U.S. ground forces into Laos without congressional approval—and that just wasn't going to happen. The new law was a definite sign that support for the war was waning, and executive power was going to be forcibly curbed. Congress also controlled funding and without money there would be no fight.

The invasion itself was planned as a sort of Asian version of Operation Market Garden, the leapfrogging airborne assault on Holland during World War II. For the Laotian version there would be two main phases. The first involved reopening High-

---

*The name came from the village of Lam Son, the birthplace of a legendary Vietnamese who defeated the invading Chinese in 1427. The numerical designation was derived from the year, 1971, and Route 9, which was the main attack axis.

way 9, reoccupying the Khe Sanh combat base, and securing the countryside up to the Laotian border. One minute after midnight on January 30, 1971, the 1st Battalion of the U.S. 77th Armored left Dong Ha and headed west down Route 9. In an astounding display of technical prowess, American combat engineers repaired the road and rebuilt dozens of bridges. By February 1 the road was open to Khe Sanh, and three days later it was clear to Laos. Rather than repair the old airstrip at Khe Sanh, the engineers simply constructed another. The first C-130 landed on February 4, though significant improvements had to be made before heavy cargo could be brought in. Phase One was an unqualified success and ARVN units had begun moving forward during the final days of January.

The biggest problem facing them was that Hanoi knew all about Lam Son 719—and had since late December. Even before the operation kicked off, General Abrams and the White House were aware that there was no element of surprise. ARVN generals had openly discussed the operation and had even made official requests for reconnaissance photos of the Route 9 area west into Laos. As Abrams himself said, "The bulk of the enemy's combat units were in the vicinity of Tchepone and could be expected to defend his base areas and logistics centers against any allied operation."

So they did. Elements of three NVA divisions began moving in north and south of the road while a Viet Cong regiment deployed near the border. The ARVN advance began on February 8 and, though it progressed initially, soon bogged down. Some of the difficulty lay in the road past the border, which the Americans had not been permitted to repair. There was also a perennial fuel shortage for the seven hundred U.S. helicopters needed to airlift men, and, of course, the weather. Some ARVN officers were also overcome by cautiousness, and 1st Armored

Brigade's commander simply stopped and did not advance farther than Ban Dong.

Unfortunately for the ARVN, General Le Trong Tan commanded Military Region 4 and was probably the best field
commander the NVA possessed. A combat veteran of vast experience, the general believed in leading from the battlefield,
which he did. By March 6 the ARVN had, with heavy U.S. air
support, managed to push into Tchepone, but there was no way
to hold it. Tan brought up five divisions totaling some 40,000
men, with artillery and Soviet T-54/55 tanks. Fearing an an-
nihilation and extensive casualties, which would impact his
upcoming election, South Vietnamese president Thieu ordered
a withdrawal on March 16, 1971. A week later most of the
ARVN survivors had crossed the border back into Vietnam,
and by April 6 the newly renovated combat base at Khe Sanh
was again abandoned. Casualty figures are ambiguous since
ARVN commanders underreported their losses, and there were
supposedly no Americans in Laos to keep count.

U.S. losses, mostly helicopter pilots, were 215 killed in action,
with 1,149 wounded. Best sources have the South Vietnamese
losing 1,500 to 8,000 dead, with 5,000 to 12,000 wounded. It
is known that despite 107 choppers destroyed during 160,000
sorties, the ARVN clearly demonstrated that it was not up to
fighting the NVA. Lam Son 719 shattered morale and with
it any hope of long term self-actualization by the South Vietnamese. On April 7, 1971, Richard Nixon would announce,
"Tonight I can report that Vietnamization has succeeded!" The
president was correct, but not in the way he intended. Vietnamization would eventually happen, but it would come from
Hanoi, not Saigon.

Yet Hanoi's international position had worsened considerably since Rolling Thunder ended. Its two main communist

allies, Red China and the Soviet Union, were still slashing at each other across their disputed border and there were now forty-four Soviet divisions in the region. Aggravated and encouraged by Chairman Mao's Cultural Revolution, belligerent Chinese militancy had remained high but with considerable cost. The Red Guards, basically armed youth gangs, had been permitted to run rampant over the land to destroy the "Four Olds": culture, customs, traditional habits, and ideas. Mao considered these a threat to his new China and, like Stalin before him, would tolerate no rival to his own personality cult.

Yet as the reality of global isolation set in, combined with intellectual stagnation and a vast economic paralysis, the situation had to change. Without international recognition there would be no foreign trade, and Mao's ideology would die in hungry stomachs. Beijing was well aware that the United States held the key to the legitimacy that would keep its government in power. Quietly traveling to China in mid-1971, Henry Kissinger set the stage for the next unprecedented step: Nixon's own visit in early 1972, which was publicly announced in July.

By October 1971, the White House had proposed a cease-fire to Hanoi, to be followed by a prisoner exchange, and internationally supervised elections in South Vietnam. The complete withdrawal of U.S. troops would also occur within six months pending negotiations and subsequent North Vietnamese actions. It was also announced that the American president would travel to Moscow in May 1972 for a summit with Secretary Leonid Brezhnev. With their own economic and internal logistical difficulties, the Soviets were increasingly desperate for American grain. They also needed to divert a sizable portion of their budget from defense to domestic programs, and to do this Moscow needed the United States to sign the Strategic Arms Limitation Treaty (SALT).

The president believed that the net results of these diplomatic efforts would be Hanoi's isolation and, more important, noninterference by Beijing or Moscow in any future American Southeast Asian operations. In short, Red China and the Soviet Union needed détente with the United States more than they needed ideological solidarity with the Democratic Republic of Vietnam. As it turned out, Nixon was quite correct.

CHAPTER 11

DEATH FROM ABOVE

"ZODIAC ZERO ONE . . . Buffs are in sight. Nose, thirty miles." Lieutenant Colonel Ed Rock released the mike switch and squinted east against the rising sun.

"King copies. Cleared to join, your discretion."

The pilot went to full MIL power and turned to point directly at the incoming flight of bombers. They were easy to see, even at 35,000 feet. Above the contrail layer, the B-52s caught the morning sun and were much darker than the powder blue sky over the South China Sea. It was September 20, 1972, and his single F-105G was fragged to escort a cell of three B-52s on an Arc Light mission.

"Ya see 'em, OB?"

In the backseat Major Mike O'Brien, unanimously known as "OB," leaned sideways and stared up past Rock's head. "I got 'em," he replied calmly after a minute. "Cell of three . . . in trail."

Rock's eyebrows knitted together and he squinted again. "I only see the first two," he grumbled and yawned. They'd taken off from Korat at 0630, hit the tanker in the Peach track, and then pressed into North Vietnam.

"You're a lot older than I am."

The pilot frowned, opened his mouth to say something back, then smiled. Shaking his head, he sighed and eased the F-105G's nose up a few degrees. If he pulled too hard they'd lose airspeed and he'd have to use afterburner to make the intercept. That meant less fuel for more rewarding activities like killing SAMs.

"Yeah. You never know when an old guy like me might just keel over. Especially on short final, at night, in the rain . . . or something like that. Then what would ya do?"

OB laughed. Like all the guys in the 17th Wild Weasel squadron he thought a great deal of Ed Rock and couldn't ask for a better commander. They might joke with him about being an old guy, but the man had been around. He'd started in F-86s, then flown the F-104, the F-100 Super Sabre, and finally the Thud. Ed had been in the second Weasel class back in '66, and had done a tour over here during the early hairy days of Rolling Thunder. He'd been back in Thailand since the spring and had taken command of the 17 Wild Weasel Squadron on April 24, 1972.

"What was Weaseling like with an open cockpit? I mean, did you have to wear heavy clothes to stay warm?"

"Nah," Ed said with a laugh. "When we landed we just all went to see your mother." He nudged the stick left and aimed the jet in front of the approaching bombers. Like pulling lead on a gunshot.

"So you could be my dad?"

"I've seen you in the shower. There's no resemblance." At twenty miles Ed could see the third Buff, about a mile behind the second one, and the highest in the cell. They were so *big*: eight engines each and weighing an astonishing 265,000 pounds fully loaded. These Buffs had flown all the way in from Anderson in Guam and had been airborne for about seven hours already. Crazy.

"Got an EW signal . . . weak. Left eight o'clock." The EWO lifted his head and glanced back off the left wing at the coast. Correlating the rough azimuth to geography he added, "Ah . . . up around Vinh."

"Copy that." Joshing aside, the two Weasels were all business now. Rock checked his wing tanks again, turned up the brightness on his APR-35 threat display, and wriggled his fingers. Keeping his heading, he let the lead B-52 drift back until it was directly off the Thud's nose. Holding the picture till ten miles, he began an easy turn of 3 to 4 g's, and ended up pointed straight down the lead bomber's left wing at five miles. For a moment they all seemed to hang in space, the big, dark jets stark against the sky and the green smudge of Hainan Island on the northern horizon. The bombers were staying well south of it and for good reason. It belonged to the Chinese and they'd shot down several U.S. aircraft for inadvertently violating the airspace.*

Mike O'Brien watched in admiration from the backseat. There was a whole complicated series of angles and measurements they'd all been taught to make midair rejoins work out, but the pilot was doing it in his head. At five miles they were lined up right down the wing line. The other two jets were stacked up like stair steps about a mile apart, and all three were headed west toward the North Vietnamese coast. Each B-52 had eight

---

*The first combat loss of an F-104 occurred on September 20, 1965, when Captain Phillip Smith of the 436th TFS (Black Aces) inadvertently strayed over the island during bad weather. He was shot down by a Chinese J-6 (MiG-19) and spent nearly eight years as a POW in China. He was released on March 15, 1973.

engines and they all trailed thin gray smoke. Pulling lead again, Rock bumped up slightly so he was now looking down on the bombers at two miles away.

"Big and ugly." OB was watching them, too. "Sure would hate to be on the receiving end of whatever they're carrying today."

Ed eased the throttle back, overbanked, then rolled out so he could see better. You could fit five F-105s between the B-52's wingtips.

"D-model Buffs." He added a bit of power and began angling in toward the leader. "Hundred and eight bombs each. Eighty-four Mk-82s in the belly and twenty-four Mk-117s under the wings there."

OB did the math in his head and whistled. "Sixty thousand tons of bombs . . . sorta makes our six thousand pounds look wimpy."

"Maybe." Rock slid smoothly in, joined up on the bomber's left wingtip, and let his eyes roam over the other jet. It was even more monstrous up close. "But they can't kill SAMs . . . or MiGs," he added, matching the airspeed exactly so the F-105 hung in space beside the B-52.

"We look like a hummingbird next to a hippo." OB chuckled and Rock nodded. There were two faces peering at them from the Buff's cockpit, so the fighter pilot and bomber pilot stared at each other. Two men, likely with similar backgrounds, from similar towns in the United States, crossing paths for a few minutes over enemy territory on the other side of the world.

Lifting a gloved hand he saw the bomber pilot wave back. Twenty miles off the North Vietnamese coast was no place for daydreaming, so Ed smoothly pushed the throttle up, dropped the nose, and accelerated. Leaving the bombers behind, the Thud dropped through the contrail layer, then leveled off at

20,000 feet. Headed nearly due west, Ed set the throttle to hold 500 knots and stared at the coast. The last turn point before the Buff's objective, called the initial point, was the mouth of the river just south of Dong Hoi. From there the bombers would turn south toward their target, an NVA encampment just east of the Ho Chi Minh Trail.

"Still got that EW radar up north?"

OB had been watching that. His main source of information—when he wasn't being shot at, that is—was the rectangular APR-35 in the center of his main console. Designed to replace the ER-142, it was also a panoramic receiver used for spectrum analysis. Selectable in three frequency bands, E/F, G, and I, the APR-35 could detect most of the Fansong signals, the Firecan, and other systems like the Side Net. Once a signal was detected the EWO could analyze the frequency and derive pulse width, power, and the specific PRF of a threat. This permitted collection of very accurate ELINT, which was recorded and dissected on the ground. The panoramic receiver provided very good threat discrimination in a high-threat environment—time permitting.

"It's a two-point-six-five-gig signal . . . bearing three-three-zero for about eighty miles."

Rock angled to the right so he'd cross the coast north of Dong Hoi. "Try to remember that I don't have an eighty-pound head. In English, please."

OB chuckled again. Based on the PRF he knew exactly what it was. He'd seen this one before and, like a good EWO, was able to fingerprint a given radar. "Side Net . . . height finder radar and based on the range I'd say it's the one up around Vinh. Probably on the top of one of those hills south of the town."

Made sense, Ed knew. Any increase in height would improve

the coverage of the radar and according to the latest intelligence there was a semipermanent SA-2 battalion near Vinh. Rolling out, he glanced over the right wing up the coast at Route Pack Two. Any SAM threats would likely come from that direction, so he'd placed himself between it and the Buffs. If anything was fired, hopefully it would be at the Weasel. Of course, there could be a stray SAM battery down toward the DMZ as well. With the North Vietnamese it was best not to take a chance.

"Feet dry," Rock said as they crossed over the coastline.

Mike O'Brien glanced right. The coastline curved into a jutting triangle that roughly marked the beginning of Route Pack Two. *Maybe we'll go up there next,* he thought, then looked back at his scope. The APR-35 was empty again and OB glanced at the two round, three-inch displays above the panoramic receiver. Essentially a much-improved version of the old Vector IV, the APR-36 Launch Warning Receiver (LWR) was on the left. Launch indications were literally lifesavers since C-band missile guidance beams were below the coverage of the APR-35. This meant the only warnings came from the APR-36 or a pair of eyeballs. The attack scope was an identical three-inch display on the right side above the APR-35. Used to correlate signals and isolate specific threats, this targeting information was then handed off to the STARM.

The solitary Wild Weasel crossed the beach at 500 knots heading west. From 20,000 feet Ed had a perfect view of the Truong Son mountain range off the nose. Knobby and rugged, the hills generally ran north to south but it was the valleys that were dangerous. The eastern routes of the Ho Chi Minh Trail twisted their way alongside rivers, through caves, and under triple-canopy forests. Ed raised his visor and reached up to a little horizontal box in the center of his windscreen along the canopy bow. He turned up the volume for his APR-36 display, then reached to the ALR-31 box mounted next to his right mirror. As he dialed the lights to full bright, the pilot flickered his eyes around the cockpit to his other switches and was satisfied.

"EW," O'Brien called from the back. "Right three o'clock. Weak."

"Same site?"

"Probably. It's not close. Not too exciting, huh?"

Rock was watching the lake on the east side of the foothills. Flying over enemy territory was always exciting to some degree, but he knew what OB meant. Not like Thud Ridge and Route Pack Six, for sure.

"Here we go." He shoved the throttle forward to MIL and rolled up to the left. Both men grunted against the 5 g's and Rock dropped the fighter's nose. National Route 1, deserted as always, disappeared beneath the wings as he sliced down and left. When the g-suit began squeezing his legs, Ed pulled the power and held 540 knots. Snapping upright, they leveled off heading south at 15,000 feet right down the ridgeline. Rock leaned forward, left hand firm on the throttle and the other around the stick. Laos and the mountain passes were east and off to his left the flatlands smoothed out toward the beach.

According to his HSI the distance to the target was twenty-nine miles. Glancing back over his left shoulder he tried to find the Buffs but couldn't. They were invisible much higher up in the rising sun, so Ed shrugged and did the math in his head. If they flew their black line, and that was always something you could count on from SAC guys, then they'd be about five miles behind him. Nodding, he began methodically searching the ground: Left side close, then far. Then right side close, then far. Looking for barrel flashes, smoke trails, or just anything out of the ordinary, he saw nothing, even along the trail three miles below him. It was a perfectly peaceful dawn in North Vietnam. Then he thought of the B-52s and their 180,000 pounds of bombs. *Not for long.*

ED ROCK WAS back in Southeast Asia hunting SAMs because six months earlier, on March 30, 1972, more than 200,000 North Vietnamese soldiers surged across the border to invade South Vietnam. Hanoi called it Nguyen Hue after a legendary military hero, but to the Americans it would be known as the Easter Offensive. In direct violation of the 1968 bombing halt conditions, this was seen as an overt act of aggression and Hanoi badly miscalculated its effects, both militarily and diplomatically.

However, such an invasion was not totally unexpected, and after NVA attacks on Saigon in December, Nixon ordered supply depots below the 20th parallel destroyed. The president was quite clear when he stated that "we cannot expect the enemy to negotiate seriously with us until he is convinced nothing can be gained by continuing the war." He also officially informed Moscow and Beijing that any communist attack would be met by the American military. Being quite satisfied with Nixon's February trip to their country, the Chinese adopted an official "posture of indifference" and showed no signs of interfering. Concerned about the Soviets, the White House bluntly stated that Soviet support for any invasion would jeopardize the upcoming Moscow summit. To back up his words, thirty-seven B-52s deployed to Guam and Thailand while an additional eighteen USAF F-4Ds were moved in theater from the Philippines.

The North Vietnamese had agreed to the additional negotiations but kept changing the date. First it was to be after

March 15, then March 20, and Hanoi finally agreed upon mid-April, knowing full well that the Nguyen Hue offensive would commence on March 30, 1972. When the invasion happened Nixon ordered immediate reinforcements to slow the advance and give the ARVN a fighting chance. The 36th TFS (Flying Fiends) came in from Osan Air Base, Korea, to join the 366th TFW at Da Nang. The Navy already had two carrier air groups on station with the USS *Hancock* and *Coral Sea,* but more were on the way.

In early April 1972, a stream of USAF aircraft departed the United States and headed west under Operation Constant Guard I. Part of this first group were twelve F-105G Wild Weasels from the 561st TFS, McConnell Air Force Base, Kansas. Home to the 23rd Tactical Fighter Wing, McConnell was led by none other than Colonel Garry Willard, the first Wild Weasel commander. The 561st Tactical Fighter Squadron, under the command of Lieutenant Colonel Ed Rock, deployed on April 12 bound for Hawaii, then Korat, Thailand. Five other Constant Guard deployments would occur through the fall of 1972. Additionally, the Navy added four carrier groups built around the USS *Kitty Hawk, Midway, Saratoga,* and *Constellation.* The Marines also forward-deployed two A-4 squadrons to Bien Hoa and three squadrons of Phantoms to Da Nang.

These forces would all play a decisive role in the months to come but made little difference in the beginning since the three-pronged NVA assault was timed to coincide with the winter monsoon. Lunging across the DMZ, the enemy swept into the Quang Tri province and under low clouds, which precluded air support, they captured the regional capital. Continuing south toward Hue, the North Vietnamese Army's ultimate objective in the top of South Vietnam was the port of Da Nang.

On the same day Quang Tri fell, the ARVN commander

was relieved and replaced by Lieutenant General Ngo Quang Truong, South Vietnam's ablest soldier.* Falling back on Hue, Truong added reinforcements, so as the weather cleared and massive U.S. air support resumed, he was able to halt the advance by early May. The southern thrust began on April 5 with the NVA 5th Division striking east from Cambodia along National Route 1. As they advanced through Binh Long, Tay Ninh was overrun and the NVA continued toward An Loc. ARVN resistance, plus renewed air support, stopped the assault and by June 12 the siege of An Loc had been lifted. In the Central Highlands some 50,000 men of the NVA 30th, 2nd, and 3rd divisions struck hard, driving north of the Drang valley toward Kon Tom and Pleiku. In the face of failing ARVN II Corps leadership the enemy advance appeared wildly successful until the American director of the Second Regional Assistance Group, the redoubtable John Paul Vann, took command himself. Ordering troop movements and reinforcements and resupplying what units he had remaining, Vann also coordinated tactical air support and halted the enemy.† By early June the battle in the Central Highlands was over and the enemy had melted back across the border.

In many places ARVN units fought bravely and extremely well, yet in many other engagements they did not. Ignored for so long under Westmoreland, the ARVN did not receive modern weaponry in sufficient numbers and proper training until Creighton Abrams took over MACV. Even so, some units were composed of recaptured deserters and convicts while

---

* General Norman Schwarzkopf called Truong "the most brilliant tactical commander I've ever known."
† After winning the battle, this remarkable man was on his way back from Saigon when his helicopter went down in bad weather. John Paul Vann was forty-seven years old.

others, though willing, had no real training or competent leaders. As mentioned, upper leadership had always been a problem
since Saigon feared successful commanders such as Ngo Quang
Truong. As long as the Americans were in country, they would
bear the brunt of combat operations, so, Saigon reasoned, there
was no reason to build up a strong military that might one day
threaten its own government.

However, by Easter 1972, American largesse had long run
out and President Thieu had done little to prepare for the day
he'd be on his own. Nixon had continued his promised withdrawals, so by the spring of 1972 there were fewer than 70,000
U.S. troops in South Vietnam.*

As with the Tet Offensive in 1968, the invasion was ambitious and audacious. Yet once again the NVA's lack of experience with larger force operations played a major role in
its failure. Tactical coordination was lacking and there was
no question that the Americans still ruled the sky. Like many
before (and since), Hanoi grossly underestimated the speed
and power of the U.S. response and had committed its entire
army to a conventional battle. Suffering nearly 100,000 casualties, the NVA also lost most of its 250 tanks. The offensive
did not win the war but Hanoi did gain a bit of the western
border and all four of South Vietnam's northern provinces.
This meant the extension of both NVA supply lines and air
defenses, which would have dire consequences for the future
of South Vietnam.

Despite the military setbacks, the DRV was hardly defeated.
Nearly four years without air attack had permitted the repair of
northern infrastructure, restructuring the military, and stock-

---

*This had followed an annual reduction of 75,000 to 150,000 men per year
since the wartime high level of 536,100 in 1968.

piling considerable war supplies. The North Vietnamese had added to their war chest a new surface-to-air missile called the Strela—meaning "Arrow" in Russian—and it was a nasty surprise for several reasons. First, it was man-portable and mass produced, so equipping hundreds of soldiers with it was easy. Weighing just over twenty pounds, it was under five feet long and could hit targets up to altitudes of 10,000 feet. Second, it used infrared emissions from the target for guidance and therefore did not need supporting radar. As it tracked heat sources, the missile's seeker was impervious to electronic countermeasures like jamming pods or chaff.

Called the SA-7 by NATO, it was a simple weapon to operate. The soldier held it on his shoulder like a bazooka and switched on the thermal battery. Using an optical sight, he then placed the crosshairs on the target and depressed the trigger to the first detent. If the seeker could identify a valid heat source and track it, then the operator saw a light in the sight accompanied by a buzzer. Depressing the trigger all the way back, the SA-7's interlocks would release if the heat signal was still strong enough, and then the missile would launch. If not, the buzzer would change tone and the operator would have to try again.

Not particularly fast or sophisticated, the Strela worked best on the battlefield against helicopters and slower, propeller-driven aircraft like the A-1 Skyraider. U.S. and VNAF pilots identified 528 missile firings between March 1972 and the end of the war, with 45 aircraft reported lost. Of these, only two were jet fighters: a VNAF F-5 and a Marine T-A4F. The two-seat Skyhawk was on a FAC (Forward Air Control) mission northwest of Hue when it discovered an enemy tank and began to strafe. Pulling off target, it was hit in the belly by an SA-7 yet managed to make it to the coast, where both men ejected.* The Strela's 1.3-pound warhead was usually too small to bring down the heavier jets, but it was deadly enough to smaller aircraft. In addition to using decoy flares whenever possible, American maintenance crews rigged diffuser shields on helicopters that deflected hot exhaust gases into the rotor wash to diminish the heat signature. Jets relied largely on maneuvering or avoidance when it came to the new IR missile and still regarded the radar-guided guns and SAMs as their primary threats.

As the Fansong system became better known, its weaknesses were well exploited. In addition to the advances in electronic countermeasures and jamming pods, pilots had also developed a "last-ditch" maneuver. They'd always known that if the SA-2 could be seen with enough time it could usually be defeated—at least the first missile or two. Treating it like a dogfight, pilots figured they could defeat it by forcing the missile to make energy-consuming guidance corrections and then outmaneuvering it. Turning to put the missile at his ten o'clock or two o'clock position, the pilot would dump the nose down to about 45 degrees and go to MIL power. Accelerating downhill and changing position in three dimensions forced the missile to correct accordingly. After four to five seconds the pilot would go to afterburner, pull up 45 degrees, and turn to keep the missile at ten o'clock or two o'clock. This forced more corrections from the SA-2, slowing it down, generating angle problems, and playing havoc with the Fansong. At about a mile, with just seconds remaining till the intercept, the pilot would plug in the burner and initiate a maximum-g, rolling pull into the missile. With its four-second command lag time the SA-2 couldn't correct

---

*Captain W. E. Ramsbottom and CWO2 Bruce Boltze were both picked up safely.

and would hopefully pass by beyond lethal range. If it passed close enough the proximity fuse could detonate the warhead and cause damage, but this was certainly less dangerous than a direct hit. These countertactics were best used with jamming since keeping sight of missiles in a big sky during a fast-moving, multidimensional air battle is hardly easy. Preemptive and reactive chaff would be a great help, but USAF fighters didn't have internal dispensers until late in the war.

The Navy usually led the Air Force in electronic combat and countermeasure development and this was no exception. When radar-guided anti-aircraft threats began proliferating back in the early 1960s the Navy issued a formal requirement for a chaff dispenser.

Aware that the speed of jet aircraft required forced chaff ejection for effective blooming, Vic Kutsch of the Naval Research Laboratory developed a system that used 37 mm shells to fire the cartridges. Goodyear adapted this into the ALE-29, a 30-barrel, forced chaff dispenser. This was replaced in 1966 by the Tracor ALE-29A dual chaff/flare dispenser and fielded in operational naval air units.

By 1972 the USAF had awakened to the tactical uses of chaff and utilized externally mounted containers on F-4 Phantoms. Several hundred pounds of chaff were packed into the MK-129 leaflet canister, which was then dropped from a specific altitude and detonated by an airburst fuse. This would ignite primacord, splitting open the canister and scattering the chaff. The resulting cloud would blank out entire sections of the enemy radar picture and made target acquisition and GCI guidance nearly impossible. All of this was worked out in advance based on the winds, enemy radar coverage, and strike package routes.

The timing of these developments was good.

Angered over the Easter Offensive and determined to end

the war, Richard Nixon once again unleashed American air-power over North Vietnam. Operation Linebacker was to be an attention getter, a stark example of what the DRV could expect if it did not satisfactorily and honestly negotiate. A warning that the United States had had enough and that he, the president, was not afraid to use more force than Hanoi could imagine. As Nixon would say to Kissinger regarding Hanoi, "In a nutshell you should tell them that they have violated all understandings, they stepped up the war, they have refused to negotiate seriously. As a result, the President has had enough and now you have only one message to give them—settle or else!"

On May 8, 1972, six A-7 Corsairs from VA-22 (Fighting Redcocks) and VA-94 (Mighty Shrikes) with three A-6 Intruders from VMA 224 (Bengals) launched from the USS *Coral Sea* to execute Operation Pocket Money. Heading directly at Haiphong, at 0859 the jets dropped thirty-six aerial mines into the harbor approaches. At 0900 the American president went on national television to state, "The only way to stop the killing is to take the weapons of war out of the hands of the international outlaws of North Vietnam."

These first mines were set with seventy-two-hour delayed fuses to afford foreign ships in the harbor a chance to leave. Some did, though Soviet ships in the harbor did not move, and those inbound to Haiphong returned to their ports. Preventing resupply of the DRV was a primary goal of Linebacker and to this end another eleven thousand mines would be dropped to bottle up Than Goa, Hon Gay, Vinh, Cam Pha, and Haiphong. Using newly fielded laser-guided or electro-optical bombs, F-4 Phantoms from the 8th TFW hit many vital targets including the infamous Dragon's Jaw and Paul Doumer bridges.

The idea was to prevent reinforcements by sealing up North Vietnam while destroying what was already on hand. It made sound military sense and was successful largely because Nixon gave the Joint Chiefs clear-cut goals, then stayed out of the way and let them figure out how to best meet those objectives. Though the president approved a master target list, the military was free to attack any of the targets when and how they saw fit. New technology like improved jamming pods, chaff, and precision munitions all helped. So did sound air-to-air tactics, at least from the Navy, and dedicated Wild Weasels to fight the SAMS. The tragedy was that this type of campaign could have been executed in 1965 and saved seven years of warfare, billions of dollars, and tens of thousands of lives. As it was, the 41,653 sorties flown and the destruction caused by another 155,000 tons of bombs did indeed get Hanoi's attention. By August 1972 peace talks in Paris resumed, though, unlike his predecessor, Nixon did not halt the attacks and the fighting continued.

"COMIN' RIGHT." ED Rock paused, then flicked his wrist and sent the F-105 into an easy turn west toward the Laotian border. He'd flown down the run-in heading toward the B-52 target area but didn't want to overfly it and alert those on the ground. He knew there were thousands of eyes down there beneath the trees, looking up, watching and listening. The NVA and VC hated the bombers and the Arc Light strikes; there was no sound, nothing to see, and no warning. One second there was the quiet, heavy air of Vietnam, then the oxygen was sucked from lungs and eyeballs were popped out from the pressure of tons of bombs. Bodies were pulped or vaporized outright, and millions of wooden shards sliced through skin and bone as the trees exploded. Ed planned to continue arcing around to the west, then turn east toward the coast to cross in front of the Buffs as they dropped. From there if he spotted anything being shot upward he'd instantly attack.

"Back to the left." Rock banked up and headed southeast, paralleling the B-52 run in heading.

"What a mess," OB remarked, staring down at the undulating green terrain. Narrow, twisting paths could sometimes be seen but these were only the bigger trails. There were thousands of others beneath the trees, not to mention the caves. A faint, bluish haze hung over the low areas, undoubtedly from fires that they also couldn't see.

"Do you think it's working, Ed?"

Rock was staring off to the right as well toward the Ban Karai Pass. He'd heard the Revak/Goldstein hundred-mission story and knew the F-4, Grommet something, had gone down over there. Maybe three miles away from where he was now. He shook his head. Now they were back to roaming at will over North Vietnam.

"It works. It always works." He looked away from the pass, checked his watch, and began an easy left bank. "It'll work a lot better nine months from now when I go home."

The EWO chuckled. *Fighter pilots.* "Not *that.* I meant bombing the trail."

Tough question. The colonel knew that in the past three years more than 1.2 million tons of ordnance had been dropped on the area below him. Rock also knew that after Rolling Thunder ceased most of the vast American air effort had been shifted to interaction along the trail. From 1969 to 1970 this amounted to more than 825,000 tons of bombs and 198,000 sorties; lots of dead monkeys, lots of big trees turned into toothpicks, but no one was quite sure how much damage had been done.

"They're still coming, aren't they? That's part of what today is all about."

Glancing at his watch again, Ed pictured the strike as if he were looking down on a map. The Weasel was about ten miles north of the DMZ heading southeast. Five miles off the right wing was Laos, and the beach in Route Pack One lay twenty miles to his left. The B-52s had already crossed the coast and turned south, so they'd be forty miles back. Ed and OB had been briefed that this particular target was a huge stockpile of essential material, maybe for another invasion of the South. Much of this had been brought in by sea through Group 959, the North Vietnamese naval infiltration organization, and were high-value items. Large-caliber anti-aircraft guns, spare SA-2 missiles, radars, plus medical supplies and weapons. These were all things that were difficult to transport, so getting them here, a few miles north of the DMZ, had been time consuming and expensive. From this point Group 559, the NVA transportation command, would separate and disperse the stuff down different sections of the trail, so it was vital to destroy the depot intact. Because the North Vietnamese were masters of deception and camouflage this area had never been hit before. Ed could only imagine how the Seventh Air Force had found out about it.

"DMZ off the nose." The pilot checked the fuel, ran his eyes over the engine gauges and switches again, then looked east off his left wing. The scopes in the back were blank so OB watched for gunfire and muzzle flashes. If they saw any then he and Rock could come back for a visit after the Buffs left.

"I think the target is off the left wing . . . maybe three miles." Mike O'Brien was staring at his map. Ed looked, took in the area just off the main trail, and nodded. It was a little river valley maybe two thousand feet wide, but relatively flat and heading straight south.

"Yeah . . . supposed to be right off that little pass through the mountains along the hillside before the terrain gets really rough."

OB squinted as it passed farther off the tail and disappeared behind them. "Pretty good place to hide stuff . . . but I couldn't see a thing."

"Hopefully you will in about four minutes."

They continued south across the DMZ for a few miles. Approaching the hills north of the old Khe Sanh combat base, Ed added power and banked up to the left. The base had been abandoned after Tet and remained vacant until the ARVN invasion of Laos in February 1971. As far as he knew, it was deserted again and had been for about eighteen months. Rolling out, Rock pulled the power back to hold 480 knots, leveled off at 15,000 feet, and wriggled his butt into a more comfortable position.

Off the nose the higher terrain broke apart and sloped away eastward toward the coast. Leatherneck Square, the old Marine bastion against DMZ incursions, was off the nose about ten miles away. He couldn't really make it out but thought the more prominent rock formation to the northeast was Con Thien—the Hill of Angels. Mike O'Brien had been gazing off the right wing at the rugged, bloody valley where armies clashed and so many men had died. There was a flat area in the river bend dominated by a jagged karst outcropping. It looked like a gray nipple surrounded by green fur. Roads, and what appeared to be an assortment of revetments, were still plain to see. The karst mound looked fairly high, maybe seven or eight hundred feet. He tapped the canopy.

"What's that at two o'clock? Not Khe Sanh, is it?"

Rock glanced right and shook his head. "Nope. The firebase is over that next ridgeline to the southwest . . . maybe five miles. That"—he knew the spot—"is the infamous Rockpile. Comin' left."

He arced the Thud back around to the north. They were now in that no-man's-land between Route 9 and the DMZ and there wasn't supposed to be anything here that could shoot them—but it had happened before. The North Vietnamese were unpredictable when it came to their SAMs, and there had been persistent speculation that a battery was down here someplace. It made sense tactically since there were lots of flights transiting the area, and many were indefensible helicopters or helpless transports.

"One minute, Ed," OB called out. His displays were still empty of signals so the EWO was watching the clock. The pilot nodded, ran a practiced eye over the cockpit again, then bumped the throttle up very slightly. Both men stared out at North Vietnam, impressed, as always, by the stark contrasts. Beyond the jagged Troung Son ridge, the sage green terrain lightened as it sloped to the beach and beyond the coast sunlight shimmered off the Gulf of Tonkin. To the left of the Weasel, the mountains rose steeply, then dropped away in a series of irregular, V-shaped valleys before climbing again. It was darker, too. Much darker. Indian Country.

"Five . . . four . . . three . . ."

The Weasel had just crossed the DMZ and the B-52 target was at their left ten o'clock. Ed focused intently on the saucer-like area between the mountains and just east of the river.

"One . . ."

They both watched expectantly but nothing happened. Rock had a fleeting thought that they were covering the wrong target and glanced down at his kneeboard.

"Holy shit!" OB's eyes widened and both men blinked. The foothills were exploding. One second all had been quiet, green, and seemingly empty. Now it was on fire. Not just fire, but smoke boiling upward and tracers shooting off as ammunition cooked off.

Rock whistled softly, eyes wide. It was now plain to see that the depot was larger than any he'd ever seen—maybe a half mile square. The illusion of camouflage had been magnificent, and what he'd taken as normal forests had been a vast array of netting; cleverly woven into trees to conceal the stockpile. It had been perfectly located. Material brought in by sea could get as far as Dong Hoi, which was about fifteen miles up the coast. The stuff could be off-loaded and floated down the river to within ten miles of this place. From there it was packed overland through dozens of smaller passes and consolidated here to await the trip south.

Not anymore. It was the most successful B-52 strike he'd ever seen and the whole little valley was on fire. Black smoke rolled up the hillsides and was beginning to lift over the mountain. It would be seen for miles and they would know. *They'd know we're still here ready to kick the shit out of them.* There was another series of explosions as the last of Buff's bombs slammed into Vietnam: 60,000 pounds of destruction that punched holes into the earth, sent pieces of men cartwheeling into the trees, and destroyed weapons intended to kill Americans. He shrugged his shoulders and tried to spot the Buffs. Knocking off this place would certainly hurt the NVA and whatever nastiness they had planned next.

"Well," OB finally said. "What next?"

Rock grinned, angling away toward the coast and deeper into North Vietnam.

"Let's go hunting."

CROSSING BACK OVER the hills, Ed suddenly rolled the Thud up on its left wing and stared down at the earth.

"What's up?" OB hung sideways and looked at the ground. There was a blue-gray lake just past the mountains but no smoke trails or muzzle flashes.

Skidding the jet on its wing and tail, the pilot found the

pimply hills east of the lake. "There . . . see the smaller set of hills in the middle? That cleared area at the base . . . I hit a SAM there in 1966. Be six years ago next month . . . October."

"I was in high school, Rock."

He actually hadn't been, but it sounded funny. Nevertheless, he found the area and noticed it was pockmarked with craters. Ed flipped the fighter upright and continued toward the coast. "Looks like something plastered it. Buffs?"

"Yep. Never been active since, I think."

Leveling off at 10,000, they crossed the coast a minute later and turned north toward Route Pack Two. There were rumors of a new SAM, which the Russians called the S-125 and NATO named the SA-3. With a two-stage rocket motor it was supposedly much more maneuverable than the SA-2 and the new radar was capable of tracking a half dozen aircraft. Deployed within the Soviet Union since the mid-1960s, it had long been expected in Southeast Asia but no one had seen it. Personally, he thought the Soviets were afraid the SA-3 would fall into Chinese hands so they wouldn't export it.

"I sure am looking forward to flying up a real beach again soon," OB remarked, staring off the left wing. Rock nudged the throttle to hold 480 knots, checked his fuel, and blinked against the morning sun.

"Yeah. Linebacker really kicked the crap outta them. Might all be over soon."

"You think?"

Ed looked at the mountains, then north. "Would've been nice to have it all over a few years ago. We're not doing anything now we couldn't have done then."

The EWO nodded gloomily and scanned his displays again. That was certainly true and guys were still dying. "Would've saved a lot of good guys."

Rock knew he was thinking about Captain Tom Zorn and First Lieutenant Mike Turose. Three days ago, on September 17, they'd been up in the Bac Giang province north of Haiphong. Hit by an SA-2, Zorn nursed the crippled Weasel southeast out over the water, trying to get far enough to ditch at sea and be picked up by the Navy. But the SAM had hit the engine section and the fighter made it less than fifteen miles off the coast. They ejected safely, two parachutes were observed, and both men came down near some islands off the mouth of Ha Long Bay. The islands were part of the Cat Ba archipelago and unfortunately home to thousands of fishermen. Rock sure hoped the pair had been captured and turned over to the North Vietnamese Army. Zorn was from Georgia and Turose, one month past his twenty-fourth birthday, was from Ohio. There had been no word yet and as their squadron commander Ed took the loss hard.*

Looking ahead he checked that his threat warning volume was all the way up. The Weasel was barely offshore coming up from the south, and the tan sand off his left wing contrasted starkly against the blue-green Gulf of Tonkin. The gray ribbon of National Route 1 paralleled the beach, running into the lead-colored water of the Gianh River. There was a ferry crossing there at Quang Khe, vital to the movement of supplies toward the DMZ, and the Vietnamese Navy kept patrol boats nearby to protect the sampans. Stifling a yawn, Rock glanced off the coast, hoping to see any of the little boats. With bombing officially resumed, targets of opportunity were approved for attack and you just never knew.

He frowned.

---

*Whether they both drowned or were killed by locals, neither man was ever seen again.

Raising the visor, he narrowed his eyes at the gulf. There it was again. Something caught the sun and glinted, white or gray, against the blue water. Rock's wrist moved slightly and he nudged the fighter a bit farther offshore.

"OB . . . look at right two o'clock . . . about three miles or so."

After a moment the EWO replied, "Don't see a thing but water. What is it?"

"See that cloud shadow on the water . . . the big one . . . look about halfway between it and the beach. Something shiny is floating in the water."

Mike O'Brien was always amazed at the pilot's vision. If Rock thought there was something there, then there probably was. He was opening his mouth to admit defeat when something flashed on the gently rolling waves. Something very white against the darker water.

"I got it! Dunno what it is, though."

"Is the scope clean?"

The EWO's eyes flickered inside to the APR-35, then up to the APR-36. Even the early warning stuff was silent. "Yep."

"Let's go have a look."

Past Quang Khe, the coastline arced to the east, jutting gracefully into the gulf. Ed angled to the right, aiming at the smudge of a small island several miles offshore. This way the sun would be off his right shoulder rather than in his face, and if there was something down there he'd have a better chance of seeing it. Dropping a few thousand feet lower, Rock leveled at 8,000 feet, unwilling to go lower and burn fuel. As he peered off the nose, the rolling blue waters of the gulf were dotted with darker patches from the clouds overhead. Sunlight gleamed from the wavetops and he lost sight of the object. Then it reappeared and he instinctively pulled the throttle back to slow down.

"There . . . left eleven o'clock . . . about a mile."

OB nodded. "I got it. Can you tell what it is?"

Rock bunted over now, eased the power back, and dropped the nose. Leaning forward, he squinted, then rolled up slightly. There. Something small and white bobbing on the wavetops. At 3,000 feet up and a half mile away he knew . . .

"It's a helmet. A white Navy flight helmet."

"Sonuvabitch . . ."

The Thud dropped a little lower and Ed banked up, bringing the fighter around in a swooping left turn. Staring straight down the wing, he saw an arm raise and slowly wave. By 1972 all USAF helmets had been painted olive drab but the Navy still retained its peacetime white. He'd always thought that was stupid, until now—maybe this was why. Twitching the stick, he waggled the wings, went to MIL power, and pulled the nose back up. Knowing OB would jot down the coordinates, he climbed toward the Vietnamese coast and keyed the mike.

"King . . . King . . . this is Zodiac Zero One."

Headed right at the mouth of the Gianh River, he was passing 8,000 feet when the other aircraft replied. King was short for Combat King, a modified HC-130 that served as a command and control platform. It could air-refuel helicopters and with an impressive radio communication suite it could talk to just about anyone. They often served as rescue coordinators and as O'Brien passed the information, Rock could tell this one was on the ball. Leveling off again at 10,000 feet, they flew a little north of Quang Khe. Turning left to parallel the shoreline to the south, he snapped upright before they got to the ferry. He'd survived too long to be assholed by a SAM on the beach.

"Zodiac . . . King."

"Go ahead."

"Red Crown was passed the info and is coordinating. Say playtime."

Ed's eyes flickered to his fuel gauge. "Ah . . . thirty mikes with no AR. If you can get us a tanker we'll stay all day."

"Copy . . . I'll work it."

Red Crown was the Navy equivalent of King, so apparently this would be their show. Well south of the river now, Ed banked up left and headed out to sea again. He'd decided on a short racetrack pattern and would fly the outbound leg at 400 knots. This would give him more time to keep the pilot in sight and would save some fuel. The Navy flier was only about four miles off the coast and they had no trouble spotting him this time. Turning back inbound, he pushed the throttle up to 480 knots. More speed for a threat reaction and less time with eyes off the downed pilot. Why, he wondered, had there been no emergency beacon?

As they neared the coast, OB saw several white scratches on the water. It took a minute before he realized they were wakes . . . wakes from boats. "Rock . . ."

"I see them."

"Patrol boats?"

The pilot saw about a dozen small craft heading out from the little port by the river. Three to four up front were all painted the same dark shade of gray. Plainly military and plainly much faster than the others trailing behind.

"Uh huh."

Cranking up on one wing he passed overhead and then looked east. They were obviously heading out toward the Navy pilot.

"Must've seen his chute," OB remarked. "Looks like we got here just in time."

"Now we know why there was no beacon. He turned it off."

"Well . . . I guess we can't let them have him, can we?"

"Nah. We need the Navy around to make us look good in the bar."

"So we should save him?"

Rock chuckled and cinched his oxygen mask back up. "Yeah . . . guess so."

Relaying the situation to King, Rock eyeballed the boats and decided to swing around to the south, drop low, and attack from the east with the sun behind him.

"Triple A! Right one o'clock!"

His head snapped right and immediately picked up the airbursts. Lots of ugly white puff balls but also some bigger, darker smears closer to the fighter's altitude. Had to be 85 mm or 100 mm junk from batteries near the ferry, so he edged farther offshore, extended south another mile, then turned back out to sea.

"We'll head out for one minute then turn back in and attack east to west."

OB nodded. The lead boats were doing about 25 knots, which was nearly 30 miles per hour. Doing the math in his head he figured they'd get to the pilot in less than ten minutes. If he and Rock hit the boats two miles out of port, they'd be beyond the range of the shore batteries. That meant in about two minutes. He stared around the front ejection seat at the pilot's helmet and shook his head. Ed had figured all that out while keeping sight of the Navy guy, dodging anti-aircraft fire, and talking to King.

Out of habit, Rock touched the MASTER ARM switch then glanced at the orange gunsight on the combining glass. It was a gyroscopic, lead computing sight that theoretically used radar ranging. Fine for air-to-air, when it worked, but he preferred the 1,500 foot stadiametric sight for strafing. Twisting in his seat, Ed looked back at the line of boats and figured they were about a mile and a half offshore. It was time.

Playing the turn, the pilot stayed level through the first half, then, as the sun showed under his right wing, he dumped the nose and tugged the throttle back a few inches. Passing over the bobbing white helmet, Rock over-rotated, steepened the bank, and rolled in.

"Four thousand feet," OB called.

The boats were about a mile and a half due west and still heading east. Rock decided that they hadn't seen the Thud yet because of the sun. Smiling a little, he lowered the nose a few degrees and kept the throttle where it was. As the fighter's nose came even with the river mouth, the coast, and the white wakes, Ed rolled upright. Eyes flickering to the instruments, he saw the orange gunsight was mostly washed out from the glare behind him. *It didn't matter.*

Thirty-two hundred feet, 490 knots, and a mile away from the boats.

Leaning forward, strung tight but still loose, the pilot found the closest wake and focused on the dark spot in front of it.

"Twenty-five hundred feet."

Ignoring the gunsight he used the long, pointed pitot tube on the Thud's nose to aim. The idea was to make the tube and the target come together by 1,000 feet in altitude and 1,000 feet or so laterally. Instantly judging closure, distance, and his aim, Ed found the spot on the water where everything would meet and he played controls to put the jet there.

At 520 knots and 1,500 feet he bumped the throttle back, fanned open the speed brakes, and finessed his aim. The patrol boat was plain to see . . . it was actually a motor launch, about sixty feet long, dark gray, and had something yellow mounted just forward of the open wheelhouse.

Almost . . .

His right forefinger was curled lightly around the trigger and Ed smiled again when the pitot tube touched the bow.

Now! He squeezed the trigger.

"BRRPPP."

Six 20 mm barrels rotated and fired, spitting shells out that traveled the thousand-foot distance in a third of a second. Releasing the trigger, he bunted forward slightly, aimed at the yellow thing on the deck, and fired again as the first burst hit the boat.

"BRRRRPPPPPPPPP."

The combined bursts spat out some two hundred rounds of 20 mm shells and the first group hit before the second left the barrels. The North Vietnamese launch disappeared under waterspouts and oily black smoke. Pulling the nose straight up, Rock shoved the throttle forward to MIL and as the nose came through the horizon he rolled hard left. The Vietnamese hadn't seen the big, mottled green and tan fighter till he'd dropped down on their heads and opened fire.

But they saw the Weasel now.

"Yeah!" OB yelled from the pit as Ed snapped upright. With the sun on his left cheek they headed south at about 3,000 feet. As he bunted forward again, dirt and a cigarette butt floated up from the floor, but the pilot ignored them. Kicking the right rudder, he skidded the jet sideways, banked up hard, and looked back.

The launch had been quite literally sawn in half and both big sections were bobbing dejectedly on the waves. Fuel and oil from the shattered tanks left burning patches on the water. The other boats turned wildly, trying to zigzag evasively, and Rock laughed.

"Zodiac . . . this is King."

Ed reversed his turn and came back to the left in a tight, 5-g circle. "Go ahead for Zodiac," he replied, checking the fuel: 5,500 pounds. They'd either have to tank or return to Korat.

"Zodiac, this is King . . . no tanker available. Repeat, no tanker."

Spinning through south he kept two miles away from the

milling boats. Rock had never heard of anyone using an SA-7 over water, but it was certainly possible. Holding 480 knots he replied tersely, "Copy that . . . you'll need to divert a flight for top cover. Zodiac is RTB in three mikes."

"Zodiac, King . . . roger that. Angel One One is ten out. Blue Three One is en route for cover. Two Alpha Sevens . . . believe the DP is one of theirs."

So the DP, the downed pilot, was an A-7 Corsair jock. Ed had no idea what squadron Blue was and it didn't matter. What did matter was that the Angel, the rescue helicopter, was inbound with some fighters to protect him.*

"Copy all. We'll make a pass on the way out. One boat destroyed and we'll get another."

"We can't leave that guy, Rock."

"I know. We'll stay till the Corsairs get here. We'll use a new Bingo of two-point-five for Da Nang if we have to."

OB swallowed: 2,500 pounds to go . . . he looked at his map . . . 150 miles. He exhaled and decided not to worry about it. Ed knew what he was doing and had done it many times before. He checked his displays again and looked off to the southeast toward Yankee Station. The carriers were out there somewhere and so was the—

"Sonuvabitch."

"What?" Rock was still padlocked on the boats, playing the turn again. The North Vietnamese hadn't gone any closer to the floating pilot but were plainly looking for their own survivors.

"Chopper. Right three o'clock low. Northwest bound. Probably five miles away."

"Anyone else?"

---

* As it happens, the A-7 was not from VA-153 (Blue Tail Flies) but from VA-155 (Silver Foxes). Both squadrons were off the USS *Oriskany*.

OB squinted harder. The sunlight had also caught the lighter-colored helicopter and made it easy to see. Probably a Sea King, he thought. Bulbous kind of bumblebee-looking thing. "Not that I can see."

"Hold on."

Rock snapped the fighter up, rolled in again from 3,500 feet, and keyed the mike. "King . . . Zodiac is in on the boats . . . relay five boats remaining . . . approximately two miles west of the pilot. We've got the chopper in sight."

He popped upright and smoothly lowered the nose a few degrees. The wind was blowing the smoke toward shore so he picked up the largest boat remaining that he could see. This time the North Vietnamese saw the Thud and promptly abandoned their search. As they wheeled around for the coast, wakes boiled up and they went to full throttle. Rock chuckled. *Like that was gonna help.*

Three thousand feet and a bit over a mile away. He nudged the stick forward, dumped the nose, and lined the pitot boom up on the trailing wake. Walking the throttle back a few inches, Ed held 500 knots in the dive and watched the water from the corners of his eyes.

"Zodiac." A new voice filled his helmet but Rock never looked away from the fleeing boat. "Blue Three One has you in sight. In from the southeast, high."

Two thousand feet and half a mile. Rock could see four or five men on the back of the launch waving their arms . . . or weapons. He fanned the speedbrakes and slowed to 450 knots, easing the pitot boom up to the base of the wake.

"Roger that, Blue. We'll be finished in thirty seconds, then off to the southwest. Your pilot's behind me about a mile."

Passing 1,500 he pushed the throttle up to MIL and aimed at the bow of the boat. A fast-moving receding target was tricky without a computing gunsight but he still couldn't see his because of the sun. Rock actually never thought about it—he'd started out flying F-86s in Korea so marksmanship was second nature. At 1,000 feet back he kept the pitot boom centered on the boat but pulled the tip up a few inches, leading the target. A few muzzle flashes sparkled but he ignored them.

"BRRRRRRRRPPPPPPPPPPPP."

Releasing the trigger, he instantly went to MIL, pulled up and over to the left, then leveled off. OB laughed from the back and Rock grinned. The second launch looked like a giant chain saw had hit it. The bow was gone and it had flipped over on its side, orange flames showing through the oily black smoke. Holding the fighter level until he reached 500 knots, Ed smoothly pulled back and started to climb. Putting the big mountain peak ahead on his nose, they were passing 8,000 feet as they crossed the coast.

"King . . . Zodiac is RTB. Bingo."

"Copy all . . . sorry about the tanker. Good work!"

Rock clicked the mike and nodded. They *had* done good work, and if he and OB hadn't happened along the Navy pilot would likely be tied up naked in the bottom of one of these boats.* Above 15,000 feet he pointed toward the Ban Karai Pass, shallowed the climb to hold 450 knots, and dropped his mask.

"Heading?"

"About ten left for Korat . . . three hundred ninety miles."

Looking left, he could see clear south to the DMZ and Rock thought of the battlefields down there. Khe Sanh, the Drang

---

*Lieutenant Stan Bloyer of VA-155 would survive the war and get married. Remaining in the Navy, he would command VA-83 and then Carrier Air Wing Six during Operation Desert Storm. Stan Bloyer retired as a captain (O-6) and passed away in March 2012.

valley, A Shau, and all the others with American blood on them. His eyes wandered up the Bolavens Plateau to the Truong Son range in front of him. The trail was still down there, despite the bombs, the electronic wizardry, the years, and the lives.

Passing 20,000 feet, Rock gazed north along the Gianh River valley to the mouth of the Mu Gia Pass. Some 250 miles beyond that lay Hanoi, the Red River valley, and Thud Ridge, where he'd fought during the savage days of 1966. The SAM had been an unknown, deadly foe, and he remembered the haggard faces of those first Weasels as they passed on what they'd learned. He thought of the amazingly fast, low-level attacks with iron bombs, cannons, and guts. The men, civilian and military alike, who'd created and tested the Vector equipment that gave the Weasels a fighting chance. Hunter Killers like himself who'd used themselves as bait, outflown the MiGs and missiles, then killed the sites.

He passed 25,000 on his way up to 30,000 and gazed off to the right again. Way up north toward Barthelemy Pass, a low quilt of clouds covered the ground. Smoky and soft, it rolled with the terrain, pierced only by the high, dark peaks of North Vietnam. Then he saw them. Images and faces from the past played like a movie against the gray background. John Pitchford and Bob Trier, the first Weasels killed in action; the redoubtable, unquenchable Allen Lamb alongside Garry Willard and Rick Morgan, the quiet professionals. Jack Donavan's immortal "You gotta be shittin' me!" rang in his ears, along with faint, ghostly voices singing "The Balls of O'Leary."

He saw bright afterburner plumes spearing through the darkness of a predawn launch; missiles sliding across the sky like lethal, silver splinters to penetrate, to burn, and to kill. Calmly frantic radio calls; urgent warnings, pleas for help, and that awful heavy silence after a fight. Ed saw faces, too.

Cheek-splitting grins under big, bushy mustaches and boonie hats pushed back on sweaty hair. Laughing, exuberant men drinking hundred-mission champagne under the nose of a dirty Thud as another pair of Weasels survived to return home. Other faces, too: shocked, tearful women and the blank, uncomprehending faces of children when they were told Daddy wasn't coming home.

He blinked several times and the images faded.

Once again the cloud deck was just a cloud deck and he was headed back to Korat. Taking a deep breath, he smelled the dry oxygen mingling with the rubber in his mask. Jet fuel, hot plastic, and the stale odor of his flight suit were all familiar and comforting. It was worth it. It *had* to be worth it. Like many others, Ed Rock wasn't really fighting for political objectives or for the South Vietnamese. He was fighting for his life and the lives of those with him. Fighting for all the men who strapped themselves into aircraft and took off into the guns and the SAMs. Men who chose to go in harm's way because it was a duty; because it was their profession. Many had gone down fighting. Some were recovered, some were prisoners, and, he sighed, some were gone forever.

EPILOGUE

NINE DAYS LATER Lieutenant Colonel Jim O'Neil and Captain Mike Bosiljevac weren't so fortunate. Flying as Crow 01, they were escorting a SAM strike northwest of Hanoi when one of the other fighters was lit up by a Fansong. By this time the enemy had perfected their multi-radar tactics so the SA-2 they were attacking was not the site actually shooting. Mining Haiphong Harbor and blockading the North Vietnamese coast had been very effective. Spare missiles were in short supply and every shot counted. Fansong operators could also recognize the distinctive loft profile used by Weasels when employing anti-radiation missiles. In the Shrike's case, they could detect the metallic residue in the missile's exhaust following a launch.

The North Vietnamese hated Weasels and targeted them whenever possible, so when Crow 01 turned in to attack, another SA-2 had already been fired. Before Colonel O'Neil could shoot, the SAM hit the F-105G in the belly. Amid the glowing warning lights and nose, O'Neil turned immediately southwest toward the Laotian border and nursed the jet as far as possible. Trailing smoke, they limped across the Red River to the southern slopes of Ba Vi Mountain before the fire burned through the warning circuits and the Thud began shuddering.

Just short of the Black River and twenty-five miles west of Hanoi, both men ejected and came down south of the old Spring High missile sites. Colonel O'Neil had seen Mike Bosiljevac alive on the way down; his EWO had deployed the seat kit and cut away his extra parachute lines to better steer. By a strange twist of fate they landed five miles from Allen Lamb's first SA-2 kill nearly seven years earlier. After being captured, the pilot had asked a guard about his backseater and was told that "he is alive, well, uninjured, and luckier than you." In another enduring tragedy of the war, Captain Bosiljevac was never again seen alive by Americans.*

The two great air campaigns that defined the Wild Weasels and the Vietnam War are usually written as though they were completely dissimilar operations. Rolling Thunder is viewed as a case study of political meddling in military operations, while Linebacker is often portrayed as a vindication of what airpower can accomplish if permitted to do so. These are somewhat oversimplified notions and, as it turns out, not wholly accurate. Yet after all, it was essentially the same U.S. military fighting in the same place against the same general threat. So what happened?

The overarching difference is that Rolling Thunder was in-

---

*Under extremely peculiar circumstances, Michael Joseph Bosiljevac's remains were returned in September 1987. He was finally laid to rest in Omaha, Nebraska, on February 10, 1988.

tended to influence a foreign policy decision through the use of force, while Linebacker was initiated to meet a specific military objective.

To be fair, there were geopolitical differences between 1965 and 1972. Johnson and McNamara badly feared that an escalation with the Soviet Union and Red China would lead to a global atomic Armageddon—World War III. This severely influenced the war by unnecessarily limiting Rolling Thunder. Détente with both communist nations, and 440 million bushels of wheat sold to the Soviet Union, removed this variable, so Nixon had much greater freedom of action than his predecessor. Yet the current president had to contend with domestic issues that Johnson, at least in the beginning of his tenure, did not. True, American public opinion had been greatly mollified by troop withdrawals, but there was still discontent. Also, Nixon was certain that early in the next year Congress would cut funding for the war, so anything he planned to do had to be done by the end of 1972.

This, as much as any of the other factors acting on the president, was the impetus behind what followed. As a show of good faith toward pending negotiations, Nixon had suspended bombing above the 20th parallel on October 23, 1972, but he did not halt the air campaign. He was aware that the Saigon government's intransigence was a real issue so he simply bypassed the South Vietnamese and had Henry Kissinger bargain for both parties. Washington proposed an in-place cease-fire with NVA troops remaining in the South, a prisoner of war exchange, and an American withdrawal. For their part, the North Vietnamese agreed to a National Council of Reconciliation and Concord that would supervise elections and work toward a peaceful coexistence. Kissinger balked at NVA soldiers staying in South Vietnam, then recanted under the utterly implausible condition that they not be resupplied. He was enthusiastic enough to state, to his later embarrassment, "We believe that peace is at hand. We believe an agreement is in sight."

In reality, the DRV had finally realized that if they agreed to nearly everything the White House demanded, the Americans would just leave at this point. Underestimating Richard Nixon, Hanoi overplayed its hand and in the recent light of Linebacker I, this was a risky proposition. In any event, October and November were consumed with quibbling and subterfuge, though in truth Nixon was in no hurry to proceed until after the U.S. election. While this was practical from a political standpoint, continuing to risk American lives and delaying the anguish of our POWs for political timing was deplorable.

However, by December 14 Nixon had had enough and gave Hanoi seventy-two hours to talk seriously. He'd been reelected, nearly all the U.S. ground troops were home, and it was time to finish this. Directing the chairman of the Joint Chiefs, Admiral Thomas Moorer, to plan a series of massive air strikes, the president made himself very clear by saying, "I don't want any more of this crap about the fact that we couldn't hit this target or that one. This is your chance to use military power to win this war, and if you don't, I'll hold you responsible."

On the afternoon of December 18, 1972, the first of twenty-eight B-52s rumbled down the runway at Anderson Air Force Base, Guam. Trailing heavy black smoke, the bombers lifted off ninety seconds apart, and forty-five minutes later the island air base was silent. With more than 1,500 miles to go, the big jets would refuel, fly a circuitous route to deceive the North Vietnamese, and reach their target some seven hours later. Twenty-one other B-52s would come from southern Thailand, and with a shorter distance to fly the crews were eating lunch while the Anderson jets took off. Both groups were heading to the same place—Hanoi.

Soviet spy trawlers hovering in international waters off Guam passed the takeoff time and numbers of bombers just as they'd done for years. Local agents in Thailand near U-Tapao Airfield did the same when the second package got airborne. There was no hiding from the North Vietnamese; they would know the B-52s were coming and would plainly see them on radar. Given that, and the relatively small size of the country, feints and diversions from high-altitude bombers were an unnecessarily risky waste of time.

Yet that's exactly what the SAC planners mandated: an Arc Light route across South Vietnam that went north to the Chinese border, then turned southeast down Thud ridge toward Hanoi. Worse still, all the bombers followed the same route, made the same turn off target, and followed each other out. One big daisy chain, with subsequent waves following identical routes to the same targets exactly four hours apart. Most of those who saw the plan were stunned by its stupidity, and the fighter pilots were apoplectic. The really shocking aspect of it was that the commander of SAC was himself a former fighter pilot.

Unquestionably a brave officer during World War II and a fine tactician in single-seat fighters, General J. C. Meyer had no business commanding strategic bombers.* He was accustomed to a world where pilots made decisions on the spot and didn't rely on generals sitting in a command post 7,900 miles away. Worse, when the "top-down" SAC system failed he did nothing to change it. Add to that the fact that none of the other

---

*With twenty-four confirmed kills, J. C. Meyer was the fourth highest scoring American ace in Europe.

top bomber generals had any recent combat experience, and none at all flying jet bombers under fire. Like the earlier USAF philosophy that a "pilot was a pilot," this idea that a "general is a general" and could command anything, regardless of his experience, was absurd. Unfortunately, the SAC culture was to salute smartly and carry on unquestionably, and that's precisely what they did. In fact, Anderson's wing commander, Colonel James McCarthy, threatened to court-martial any pilot who maneuvered once they started their bomb run.* This was going to be an issue from the beginning.

Like everyone else, the Weasels were appalled.

The basic idea for the first few nights was to launch preemptive antiradiation missiles at known SAM sites. There were three big problems with that. First, preemptive shots were primarily based on timing, especially when the Weasels and B-52s had no direct communications with each other. So if the bombers were late, and they were, then the Shrikes and STARMs were wasted. Second, there was no such thing as a "known" SAM site. Real-time intelligence in 1972 consisted of eyeballs and electronic emissions, so until a missile was fired its location was uncertain. Third, as mentioned, the Vietnamese air defense operators were well aware of the Weasels and used many countertactics to entice ARM shots. The easiest and most common method was to have a few Fansongs act as decoys by powering up when Weasels approached. Once an ARM shot was detected, the Fansong simply shut down and the missile went stupid. If the radar was hit, it wasn't collocated with a SAM, so no real immediate combat degradation occurred. The North Vietnamese could also track jamming pods with their

---

*During the post-Linebacker "victory tour" conducted by Meyer and his staff, McCarthy was awarded the Silver Star for flying two combat missions.

Spoon Rest EW radars, and then pass the rough information to Fansong target trackers. This turned out to be particularly effective against the B-52s because of the size of the jamming strobes.

By late 1972, there were nearly forty EW radars strung out across North Vietnam, providing all sorts of information. With a shortage of ARMs and the higher priority of protecting bombers, these EW/GCI sites weren't actively targeted. EB-66 aircraft did what they could to jam but there was simply no way to totally conceal the bombers. At the time of Linebacker II, the North Vietnamese capital was protected by three SAM regiments from the 361st Air Defense Division. Between them there were ten SA-2 batteries augmented by thousands of anti-aircraft guns. Northeastern approaches to the city were covered by the 261st Regiment, and those to the west and south by the 274th and 257th regiments, respectively. Bombers inbound above 30,000 were safe from smaller-caliber Triple A but could be hit by the 85–100 mm variety.

Night raids were planned to minimize the danger from MiGs, yet, unbelievably to the veteran fighter pilots, the B-52s flew in over Vietnam with their lights on. Used in peacetime for safety reasons, the red rotating beacons helped pilots see each other and avoid collisions. Undoubtedly, North Vietnamese MiG-21s appreciated the help in visually acquiring their targets. Fortunately, though the moon was full there was a solid undercast at 10,000, so visual sightings from the ground weren't possible. Also, newly arrived F-111s were hitting nearby NVAF airfields and very few MiG pilots were night qualified anyway. The real danger was always from the SAMs.

Besides having Weasels for escorts, SAC tried several things to mitigate the threat. A protective corridor was laid by Phantoms carrying chaff dispensers that, theoretically, would have

trashed all the North Vietnamese radar scopes in the area. Unfortunately, the winds at altitude were stronger than predicted
and coming from a different heading, so the chaff did not cover
the planned routes. Things like this happen, so combat aviators
are expected to adapt and overcome. Again, SAC culture over-
rode the bomber pilot's better instincts and, afraid to deviate at
all from the plan, they pressed in, relying on jamming for safety.

There were several issues with this. First was burn-through,
the range that jamming can be penetrated. As the big jets approached Hanoi, they got close enough for the Fansongs to see
through the countermeasures and lock on to the bombers. Also,
as the B-52s neared their targets they had to open their bomb
bay doors, thus exponentially increasing their radar cross section, and making them easy to see. Several other relics of the
Cold War cost the bombers dearly. First, the normal procedure
after dropping a *nuclear* bomb was to immediately turn hard
away after release to avoid the explosion. There was absolutely
no need to do this with *conventional* bombs in Southeast Asia,
especially when the planned turn headed the B-52s directly into
a 100-knot jet stream. This delayed their target area egress by
slowing them down and made the bombers even more vulnerable. The actual turn itself didn't help the situation, either. ECM
antennas on B-52s were all angled downward to counter predicted Soviet threats during nuclear penetration missions. So
as the bomber rolled up in a turn, the antennas were pointed
at the sky, not at the ground. The resulting "hole" in jamming
coverage again made the bombers highly visible on radar and
extremely vulnerable to SAMs. None of these factors was accounted for by General Pete Sianis, the SAC Deputy Chief of
Staff for Operations, or his mission planners.

In retrospect, the first three nights of Linebacker II were
planned as logistical exercises rather than combat missions.

This might be forgiven on the first night of new war, but not after eight years of conflict, when there were ample sources of information about fighting the North Vietnamese. SAC simply believed that they knew best; they knew bombers and that's what this was—a bomber campaign. But there was absolutely no excuse for this attitude after December 18, when all the planning errors, tactical deficiencies, and results became known. Competent, professional combat officers learn from their mistakes or they don't survive, and that's exactly what happened. Five B-52s were hit by SAMs that first night and three went down. SAC refused to heed advice, had no process to get feedback from combat crews, and simply didn't care to. SAC headquarters was always right; it had to be right or their world made no sense.

The Weasels tried to save the bombers but were severely limited by the North Vietnamese response to Linebacker II. Due to a shortage of missiles, the 361st Air Division initiated a practical solution; MiGs, which had limited night capability anyway, would handle the majority of daytime defense, while SAMs would generally be saved for the evening B-52 raids. Both would be supplemented by anti-aircraft guns. The lack of plentiful daytime emissions from Fansongs and Firecans meant Hunter Killer teams had few radar targets.

Indeed, as a result Captains Bob Tidwell and Denny Haney of the 67 TFS (Fighting Cocks) managed a scheduling change to fly night missions. Flying the F-4C Wild Weasel, they were part of a six-jet, nine-crew detachment that deployed to Korat in September. The Wild Weasel IV program had a rough start and the equipment hadn't been satisfactorily installed until mid-June 1968. Operational testing was finished a year later at the 4537th Fighter Weapons Squadron and thirty-six converted jets were formed into two squadrons to be sent overseas. Twelve

Phantom Weasels initially went to the 80th TFS (Headhunters) at Yakota Air Base, Japan. These were subsequently transferred to the 67th TFS in 1971, and six deployed to Thailand in the fall of 1972.

The F-4 had been designated as the follow-on Weasel back in 1966. With the F-105 out of production there was no way to replace combat losses and a more advanced avionics suite was needed. Also, the USAF realized it had entirely too many different types of aircraft and was making an effort, albeit unsuccessful, to consolidate airframes. In any event, the F-4C carried the ER-143 panoramic receiver, the ALR-46 RWR, and the same basic APR-25/26 system used in the F-105F. It required no self-protection from MiGs and could employ all the normal F-4 air-to-air and air-to-ground ordnance. Due to internal electronic configuration issues it could not shoot the standard ARM, so its only antiradiation capability was the AGM-45 Shrike. Clearly the Phantom had a ways to go as a true Weasel, but it would get there.

Setting up twelve to twenty miles away from Hanoi, Bob and Denny would then troll for SAMs. One night they'd been told that the last MiG had landed and all was quiet—briefly. Then up came the Firecans and a few Fansongs. Flying directly toward Hanoi at 450 knots, the Phantom looked threatening and tried provoking the SAMs. But any missiles fired at a Weasel were not available against the bombers, so battery commanders usually held out for juicier targets. With a dark sky and good moon, Denny and Bob had an excellent view of the countryside all the way through Haiphong to the Gulf of Tonkin. Everything was blacked out, of course, except for Christmas Eve, when both cities were ablaze with lights. One possibility for this was a visit to Hanoi by singer Joan Baez and several other American entertainers. Perhaps the lights were deliberately turned on to attract the bombers. After all, if Baez and crowd were accidentally killed, then perhaps the North Vietnamese might hope for a backlash against the White House. Running short of surface-to-air missiles as they were, such a desperate notion likely seemed logical, though it's doubtful that Nixon would have cared much about a folksinger and her entourage.

A night launch of a SAM is impossible to miss, so Denny and Bob had front-row seats for the eight hundred or so missiles launched during the Christmas bombings. The initial brilliant white flash is followed by a tight, multicolored fireball that rapidly stretches into a long, dark orange tail. Picking up speed, it actually streaks across the sky like a comet headed up rather than down. This is good because if you can see movement, called line of sight, across your canopy, then the SA-2 is probably after someone else. Early in the launch it's hard to tell, but after a few seconds this is obvious—at least for the first missile. If the thing transitions from a tailed comet to a flaming doughnut, the missile has corrected and is trying to pull lead for an intercept.

On the first night of Linebacker II more than 120 SAMs were launched. Due to the missile shortage there were fewer of these over time, yet Bob and Denny counted at least 70 firings on this particular mission. As they capped, trolled, thrust, and feinted, the Weasels still weren't able to bait a Fansong into shooting—yet. Unfortunately, the area west of Hanoi and south of the Red River was defended by four SA-2 batteries of the 257th Air Defense Regiment. Perhaps they were tired of waiting for B-52s, or maybe they were just angered by the F-4 overhead. In any case, Nguyen Chen, commander of the 78th Missile Battalion, had had enough. His site was situated south of National Route 114 about twelve miles west of Hanoi, very close to where the Weasel turned.

Reacting instantly, Bob and Denny threw the Phantom sideways, dumped the nose, then rolled and pulled back hard into the missile. Stars spun and the g-force grayed their vision but there wasn't time for anything else and the SAM passed so close that both men saw flaming blobs of propellant dripping off the tail. For some reason the proximity fuse didn't function, which is the only reason they survived. Gasping for breath and thoroughly pissed-off, they wheeled around and fired both Shrikes down the radar's throat.

By the tenth day of bombing there were few targets remaining. One was actually a shack, complete with a pigsty, near a railroad siding, and it was obliterated by three bombers that flew fifteen hours to do it. Linebacker II officially ended on the morning of December 30, 1972, though the last missions had been flown the night before. During the eleven-day campaign, 795 B-52 sorties were flown and fifteen of the big bombers were lost. A self-congratulatory SAC headquarters proclaimed victory and, ever ready to manipulate math for accolades, declared a loss rate of *only* 1.9 percent. The problem with this was that only 372 of the total missions were flown to Hanoi. The actual loss rate was 4.3 percent and all fifteen B-52s went down near the city. This, along with many other facts and lessons learned, was buried and, SAC fervently hoped, forgotten.*

Linebacker II was over but combat operations would continue south of the 20th parallel until a peace agreement was reached. Fortunately, the shock of the bombing, combined with a shortage of SAMs, produced the incentive to continue negotiating. The North Vietnamese had actually indicated by Decem-

---

*Marshall L. Michel's *The Eleven Days of Christmas* and Dana Drenkowski's article "The Tragedy of Linebacker II" are highly recommended for further reading.

ber 26 that they'd had a bellyful of bombing, yet Nixon kept it up to ensure they'd gotten the point. Henry Kissinger and North Vietnamese diplomat Le Duc Tho met in Paris and by January 23 they had agreed to terms. On January 27, 1973, the Paris Peace Accords were signed by the United States, the South Vietnamese foreign minister, the minister of foreign affairs from the DRV, and the Provisional Revolutionary Government of the Republic of South Vietnam—the remnant of the National Liberation Front and Viet Cong.

The very day the accord was signed, a Navy F-4J off the USS *Enterprise* went down, killing Commander Harley Hall, former Blue Angel and commanding officer of VF-143 (Pukin' Dogs). His backseater, Lieutenant Commander Phillip Kientzler, became the last naval aviator taken as a prisoner of war. Twenty minutes after the Phantom went in, Nail 89, an OV-10A Bronco, was diverted over the Cua Viet River area to cover the rescue. Hit by an SA-7, both pilots ejected and multiple sources admit to seeing two good parachutes. Voice contact was made with First Lieutenant Mark Peterson, yet nothing further was heard from him or Captain George Morris ever again.

Strike missions into South Vietnam would end on January 28, 1973, and the war was officially over. More correctly, overt American military support in Vietnam temporarily ceased, though fighting continued in Cambodia and Laos. The last *acknowledged* American fliers killed in Southeast Asia were Captains Sam Blackmar Cornelius and John Smallwood from the 336 TFS (Rocketeers) out of Ubon. Their F-4E went down on June 16, 1973, between the Sepok and San rivers in central Cambodia. There were persistent, credible rumors that they had survived, but since Washington never sought the release of Americans captured in Cambodia, no official action was ever taken. Their fate, as with so many others, remains unknown.

The Paris Accords enabled Nixon to pull out of Southeast Asia and bring our long-suffering POWs back home. It would not, and did not, stop the conflict for the Vietnamese. Communist troops were permitted to remain in place in the South, thus firmly setting the stage for the republic's eventual collapse. Though Nixon promised President Thieu that he would again commit U.S. airpower should it become necessary, his guarantee evaporated in the face of a scandal that cost him his presidency.*

None of this mattered much to the first group of Americans who left Hoa Loa Prison, the infamous Hanoi Hilton, in February 1973. They were loaded, somewhat disbelievingly, into buses and taken across the Long Bien bridge to Gia Lam airport on the eastern side of the Red River. Those imprisoned the longest were released first. Jim Thompson, a Special Forces officer, had been held since March 1964—nearly an entire decade. Navy pilots Everett Alvarez and Jim Stockdale were there, as was Ernie Brace, a former Marine captain who'd been flying as a civilian when shot down over Laos.

Days later, on March 4, 1973, Wild Weasels Leo Thorsness and Harry Johnson walked out of the Hanoi Hilton and boarded the bus. It had been nearly six years since they'd gone down in the Phu Tho province northwest of Hanoi, and they desperately hoped the nightmare was truly over. Three and a half hours after departing Gia Lam, the C-140 transport landed at Clark Air Base in the Philippines, and the first part of their homecoming came true. Stepping out onto a red carpet amid hundreds of American flags and cheering people, Leo, Harry, and all the others were free at last.

The next stop was the hospital and the first of several beau-

---

*In fact, the White House ordered bombing to resume in April 1973 but this was canceled due to the growing Watergate controversy.

tiful sights. Children's colorful, crayon drawings festooned the walls and the rooms were sparkling clean. Crisp sheets were on the beds and each room had something none of them had seen for years—a bath with real porcelain toilets. Leo later wrote, "It was addictive—I flushed it again, again, and again." But the best part was that the doors didn't lock from the outside, and Leo could come and go as he pleased. Finally the moment came he'd dreamed of since April 30, 1967. Getting a line through to the States, he waited, mouth dry and heart pounding, while his home telephone rang. Weak with relief, *she* answered and he swallowed, breath short.

"Leo, is that you?"

Grinning from ear to ear, the fighter pilot said what he'd planned for six years to say. "Gaylee, I would have called sooner . . . but I've been all tied up."

Held up in Hawaii an extra day with a high fever, Leo Thorsness finally came home on March 10, 1973. Despite destroyed knees and a badly injured back, he stepped off the transport at Scott Air Force Base, Illinois, all on his own. His lovely wife and beautiful daughter, Dawn, were standing at the end of another red carpet . . . waiting. Describing the moment years later he wrote, "Gaylee was first to reach me. Then Dawn. As they held me, I felt at last that my life, which had gone to sleep, was awake again." *

WITH THE WAR'S end, Denny Haney, Bob Tidwell, and the rest of the F-4C Wild Weasel detachment left Korat for Okinawa

---

*Needing multiple surgeries to repair his injuries, he passed much of the time in bed by reading *World Book Encyclopedias* to fill in the lost years. Leo Thorsness was awarded his nation's highest honor, the Congressional Medal of Honor, for his actions on April 19, 1967. Leaving the USAF, he would serve as director of civic affairs for Litton Industries, and as a state senator for the state of Washington.

about the same time the first POWs began flying home. In April 1973, eleven months after assuming command of his squadron, Ed Rock was given a long-deserved rest and promotion to Deputy Commander of Operations for the 388 TFW. A month later, on May 19, he flew his 183rd, and final, F-105 combat mission; 164 of these had been over North Vietnam. Ed Rock left Korat for the last time on June 16, 1973, on his way to the Tactical Air Warfare Center (TAWC) at Eglin Air Force Base, Florida.

Military Assistance Command, Vietnam (MACV) was disbanded that same spring and, somewhat prophetically, Seventh Air Force headquarters was relocated from Saigon to Nakhon Phanom, Thailand. The last recorded American combat mission, a flight of USAF Corsairs, returned to Korat on August 15, 1973, after striking targets in Cambodia. A Disco EC-121T was the last plane to land, officially ending the air war and an amazing chapter of American history.*

All told, the combined services flew 6,377,903 *fixed-wing* combat sorties from April 1965 through March 1973. Combat losses from the U.S. Air Force, Navy, and Marine Corps would stand at 2,317 fixed-wing aircraft.† Nearly 30 percent of these aircraft went down during strike missions while the combination of close air support, armed reconnaissance, and flak (air defense) suppression missions accounted for another 56 percent. Small arms, automatic weapons, and anti-aircraft artillery fire brought down 1,761 of the total fixed-wing losses over North Vietnam, Laos, and South Vietnam. Clearly, flying close to the

---

*A specially modified Constellation, the Discos were used for airborne early warning against MiGs.
†More than 5,000 rotary-wing aircraft and some 2,000 crew members were lost in action through 1975.

guns, even in sophisticated jet fighters, was as dangerous during Vietnam as it had been in all previous wars.

For a variety of reasons there is no completely accurate accounting of the surface-to-air missiles fired during seven years of conflict. First of all, when one is shot at, it's not a priority to keep count, only to survive. After-action reports are often colored by the stress of combat and sometimes veracity unintentionally suffers. ELINT is similarly unreliable in this respect because an emitting radar doesn't necessarily mean a missile has been fired. Also, since there are many aircraft in a strike package there are a corresponding number of opinions as to the battlefield results. It is entirely normal for the same missile to be counted several times since it was seen from many viewpoints. North Vietnamese air defense units were prone to overreport the number of SAMs fired to give the impression they were fighting as hard as possible and to receive replacement missiles from the Soviet Union. Soviet figures from the Main Intelligence Directorate of the General Staff tend to be underreported in order to boost lethality claims.

The best estimate is about 5,800 SA-2s employed in combat between 1965 and 1973. According to the Center for Naval Analyses, the combined service loss rate due to SAMs for the entire war was 9 percent, or about 209 fixed-wing aircraft. The SA-2 had its best kill rate, about 10 missiles per aircraft destroyed during 1965, before the Weasels arrived in force. It would never be this low again. At the height of the air war in 1967–68, nearly 2,100 missiles were fired. They brought down 71 aircraft, or about one for each 31 SAMs expended. When the bombing of the North resumed in 1972, SAM employment spiked at 2,059 missiles fired. This meant 35 SA-2s were now fired for each of the 73 U.S. aircraft lost that year. Better tactics, countermeasures, and ECM all played vital roles in this, yet without Hunter Killers present the number of aircraft lost would certainly have been greater.

Interestingly, despite better electronic countermeasures the Navy's 15 percent loss rate to SAMs was more than twice that of the Air Force. The Navy conducted 161,586 total attack sorties over heavily defended North Vietnam, with 36,536 dedicated electronic warfare missions supporting them. The Air Force flew almost an equal number of EW support missions, but recorded 190,245 attack sorties. Navy attacks also came straight in from the Gulf of Tonkin and had very short times over hostile territory, whereas USAF strikes nearly all came in from hundreds of miles overland. Following the Black Friday Iron Hand shootdowns in 1965, Navy planners were understandably cautious regarding defense suppression, choosing ARM and ECM technology whenever possible over direct attacks on SAM sites. Jamming and suppression were used only during package vulnerability windows rather than the Air Force's Wild Weasel concept of killing the radars. There should have been fewer proportionate Navy losses to the SAMs, but there were not. The final numbers speak for themselves and validate the Hunter Killer mission without question.

Yet the price was high.

Thirty-four F-100 or F-105F/G jets were lost as a result of enemy action between 1965 and the end of the war. From Wild Weasel I through Wild Weasel IV-C, there were only about 150 aircraft modified to hunt and kill SAMs and never more than seventy-five pilots and EWOS in theater at any given time. Of the 68 Hunter Killers who went down, 30 were killed in action, 19 became prisoners of war, 2 died in captivity, and 17 were rescued. Shortsightedness cost America the initial edge against the SAMs, and the sacrifices of the Weasels bought time to recover and to beat the new missiles. In the end, it was what they did, and what they were prepared to do for all of us, that truly matters. As Colonel Ed Rock would say in 2014:

All of these men are heroes because they were willing to make a sacrifice, and take a risk by doing something that most people would not even attempt. They were truly brave, selfless, generous in spirit, and gave as much as possible to save the lives of others.

Some were welcomed home and others, to our national shame, were not. Yet despite everything stacked against them, the Hunter Killers attacked the guns and the missiles head-on, and they *did* win. The rationale behind the Vietnam War might have been ambiguous, but the courage of those who fought it was not. Certainly as long as America has men like this, it shall remain America. Their legacy still lives on today, and when we once again go to war against those who would destroy us then we will know what to do—men like the Hunter Killers showed us how.

"First In, Last Out."

ACKNOWLEDGMENTS

THIS BOOK ABSOLUTELY could not have been written without the firsthand knowledge, personal accounts, and extraordinary patience of the men described herein. Time and again I turned to them all with an obscure question, a clarification, or endless requests to repeat things they'd already told me before. As a fighter pilot myself I could write about air combat, about dropping bombs, strafing and, above all, Wild Weaseling—in the context of the Gulf Wars. But I'd never flown a Thud or a Hun, or fought the North Vietnamese. So it is to these men that I owe my profound thanks for dredging up memories, reliving the bad times and the brave times, then sharing all that with me so I could pass it on. The pilots and Bears in this book are all superb examples of what the military should produce in combat officers and it has been my privilege to make their acquaintance. It is impossible to mention all the fine men involved in this conflict and for my inadvertent omissions, please accept my profound apologies.

Ed Rock, fighter pilot and editor of *First In Last Out: Stories by the Wild Weasels,* gave up an incredible amount of time ensuring that the details were correct, proofreading, correcting my errors, and answering literally hundreds of questions. Research is fine, but there is simply is no substitute for firsthand sources from those who had been there and done that. Thank you, Ed.

Stan Goldstein gave freely of his time, expertise, and knowledge. An inexhaustible source of contacts, he always knew someone who could answer my interminable, pesky questions. Going far beyond that, he sacrificed a considerable amount of time on the golf course to track folks down for me. Incidentally, despite my own fighter background (or perhaps because of it!) several of these people would only consent to speak because of Stan's introductions. He was also a proofreader, sounding board, and reality checker rolled into one extraordinary, humorous individual.

Allen Lamb was kind enough to put me up for several weekends, share his single malt scotch, and relive his experiences as a Hunter Killer during Wild Weasel I. He and his lovely wife, Frances, also provided a considerable amount of personal photographs, papers, and maps—without which this book would not be what it is.

Howard Plunkett is an amazing source of information regarding the Vietnam war in general, and specifically for anything pertaining to the F-105. I will presume to say that the man knows everything about Thud operations in Southeast Asia, and no author could wish for a better source of hard data. Howard also kindly agreed to read each chapter as I finished and his blunt, accurate, and wholly necessary corrections have saved me much embarrassment. He has my unflagging admiration and gratitude.

Another wonderful man, former USAF Flight Surgeon Dr. Phil Steeves, freely volunteered his time to read every chapter, offer insights, and discreetly point me in the right direction. A Yale-educated consummate gentleman, his tact and diplomacy in a world of large egos is truly astounding and sincerely appreciated.

Vic Vizcarra, former Thud driver, made the "Spring High"

chapter possible. A computer simulation had been created of that particular pivotal mission, and Vic was kind enough to let me use it to get every detail correct. As an author, having such a remarkable tool, as well as getting insights from the men who flew the actual mission, was invaluable.

Chapter seven, "A Full Day's Work," was only possible due to the assistance of Leo Thorsness and Jerry Hoblit. Each took the time to look at my sketches, review the writing, and dredge up memories of a very bad day long ago. My personal thanks and best wishes to both men.

Being able to discuss the "Bauman Mod" and its implications was only possible because Weldon Bauman cheerfully volunteered his expertise and time. Twenty-five years after the fact, the fighter jets I flew all had derivatives of his extraordinary contribution, and it is no exaggeration to say that the modification he created makes modern Weaseling possible.

Denny Haney was kind enough to "close the loop" for me regarding Linebacker II and the combat debut of the F-4C Weasel. A fine writer himself, Denny's lucid account, technical memory, and details (like Hanoi's lights on Christmas Eve), were greatly appreciated.

Among the many others who deserve very public acknowledgement for their contributions are Guy Aceto, George Acree, Jack Broughton *(Thud Ridge, Going Downtown,* and *Rupert Red Two)*, Marty Case, Liz Carroll, Paul Craw, Bill Freeman, Ben Fuller, Bruce Giffin, H. Lee Griffin, Russ Greer, Dan Hampton Sr., Biddie Hampton, Chuck Horner, Mike Jackson, Patti King, Bob Klimek, Frances Lamb, Bob Lilac, Rich McCubbins, Dr. John Mearns, Erica Mearns, Dave Moody, Rick Morgan, Paul T. Mudge, George Nolly (author of the Hamfist series), John Revak, Don Shepperd, Joe Telford, Erin and Frank Thompson, Ken Wicks, Garry Willard, and Darrel Whitcomb.

A special thanks to Greg Anderson, Marilyn Chang, and Matthew Burchette of Wings Over the Rockies Air and Space Museum in Denver; Josh Staff of the Cradle of Aviation Museum on Long Island, and Gary Lewi of the American Airpower Museum. Also Richard Poulsen, managing editor of Squadron Signal Publishing and Lou Drendel, author and very talented aviation artist.

As always, my sincere gratitude and appreciation to the talented group at HarperCollins: my publicist, Lauren Jackson, for making me look better than I really do; art director Rich Aquan for his superb cover; editorial assistant Nick Amphlett for his ability to juggle the details; my editor, Peter Hubbard, for his endless patience, skill, humor, and ability to transform raw ideas into new books; and, finally, to William Morrow's publisher, Liate Stehlik, for giving everyone in this paragraph the chance to tell a story that needed to be told.

GLOSSARY OF TERMS AND ACRONYMS

AAA: Anti-Aircraft Artillery. Also called "Triple A."

AI: Airborne Intercept radar used on board fighter aircraft.

ARC LIGHT: B-52 strikes during the Vietnam War.

ARM: Anti-radiation missile used against radars.

BARCAP: Carrier Combat Air Patrol. Defensive fighters placed between vulnerable aircraft and probably MiGs.

BEAR: A nickname for a Wild Weasel Electronic Warfare Officer.

B Scope: A radar display that depicts range vertically from the base of the scope. Azimuth is shown left and right of the display's center line.

BIG EYE: Known also as "College Eye." EC-121D aircraft used for surveillance and airborne early warning over North Vietnam.

BINGO: Pre set fuel limit to egress a target area and get to a tanker or return to base.

BUFF: Big Ugly Fat Fucker. A B-52 bomber.

BURN THROUGH RANGE: The slant range to a target at which a radar can 'see' through jamming or countermeasures.

CAW: Carrier Air Wing.

CEA: Circular Error Average. Average radial distance of a bomb impact measured from the target.

CEP: Circular Error Probable. Measures the precision of a weapons system by calculating the radius of a circle within which 50 percent of all weapons attempts are expected to fall.

CHAFF: A decoy composed of metal foil or metal coated diploes that will hopefully produce false radar returns or cause a radar to break its lock on a target.

CV: Designation for a U.S. aircraft carrier.

DECEPTION JAMMING: A countermeasures technique which detects radar signals, alters one or more characteristics, and re-radiates them to defeat or mislead the tracking radar.

DIXIE STATION: U.S. Navy operating area in the South China Sea off the coast of the Republic of South Vietnam.

DME: Distance Measuring Equipment.

DMZ: Demilitarized Zone. For Vietnam the 17th parallel was temporarily set during the 1954 Geneva Accords and became a de facto border.

DRV: Democratic Republic of Vietnam.

ECM: Electronic Counter Measure. Any equipment or technique utilized to negate, deceive or disrupt radar operations.

ELINT: Electronic Intelligence.

EW: Early Warning system. In the context of this book it is a long-range surveillance radar.

EWO: Electronic Warfare Officer.

FAC: Forward Air Controller. Responsible for calling in and managing close air support air strikes.

FANSONG: Fire control and tracking radar for the SA-2 missile system.

GCI: Ground Controlled Intercept. A system whereby a radar ground controller uses extensive voice commands to vector fighters onto targets.

GOMER: Slang for the enemy.

GUIDELINE: NATO term for the V-75 SA-2 missile system.

HUN: Nickname for the F-100 Super Sabre.

HUNTER KILLERS: Specially equipped USAF fighters who locate and kill enemy radars, missiles, and anti-aircraft guns.

IDENT: A request to identify an aircraft using onboard IFF systems.

IFF: Identification Friend or Foe equipment. Basically a coded transponder signal which can be interrogated and used for hostile or friendly aircraft identification.

INS: Inertial Navigation System.

IRON HAND: A term used by both the USAF and USN to identify missions that specifically attacked SAM sites.

MiGCAP: A primarily offensive Combat Air Patrol.

MONOPULSE: A radar which radiates a pair, or two pairs, of parallel beams and then measures the difference in the strength of the target return.

MUSIC: Brevity/secure term for friendly jamming.

NOTAMS: Notices to Airmen. Safety of flight information read by aircrews prior to flying.

NLF: National Liberation Front. Political arm of the South Vietnamese communist movement.

NOISE JAMMING: A countermeasures technique used to screen radar return echoes by using radiated power to obscure a target or a sector.

NVA: North Vietnamese Army from the period following the French Indochina War through the fall of Saigon. Alternately referred to as the Viet Minh (1946–1954) and the People's Army of Vietnam (PAVN).

PACAF: Pacific Air Forces.

PRF: Pulse Repetition Frequency or the number of pulses per second transmitted by a radar.

PRI: Pulse Repetition Interval.

RHAW: Radar Homing And Warning receiver.

RWR: Radar Warning Receiver.

SAM: Surface-to-Air Missile.

SEA: Southeast Asia.

TACS: Tactical Air Control Squadron.

TFS: Tactical Fighter Squadron. Usually three per wing, but this varies.

TFW: Tactical Fighter Wing. A wing is composed of the flying squadrons, maintenance units of all types, and logistical/administrative support.

THUD: Nickname for the F-105 Thunderchief.

TRS: Tactical Reconnaissance Squadron.

USAF: United States Air Force.

USMC: United States Marine Corps.

USN: United States Navy.

VA: Designation for a Naval Attack squadron.

VC: Viet Cong. South Vietnamese communists.

VF: Designation for a U.S. Naval fighter squadron.

VHF: Very High Frequency.

VMF: Designation for a U.S. Marine Corps fighter squadron.

VMFA: Designation for a U.S. Marine Corps fighter attack squadron.

VNAF: Vietnamese Air Force. Also the Republic of South Vietnam Air Force.

VPAF: Vietnamese People's Air Force. Also the North Vietnamese Air Force.

WILCO: Brevity phrase for "Will Comply."

WILD WEASEL: Elite U.S. Air Force fighters who find and destroy enemy radars, SAM sites, and anti-aircraft emplacements.

WSO: USAF term for a Weapons System Operator in two place fighter aircraft.

YANKEE STATION: U.S. Navy operating area in the northern Gulf of Tonkin off the coast of North Vietnam.

APPENDIX A

WILD WEASEL COMBAT LOSSES, VIETNAM: 1965–1972

1965 - 1966

DATE	AIRCRAFT	WEASELS	UNIT	DOWNED	STATUS
20-Dec-65	F-100F 58-1231	Capt John Pitchford Capt Bob Trier	6234th WW Det 6234 TFW	AAA	POW KIA
23-Mar-66	F-100F 58-1212	Maj Clyde Dawson Capt Don Clark	6234th WW Det 6234 TFW	AAA	KIA KIA
6-Jul-66	F-105F 63-8286	Maj Roosevelt Hestle Capt Charles Morgan	13 TFS 388 TFW Korat	AAA	KIA KIA
23-Jul-66	F-105F 63-8338	Maj Gene Pemberton Maj Ben Newsom	354 TFS 355 TFW Takhli	SA-2	KIA KIA
7-Aug-66	F-105F 63-8358	Capt Ed Larson Capt Mike Gilroy	354 TFS 355 TFW Takhli	SA-2	Recovered Recovered
7-Aug-66	F-105F 63-8361	Capt Bob Sandvick Capt Thomas Pyle	354 TFS 355 TFW Takhli	AAA	POW POW
17-Aug-66	F-105F 63-8308	Maj Joe Brand Maj Don Singer	354 TFS 355 TFW Takhli	AAA	KIA KIA
4-Nov-66	F-105F 63-8273	Maj Robert Brinckmann Capt Vincent Scungio	13 TFS 388 TFW Takhli	AAA	KIA KIA

1967

Date	Aircraft	Weasels	Unit	Downed	Status
29-Jan-67	F-105F 62-4420	Maj Larry Biediger 1Lt Claude Silva	354 TFS 355 TFW Takhli	Battle Damage	KIA KIA
18-Feb-67	F-105F 63-8262	Capt Dave Duart Capt Jay Jenson	13 TFS 388 TFW Korat	SA-2	POW POW
10-Mar-67	F-105F 63-8335	Maj Dave Everson Capt Jose Luna	354 TFS 355 TFW Takhli	AAA	POW POW
19-Apr-67	F-105F 63-8341	Maj Tom Madison Maj Tom Sterling	357 TFS 355 TFW Takhli	MiG-17	POW POW
26-Apr-67	F-105F 63-8277	Maj John Dudash Capt Alton Meyer	333 TFS 355 TFW Takhli	SA-2	KIA POW
30-Apr-67	F-105F 62-4447	Maj Leo Thorsness Capt Harry Johnson	357 TFS 355 TFW Takhli	MiG-17	POW POW
7-Oct-67	F-105F 63-8330	Capt Joe Howard Capt George Shamblee	44 TFS 388 TFW Korat	MiG-21 AAA	Recovered Recovered
5-Nov-67	F-105F 63-8302	Maj Dick Dutton Capt Mike Bosiljevac	333 TFS 388 TFW Korat	AAA	POW * Died in captivity
18-Nov-67	F-105F 63-8295	Maj Oscar Dardeau Capt Ed Lehnhoff	44 TFS 388 TFW Korat	MiG-21	KIA KIA
19-Nov-67	F-105F 63-8349	Maj Gerald Gustafson Capt Russell Brownlee	333 TFS 355 TFW Takhli	SA-2	Recovered Recovered

1968 - 1969

Date	Aircraft	Weasels	Unit	Downed	Status
5-Jan-68	F-105F 63-8356	Maj Jim Hartney Capt Sam Fantle	357 TFS 355 TFW Takhli	MiG-17	KIA KIA
18-Feb-68	F-105F 63-8293	Maj Michael Muscat Capt Kyle Stouder	44 TFS 388 TFW Korat	AAA	Recovered Recovered
29-Feb-68	F-105F 63-8312	Maj Crosley Fitton Capt Cleveland Harris	44 TFS 388 TFW Korat	SA-2	KIA KIA
15-Jul-68	F-105F 63-8353	Maj Gobel James Capt Larry Martin	44 TFS 388 TFW Korat	AAA	POW KIA
30-Sep-68	F-105F 63-8317	Capt Cliff Fieszel Maj Howard Smith	333 TFS 355 TFW Takhli	AAA	KIA KIA

1970 - 1972

Date	Aircraft	Weasels	Unit	Downed	Status
28-Jan-70	F-105G	Capt Richard Mallon	354 TFS	AAA	KIA
	63-8329	Capt Bob Panek	355 TFW Takhli		KIA
21-Feb-70	F-105G	Maj Gerald Hurst	357 TFS	AAA	Recovered
	63-8281	Capt Clive Bevan	355 TFW Takhli		Recovered
21-Nov-70	F-105G	Maj Don Kilgus	6010 WWS	SA-2	Recovered
	62-4436	Capt Clarence Lowry	388 TFW Korat		Recovered
10-Dec-71	F-105G	Maj Robert Belli	17 WWS	SA-2	Recoverd
	63-8326	LTC Scott McIntire	388 TFW Korat		KIA
17-Feb-72	F-105G	Capt Jim Cutter	17 WWS	SA-2	POW
	63-8333	Capt Kenneth Fraser	388 TFW Korat		POW
16-Apr-72	F-105G	Capt Alan Mateja	17 WWS	SA-2	KIA
	63-8342	Capt Orvin Jones	388 TFW Korat		KIA
11-May-72	F-105G	Maj William Talley	Det 1 561 TFS	MiG-21	POW
	62-4424	Maj James Padgett	388 TFW Korat		POW
29-Jul-72	F-105G	Maj Tom Coady	17 WWS	Battle	Recovered
	62-4443	Maj Harry Murphy	388 TFW Korat	Damage	Recovered
17-Sep-72	F-105G	Capt Thomas Zorn	17 WWS	SA-2	KIA
	63-8360	1Lt Michael Turose	388 TFW Korat		KIA
29-Sep-72	F-105G	Lt Col James O'Neil	17 WWS	SA-2	POW
	63-8302	Capt Mike Bosiljevac	388 TFW Korat		* Died in captivity
16-Nov-72	F-105G	Capt Ken Theate	Det 1 561 TFS	SA-2	Recovered
	63-8359	Maj Norman Maier	388 TFW Korat		Recovered

TOTAL COMBAT LOSSES

Aircraft	KIA	POW	Recovered	Died in Captivity
34	30	19	17	2

APPENDIX B

AIRCRAFT LOSS TABLES

FIXED-WING COMBAT AIRCRAFT LOSS TABLES (JANUARY 1962 - JUNE 1973)
Source: Center for Naval Analyses

US NAVY

Aircraft	North Vietnam	South Vietnam	Laos	Other/Unknown	Total
A-1	36	4	6	2	48
A-4	172	4	16	3	195
A-6	38	1	10	2	51
A-7	39	3	13	0	55
F-4	64	4	6	1	75
F-8	54	3	1	0	58
Other	41	8	6	1	56
	444	27	58	9	538

USMC

Aircraft	North Vietnam	South Vietnam	Laos	Other/Unknown	Total
A-4/TA-4	7	51	4	0	62
A-6	10	4	1	1	16
F-4	7	47	11	0	65
F-8	2	7	1	0	10
Other	3	15	0	2	20
	29	124	17	3	173

USAF

Aircraft	North Vietnam	South Vietnam	Laos	Other/Unknown	Total
A-1	18	45	93	3	159
F-4	193	61	109	13	376
F-100	16	140	29	6	191
F-105	281	1	52	0	334
RF-4	38	10	22	2	72
O-1/O-2	5	130	29	7	171
Other	67	147	73	16	303
	618	534	407	47	1606

| Grand Totals | 1091 | 685 | 482 | 59 | 2317 |

COUNTRY WHERE LOSS OCCURRED
Source: Center for Naval Analyses

North Vietnam	47%	
South Vietnam	30%	
Laos	21%	
Unknown	2%	

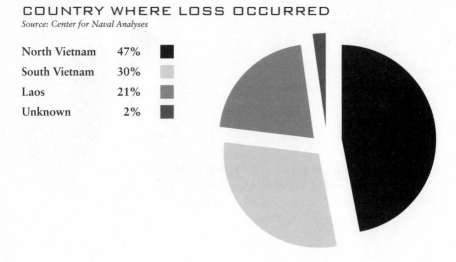

WEAPON CAUSING LOSS
Source: Center for Naval Analyses

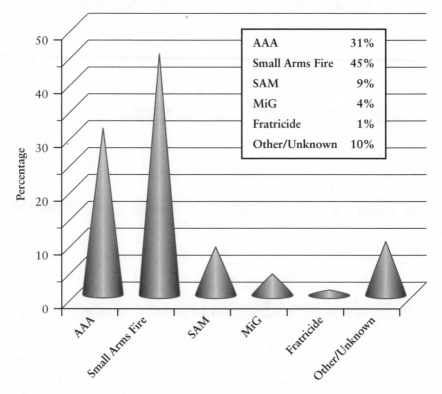

AAA	31%
Small Arms Fire	45%
SAM	9%
MiG	4%
Fratricide	1%
Other/Unknown	10%

WILD WEASEL COMBAT LOSSES BY CAUSE 1965-1973

Source: Howard Plunkett Database and Center for Naval Analysis

AAA	38%	
MiG	18%	
SAM	38%	
Other	6%	

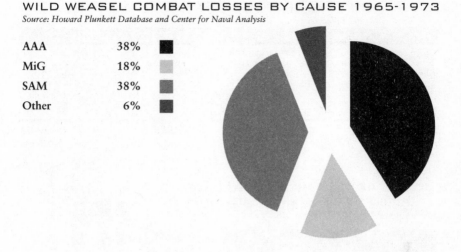

SAM BATTALION STRENGTH - NORTH VIETNAM (1965-1968)

Source: U.S. Defense Intelligence Agency

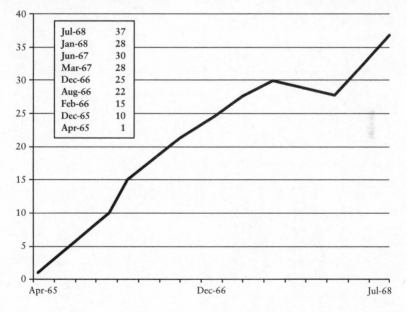

Jul-68	37
Jan-68	28
Jun-67	30
Mar-67	28
Dec-66	25
Aug-66	22
Feb-66	15
Dec-65	10
Apr-65	1

SA-2 COMBAT EFFECTIVENESS – VIETNAM 1965-1973

	1965	1966	1967	1968	1969	1970	1971	1972	1973	Total
Missiles fired	109	590	1894	376	16	23	136	2032	72	5248
Aircraft claimed	87	186	411	96	2	2	32	415	62	1293
Actual losses	13	34	61	12	0	1	7	72	3	203
Missiles per aircraft kill	8.4	17.3	31	31	-	23	19	28	24	26

Source: U.S. Department of Defense and the Center for Naval Analyses

TOTAL VIETNAM WAR CASUALTIES
(AUGUST 1964-JANUARY 27, 1973)
Source: U.S. Department of Defense

	Combat Deaths	Non-Combat Deaths	Non-Mortal Wounds
USAF	1,741	842	931
US Army	30,922	7,273	98,802
Marines	13,084	1,753	51,392
Navy	1,631	931	4,178
	47,378	10,799	155,303

THE BAMBOO DRAGON: BACKGROUND NOTES ON HO CHI MINH, FRANCE, AND THE ORIGINS OF THE VIETNAM WAR

IN 1911, AT the age of twenty-one, Ho Chi Minh sailed from Saigon on the *Amiral Latouche Treville,* a French freighter bound for Marseilles. A wanderer, writer, and jack of all trades, Ho would not see Vietnam again for three decades. After a year in France, he left for the United States, spending another twelve months in San Francisco and Boston. Returning to Europe, Ho became a pastry chef at London's famous Carlton Hotel before again taking up residence in Paris. Mixing with French socialists, he wrote articles and penned a wickedly satirical play called *The Bamboo Dragon.**

When the Great War ended and the Treaty of Versailles delegates arrived in Paris, Ho rented a tuxedo and tried to see President Woodrow Wilson, whom he greatly admired for

---

*It played a single performance.

his democratic principles, but was unable to gain admittance. Unable to put down roots, he left for Moscow in 1924 and would meet Lenin, Trotsky, and other prominent Soviet leaders while adding Russian to the fluent French, English, and Cantonese he'd already mastered. Yet during the traveling decades Vietnam never left his thoughts and, in 1941, as the world went back to war, he crossed from China into the Tonkin province and finally came home.

That summer, through the Atlantic Charter, both Winston Churchill and Franklin Roosevelt vowed to "see sovereign rights and self-government restored to those who have been forcibly deprived of them." A grand statement, but one constructed more to instigate rebellion than as a genuine end to colonialism. Churchill in particular was utterly dedicated to the preservation of the British Empire and had no desire to liberate anyone.* The United States, whose main concern at present was to win World War II, and overly selective about allies, as support for the Soviet Union demonstrated. Though eminently practical, Ho Chi Minh believed the idealism of the charter, so without hesitation he declared against the Japanese and began to fight.

However, he miscalculated the negative impact of his communist status and the reaction that this provoked in U.S. decision makers. The ideological genie of communism was every bit as evil to those in the late 1940s and 1950s as global terror is today. With World War II ending, the necessary but strained coalition with Moscow would not last. An enormous, well-armed, and belligerent Soviet Union was a very real threat, as was the bloody struggle in China between Chiang Kai-shek's national-

---

*In 1919, Secretary of War Winston Churchill sanctioned the use of poison gas against the Kurds. It was not actually employed.

ists and Mao Zedong's communists. Indochina became an ideological line in the sand for Paris, and the United States wasn't interested in interfering.

Yet.

Retrospectively, then, Ho's enthusiastic welcome of American OSS agents in 1945 is truly sad, and there is a sense that the future U.S. military involvement in Vietnam might have been avoided with a bit of intelligent, far-thinking political support.* The tragedy of missed opportunities would become a recurring theme in Southeast Asia. Those on the scene could certainly see it; American captain Archimedes Patti helped Ho draft up his own declaration of independence, unashamedly borrowing from the United States with "We hold the truth that all men are created equal. That they are endowed by their Creator with certain unalienable rights, among them life, liberty and the pursuit of happiness."

At one point, Ho even applied for a U.S. visa and had personally received a signed photograph from Claire Lee Chennault, of Flying Tiger fame, whom he greatly admired. During a July 1945 covert mission, Paul Hoagland, an American medic with the OSS, most likely saved Ho's life from malaria and dysentery. Following the Japanese surrender in August, with French credibility nonexistent, Ho Chi Minh had reasonable expectations for the success of his independence movement. Earlier in the year, Boa Dai, the last Vietnamese emperor, had abdicated in favor of the Viet Minh, stating, "I would rather be a simple citizen of a free country rather than the king of a subjugated people." A noble sentiment, but his decision likely had more to do with personal survival than with principle.

In any event, the way seemed clear as Ho now stood in Ha-

---

* Office of Strategic Services—predecessor of the Central Intelligence Agency.

noi's Bao Dinh Square and declared independence on September 2, 1945. By filling the power void in Vietnam, he had hoped that Washington, in the postwar spirit of freedom sweeping the world, would support him. He didn't regard the United States as a threat, stating that it was "a democracy without territorial ambitions." Ho also openly stated he would have in his country "a million American soldiers . . . but no French."

Unfortunately, he overestimated world interest in Vietnam, misread French postwar intentions, and underestimated Washington's commitment. In fairness to the White House, potential conflicts with a nuclear-armed China and ongoing competition with the Soviet Union far outweighed ideological sympathy with colonial Vietnam. In fact, it was this very threat vis-à-vis Moscow that prompted U.S. support for the French in Indochina. Ships, aircraft, maintenance, and, above all, money were provided to Paris in the hope that a French-controlled Vietnam would remain a deterrent against the rising communist movement in China.

This situation was brought to a head by the terms of the Potsdam Agreement and the disposition of Japanese forces surrendering in Vietnam. Those north of the 16th parallel were to be disarmed by Chiang Kai-Shek's Nationalists, and to that effect some 300,000 rapacious Chinese soldiers crossed the Tonkinese border headed for Hanoi. Looting, raping, and pillaging became common, so northern Vietnamese communists immediately began fighting back. Japanese soldiers in the southern provinces were disarmed by British general Douglas Gracey's 20th Indian Division, which had been diverted on its way home to keep the peace.

Cochinchina, the southern zone containing Saigon, was the real problem.

Ho subsequently found himself boxed in geopolitically and,

as he saw it, betrayed diplomatically. French troops were back in the South and the Chinese were brutalizing the North. Beset on both sides, in 1946 Ho cut his losses and compromised with Paris. If Vietnam's independence was recognized and the Chinese would withdraw, he would garrison 25,000 French soldiers for five years. It was, he felt, the lesser of two evils, and Ho pragmatically reminded his opponents that "the last time the Chinese came they stayed a thousand years. The French are foreigners. They are weak. Colonialism is dying. The white man is finished in Asia. But if the Chinese stay now, they will never go. As for me, I prefer to sniff French shit for five years than eat Chinese shit for the rest of my life."

Paris then declared Vietnam a "free state" within the newly created and grandly titled French Union. Again, Ho Chi Minh was betrayed by the French, who had no intention of leaving Indochina and were using the Vietnamese resistance movement to rid themselves of the Chinese. Certain they could conquer Vietnam anytime they chose to, Beijing agreed to withdraw after the fall opium harvest, and if France would relinquish Shanghai. With Washington's full support, the French agreed and the deal was quietly done. Then abrogating their own agreement, in May 1946 France established a separate government for Cochinchina—as always, with Washington's collusion.

UNIFYING THE COUNTRY under the auspices of the French Union meant occupying and subduing Ho Chi Minh's Democratic Republic of Vietnam. Militarily, the next few years were generally spent in a tit-for-tat fashion as the French tactically experimented with various commanders. Forts were constructed in the northern frontier area, particularly along Route Coloniale (RC) 4, which ran north from Hanoi to Cao Bang, on the Chinese border. The goal was to disrupt arms and ammunition flowing in from China while Operation Lison aimed at defeating enemy strongholds between the Black and Red rivers. French troops now controlled the fertile rice lands of the Red River delta and forced the Viet Minh back into the hills—temporarily.

Yet despite their long experience in Indochina, the French never learned quite how to fight the Vietnamese. Fixed fortifications were even less effective in Indochina than they had been against the Germans in 1940. A mobile enemy, with room to infiltrate and maneuver, could go around them, ambush patrols, or cut them off. Or all of that—which is precisely what the Viet Minh did. There was little air support at the beginning of the conflict, and what eventually appeared came from the United States, along with mechanics and support personnel. Helicopters had not yet made a significant tactical appearance on any battlefield and, as the Americans later discovered, were really the only effective means of transport and supply. The terrain was ideally suited for native defenders who could live off the land and walk to a fight and didn't rely on the trucks, tanks, and heavy equipment that became useless during Vietnam's rainy season.

Time, as always, favored the Vietnamese since French domestic support for the war was problematic, at best. Initially, French nationalists had enthusiastically beat the war drums, hoping to erase the shame of defeat and collaboration from World War II. Mortally afraid of appearing weak and realizing that weakness in Indochina would encourage rebellions in her other colonies, France had begun strengthening its CEFEO* from 50,000 to about 150,000 men by 1949. But patriotic

---

*Corps Expéditionnaire Français en Extrême-Orient.

fervor thinned rapidly against the economic realities of postwar France and Ho was well aware of this. Paris attempted to offset this by appealing to Washington for aid, and most Americans in 1949 would have been shocked to learn that they were subsidizing more than 30 percent of the war's expense.

French politicians also misunderstood, as would their American counterparts a decade later, that to the Vietnamese this was *war*, not a conflict. A war of independence from colonialism; a war of reunification that they were prepared to fight and die to achieve. This caused immediate issues with French field commanders, who did not receive supplies and the reinforcements needed for combat. This was partially due to France's tottering economy, but also to the higher prioritization of the Soviet Union and Germany to European security issues. Paris wasn't alone in this; Washington also considered Indochina a sideshow compared to the threat of an East-West war in Europe. Additionally, President Harry Truman was a stalwart Europeanist and did not actively oppose French and British colonial interests.

Paris was quick to paint the struggle in Southeast Asia in flaming communist red to play on U.S. fears of spreading Chinese and Soviet influence. In late October 1949, as Chinese Nationalists under Chiang Kai-Shek were defeated, Mao Zedong declared the formation of the communist People's Republic of China, alarming Washington. This was exacerbated in April 1950 when Beijing signed an assistance pact with the Viet Minh. Full-scale panic then set in during June when ten North Korean divisions crossed the 38th parallel heading south toward Seoul. The city fell two days later and the United States found itself back at war. Britain was thoroughly enmeshed with India and Pakistan, so France was left unhindered to do as she pleased in Indochina.

General Marcel-Maurice Carpentier, a World War I veteran who fought with the Free French during World War II, rightly concluded that the existing line of frontier forts was ineffective. In the fall of 1950 he planned a rollback withdrawal, north to south along Route Coloniale 4, of all the emplacements. General Vo Nguyen Giap, the Viet Minh field commander, moved rapidly to disrupt the move and cut the French to pieces. A lawyer by profession with no military schooling, Giap had learned his new trade rapidly and proved a naturally gifted general. He also intimately knew the terrain and had the advantages of regular aid from China and the local population.

Despite fierce resistance from the Foreign Legion garrisons and paratroopers, many of whom were World War II veterans, Giap's twenty battalions annihilated the defenders. Nearly 7,000 French soldiers began the southward trek and barely 600 survived. Captured intact, the main frontier arsenal at Lang Son contained enough weapons to supply a 10,000-man division. Neutral or uncommitted Vietnamese now openly considered whether they might be better off supporting Ho Chi Minh against the French.

Buoyed by his successes, Giap then mistakenly attempted to fight the French on their own terms, in open country, and was severely mauled. Against American-supplied heavy weapons and aircraft Giap lost nearly half of his regular infantry. However, learning his lesson, the general put together three divisions, boosted operations in Cochinchina to assault the French rear, and took to the hills. As guerrilla operations extended into the Thai highlands and northern Laos, the new French commander, Henri Navarre, launched a series of small, quick operations against the Viet Minh.

By 1953 several pivotal outside events had occurred that would impact the outcome of the First Indochina War and set the stage for a conflict with the Americans. Joseph Stalin had died in March and the Soviet Union, seeking to cast aside its pariah status, openly suggested resolving European security issues that troubled the Western powers. There were ulterior motives with this, of course, such as keeping France and West Germany out of any anti-Soviet military pact, but it was a start.

China was a wild card for several reasons. First, Beijing was certain that the French would lose in Indochina and was equally sure that the United States would step into the void. The Chinese knew they could deal with the French, militarily or diplomatically, but as the Korean War had proven, the United States was a different matter. Also, Mao's communist economy was failing and Beijing desperately needed trade with the West if the new government was to survive. This hadn't been possible while the Korean War persisted, but that conflict had been concluded following the July 1953 armistice.

As for the United States, President Dwight D. Eisenhower had taken office the year prior promising to end the war in Korea. After agreeing to stop fighting in one Asian country, he couldn't very well start again in Indochina, despite Paris's wishes. Also, by this time French military ineffectiveness and duplicitous diplomatic behavior were wearing thin. John Foster Dulles, the U.S. secretary of state and ardent crusader of communist containment, had arranged $500 million in aid to France with the understanding that any peace negotiations with the Viet Minh would be delayed. Paris simply took the money and ignored the conditions. None of this sat well with Eisenhower as Washington was now paying 40 percent of French expenses in Indochina, more than $100 million per year, and it still wasn't enough for a victory.

So with the foreign and domestic tide turning against them, Paris ordered Navarre to rapidly conclude the war. Faced with morale problems, low supplies, and a reenergized enemy, he formulated what became known as the Navarre Plan. The general envisioned an "air-land" base constructed deep in the heart of Viet Minh territory, a fortified striker camp that could be resupplied by air. He chose the only flat land in the region, an eleven-by-five-mile valley near the Laotian border containing an old Japanese airstrip near a wretched little town the Vietnamese called Dien Bien Phu. Navarre believed his air-land base could connect French garrisons in northern Vietnam with Sam Nuea in Laos. This would severely disrupt Viet Minh supplies of rice and munitions and, most important, would halt the wide-scale opium trafficking that provided a major source of Hanoi's revenue. Drug money was then used to purchase some six thousand tons of armaments, and food each month from China.

Navarre, as an ex-cavalry officer, believed implicitly in fire and maneuver tactics, so he'd convinced himself that such a base would also draw the Viet Minh onto open ground. Anticipating mass wave attacks reminiscent of World War I, he planned to then destroy the enemy with artillery, or the ten M-24 Chaffee light tanks he'd airlifted into the valley. It looked good on paper from an air-conditioned headquarters in Saigon, but several of his highly experienced combat officers knew better. Navarre's maps didn't depict the thick, tangled brush that broke up fields of fire, nor show the effects of the miserable spring weather. Monsoon season was fast approaching with its torrential, soaking rains and French intelligence was finding evidence of a massive Viet Minh buildup. But Navarre shrugged it all off, confident in his tanks, artillery, and American-supplied air transport.

So at 0500 on November 20, 1953, a solitary C-47 Dakota lifted off from Hanoi and arrived over Dien Bien Phu by 0700. Three generals on board (Navarre was not among them) decided that despite fog covering the valley, the drop, called Operation Castor, could proceed. Sixty-five more Dakotas finished loading 1,800 French paratroopers, five battalions in all, and took off in two waves. By noon, Major Marcel Bigeard, a tough, up-from-the-ranks veteran combat officer, jumped with his 6th Colonial Commando Parachute Battalion and the battle was officially joined.

Initially taking the village and shoring up the defenses, the French then waited for the enemy to come—and so they did, but not in the way Navarre planned. General Giap, who rode between the valley and Ho's headquarters on his horse, did what the French considered impossible. Using captured American trucks, provided from the Chinese by way of Korea, he brought his heavy weapons as far forward as the roads allowed. Off-loading 140 howitzers, 80 recoilless guns, rocket launchers, and about 50 heavy mortars, the Viet Minh promptly disassembled them. Distributing the components among tens of thousands of porters and solders, they hiked through the highlands onto the hills overlooking Dien Bien Phu. Under thick cover Giap assembled 120,000 men, 200 anti-aircraft guns, and hundreds of thousands of artillery shells. The 10,000 French soldiers, hunkered down in their string of pillboxes, failed to appreciate the scale of the deployment.

Then it began to rain. And rain.

Clouds lowered and resupply by air became problematic. Some 36,000 tons of material were required to sustain the fort, yet barely 4,000 were delivered. The hard-packed valley floor that was supposed to allow armored maneuver became a wet, clutching morass, and the tanks remained stuck in place. Incredibly, the French commander also neglected to dig in his twenty-nine pieces of field artillery, or adequately entrench his thirty heavy mortars. This was hardly surprising given that Colonel Christian Marie Ferdinand de La Croix de Castries was, like Navarre, a cavalry officer. He trusted the artillery commander to site his own guns, and when Colonel Charles Piroth pompously stated that "no Viet Minh cannon will be able to fire three rounds before being destroyed by my artillery," de Castries believed him.*

After tightening the siege for another month, Giap launched his attack on the afternoon of March 13, 1954. Following an intense artillery barrage, the Viet Minh 312th Division used a network of carefully constructed tunnels to assault pillbox "Beatrice," which finally succumbed just after midnight.† A single afternoon of fighting was enough, and the French plaintively begged the United States for help. Paris was finally aware that the garrison would not survive and absolutely did not want to enter the upcoming Geneva Conference from a position of weakness.

Despite the insertion of the 5th Parachute Battalion on March 14, the French pillbox "Gabrielle" fell the next day. Colonel Piroth, the optimistic artillery commander, met the tactical situation by lying down in his tent with a hand grenade and blowing himself apart. Some 4,300 additional paratroopers jumped in during the next month, but after "Ann-Marie" was taken the Viet Minh were able to place 37 mm anti-aircraft guns on the hillside near the airstrip. During the next fifty days more than 10,000 close air support and evacuation sorties would be flown, but to no avail. Forty-eight aircraft would be lost and another 167 damaged as the French attempted to break the siege.

---

*An amazing viewpoint to take, given that both men were World War II veterans who had witnessed the limitations of fixed fortifications during the ten days it took for the German Wehrmacht to defeat the French Army in 1940.
†The pillboxes were all named for de Castries's local mistresses: Beatrice, Gabrielle, Huguette, Ann-Marie, Francoise, Claudine, Isabelle, and Eliane.

By May 4, Giap managed to bring up his Soviet-made Katyusha rockets and began systematically shredding what remained of the miserable camp. Two days later the skies cleared and a French fifty-plane relief airdrop was flown into the valley. Nearly 200 tons of food, medicine, and ammunition floated down into the trees, most of it directly to the Viet Minh. More than one hundred American-made B-26 Marauders, Hellcats, Bearcats, and Corsairs attacked the hillsides surrounding Dien Bien Phu, but it was much too little and entirely too late. By late afternoon on May 7, with little ammunition and no real options remaining, de Castries sent the following message: "We're blowing up everything. Adieu."

The radio operator added a *"Vive la France!"*

Including reinforcements, 15,709 French soldiers, legionnaires, and auxiliaries ended up fighting in that narrow, bloody valley. A handful escaped to Laos, nearly 1,200 deserted, and Giap permitted the Red Cross to evacuate 858 of the most severely wounded. By nightfall on May 7, as the red Viet Minh flag was raised, 11,721 prisoners, half of them wounded, were shuffled off through the trees to prisoner camps in North Vietnam.* Of these a mere 3,290 were repatriated four months later, in September 1954. Beginning with 120 transport aircraft and 227 fighters, the French lost 56 destroyed and nearly 200 damaged. Of the casualties sustained by the five Viet Minh divisions engaged at Dien Bien Phu, there are no accurate records. French claims are exaggerated and Hanoi's admissions are underestimated. Still, it seems likely that about 8,000 were killed and some 15,000 wounded, with an unknown number later perishing from poor medical care.

---

*Many were tortured in Camp 113 (Lang-Kieu) prison by a fellow countryman named Georges Boudarel: philosophy teacher, communist, and traitor.

On May 8, while de Castries and his battered men staggered through the steaming, stinking trees on their way to oblivion, the Geneva Conference opened. It was an attempt, although one laced with subterfuge and private agendas, to resolve the situation in Indochina. The French defeat certainly complicated matters, and the Viet Minh were in no mood to compromise. However, Hanoi's backers in China and the Soviet Union were. The United States had detonated the H-bomb at Bikini Atoll several months earlier, so both communist governments were quite rightfully leery of American military power. Also, as mentioned, the Chinese much preferred French influence in Indochina rather than a U.S. foothold just across its southern border.

In the end, France gained at Geneva what it failed to gain through combat while the Viet Minh lost through diplomacy much of its victory in the field. Vietnam would be *temporarily* partitioned into northern and southern regions at the 17th parallel, pending the reunification that would follow a 1956 national election. Ho retained control of the North while French forces were to remain in the South. It was likely the best resolution possible at the time since it stopped the fighting and provided some hope for the future. France, the USSR, Laos, the People's Republic of China, Cambodia, and Ho Chi Minh's Democratic Republic of Vietnam were all signatories. South Vietnam and the United States were not.

Unfortunately, it became rapidly apparent that the U.S.-backed prime minister in Saigon, Ngo Dinh Diem, had no intention of complying with the Geneva settlement. As soon as he returned to Saigon in July 1954, Diem began replacing key government officials with friends, backers, and family members. Hopelessly out of touch with the needs of the people, and not interested in a rapprochement with the North, Diem was a disastrous choice. Opposition to him grew daily, an unlikely assortment of religious and political sects thrown together by a hatred of the French, the communists, and the Saigon regime.* Though the U.S. Joint Chiefs opposed intervention and the training of Vietnamese troops, they were overruled by the White House. In all fairness, it must have seemed that if the fragile Saigon government fell, the entire South would be ripe for a communist takeover, so with U.S. help the first coup attempt was crushed. In late October 1955, Diem proclaimed himself president of the newly created Republic of Vietnam.

To no one's surprise, Paris proved utterly unequal to the task of managing Indochina, especially without American funding and equipment. In the wake of Dien Bien Phu, the French gave up again and pulled out of Vietnam in April 1956, creating a void that had to be filled. Amid long-term economic turmoil coupled with a deeply conflicted national identity crisis, France would subsequently lose Cambodia, followed in 1956 by Morocco, Laos in 1957, and finally Tunisia in 1962.

Diem justified his failure to hold the mandated 1956 elections by asserting they would never be "fair." The Eisenhower administration backed him with a $300 million assistance package, then permitted him to ban political parties and public gatherings and to rule by decree for six years.† Colonel Edward Lansdale, a former OSS officer, was sent to create the Saigon military mission and to ensure Diem's survival by rigging the next election. Lucky red ballots were used for Diem while any opponents were forced to use "evil" green paper. Green votes were often thrown away or destroyed outright; coercion was actively practiced, and in Saigon the final tally for Diem was greater than the number of eligible voters.

---

* Cao Dai, Hoa Hao, and the Binh Xuyen, among others.
† Two new political parties were formed—both controlled by Diem's brothers.

With the United States as his bodyguard, Diem defied China and dismissed the Geneva settlement, which he'd never signed anyway. In a rather unorthodox effort to keep peace the Soviet Union, with Hanoi's approval, proposed a permanent partition of Vietnam at the 17th parallel. If accepted, this certainly would have eliminated the immediate pretext for war and perhaps avoided it altogether. Not surprisingly, the White House refused the whole partition idea since it ran contrary to the anticommunism that was the lifeblood of Washington at the time. This inconsistent position has never been rationalized given U.S. support for the Soviet Union during World War II and recognition of Tito's communist government in Yugoslavia.*

But not Vietnam.

On both sides of the 17th parallel things were going badly. Ho Chi Minh initiated a disastrous series of land reforms that only exacerbated the North's shaky economic conditions. Continuous war had destroyed ports, railheads, rolling stock, bridges, and factories. The exodus of some 625,000 teachers, priests, business owners, and medical professionals also drained much of the region's intellectual talent. Being cut off from the South also deprived the North of its primary rice supply, causing severe food shortages. Both Hanoi and Saigon resorted to military force to keep order, though Diem was generally worse since he never modified his position or explored other options. This led to numerous coup attempts, domestic distrust, and a spreading disenfranchisement among the peasantry.

Still stung by the Geneva betrayal, Hanoi capitalized on Saigon's problems by sending thousands of southern-born insurgents, many of them Viet Minh combat veterans, back into

---

*In fact, a substantial aid package was approved in 1951 when President Truman backed Yugoslavia's bid for a seat on the UN Security Council.

Cochinchina after December 1960. Organizing an effective propaganda system, they armed and trained supporters, then began conducting guerrilla operations. Hanoi called them the National Liberation Front for the Liberation of South Vietnam, and the fighting branch of this movement was the People's Liberation Armed Forces (PLAF).

To Saigon and the west they became known as the Viet Cong.

NOTES AND SOURCES

PROLOGUE

I was greatly aided in writing this from the NVA point of view through a document brought back from Hanoi by Mr. Bruce Giffin—the nephew of Ross Fobair (Leopard Two). I was able to get the real names and, even accounting for the Soviet penchant to exaggerate, some specific weapon and targeting information.

By using that, with what has been declassified from our own sources, and my own experiences as a Wild Weasel, I was able to reconstruct most of that fateful day. Colonel Vic Vizcarra, whose invaluable assistance is evident in Chapter Two, was also airborne the same time as Leopard flight and heard most of this on the radio. He was able to correct a few details from the unimpeachable standpoint of an eyewitness—or in this case, an ear witness.

As for the SA-2, the Nellis AFB Threat Museum has most surface-to-air missiles made by the Soviet Union. Being able to sit in the vans and climb around on the radars was instrumental in writing about it from the viewpoint of an operator.

There are also several good technical books, including Steven Zaloga's *Red Sam: The SA-2 Guideline Anti-Aircraft Missile* and Peter Davies' *F-105 Wild Weasel vs. SA-2 "Guideline" SAM*.

Dr. Alfred Price's *War in the Fourth Dimension: US Electronic Warfare from the Vietnam to the Present* is a lucid, comprehensible account of basic principles and history from 1964 onwards.

CHAPTER ONE—Spring High

This chapter would not have been possible without the indispensable assistance of Vic Vizcarra, Col, USAF (ret.), Marty Case, LtCol, USAF (ret.) and Paul Craw. All three men were F-105D pilots with the 80th TFS (Headhunters) and 563rd TFS (Ace of Spades) respectively. They all flew the Spring High mission and volunteered their time and memories to ensure it was written accurately.

Republic F-105 Thunderchief (Osprey Publishing, 2012), by Peter Davies is an excellent source of general technical information. See the 'Design and Development,' pp. 5–18, for a good overview of political and technological constraints at the time. I am indebted to Mr. Greg Anderson, Marilyn Chang and

Matthew Burchette of the Wings over the Rockies Museum in Denver for permitting me to sit in their beautiful F-105 Thunderchief and write. The Cradle of Aviation Museum in Long Island, New York, was kind enough to let me rummage through their records, photographs and technical documents.

CHAPTER TWO—Hitchhiker in a Hailstorm

Unless one is writing a textbook, I firmly believe that an understanding of the larger historical and geopolitical issues surrounding major events are required to comprehend why and how combat is accomplished.

Two superb books on the overall history of Vietnam from 1945 onwards are Stanley Karnow's *Vietnam—A History,* and Dr. John Prados's *Vietnam.* Many of Ho Chi Minh's quotes come from "The Light that Failed," and "The War with the French," both chapters in Karnow's book. Much of the synopsis came from *Lords of the Sky,* pp. 426–432.

Lords of the Sky pp. 426–441, also contains a concise summary of the abortive French actions around Dien Bien Phu in 1953–54. The same section details the 'big picture' around America's initial involvement in Southeast Asia.

Background on Lyndon Johnson and Robert Strange McNamara came from many sources. One of the more poignant books is H.R. McMaster's *Dereliction of Duty;* pp. 50–52 in particular describe Johnson's spin doctoring regarding his brief time in the military.

CHAPTER THREE—Wild Weasel

I am indebted to Allen Lamb for permitting me to spend several weekends with him, allowing me to get his extraordinary story directly from the man himself. His patience with my endless questions was truly remarkable and well appreciated. Rick Morgan, who flew with Allen on his second SAM kill in February 1966, reviewed my F-100 chapters for accuracy. There are no better sources than the men who flew the missions. Technical data for the Hun is abundant, but I found Peter Davies's *F-100 Super Sabre Units of the Vietnam War* to be readable and informative. Again, my thanks to Wings over the Rockies Museum for permitting me access to the cockpit of their Hun.

Mr. Greg Anderson, Marilyn Chang and Matthew Burchette of the Wings over the Rockies Museum in Denver allowed me to ravage their reference library and permitted me to sit in the cockpit of their F-100, think of SAMs, and write.

CHAPTER FOUR—Charlie and SAM

Kenneth Werrell's *Archie to SAM,* provides an excellent, big picture view of anti-aircraft systems development. For more specific works see Peter Davies' *F-105 Wild Weasel vs. SA-2 "Guideline" SAM* and Steven Zaloga's *Red Sam: The SA-2 Guideline Anti-Aircraft Missile.*

The evolution of Wasserfall and its implications for the modern SAM are introduced in Werrell's *Archie to SAM,* pp. 114–119, which also contains very good summaries of anti-aircraft statistics from World War II, Korea and Vietnam.

Colonel Ed Rock's anthology *First In, Last Out: Stories by the Wild Weasels,* is a remarkable account (in their own words) from the men who made the Weasel program succeed. Covering a wide range of topics, the technical chapters from Dr. John Grigsby pp. 26–83, and Joe Telford, pp. 101–135, were particularly helpful.

CHAPTER FIVE—Hunter Killers

Colonel Ed Rock graciously consented to many interviews, both verbally and electronically, to recount this mission.

CHAPTER SIX—Make Mud not War

Weldon Bauman, creator of the lifesaving "Bauman Mod," gave much of his time and expertise during a series of verbal and electronic interviews. Colonel Ed Rock's *First In, Last Out* was again utilized extensively for technical details by those who used the equipment. Those wishing more information see pp. 271–277 for the account by Paul Chesley and Weldon Bauman. *The Limits of Airpower,* by Mark Clodfelter contains an excellent chapter called "An Extended Application of Force," pp. 73–116.

John Prados's *The Blood Road* has a fascinating chapter called "Pinball Wizards," pp. 267–285 detailing much of the attempted science on the ground in South Vietnam and Laos.

CHAPTER SEVEN—A Full Day's Work

Colonel Leo Thorsness and Colonel Jerry Hoblit were both kind enough to directly assist with this chapter. Extensive interviews were conducted with both men, and a great deal of detailed information was exchanged both verbally and electronically. Jerry Hoblit is currently writing *YGBSM! A History of the Wild Weasels,* and was very generous with his materials.

Surviving Hell, A POW's Journey by Leo Thorsness was an excellent source for the mission's background. Peter Davies's *F-105 Thunderchief MiG Killers of the Vietnam War,* pp. 65–76, also contains an account which includes rare details of the Thud dogfight. Similarly, *MiGs over North Vietnam,* by Roger Boniface provides an inside look at the Vietnamese People's Air Force. See chapters two and three, specifically pages 4–24.

CHAPTER EIGHT—The Year of the Monkey

Delving into the Tet Offensive means closely examining events on both sides of the actual January 1968 fighting. John Prados, *The Blood Road,* is excellent background as is Edward Murphy's *The Hill Fights: The First Battle of Khe Sanh,* pp. 1–120. Gordon Rottman, who served with the 5th Special Group in

Vietnam, authored *Khe Sanh 1967–68*, a very focused look at the siege of the Marine combat base.

Similarly, *Con Thien, the Hill of Angels* by James P. Coan is another invaluable source from an eyewitness. Karnow's *Vietnam* and John Prados's *Vietnam: the History of an Unwinnable War*, both supply much of the timing and detail surrounding the regional Tet attacks. Andrew Wiest's *Rolling Thunder in a Gentle Land*, pp. 157–172, provided concise insights into both General Westmoreland and General Abrams, especially the contrast between their strategies for winning the war.

CHAPTER NINE—Warts on a Frog

Personal interviews were graciously supplied by both Stan Goldstein and John Revak. Ed Rock's *First In, Last Out* also contains valuable background on the missions and men discussed. Hobson's *Vietnam Air Losses*, used in conjunction with the POW Network Biography section, and Howard Plunkett's extensive F-105 database provided the technical details.

Brigadier General Soutchay Vongsavanh's *Military Operations and Activities in the Laotian Panhandle* is a very good, albeit dry, source of information regarding the border area.

Prados's *The Blood Road*, pp. 311–350, contains fascinating accounts of the Cambodian and Laotian invasions.

CHAPTER TEN—Winds of Change

Vietnam Air Losses by Chris Hobson, pg. 197, contains a synopsis of Seabird Two's loss on January 28, 1970. Information about the F-105G was obtained from interviews with Colonel Ed Rock, Peter Davies's *F-105 Wild Weasel vs. SA-2 Guideline SAM*, and from Republic Aviation technical publications (procured with the kind assistance of the Cradle of Aviation Museum and Wings over the Rockies Museum).

The best sources of background information regarding the war in 1970 is Oliver Stone and Peter Kuznick's superb work *The Untold History of the United States*, pp. 355–390; Prados's *The Blood Road*, pp. 287–309; and Clodfelter's *The Limits of Airpower*, pp. 147–176.

CHAPTER ELEVEN—Death from Above

The story of Zodiac 01 was compiled from Colonel Ed Rock's mission data cards, verbal and electronic interviews, and Hobson's *Vietnam Air Losses*, p. 237. Interestingly, Hobson was unable to name the A-7 pilot involved, but this information was discovered by Paul T. Mudge, J.D., MPH, PhD, and former Marine Skyhawk pilot.

The political summaries were derived from numerous sources; the Library of Congress, the National Archives, John Prados's *Vietnam*, pp. 404–454, and Mark Clodfelter's *The Limits of Airpower*, pp. 147–176.

EPILOGUE

Information for both Rolling Thunder and the Linebacker operations is prolific. In summarizing these by comparison, Colonel Dennis Drew's *Rolling Thunder 1965: Anatomy of a Failure,* provides an abbreviated, but concise analysis.

The 11 Days of Christmas, by Marshall L. Michel III offers a comprehensive and very pointed assessment of Linebacker II, specifically pp. 86–122; "Denouement," pp. 217–231; and "Retrospective," pp. 232–238. Clodfelter's *The Limits of Airpower,* pp. 177–202, examines the Christmas bombings and their effect on peace negotiations.

Denny Larsen, USAF LtCol (ret.), was kind enough to provide his personal Linebacker experiences, and Colonel Ed Rock's *First In, Last Out* was again an invaluable reference for Wild Weasel IV operations.

The Center for Naval Analysis report titled *U.S. Navy, Marine Corps, and Air Force Fixed-Wing Aircraft Losses and Damage in Southeast Asia* is a superb single source for accurate statistical data. However, this was supplemented by Department of Defense and USAF Operational Summaries when needed.

APPENDIX C—The Bamboo Dragon

Historical references for Southeast Asia are plentiful yet few are as well written as Dr. John Prados's *The Blood Road: The Ho Chi Minh Trail and the Vietnam War,* pp. 2–61. The pages mentioned are an excellent summary of Vietnam during the period between the 1954 Geneva Accords and American intervention in the early 1960s. Also, *Vietnam at War* by Phillip B. Davidson, and Stanley Karnow's *Vietnam,* specifically chapter four, "The War with the French," is a very detailed primer for those wishing to understand the regional background leading up to the war.

BIBLIOGRAPHY

ACIG. *Indochina Database: U.S. Air to Air Victories During Vietnam, Part One.* September 16, 2003. http://www.acig.org/artman/publish/article_243 .shtml, accessed October 22, 1014.

Addington, Larry H. *America's War in Vietnam: A Short Narrative History.* Bloomington: Indiana University Press, 2000.

"Air War over Vietnam and Lessons Learned." http://forums.navalwarfare.net, accessed July 20, 2013.

Anderson, John D. *A History of Aerodynamics.* Cambridge: Cambridge University Press, 1997.

Aviation History Online Museum. http://www.aviation-history.com, accessed February–July 2013.

Bauman, Weldon. Interview by Dan Hampton about the Bauman Modification, conducted October 4, 2014.

Beachy, Robert. "Ferrets, Ravens & Weasels." http://hud607.fire.prohosting.com /uncommon/reference/usa/sead.html, February 3, 2013, accessed August 2013.

Blackburn, Lonnie M., and Gary B. Long. *Unlikely Warriors: The Army Security Agency's Secret War in Vietnam 1961–1973*. Bloomington, IN: iUniverse, 2013.

Boniface, Roger. *MiGs over North Vietnam: The Vietnam People's Air Force in Combat, 1965–75*. Mechanicsburg, PA: Stackpole Books, 2008.

Boyne, Walter, and Philip Handleman. *Brassey's Air Combat Reader*. London: Batsford Brassey, 1999.

Brodie, Bernard. *Strategy in the Missile Age*. Princeton, NJ: Princeton University Press, 1959.

Broughton, Jack. *Going Downtown*. New York: Pocket, 1990.

———. *Thud Ridge*. Manchester, England: Crecy, 2006.

Budiansky, Stephen. *Air Power*. New York: Penguin, 2004.

Busboom, Lieutenant Colonel Stanley. *Bat 21: A Case Study*. Carlisle Barracks, PA: U.S. Army War College, 1990.

Campbell, John M., and Michael Hill. *Roll Call: Thud*. Atglen, PA: Schiffer, 1996.

———. *USAF Operations Report*. Washington, DC: USAF, 1973.

"Carriers: Airpower at Sea." http://www.sandcastlevi.com/sea/carriers, accessed May 15, 2013.

Case, Martin. Interviews by Dan Hampton about the Vietnam Air War, 1965, conducted August 31 through October 27, 2014.

Cecil, Paul Frederick. *Herbicidal Warfare: The Ranch Hand Project in Vietnam*. New York: Praeger, 1986.

Chinnery, Philip D. *Life on the Line: Stories of Vietnam Air Combat*. London: Blandford Press, 1998.

Clay, Major Wayne J. *Electronic Countermeasures: Should We Reorganize Our Thinking? (Secret) Declassified*. Thesis. Maxwell Air Force Base, AL: Air University, 1968.

Clement, Major Robert A. "A Fourth of July in December: A B-52 Navigator's Perspective of Linebacker II." Research paper. Maxwell Air Force Base: USAF Air Command and Staff College, 1984.

Clodfelter, Mark. *The Limits of Airpower: The American Bombing of North Vietnam*. New York: Free Press, 1989.

Coan, James P. *Con Thien: Hill of Angels*. Tuscaloosa: University of Alabama Press, 2004.

Coonts, Steven. Interview by Dan Hampton on USN SAM suppression during Vietnam. September 6, 2013.

Cooper, Chester L. *The Lost Crusade: America in Vietnam*. New York: Dodd & Mead, 1970.

Correll, John. "Daylight Precision Bombing." *Air Force Magazine*, October 2008, pp. 60–63.

Davidson, Phillip B. *Vietnam at War. The History 1946–1975*. Oxford: Oxford University Press, 1988.

Davies, Peter. *F-105 Wild Weasel vs SA-2 "Guideline" SAM, Vietnam 1965–73*. Oxford: Osprey, 2011.

———. *F-4 Phantom II vs MiG-21*. London: Osprey, 2008.

————. *Republic F-105 Thunderchief.* Oxford: Osprey, 2012.

Davies, Peter E., and David W. Menard. *F-100 Super Sabre Units of the Vietnam War.* Oxford: Osprey, 2011.

Director of Operations, USAF. *History of Air Defense in North Vietnam. (Secret) Declassified.* PACOM Intelligence Digest. Washington, DC: USAF, 1970.

Dorr, Robert F. *Phantoms Forever.* London: Osprey, 1987.

Dramesi, Lieutenant Colonel John A. *Code of Honor.* New York: Norton, 1975.

Field, Alexander J. "The Most Technologically Progressive Decade of the Century." *American Economic Review* (September 2003): 399–413.

Flack, Ronald. *Fundamentals of Jet Propulsion with Applications.* New York: Cambridge University Press, 2005.

Flintham, Victor. *Air Wars and Aircraft: A Detailed Record of Air Combat, 1945 to the Present.* New York: Facts on File, 1990.

Francillon, René. *Tonkin Gulf Yacht Club: US Carrier Operations off Vietnam.* Annapolis, MD: Naval Institute Press, 1998.

Fromson, Murray. "Name that Source." *New York Times,* December 11, 2006.

Giffin, Bruce. Interviews by Dan Hampton about Captain Ross Fobair, conducted June 12 through September 25, 2014.

Goldstein, Stan. Interviews by Dan Hampton about Wild Weasel III, conducted August 21 through December 1, 2014.

Good, Major William, USMC (ret.). Interview by Dan Hampton on Marine combat aviation in Vietnam, August 25, 2013.

Grossnick, Roy A. *Dictionary of American Naval Aviation Squadrons.* Vol. 2. Washington, DC: Naval Historical Center, Department of the Navy, 1999.

Guenther, R. C. "North Vietnamese SA-2 System, Development and Role (Secret) Declassified." *Defense Intelligence Digest,* February 1971, p. 7.

Hampton, Dan. *Lords of the Sky.* New York: HarperCollins, 2014.

Hoblit, Colonel Jerry. Interview by Dan Hampton about April 1967, conducted October 12, 2014.

Hobson, Chris. *Vietnam Air Losses.* Hinckley, England: Midland, 2001.

Hoopes, Townsend. *The Limits of Intervention.* New York: David McKay, 1969.

Horner, General Chuck. Interview by Dan Hampton about July 27, 1965, conducted October 1, 2014.

Karnow, Stanley. *Vietnam: A History.* New York: Penguin Group, 1983.

Kissinger, Henry. *The White House Years.* Boston: Little, Brown, 1979.

Klimek, Colonel Bob. Interview by Dan Hampton about Wild Weasel I and III, conducted November 22, 2014.

"Klusmann Report." *Homecoming II Project.* POW Network, May 15, 1990.

Lamb, Allen. Interview by Dan Hampton on the first Wild Weasels, September 9/10, 2013, and May 16/17, 2014.

Lavalle, Major A. J. C. *Air Power and the 1972 Spring Invasion.* Washington, DC: Office of Air Force History, 1985.

Lenski, Brigadier General Al. *Magic 100: An F-105 Fighter Pilot's 100 Combat Missions in Vietnam.* Paducah, KY: Turner, 1995.

Levinson, Jeffrey L. *Alpha Strike Vietnam: The Navy's Air War, 1964 to 1973.* Novato, CA: Presidio Press, 1989.

Logan, Don. *The 388th Tactical Fighter Wing at Korat Royal Thai Air Force Base 1972.* Atglen, PA: Schiffer, 1995.

Manning, Thomas A. *History of Air Education and Training Command, 1942–2002.* San Antonio: USAF Air Education and Training Command, Office of History and Research, 2005.

McCarthy, Brigadier General James R., and Lieutenant Colonel George B. Allison. *Linebacker II: A View from the Rock.* Montgomery, AL: Air University Press, 1979.

McMaster, H. R. *Dereliction of Duty.* New York: HarperCollins, 1997.

Michel, Marshall L., III. *Clashes: Air Combat over North Vietnam 1965–1972.* Annapolis, MD: Naval Institute Press, 1997.

Morgan, Rick. Interview by Dan Hampton about Wild Weasel I, conducted May 28, 2014 and June 18, 2014.

Morocco, John. *Thunder from Above.* Boston: Boston Publishing Company, 1984.

Morris, Guy V. *Airborne Pulsed Doppler Radar.* Norwood, MA: Artech House, 1988.

Nalty, Bernard C. *Air War Over South Vietnam: 1968–1975.* Washington, DC: Air Force History and Museums Program, 2000.

Newman, Rick, and Don Shepperd. *Bury Us Upside Down.* New York: Random House, 2007.

New York Times. "Communists Quit Session in Paris." December 22, 1972, p. 1.

———. "Congress Opens: Democrats Plan Anti-War Action." January 5, 1973, p. 1.

———. "Kissinger Says Talks Have Not Reached an Agreement." December 17, 1972, p. 1.

Ngo, Lieutenant General Quang Truong. *The Easter Offensive of 1972.* Washington, DC: U.S. Army Center of Military History, 1980.

Nichols, Commander John, and Barrett Tillman. *On Yankee Station: The Naval Air War over Vietnam.* Annapolis, MD: Naval Institute Press, 1987.

Northrop Grumman, Defensive Systems Division. *The Radar Warning Story.* Northup Grumman Electronic Systems.

Olds, Christina, and Ed Rasimus. *Fighter Pilot.* New York: St. Martin's Press, 2010.

Pierson. *Corona Harvest, Tactical Electronic Warfare.* USAF, 1968–69.

Plunkett, Howard. Interviews by Dan Hampton about Wild Weasel chronology and statistics, conducted April 6 through December 29, 2014.

POW Network: Homecoming II Project. July 1990. http://www.pownetwork .org/bios, accessed June–November 2014.

Prados, John. *The Blood Road: The Ho Chi Minh Trail and the Vietnam War.* New York: Wiley, 1999.

———. "The '65 Decision: Bombing Soviet SAM Sites in North Vietnam." http://www.vva.org, January/February 2006, accessed August 2013.

Price, Dr. Alfred. *History of U.S. Electronic Warfare.* Vol. 3. [Arlington, VA]: Association of Old Crows, 2000.

———. *Instruments of Darkness: The History of Electronic Warfare.* New York: Charles Scribner's Sons, 1978.

Rasimus, Ed. *When Thunder Rolled.* New York: Random House, 2003.

Ravenstein, Charles A. *Air Force Combat Wings: Lineage and Honors Histories 1947–1977.* Washington, DC: Office of Air Force History, 1984.

Revak, John. Interviews by Dan Hampton about Wild Weasel III, conducted November 22 through December 2, 2014.

Robbins, James S. *This Time We Win: Revisiting the Tet Offensive.* New York: Encounter Books, 2010.

Rochester, Stuart I., and Frederick Kiley. *Honor Bound: The History of American Prisoners of War in Southeast Asia, 1961–1973.* Washington, DC: Office of the Secretary of Defense, 1998.

Rock, Colonel Ed, USAF. Interviews by Dan Hampton on Vietnam SAM engagement of December 1965 and Vietnam Wild Weasels, January 23 through December 21, 2014.

Rock, Ed. *First In, Last Out: Stories by the Wild Weasels.* N.p.: AuthorHouse, 2005.

Rottman, Gordon L. *Khe Sanh 1967–1968: Marines Battle for Vietnam's Vital Hilltop Base.* Oxford: Osprey, 2005.

Schlight, Colonel John. *A War Too Long.* Washington, DC: Air Force History and Museums Program, 1996.

Schneider, Major Donald K. *Air Force Heroes in Vietnam: USAF Southeast Asia Monograph Series.* Vol. 7. Maxwell Air Force Base, AL: Air War College, 1979.

Sharp, Admiral U. S. Grant. *Strategy for Defeat: Vietnam in Retrospect.* San Rafael, CA: Presidio Press, 1978.

Shepperd, Major General Don, USAF (ret.). Interview by Dan Hampton on Vietnam War, August 6, 2013.

Smith, John T. *The Linebacker Raids: The Bombing of North Vietnam, 1972.* London: Cassell, 2000.

Sparks, Billy R. *Takhli Tales.* San Bernardino, CA: N.p., 2013.

Staaveren, Jacob Van. *Interdiction in Southern Laos 1960–1968: The United States Air Force in Southeast Asia.* Washington, DC: Center for Air Force History, 1993.

Stanton, Shelby L. *The Rise and Fall of an American Army: U.S. Ground Forces in Vietnam, 1965–1973.* New York: Ballantine Books, 1985.

Steeves, Dr. Phil. Interviews by Dan Hampton, conducted March 2 through November 23, 2014.

Stimson, G. W. *Introduction to Airborne Radar.* El Segundo, CA: Hughes Aircraft, 1983.

Thompson, James C. *Rolling Thunder: Understanding Policy and Program Failure.* Chapel Hill: University of North Carolina Press, 1980.

Thompson, Wayne. *To Hanoi and Back: The U.S. Air Force and North Vietnam, 1966–1973.* Washington, DC: Smithsonian Institution Press, 2000.

Thorsness, Colonel Leo. Interview by Dan Hampton about April 19, 1967, conducted October 2, 2014.

Thorsness, Leo. *Surviving Hell: A POW's Journey*. New York: Encounter Books, 2008.

Tillman, Barrett. *Above and Beyond: The Aviation Medals of Honor*. Washington, DC: Smithsonian Institution Press, 2002.

Toperczer, Dr. Istvan. *Air War over North Viet Nam: The Vietnamese People's Air Force 1949–1977*. Carrollton, TX: Squadron/Signal, 1998.

U.S. Department of Defense. *Statistics on Southeast Asia*. Washington, DC: U.S. Department of Defense, 1972.

Van, Colonel Dinh Thi. *I Engaged in Intelligence Work*. Hanoi: Gioi, 2006.

Van Creveld, Martin. *The Age of Airpower*. New York: PublicAffairs, 2011.

Velocci, Anthony L., Jr. "Naval Aviation: 100 Years Strong." *Aviation Week and Space Technology*, April 4, 2011, pp. 56–80.

Vietnam War database. http://vietnamwar-database.blogspot.com, accessed November 2, 2014.

Visions of Victory: Selected Vietnamese Communist Military Writings, 1964–1968. Stanford, CA: Hoover Institution on War, Revolution and Peace, 1969.

Vizcarra, Colonel Vic. Interviews by Dan Hampton about Spring High mission, 1965, conducted July 12 through August 30, 2014.

Vongsavanh, Brigadier General Southchay. *Military Operations and Activities in the Laotian Panhandle*. Washington, DC: U.S. Army Center for Military History, 1981.

Werrell, Kenneth P. *Archie to SAM: A Short Operational History of Ground Based Air-Defense*. Maxwell Air Force Base, AL: Air University Press, 2005.

"World Carrier Lists." http://www.hazegray.org/navhist/carriers/, accessed June 5, 2013.

Zaloga, Steven. *Red SAM: The SA-2 Guideline Anti-Aircraft Missile*. Oxford: Osprey, 2007.

INDEX